THE WINGED HORSE

THE
WINGED HORSE

The Story of the Poets and their Poetry

By

JOSEPH AUSLANDER *and*
FRANK ERNEST HILL

With decorations by
PAUL HONORÉ
and a bibliography
by Theresa West
Elmendorf

EDUCATIONAL EDITION

DOUBLEDAY, DORAN & COMPANY, INC.
NEW YORK

To
Anabel
and
Russell

ACKNOWLEDGMENTS

In the making of a book like this the many possibilities for error can only be reduced by the kindness and vigilance of others besides the authors. We wish to acknowledge our great debt to friends who read all or portions of the manuscript and made remarks: Elsa Hempl Hill, who also made a suggestion from which the book first grew; Eunice Tietjens and Cloyd Head, Dr. Richard Burton, Maxwell Anderson, Mark Van Doren, Joseph Woods Krutch, Arthur G. Kennedy, Edith Mirrielees, Frances Theresa Russell, Dorothy Rowden, Sister Monica of the Brown County Ursulines, David Moore Robinson, George Depue Hadzsits, Henry J. Wright, Elizabeth Buckingham, and Ruth Langland Holberg.

Our critics have been responsible for many improvements in the book; they are, of course, not responsible for such mistakes as may still exist.

We have found our publishers not only very patient under long delay, but helpful also in their suggestions with regard to the book.

Our thanks must be extended to the following authors and publishers for quotations used in the text:

Messrs. Houghton, Mifflin Company for permission to reprint Helen Waddell's translation of *The Sacrifice*, from her book, *Lyrics from the Chinese*.

Messrs. The Macmillan Company for permission to reprint the Old English hymn to Erce, as translated by Stopford A. Brooke in his book, *The History of Early English Literature;* also a short passage from *Merlin*, by Edwin Arlington Robinson; from John Masefield's poems, eight lines from *Salt-Water Ballads*, seventeen lines from *The Everlasting Mercy,* two stanzas from *Dauber*, and eight lines from *The Hounds of Hell*, in *Enslaved, and Other Poems*, and from Thomas Hardy's *Collected Poems*, the poem *Waiting Both*.

Mr. Vachel Lindsay and Messrs. D. Appleton and Co., New York, for permission to reprint Mr. Lindsay's poem, *The Flower-fed Buffaloes*, from *Going to the Stars*.

Messrs. Charles Scribner's Sons for permission to reprint a brief passage from Francis Thompson's *Shelley*, and fifteen lines from the *Poems* of William Ernest Henley.

Mr. Rudyard Kipling, Doubleday, Page & Co. and A. P. Watt & Co. for permission to reprint a number of short passages from *Barrack Room Ballads*.

Messrs. Henry Holt and Company for permission to reprint two brief quotations from Carl Sandburg's *Cornhuskers*.

Messrs. Longmans, Green and Company for permission to reprint brief quotations from *The Defense of Guenevere* and *The Earthly Paradise*, by William Morris.

To Mr. Alfred Knopf, and the original English publisher, Martin Secker, for permission to reprint two brief passages from the *Collected Poems* of James Elroy Flecker.

To Mrs. Martha Dickinson Bianchi and Messrs. Little, Brown and Company for permission to reprint a number of quotations from the poems of Emily Dickinson.

Messrs. Boni and Liveright for permission to reprint the poem *Heat*, by "H. D.," and six lines from *The Waste Land*, by T. S. Eliot.

To Mr. George Moore and Messrs. Boni and Liveright for permission to reprint several pages from *Heloïse and Abelard*, by George Moore.

To Messrs. Harper and Brothers for permission to quote from the poems beginning *Your Face Is Like a Chamber Where a King* and *I Drank at Every Vine*, these being taken from *The Harp Weaver and Other Poems*, published by Harper and Brothers, copyright 1920, 1921, 1922, 1923 by Edna St. Vincent Millay.

To Messrs. Henry Holt and Company for permission to use

certain quotations from *The Shropshire Lad*, by E. A. Housman.

To Mr. Franklin P. Adams and Messrs. Doubleday, Page & Co. for permission to reprint Mr. Adams's adaptation from Horace entitled *R. S. V. P.*, and originally appearing in his volume *Tobogganing on Parnassus*.

To Mr. Conrad Aiken and The Four Seas Company for permission to reprint eight lines from *Portrait of One Dead*, in the volume *The House of Dust*, by Conrad Aiken, Copyright, 1920, by the Four Seas Company.

To Messrs. Henry Holt and Company for permission to reprint *Nothing Gold Can Stay* from *New Hampshire*, by Robert Frost.

The two Indian chants in Chapters I and II are taken from *The Path on the Rainbow*, edited by George Cronyn and Mary Austin, and published by Messrs. Boni and Liveright. The first chant is translated by T. S. Rand, the second by Matilda Coxe Stevenson.

The fragment from the hymn to Amen at the beginning of Chapter IV is E. A. Wallis Budge's translation; the fragment descriptive of the king is from the *Poem of Pentaur*, translated into English by H. D. Seymour from the German version of Henry Brugsch-Bey.

The version of the Indian shawl chant in Chapter II was generously given to the authors by Dhan Gopal Muckerji.

The quotations from Theocritus are from translations by Edward Cracroft Lefroy.

The translations from Homer, Sappho, Aeschylus, Euripides, Sophocles, Horace, Virgil, Beowulf, Dante and Chaucer, together with other fragments, were made by the authors.

The little poem, *Epitaph for a Hound*, on page 34, is adapted from the prose version of J. W. Mackail, in his *Lectures on Greek Poetry*, published by Longmans, Green and Company.

The translations of Petrarch's sonnets were made by Mr. Auslander, and the sonnet on Keats on page 302 and the verses on modern poets on page 416 are his work.

FOREWORD

WE WROTE this book because we wanted to write it.

Also, we saw that such a book was needed.

We were aware of numberless people coming eagerly to the edges of poetry, wondering what it was, what it had been. The straightest way into the knowledge of an art, as into the knowledge of a person, is to discover what has happened to it—how men have used it. But the story of poetry seemed to be scattered as hopelessly as Humpty Dumpty after his fall; it was buried in histories and biographies that were sometimes a punishment even for those who made it a business to read them; there were a thousand fragments, but no one story. Yet it was clear that anyone at the beginning of poetry, trying to find out about it, needed a single simple account of what poets had been and what they had done in the world.

We saw that millions of people of all ages shared a baffled ignorance of what poetry is. They were curious about it, often wistfully so, but they did not understand the simplicity and usefulness of poetry. They thought it was a fearful or non-sensical hocus pocus that sensible readers could not hope to know and like. We decided to make our story one that such readers would understand. We set ourselves not to write up or down, but to tell as clearly and directly as we could how poetry probably developed and what men had done with it, and to explain its forms and music as we told about its place in the past and present life of the world.

Our story might be called the story of poetry that is at home in the English language. We have gone back of history to picture the probable beginnings of poetry, and we have paused in

Greece and Rome and mediæval Europe to show what came down through these times and lands into modern English verse. The rest of the book is about poets in Great Britain and America. If we attempted more than this we would expand a book into a library, or run the risk of making our story so simple that it would be as ridiculous as it is now audacious.

For it is audacious and experimental. We have restricted ourselves to a single footnote. We have brushed through fierce scholarly wars, trying to make brief and clear and essentially true what has been long and confused and doubtful. We must have made mistakes. Still, if we have succeeded in making poetry more vivid and understandable we shall be satisfied.

Each chapter of the book is complete in itself, but at the same time makes a part of a larger story. Because it seemed most right and interesting to do so, we have built up the larger story out of the stories of single great poets. So, except for some introductory material, most chapters deal chiefly with significant singers. In selecting these, we have ignored poets whom many will consider important. In treating those we have selected, we have also ignored much.

But we have tried always to handle each poet fairly—coming without gloves or hatchets, smashing no statues, building no pedestals. Where the balance has been close between good and ill, we have tipped it toward the good.

The result seems to us something like what we deliberately sought, and we hope that it has a clarity and significance that justifies the many omissions. We have enjoyed writing the book. It has taken us again through a world of rhythmic delight, of great stories of human deeds, human souls, and human utterances, of bold striking for the truth about life. We hope there will be many readers to go after us through this world, and that they will catch some of the magic we found in it.

Joseph Auslander
Frank Ernest Hill

New York, August 29, 1927

CONTENTS

		PAGE
Acknowledgments		vii
Foreword		xi
The Winged Horse		xv

CHAPTER

I.	When Poetry Was Necessary	1
II.	How Poetry Became Beautiful	9
III.	The First Poets	13
IV.	Blind Homer.	19
V.	Pegasus in Greece	30
VI.	How Poets Invented Plays	41
VII.	The Romans: Horace and Virgil	55
VIII.	The Poetry of Heroes and Dragons	79
IX.	The Poet of Heaven and Hell	89
X.	Petrarch and His Laura	106
XI.	Pegasus in England	127
XII.	The Ballad-Makers	139
XIII.	Queen Elizabeth's Poets	147

CHAPTER   PAGE

XIV.   Will Shakespeare 164

XV.   Milton and His Angels 190

XVI.   Poetry Becomes Sensible 205

XVII.   The Poets of Nature 215

XVIII.   The Poets of Nature (Continued) . . . 233

XIX.   "Childe Harold" 255

XX.   The Sun Treader 265

XXI.   Beauty Is Truth, Truth Beauty 283

XXII.   Lord Tennyson 303

XXIII.   The Brownings 316

XXIV.   The Poet of Ravens and Lost Ladies . . 333

XXV.   "I Sing Democracy" 348

XXVI.   Under Steam and Stone 365

XXVII.   Under Steam and Stone (Continued) . . 389

XXVIII.   Pegasus in To-morrow 414

Reading Lists

Anthologies 421

Studies 423

References 431

Index 441

Long ago the Greeks told the story of the winged horse Pegasus: How Pegasus was caught and tamed by Pallas Athenæ, Goddess of Wisdom, and how the hero Bellerophon came seeking him.

"If I had a horse with wings," said Bellerophon, "I could kill the Chimæra, the monster that destroys men with her breath of fire."

Then Pellas gave Bellerophon a golden bridle and showed him where Pegasus was drinking at a magic well. When the winged horse saw the bridle he came willingly to Bellerophon and let the young man put the bridle on him and ride him. Swinging down from the air on Pegasus like an arrow of lightning, Bellerophon smote the monster and slew her.

This story the Greeks used when they spoke of poets and poetry. For they saw how great singers rose on wings of imagination, leaving the world of ordinary words and men, and striking with lightning strokes of truth through littleness and lies and evil. And they made the winged horse the swift steed of poets, the symbol of song.

THE WINGED HORSE

CHAPTER I

WHEN POETRY WAS NECESSARY

I

When men first made poetry, it was very different from what it is to-day.

To-day we think of poetry as something to amuse us, or as something that says beautifully for us things that we have felt but could not say.

Usually, we see it in newspapers or magazines, or in slender books that few people seem to read. It is not what we would call a useful thing. It will not run plows or turn the wheels of factories. It will not speed up an automobile or tell a young man or a young woman how to succeed in business. The captain of an ocean liner, starting across the sea, does not say a poem as his ship leaves the dock, and of the millions of people making gardens every spring, it is safe to say that none of them recites a verse as he covers his seeds with earth.

But when poetry was first made, people used it for things very much like these. They were sure that they could not sow wheat or barley, go out to sea in a ship, make their gods hear them, get well if they were sick, or fight their enemies without poetry.

They might not have thought of poetry in just this way. For

a long time, they didn't even know they were making it. But whatever these people did that was of any importance began or ended in poetry. If someone could have destroyed their poetry, they would have been as frightened and helpless as men would be to-day if all the newspapers, theatres, schools, and churches should suddenly and mysteriously be blotted out.

II

We do not know how people first began to use poetry, but we can imagine.

There is the case of fighting. Thousands of years ago, before cannon and airplanes and battleships and poison gas had been dreamed of, men fought their wars with such weapons as they knew. Naturally, when a battle got started, every fighter was excited. He was fighting for his life. He shouted to his friends to encourage them and shouted at his enemies to frighten them. If his club crashed through the shield of a foeman, if he sent a spear to its mark, he roared his triumph.

Men who were fighting got the habit of shouting certain things that they liked. They may have shouted the name of their tribe or their god. Perhaps they yelled something to sharpen their own anger or to ridicule their enemies. There was probably a great deal of bellowing back and forth.

It was like certain games that we still play. Long ago the children playing these games shouted things they felt like saying. As a result, there is one game which we cannot play nowadays unless some of the players cry out:

> I'm a robber, I'm a thief,
> I don't care for the old police,

and in another game there is a refrain:

> I had a little dog and he wouldn't bite you,
> And he wouldn't bite you,
> And he wouldn't bite you—

and so on.

In the same way the first war cries came to be used, and war songs must have grown in a similar fashion. They grew the faster because, before a battle, each army came shouting, and the two often stood for some time singing and taunting each other. Of course, any two crowds will do the same thing now, adays. The yells are tossed back and forth between college freshmen and sophomores before a class rush, and at football games the cheer leaders and the rooting sections are busy. The rooters don't do the actual work, as the fighters in the armies did, but there is a similarity between their yells and the old war cries.

People who are excited and shout things are likely to shout them in a peculiar way. An angry child will often say a few words over and over. He may have been locked in a room by his brothers and sisters. He will begin crying:

> I want to get out
> I want   to get *out*
> I *want*   to get OUT—

and soon it becomes a kind of song. It has what we call rhythm. That is, it has certain words said together, and some of them said more loudly than others. There are also longer pauses between some words than others. It is true that everything we say has rhythm. We don't say:

> theothernightIsawamovie

all in a gulp, but probably something like this:

> The other *night*   I saw   a MOVie.

But the more excited we are, the more likely it is that we shall give a *decided* rhythm to what we say. It was so with the men who made war cries.

It was particularly so before battles, when they were thinking about fighting. For sometimes it took the warriors a long time to make up their minds to fight. Often they didn't enjoy the idea of being wounded or killed any more than many of us do to-day. So they got together when they thought of making war, and talked or danced until they felt brave and wanted to fight or were willing to give up the idea. The Indians used to do this. Of course, they got excited and shouted things over and over, and when one Indian said something the others liked, they would shout it after him, and perhaps at some other war council they would remember it and start shouting it again.

There were plenty of exciting things to say. The warriors believed, for instance, that there were gods of battle who could help them or hurt them. It was important to ask these gods to put strength into their arms when they struck, or guide their arrows straight. And perhaps it would not be exactly the right time to fight, and if the gods were asked, they would show by some sign whether or not the favourable moment had arrived. If the warriors danced and asked the gods about it, and a cloud suddenly passed over the sun or moon, they might decide that the spirits were displeased about something, and put off going to war.

Besides talking to gods, the fighters could talk to one another. They could tell how brave they were, and how they would get many sheep or horses from their enemies if they won a battle. While they shouted excitedly about such things, the warriors often beat time on drums or by clashing their weapons together to the rhythm of what they said. Here is an Indian war song that shows how this was probably done:

> Death I make, singing
> *Hey-yeh! hey-yeh! hey-yeh! hey-yeh!*
> Bones I hack, singing
> *Hey-yeh! hey-yeh! hey-yeh! hey-yeh!*
> Death I make, singing
> *Hey-yeh! hey-yeh! hey-yeh! hey-yeh!*

In this song we can see how the Indians would beat their drums or strike their spears together. One warrior might say the first line, and the others would join in with "hey-yeh!"

It can be seen that the rhythm in this song is strong and clear.
All poetry has a strong rhythm.

> Double double
> Toil and trouble,
> Fire burn and cauldron bubble!

Such words, like the words of an Indian war song, make us want
to sing them. Teachers have long told children at school not to
"sing-song" the poetry they read. It is interesting to know that
the earliest poetry *was* said sing-song, and that when we read
verse in that way we are only doing what the rhythm of the
poetry makes very natural.

III

We have already mentioned other things besides fighting
that needed words to be said about them. There was seed-
planting.

To-day seed-planting and the growing of crops are a matter
of science and common sense, but they were not that three thousand years ago. The storing of seeds was often crudely managed,
chemical spraying and even proper ploughing and irrigating
were often unknown. There was a great amount of superstition
about ploughing and planting and cultivating. The seeds might
have got frozen in the winter (there were only fireplaces in most
countries), but if they failed to sprout it was a witch or a sor-
cerer who had spoiled them. If insects came to eat the crops,
a god had been displeased and had sent them as a plague.

In a similar fashion gods could send rain or keep it away as
they wished, and the wind god could make the winds either
gentle or fierce and destructive.

So the people reasoned that, if they talked to the gods and
asked them for their help, saying words to please the good gods
and words to protect the seed from the bad spirits and from
people who practised witchcraft, things would grow well.

They had little songs or chants to say when they planted their seeds, like this one which the old Saxons in England used to say:

Erce, Erce, Erce,   mother of Earth!
May the All-wielder,   Ever-Lord grant thee
Acres waxing,   upwards growing,
Pregnant with corn,   plenteous in strength;
Hosts of grain shafts   and of glittering plants!
Of broad barley   the blossoms
And of white wheat   ears waxing,
Of the whole earth   the harvest!
Let be guarded the grain   against all ills
That are sown over the land   by sorcery-men;
Nor let cunning woman change it   nor a crafty man!

There were other chants like this for the work men did. In some countries, people still say simple songs as they make rugs or vases or tools. These songs usually tell how the workers hope the things they are making will be good to use and lovely to look at. Often such chants were like the chant for the planting of the grain: they were meant to get the help of good gods or spirits and to keep bad spirits or bad men from spoiling the work.

Of course, it made the workers feel better to say such things. What they said might also help them with their work. Often the song would tell about a certain part of the work, and the worker would have to do this as he sang. Then he sang about another thing and did that, and so the song went until what he was making was finished. The song also helped him to remember what to do.

In fact, songs were made just to help people remember things. They didn't know how to write, and their songs were something like books. They kept a record of what was known. Even to-day we have rhymes which have come down through hundreds of years and tell us how to remember the number of days in a month, or teach little children to count. When all men were children their rules for working and behaving and even their laws were put into poetry for safe keeping.

There were also chants or songs for going out to sea, for marrying, and for sickness. In Africa, a tribe of Negroes called the Bantus still say these words when a boy or girl is sick:

Tsu! If it be thou who art causing our child's sickness, see here is the beer thou desirest and also some tobacco; we pray thee, leave him alone that he may recover.

The Bantu is talking to an "evil spirit" or god. When he has finished, he pours out some beer and leaves some tobacco where the spirit can get it. Of course, we have other ways of getting well when we are sick, but long ago our ancestors acted very much as the Bantus do to-day. In ancient India, for instance, the charm against fever sought to flatter the fever spirits and get them out of the body of the sick person into some small animal:

Homage be to the deliriously hot, to shaking, exciting, impetuous fever!

Homage to the cold fever, to him that in the past fulfilled desires!

May the fever that returns on the morrow, he that returns on two successive days, the impious one, pass into this frog!

Now, most of the songs and chants used in everyday life were like the war songs in one important way. They had the rhythm we have spoken of. And like the war songs, they were rhythmic because they were made for important occasions about which men were very much excited. When the chant was made for planting grain, a priest usually said it. He made certain motions that were supposed to help protect the seed. The people who watched probably saw the evil spirits flying away and imagined the good ones hearing and getting ready to help. It was the same with sickness. They were excited about the bad spirits that were causing them pain, and thought the chant was driving them away. And in each case the chant itself took on its insistent, musical beat from the feelings of those who said it and those who listened.

The old songs and chants were very crude, but they made people brave or happy or helped them work. There were chants for the birth of children and for burying people, chants of thanksgiving after eating, and chants for pulling ropes and lifting stones. The people who used them would not have known how to live without such poetry. Poetry started them doing things, it helped them as they worked, it was the speech of their gladness, it gave them their courage, it spoke to their gods, it stored their wisdom. The wheels of the early world seem to have been turned by poetry. It was necessary.

CHAPTER II

HOW POETRY BECAME BEAUTIFUL

The chants and songs men made long ago told of things they hoped to get or of things they had lost.

Both seemed very desirable to them. The warrior saying his war song pictured himself leading home captured horses loaded with furs and beads. The worker sowing seed was happy as he thought of the fields of ripe grain that might grow where he was sowing. The women who mourned the dead remembered how strong and handsome the young men had been.

All this was natural. Things we don't possess, whether we hope for them or have lost them, usually seem very precious to us.

People will often remember some place they have left, and come to believe that they love it, and that if they were there they would be happy. Sometimes they go back to it and don't like it at all. That only shows how something that is gone, whether for a time or for good, may become desirable and beautiful.

What we think or feel is likely to get into our words. The warriors in their war songs told about the much-desired things they hoped to get, and the women who mourned described the

beauty or kindness of their friends or sons. The workers described the things they hoped to make or the sunshine and
rain they hoped would come to help their crops.

We can see how this worked out from the case of a simple
thing like rain. In Arizona and New Mexico, very little rain
falls. The Indians there needed rain for their corn, and rain
seemed a lovely thing to them. So they made a song which shows
their feeling for the beauty of rain:

> Cover my earth mother four times with many flowers.
> Let the heavens be covered with the banked-up clouds.
> Let the earth be covered with fog; cover the earth with rains.
> Great waters, rains, cover the earth. Lightning cover the earth.
> Let thunder be heard over the earth, let thunder be heard;
> Let thunder be heard over the six regions of the earth!

Other chants and songs are also filled with the beauty of
what they describe. Songs sung at the birth of children are
lovely with the hope of the parents for maidens graceful and
swift-fingered at their work, for boys with suppleness and
strength that will be glorious in battle. Chants for the return
of men from the sea gleam with the quiet peace of the fields
they hope to see again, with the love on faces that are dear to
them.

Very naturally, the making of songs taught the art of lingering
over beautiful ideas, of selecting words that would sharpen the
images that were called up, and make greater the feelings that
come with them. Men liked beautiful chants better than those
that were not beautiful, and sought always to put beauty into
their charms, their prayers, their laments.

And, strange as it may seem, the result was to make poetry
even more useful than it had been. For, as poetry became more
beautiful, it became more powerful. And where at first it had
merely reassured men, giving them a sense of protection, it came
to inspire and intoxicate them until they were able to endure
or do more than ordinary men.

In Cashmere, in northern India, the people weave beautiful

shawls. Before they weave they say a poem-prayer. This prayer shows well how beauty in poetry can lift those who chant it to a new effort and a new strength. We who are far from these weavers and their work respond to the noble ending of this cry for skill and power:

> Quicken our senses,
> Make them ache
> Till they weave
> A garment soft as moonlight,
> But invincible as the thunderbolt.
> When it is wrought men will marvel and exclaim:
> "Man has not woven this beauty,
> Only madness could have made it!"

In a similar way, men and women may be given strength to suffer. When the Jews were taken to Babylon and kept there to slave for the Babylonians, they made a song that seems to have helped them to live through toil and shame and loneliness.

> By the rivers of Babylon we sat down;
> Yea, we wept when we remembered Zion.
>
> We hanged our harps upon the willows
> In the midst thereof.
>
> For they that carried us away captive
> Required of us a song;
> And they that wasted us required of us mirth, saying,
> "Sing us one of the songs of Zion."
>
> How shall we sing the Lord's song
> In a strange land?
>
> If I forget thee, O Jerusalem,
> Let my right hand forget her cunnihg.
>
> If I do not remember thee,
> Let my tongue cleave to the roof of my mouth;
> If I prefer not Jerusalem
> Above my chief joy.

Such songs may be more useful than money or food. The things we taste or wear are pleasant to our bodies, but if we are desperate with weariness or grief, we cannot sit down to a banquet or enjoy the colour and shape of a new garment. Healing words may be what we need. After we have had them, the feast will delight us and the garment be a joy.

So, as the poetry became more beautiful, it also became more useful. Yet this new usefulness had a strange quality, for with it went not only the ability to suffer or do more, but a love also for the magic of words that had given such new power. And since that time men have prized poetry for this mysterious delight that was in the sound of it, and that would not come merely from having enough to eat, or recovering from a sickness, or coming back safely from an ocean or a battle.

CHAPTER III

THE FIRST POETS

About the time people discovered that they liked their songs to be beautiful, they discovered another thing.

They saw that, in order to have poetry, it was not necessary to wait until you wanted to be helped or protected. Poetry could be made, they realized, that had nothing to do with protecting people. It could be made for pure enjoyment and chanted for pure enjoyment.

They began to make such poetry. They made poems about the battles they fought. They made poems telling how brave hunters had killed wild beasts—boars, lions, dragons. They made poems about young men and women who fell in love with one another and couldn't get married because their families were enemies. The people liked to get around a fire on a winter night, or to lie out in the fields in summer when their work was done, and listen to someone chanting such poems.

But not everybody could make poems, and not everybody could chant them well. In fact, very few could do either. Those who could soon became known.

They found that, if they could make and sing poems, they didn't have to do anything else. They could be poets. Poor people would see that they had at least something to eat and a place to sleep. Rich men and chiefs and kings would give them riches.

It is easy to understand why. When the first poets came, there were, of course, no theatres, newspapers, motion pictures, or books. The poet, in a way, was all of these.

He often went from place to place and made poems about what he had seen. He would recite a poem that told a story, playing on his harp as he recited. This was as near to the opera or the movies or a play as people in uncivilized countries could get. It was a great occasion for them. A chief or king would be well liked if he attracted poets to his house so that people could hear their stories and songs. What might be more important, the poets would like him, too, advertising his bravery and generosity. But if he didn't reward them properly, they usually went to chiefs or kings who did. Then there would be little entertainment for the chief or king who had been stingy with the poets; or for his people.

So we find in many countries that the poets were honoured, and that often they were rich and important. In Norway every great chief had his favourite poet. In ancient Ireland, some poets were ranked next to the kings themselves.

The poets soon made poetry more regular and musical than the early chants and songs had been. They introduced metre.

In a way, metre was not new, for it is only a kind of rhythm. In the earlier chants and songs the rhythm might change as the song went along. But now the poets would take one kind of rhythm and keep repeating it. There would be, instead of lines of uneven length, lines all about the same length. Each of these lines would be made up of the same number of groups of words, each group much like the other in the number of sounds it contained. We have this in our poetry to-day.

> I wandered lonely as a cloud
> That floats on high o'er vales and hills
> When all at once I saw a crowd,
> A host, of golden daffodils

falls quite naturally into lines of the same length, and the groups of sound in it might be set off like this:

```
I wan     dered lone    ly as     a cloud
That floats    on high    o'er vales    and hills
When all    at once    I saw     a crowd
A host    of gold    en daff    odils.
```

This is one kind of metre. There are four divisions in each line. Each division is called a "foot." Every foot has two syllables. Instead of calling this "metre" we could, if we wanted to, call it "regular rhythm."

There are many other kinds of meters than this given above. The poets in various parts of the world used different kinds. Sometimes one poet would use a number of kinds of metres. None of them used rhyme, as we do, but they chose carefully the words they used to make them sound beautiful, grave, or terrible. Below is an example of the kind of poetry the English made in England 1,000 years ago. It is taken from a poem about a battle the English fought with the Norsemen who had come up a river in their ships to rob the English. A Norseman left his ship to come over and try to make the English pay money to him and his companions. He waded out into the river until he could talk to the English who were on the bank, and shouted:

```
Swift-faring seamen    have sent me to thee—
Bade me to tell thee    that thou must quickly
Send rings for ransom;    well that you rather
Buy off with bracelets    the brunt of our spear rush
Than we should share    sharp burden of battle.
```

Metre like this had a swing to it and helped the poets to make songs and tell stories. They knew how the metre went, and they could fit words into it. The more they did this, the more skillful they became. The older poets taught the younger ones what they knew, and the younger poets sometimes tried doing new and different things with their poetry.

Poets had to understand men and women, as well as be skillful. They couldn't make stories and sing songs unless they felt what people suffered and could describe their joy, their hate, their courage, their sadness. Men have to know something pretty well before they can tell others about it and make them interested in what is being told. But when a poet who could sing nobly found a great story to tell, people remembered the poem he sang for hundreds and even thousands of years.

Men died, and the poet himself; swords rusted away, gold was lost and houses crumbled and fell, but the words the poet made were still remembered, and people listened to them as they sat around their fires in the winter or lay at the end of the day in the summer fields.

CHAPTER IV

BLIND HOMER

All this happened ten or twenty or thirty thousand years ago, and it is happening to-day!

That is a way of saying that poetry has been made in many places and at many different times, but that all the people who have made it have gone through much the same experience, as everybody does in learning to talk.

The Greeks and the English show how poetry grew in different places and in different centuries. The oldest of the great Greek poems is supposed to have been written about 1000 B. C., or more than two thousand nine hundred years ago. At that time the peoples who afterward blended into the English race may have been savages with no poetry but charms and war cries. At any rate, the first great poem we have in English seems to have been written between 600 and 700 A. D., or at least one thousand six hundred years later than the Greek poem. There must have been a time—long before any Greek poetry we know—when the Greeks, too, had nothing but short chants and songs. And to-day savage tribes in Africa and Australia have never got beyond making this crude type of poetry. So, in a way, the story of poetry is a complicated affair, each race having its own story.

But in another sense the story of poetry is simple. We cannot go back of what we know. And we know about people who lived long ago only through what they have left behind to tell us about themselves. We can often get an idea of their lives by digging up the ruins of their houses and studying their coins, pots, furniture, and carvings. But with poems we have only what they wrote down. The story of poetry carries us back no farther than the oldest written records of poetry.

We know poetry was made before writing was invented, that it was passed on by being memorized. But we have only such poems as were still remembered when the people who know them began to write. We are sure there were older poems, but they have not come down to us.

We have a few very ancient poems—poems from Egypt and India and China, showing that men have made their songs in many places. The Egyptians sang of their kings. A poet wrote of Rameses II:

> The youthful king . . . seizes his weapons
> And is a wall of iron to his warriors . . .
> Terrible is he when his war-cry resounds,
> Bolder than the whole world . . .
> As the grim lion in the valley of gazelles.

They made hymns to their gods—to Amen:

> When Amen casteth a spell upon the water
> And his name is on the waters,
> If this name of his be uttered
> The crocodile hath no power.
> The winds are driven back,
> The hurricane is quelled,
> At the remembrance of him
> The wrath of the angry man dieth down.

In China the poets were already busy more than a thousand years before Christ. The little poem below, translated into English rhyme, shows that they had already become politely doubtful about the religious customs from which the earliest poetry of any people usually grows:

THE SACRIFICE

We load the sacrificial stands
Of wood and earthenware,
The smell of burning southernwood
Is heavy on the air.

It was our father's sacrifice,
It may be they were eased;
We know no harm to come of it;
It may be God is pleased.

We could study poetry in other countries as strange and re-mote as Egypt or China. We could find most of it beginning with the history of its particular land, and coming down through the years to our own day. Whether we look at it in Japan, Arabia, Finland, the South Sea Islands, or Peru, poetry has its long and often exciting story.

However, this book is the book of poetry in our own language, not that of the poetry of the world. We can consider among early poems only those which have affected English and American poetry. The Greek poems alone have done this. The Greeks made the story of Pegasus, the winged horse which we use as the symbol of poetry. A Greek poet (or perhaps a number of Greek poets) made also the Iliad and the Odyssey. These are not only the oldest of great stories existing in verse, but are the first poems to which we can trace a kind of fatherhood for the poetry we write and read to-day.

Unfortunately, we know very little of the man who was said by the Greeks themselves to have made these poems. His name was Homer. The Greeks tell us that he was blind (though in some cases their artists represented him as reading!), and that, as he got old, he wandered about reciting his verses and getting food and shelter where he could. After he was dead, those who had paid little attention to him realized the power and beauty

of what he had written. All over Greece and throughout Asia
Minor and the Greek islands, people gathered in cities to hear
Homer recited. Then men in many different places said he was
their poet:

> Seven cities claimed great Homer dead
> Through which the living Homer begged his daily bread.

Nowadays, the scholars who have studied the two Homeric
poems are puzzled. Some think Homer never existed. Some
think he really lived and composed what was credited to him.
Some think he put together into two long poetic narratives
many short ballads that other and earlier singers had made.
Some think he wrote only the Odyssey.

But, in any case, we have the poems. The Iliad is the story
of a war at Ilium, or Troy. The Odyssey is a story of Odysseus
or Ulysses, a king and hero who was one of the warriors of the
Iliad.

The Iliad takes us to the camp of the Greek kings before the
city of Troy. The poem opens in the tenth year after the Greeks
or Achaians had come thronging in their ships from the Greek
islands and from Greece itself to this great town on the coast of
Asia Minor. Menelaus of Sparta had called them together. His
wife Helen, most beautiful of all women, had fled from Sparta
with Paris, one of the fifty sons of King Priam of Troy. The
Trojans refused to give her up, and the Greeks had come to get
her; but Troy had high walls, and after all the years of war, she
was still uncaptured.

So the battle continued on the great plains near the sea.
There the Greeks had beached their ships—crude boats about
the size of the tugs we use to-day for hauling coal or sand or
pulling steamers about—and there they made their tents and
walled them in with walls of stone and timber. There the
soldiers went out to battle with their shields of bronze and
leather, bearing their spears and swords and bows and arrows.
Their kings rode before them in chariots—rough jolting carts,

but shining with paint and metal—their armour studded with gold, and coloured plumes of horsehair waving from their helmets.

Now the greatest of the Greek warriors was Achilles, and the Iliad is a poem of his anger and glory.

> Sing, O goddess, the wrath of Achilles the son of Peleus,
> The wrath that was bearer of lasting woe for the host of Achaians
> Tumbling the souls of heroes down to the darkness of Hades,
> Giving their bodies to dogs and the beaks of devouring birds.

It was not with the Trojans that Achilles was angry—not at first. It was with Agamemnon, the brother of Menelaus and the general in chief of all the Greeks, who had insulted and wronged him by taking from him a slave girl Achilles had been given as a prize. Achilles, in great anger, left the council of the Greeks and swore to fight for them no more.

"The Trojans will come out and multitudes of the Achaians shall fall before Hector, the slayer of men," he cried. "Then will ye long for Achilles, and you, Agamemnon, will tear your heart within you that you wronged the best of the Achaians!"

And so it came to pass. After many combats between champions, the Trojans stormed out one day and drove the Greek army back. Many of the Achaian warriors were wounded, and Hector, son of King Priam, the greatest of the Trojans, surged with his men down to the walled camp by the shore. He hurled a great stone against the wooden gates of the wall:

> Loud rang the gates, and the bars crashed in, and the rush of the stone
> Splintered a gap. And through it, his face like terrible night,
> Leaped Hector, shining with marvel of mail that engirdled his body,
> Shaking two spears. No man could have stayed him then as he stormed
> Through the gates—nay, none but gods, and the light of his eyes
> Flamed like a fire.

The Trojans rushed in. There was a long battle, the Trojans driving toward the Greek ships, the Greeks furiously opposing them. But finally Hector beat his way to one of the vessels, and the Trojans cast fire upon it.

All this time Achilles had sat in his tent. But now his dearest friend, Patroclus, begged him with tears:

"Let me put on your armour and take your spearmen and do what I may to hearten the Achaians."

"Go," said Achilles, and Patroclus took the arms and rushed forth, shouting, at the head of Achilles' Myrmidons. When the Trojans heard him shout and saw the well-known armour he wore, they thought Achilles himself had come. They gave way, some of them flying. The Achaians quenched the blaze in the ship that had been fired and poured out after their enemies. There was a thundering of war chariots and a shouting and din of arms. And Patroclus dashed among the flying Trojans striking down princes. Many fell before him, but at last he himself was smitten, and, as he reeled from the blow, Hector dashed from the ranks of the Trojans and slew him, and took the armour of Achilles from his body.

When Achilles heard of the death of Patroclus, his grief and anger were terrible. He got new armour. He made peace with Agamemnon and went forth with the Greeks to wreak vengeance upon the Trojans, and especially upon Hector. The armies clashed, and Achilles swept in his chariot among his enemies, his spear like deadly lightning. Men fled before him, horses ran wild, while he dashed on, untiring and terrible:

Fierce as a fire that rages deep in the glen of a sun-parched
Slope, and the tall trees burn, and the flame with the wind goes whirling
This way and that, so he with the light of his spear went raging,
As if he had been a god.

He beat the Trojans back to the city and filled the river Scamander with bodies of the slain until the river god rose against him in wrath. Always he sought Hector. Once he came upon him and the two fought, but the god Apollo put a mist between them and snatched Hector away. Yet, when the Trojans fled within their walls, Hector remained without, waiting, and would not come in when Priam his father begged him, or

Hecuba his mother. But when Achilles drew near, Hector grew afraid and fled, and the two sped around the walls of Troy:

> As sweeps a hawk of the mountains, swiftest of winged creatures
> After a frightened dove, and the dove before him fleeth,
> And ever the hawk hard pressing with shrill screams darteth at her,
> Pricked by his heart to seize her, Achilles with fierce haste darted
> Ever at Hector, and Hector went flying beneath the walls
> Of the Trojans, plying swift knees.

Three times they encircled the city, and still Hector fled and Achilles pursued, and neither gained on the other:

> As in a dream one faileth in chasing a flying man—
> Fails the one who flies and likewise fails the pursuer,
> So did Achilles fail to close on the flying Hector,
> And Hector to escape.

How, finally, Achilles stopped, and Hector took courage and came against him, how they taunted each other, how Hector fought bravely, how the goddess Athene tricked him and he went down at last is a story that leaps and flames in magnificent words until the spear of Achilles, flashing like a star, brings it to an end.

The Iliad is a great poem of quarrelling and speech-making, of love and fighting. It is also a poem of grief and tenderness. We see terrible Achilles yield to the tears of aged King Priam, begging for the body of his son. We see Hector, so devastating in battle, saying farewell to Andromache, his wife, and to his child. Very tender is the passage describing how he took the boy to kiss him, and how the little one, seeing Hector's helmet,

> Screaming shrank close to the nurse, fearing the look of its father—
> The bronze of the helm, the crest of horsehair dreadfully nodding.
> Tenderly Hector smiled; Andromache smiled; and the hero
> Quickly took from his head the high-plumed helmet, and laid it
> Shining upon the ground.

No one can forget the beauty of Helen, the swift rage of Peleus's son, the coloured crests, the clanging armour, the gilded chariots and proud horses.

The story of Odysseus begins after the Greeks had finally captured Troy and burned it, and the many Greek kings had begun to sail for their homes.

Among them was Odysseus. He set out with seven ships for his island kingdom of Ithaca, but many things prevented him from reaching his country. He displeased certain of the gods, and accidents and suffering were his lot. He had adventures with the one-eyed giant Polyphemus, he met the enchantresses Circe and Calypso, he heard the sirens sing. He saw the strange sleepy land of the lotus-eaters. Some of his men went ashore here and stayed, and those sent to bring them back stayed also, and finally Odysseus himself had to go after all of them, for

> Whoever of them ate of the fragrant food of the lotus
> Thought no more to come back with news, nor of any returning,
> Longing only to stay with the Lotus people, forever
> To eat of the lotus flower, and lose the thought of departure.

Odysseus also visited the underworld where the spirits of the dead lived. Finally, he was shipwrecked in the land of the Phæacians, and crept naked through the woods and saw the princess Nausicaa playing ball with her attendants. He put a branch before his naked body, and went out to ask help. And the great king whom the Greeks thought the wisest of their warriors stood without even a garment to shield his body and said to the princess:

> But thou, O Queen,
> Pity me! See, I have come with the scars of my heavy misfortunes
> First unto thee. I know thee only of those possessing
> This city and land. Then lead me unto the city, and give me
> Some rag to wear—some coarse old robe if thou hast one with thee.

Finally, Odysseus got back to Ithaca, but he had to come disguised as a beggar. He found other kings and princes making a hotel of his palace, swaggering about insisting that his wife Penelope should marry one of them. Each wanted to get Odysseus's kingdom. The Odyssey tells how Penelope put off the suitors, and how Odysseus finally surprised them and killed them, striking them down with arrows shot from the great bow that he alone could bend.

The Iliad and the Odyssey were very important in the life of the Greeks. They were more to the Greeks than any poems we know are to us. They were recited by men trained to recite them, and people listened to them as they would to plays or music to-day. Often the rhapsodists, as the reciters of Homer were called, performed before twenty thousand people or more.

To some extent, these poems were like our Bible. In the Iliad and the Odyssey, written a little while before the Jews were beginning to set down the Bible, Homer had described how brave and wise men behaved. He had written beautiful prayers to the gods of the Greeks. He had described how courteous men and women treated their friends and the strangers who came to them.

Also he showed, in the way he wrote the poems, how to say things simply, yet with words that clashed like shields or flowed like slow music. His poems seldom waste language. They say directly what they have to say. Yet they manage to say it so well that we cannot forget it. Some poets get started making poetry and make too much of it. Homer rarely did this. He knew when to say little and when to say much. The Greeks saw how fine a thing it was to do this. "Measure [moderation] is best in all things," was their idea of conduct. These are the words Homer had put into the mouth of Menelaus, and if he was not the first to bring this sense of proportion to the Greeks, he was foremost among those who helped them to praise and to practise it. And we to-day, often dashing about with very little idea of moderation, still pause to listen to Homer's words, to talk about them and try to follow them.

The Iliad and the Odyssey were written in a metre we call hexameter. *Hexa* is the Greek word for "six." Every line of this poetry had six groups of words in it:

Thought   no more   to come back   with news   nor of any   returning
Longing   only   to stay   with the Lotus   people   forever.

There was no rhyme, but the poetry of Homer is as beautiful as
any we know. It is very musical, yet it can be strong and even
harsh. In our language, hexameters are not as satisfactory as in
the Greek. In fact, on account of differences between the English
and Greek speech, it is physically impossible for us to make
musical effects much like Homer's. Still, some idea of Homer's
metre, though not of his power and beauty, can be got from
English poems like Longfellow's *Evangeline*, or the less known
but finer poem by Arthur Hugh Clough, *The Bothie of Tobur na
Vuolich*. For the story, there are translations made from the
Greek into English, none as good as the original (for translations
never are), but worth reading. Of the better known of these
translations, none is in hexameters, but the selections given in
this chapter are translated into an English metre with a movement similar to the original Greek.

The Iliad and the Odyssey are called epics. An epic is a poem
about great events in the life of a people. The poets of many
countries have written epics, but Homer's are generally acknowl-
edged to be the greatest of all, even though they are the first we
know. We still come from reading them full of their spirit of
bravery, their wisdom, their beauty.

More than that, we still use Homer. We write stories and
poems better because of these first great poetic stories, which
have influenced the narrative poetry of the world ever since
they were made. Certainly we think and write about the people
he made for us. Perhaps Helen never lived until Homer put her
into his verse, but ever since he did so poets have written
about her, and when we think of beauty in women to-day we
think of Helen of Troy. Within the last few years new books
about her have been published.

And every day, when we think or talk, we use Homer. We
see a woman who makes people forget about the things they

ought to do and attend instead to the things she wants them to do, and we say she is a Circe. We read of a man who takes a long journey in a boat, and we say he is an Odysseus. We hear of a woman who waited years for a husband to come back, and we call her Penelope. Homer still helps us to understand people about us and the lives they live.

This is after three thousand five hundred years. Life now is not the life Homer knew. In Homer's time the women and children brought water to the house in skins and jars; when we want it we turn on a faucet. Homer's kings rode fierce horses, or jolting chariots without springs; we go in soft-tired automobiles. Then men had only torches for light; we use electricity. There were only rude fireplaces in Homer's time; we have stoves and furnaces. Gods, clothes, speech, music—all are different. Yet we read the poetry that Homer made for his world and find it still useful in ours.

CHAPTER V

PEGASUS IN GREECE

I

The Greeks described by Homer lived a life in which art and simplicity were blended. They wrought marvellously in bronze and gold and silver, leaving behind them exquisite goblets and brooches. Their vases were often shaped with a superb skill and craftsmanship. On the other hand, they ploughed with wooden ploughs, bought and sold without coined money, lived in houses without glass windows, and waged incessant wars. We wonder at times how they found leisure for carving or poetry at all. Their splendid epics show this fusion of simplicity with noble craftsmanship and high intelligence.

But eventually Greek life became richer and more elegant. And in the process of learning to fashion larger ships and cities, better houses and better governments, the Greeks invented many things. Their inventions were not like the complicated machinery Europeans and Americans have fashioned in the last few centuries, though the Greeks were the first people to understand many facts that later helped to set us on the way toward steam engines, and electric light, and airplanes. No—the great-

est of their discoveries could not even be touched with hands.
They were—

Ways of thinking.

Some of them we call now by names like geometry, history,
philosophy. Other peoples had thought about certain of these
"knowings," or sciences, but the Greeks, in each case, collected
what was known and reasoned about it and made it a body of
knowledge that was useful in human life. They did this also
with poetry. About three centuries after Homer's time, Greek
poets began to discover new kinds of verse, and the way in
which poems were made. No one has ever done so much for the
poetry we write and read to-day as the singers who sang in the
islands of the Ægean Sea and in cities on the mainland of
Greece, like Thebes and Athens, during a few hundred years of
supreme poetic activity.

II

Who were these poets?

Many names have come down to us, and very little poetry.
Of some of the singers the Greeks thought greatest, only a few
complete poems remain, and some fragments, usually quoted in
the essays or romances or histories of other writers. For poetry
had to be written down by hand or cut on stone, and war and
fire, frost and earthquakes have destroyed most of the marble
tablets and manuscript books that were made. Those remaining
are like the fragments of a beautiful broken vase. Much is dust,
much is marred or lost. The pieces will never be put together.
We can only guess what the whole was like, we shall never
know.

But from what the Greeks wrote of their poets in manuscripts that have survived, and from such poetry as we have, we
can get some idea of certain great singers.

The first is Hesiod, a poet living not long after Homer, or
perhaps in Homer's own time, among the shepherds of Bœotia.
It is possible that at the time Hesiod wrote, certain changes

that were to take place in the Greek world had already begun. We know that it was not long after Homer's day that the cities and islands began to shake off the rule of kings. They made oligarchies, or governments-of-the-few, and democracies, or governments-by-the-people. They began to pay less attention to war and more to commerce, art, games, oratory, singing, dancing, and talking.

At any rate, Hesiod wrote much poetry suited to this quieter, friendlier life. He made a kind of encyclopedia of the gods, their ancestry, birth, adventures, and habits; and for hundreds of years, the Greeks consulted and quoted his *Theogony*. He wrote also *Works and Days*, a long poem about the times to plough and sow and the way to choose a wife and educate children and go about farming and trading. Such poems drew later poets more easily into poetry about their new life. They did not forget their heroes—Odysseus and Agamemnon and Theseus and Jason, but they began to sing also of politics, trade, athletic contests, love.

As they turned to new subjects, they made a tremendously important change in poetry. One of their poets, Archilochus, began to make poems in a metre different from Homer's. He used word groups of two instead of three syllables—iambics they were called. He also used fewer feet in each line, often writing in trimeter and tetrameter (three-measure and four-measure) instead of hexameter. He began also to write poems ridiculing the faults of men and women—the beginning of what we call satiric poetry. He and other poets discovered that, not only was it possible to make one or two kinds of poetry different from the Epic verse, but that every thought or feeling could be sung in a poetry suited in metre to its own character. Epic poetry had been poetry of the race. The new poetry was personal.

One of the earliest of the new poets was Sappho. The Greeks used to say that Homer was the greatest of men who made poetry, and Sappho the greatest of women.

She lived in the island of Lesbos in the Seventh and Sixth centuries before Christ, and had there a school in which she trained young women to dance and make music and write and chant poetry. She arranged the singing and dancing for marriages. She seems to have been a beautiful and busy person, full of the joy of loving and living. Her poems were lyrics—or songs to be recited or sung to an accompaniment on the lyre. The few we have of them show great power and feeling and bear out the assertion of the Greeks that she wrote the greatest of love poetry and made lines of glowing beauty. Often she wrote in the Sapphic stanza—a form she invented herself. Her *Hymn to Aphrodite* cannot be brought from the Greek into English without the loss of much of its power and magic, but the rhythm of the poem can be suggested by this translation of the English scholar and poet, John Addington Symonds:

> Glittering-throned, undying Aphrodite,
> Wile-weaving daughter of Zeus, I pray thee
> Tame not my soul with heavy woe, dread mistress,
>   Nay, nor with anguish!
>
> But hither come, if ever erst in old time
> Thou didst incline, and listenedst to my crying,
> And from thy father's palace down descending,
>   Camest with golden
>
> Chariot yoked: thee fair swift-flying sparrows
> Over dark earth with multitudinous fluttering
> Pinion on pinion, through middle ether
>   Down from heaven hurried, *etc.*

Simpler and gently tender is the fragment about the evening star, which we possess to-day only because a writer quoted it to show how Sappho used repetition to get an effect:

> Hesperus, thou who bringest back all things
> Scattered by the bright wings of the dawn:
> Thou bringest the sheep back, thou bringest the goat,
> Thou bringest the babe to its mother's breast.

There are other poems, enough to give us a glimpse, at least, of "violet-weaving and gently smiling Sappho" as the poet Alcæus called her.

But more of what her poetry was like to the Greeks comes in such a story as was told of Solon, the Athenian poet and lawgiver. At a banquet, he heard his nephew sing one of Sappho's songs. He made the boy repeat it at once, over and over, and when he was asked why he did this, answered, "So that I may not die before I have learned it."

Thousands of other Greeks must have felt as he did. Greek potters and painters put Sappho and her lyre on vases, and Greek cities put her on their coins. And if we know too little of her or of her poetry, it is good to realize that she wrote so gloriously for those who heard more than we can hear.

Scarcely less renowned than Sappho was Simonides of Ceos, who spent many years of his life in Athens, and was famed for his choruses of victory, his elegies or poems for the dead, and his epigrams, or poems of a line or two making a sharp comment, often witty. He wrote the brief epitaph (a very short poem usually carved on gravestones) for the tomb of the 300 Spartans who died defending the pass of Thermopylæ against the entire Persian army. The Spartans had told the little band to hold the pass, and they perished to a man, carrying out this command. Simonides wrapped the sadness and admiration he and other Greeks felt into a few words:

> Go tell the Lacedæmonians, passer-by,
> That here, obedient to their words, we lie.

He could write gravely of the passing of all things into death, and he could make tender poems of little things, like his

EPITAPH FOR A HOUND

> Dead as thou liest now,
> Sealed in this tomb,
> I think the wild beasts tremble still
> Before thy white bones
> O huntress Lycas;
> And thy bravery great Pelion knows
> And splendid Ossa
> And the lonely peaks of Cithæron.

Of the Greek song writers, Anacreon was one of the most famous, making songs of wine and love. Born at Teos in Asia Minor, he went later to the rich city of Athens, where the tyrant Hipparchus, ruler of the city, made him welcome. Oddly enough one of the best known of Greek drinking songs is that made over the assassination of Hipparchus by two young men—a deed which took away Anacreon's bread and butter in Athens and sent him back home. This lyric was the Marsellaise of ancient Greece, expressing the Greek joy in liberation from tyrants, the Greek pride in democracy.

The English writer Conington has caught the singing spirit of this poem, supposed to have been made by the poet Callistratus:

HARMODIUS AND ARISTOGEITON

In a wreath of myrtle I'll wear my glaive, [sword]
Like Harmodius and Aristogeiton brave,
Who, striking the tyrant down,
Made Athens a freeman's town.

Harmodius, our darling, thou art not dead!
Thou liv'st in the isles of the blest, 'tis said,
With Achilles first in speed,
And Tydides Diomede.

In a wreath of myrtle I'll wear my glaive,
Like Harmodius and Aristogeiton brave,
When the twain on Athena's day
Did the tyrant Hipparchus slay.

For aye shall your fame in the land be told,
Harmodius and Aristogeiton bold,
Who, striking the tyrant down,
Made Athens a freeman's town.

Pindar, the great Theban poet, sang also of glorious deeds. He studied flute playing and dancing and the making of music, and learned from Athenian and Bœotian poets all he could of the art of poetry. His drinking songs and dirges, dancing songs

and pæans (poems of praise) were famous throughout Greece.
So were his odes to victors in the Olympic and other athletic
games. Stately in manner, he lifted the gorgeous Greek language
in marvellous rhythms and similes and metaphors. Much of his
poetry was doubtless chanted on semi-religious occasions and
at public celebrations, often to dancing. We have some of the
poetry, but cannot get its power and brilliance without the
flutes and lyres, the swaying bodies of young men or of maidens,
the solemn processions that must have been part of it.

The Greeks looked on Pindar as a kind of saint as well as a
poet. They put a throne for him in the temple of Apollo, and
a statue in the circus at Thebes. When the Spartans captured
and looted Thebes, they would not touch the house of Pindar,
and later Alexander the Great bade his soldiers to spare it when
in anger he destroyed the city and sold its people into slavery.

It was several hundred years after Pindar that one of the last
of the great Greek poets made a poetry quite his own. Theocritus lived in the Fourth and Third centuries before Christ
(he was probably born 316 B. C.), and not in Greece but in the
Greek city of Syracuse, in Sicily. But he was near a new centre
of Greek art and learning. Alexander the Great had conquered
Greece and Egypt and Persia, and built his capital, Alexandria,
on an island off the Egyptian coast. Here his successors held
court, and here a new Greek poetry glowed for hundreds of
years. Theocritus finally went to Alexandria, and of the poets
who belong to the Alexandrian group he is the greatest.

Theocritus, like other Alexandrian poets, made verses about
the glitter and perfume and gayety and music of the cities he
saw. These, however, were not his first poems nor his greatest.
We remember him chiefly because in much of his work he turns
from kings and heroes and elegant youths of the town and writes
of shepherds and shepherdesses. His "idyls," or brief pictorial
dialogues and stories, are of great sweetness and charm, and
ever since his time poets of other countries have written
"pastoral" (*pastor* is the Latin word for "shepherd") poetry.

But none have written with so simple, and pleasant, and clear a beauty as Theocritus. We see the goatherd asking his friend to watch the flock while he goes to say hello to his love, Amaryllis:

> The goats are tame—the least of all my cares,
> Save one, that tawny thief; keep watch upon
> His bearing, lest he butt thee unawares,

and we hear the simple countryman praying to Pan with a prayer that is half a threat:

> O goatish god, I pray you! grant my prayer,
> And in my view great Zeus is less divine:
> Reject it—at your peril—if you dare!
> And look no more for further gift of mine.

This humour, the beauty of the noontime when

> The fruit trees bend as though foredoomed to break
> With burden heavier than their strength can bear,
> And if the faintest zephyr seem to shake,
> Drop down an apple now, and now a pear,

the beauty of love-making under the trees, and the sadness of young Hylas, the friend of Hercules, dragged down by the water nymphs into a pool

> by galingale surrounded,
> With parsley and tall iris overgrown

are all in the simple, liquid poetry of Theocritus.

III

Of the poetry of poets like Sappho and Simonides, Pindar and Theocritus, we have said that little remains. Hundreds of other Greek poets are only names to us. Thousands are not even known by name. Yet to-day, when we talk of poetry, almost all of the words we use are borrowed from these Greeks.

Our terms for metre are Greek—hexameter, pentameter, tetrameter, trimeter.

The word *onomatopœia* (the suiting of the sound of words to their meaning) is Greek.

The names for the *kinds* of word groups—iambs, trochees, spondees, are Greek also.* Almost all the kinds of poetry we make bear Greek names—epic, lyric, dramatic, narrative, choric, idyllic, for example.

These facts tell their own story. They suggest what is true—that it was the Greeks who first took poetry to pieces and found how it was made and named the delicate magic machinery of it. They suggest also that the Greeks not only understood poetry, but wrote it so well that we still go to their verse to discover how to write our own.

Great poetry comes of being *lived*, and the Greeks lived theirs. In a way, these civilized Athenians and Lesbians and Thebans

---

*Word groups may vary a great deal. They may have two syllables in each group or three. In some groups the accent may be on the first syllable, in others not. Thus, in English, our "iamb" is a two-syllabled group with the accent supposedly on the last syllable:

The stag'   at eve'   had drunk'   his fill'
Where danced'   the moon'   on Mo'-   nan's rill'.

The trochee is also a two-syllabled group, with the accent on the first syllable:

Sol'dier   rest', thy   war'fare   o'er'
Sleep' the   sleep' that   knows' not   wa'king.

The whole metre of the first quotation is iambic tetrameter, because it has four feet or groups of words in the line, all iambs. The second quotation is trochaic trimeter with an extra syllable in the first line, and trochaic tetrameter in the second line.

The most generally used metre in English is iambic pentameter, or lines with five iambic feet in each. The Greeks used more frequently the dactylic and anapæstic feet—both three-syllabled. In good poetry the metre is not kept too closely, because readers would find it monotonous. The lines given below are iambic pentameter, but the accents are not always regular:

Good sir',   why' do   you start'   and seem'   to fear'
Things' that   do sound'   so fair'?   I' the name'   of truth'
Are' ye   fantas'   tical',   or that'   indeed'
Which out'   wardly'   ye show'?

In Greek poetry there were probably accents, but the length of the vowels played a more important part than in English. To some extent the long vowels corresponded to our accented syllables, and the short vowels to our unaccented syllables.

were very close to the simpler folk who planted their grain to chanted words and said verses to drive out sickness from the bodies of men or to send the souls of the dead on their way to the gods.

But the Greeks made poems less because they feared what would happen if they didn't and more because they loved the joy and ecstasy and wisdom of poetic art. They also had a feeling that no occasion of any importance, whether happy or unhappy, would be *fitly* observed without a poem. They made poems as we write letters of thanks or condolence, as we send flowers to someone we love or mourn, as we have music before our plays or speeches at our funerals. And for many occasions they developed particular kinds of poems.

The elegy was suitable for mourning.

The epitaph, as we have seen, was a short poem to be put on a tombstone.

The Greek odes were poems of a definite form made to celebrate victories in battle or at the athletic contests.

Many kinds of songs made for daily life have not come down to us at all—fifty different varieties, one writer thinks.

Probably poetry never meant so much before as it did to the Greeks, and has never meant so much since. The reciting of a poem was always an occasion. Often men and women and children flocked to the court of a palace or the broad steps of a temple, to hear the poets flinging their rhythmic words on the blue air. The singers sang alone and met in contests. They tossed jests at one another in rhythm, they told the news of other cities they had visited, they sang love songs and songs of victory.

We can mourn the loss to the world of the sparkling spirit and harmony of word, gesture, and music which these people made of poetry. Yet their words have not wholly died, and the fragments of Greek songs which we possess keep teaching us still of life and beauty. A modern poet, James Elroy Flecker, has told in poetry the miracle of this old world, reaching through time and fallen temples and forgotten cities to speak its word to us.

> We are dead, but our living was great: we are dumb, but a song of our State
> Will roam in the deserts and wait, with its burden of long, long ago,
> Till a scholar from sea-bright lands unearth from the years and the sands
> Some image with beautiful hands, and know what we want him to know.

CHAPTER VI

HOW POETS INVENTED PLAYS

In ancient Greece one of the great gods was Dionysus. He was the maker of green life on the earth, the lord of harvest time and purple grapes from which boys and girls trod red wine. When the last fruit of the year had been gathered, the folk of the Greek villages made festival in honour of Dionysus, dancing and shouting their joy that toil in the fields was over, that food was stored for winter and wine fermenting in tall jars.

The people would gather about the stone altar of the god and sacrifice a goat in his honour. In many places, they danced and sang a hymn, and it is thought that the celebration was named *tragoedia*, from *tragos*, the Greek word for "goat," and *ode* the word for "song." Sometimes the hymn would tell of the birth and death and resurrection of Dionysus, symbolizing the growth and autumnal decay and new springtime life of the fields, and sometimes the ancient heroes of the land would be honoured also. And there were boisterous worshippers who dressed themselves in goatskins and frolicked wildly in honour of the wine god. Some Greeks said that the tragoedia was in origin this rough, clowning dance.

In such celebrations there was little that resembled drama.

Negro tribes still dance and sing in the same fashion, and Indians in America, yet no plays have come of their ceremonials. But the Greeks, with their love of poetry, brought the poets into the religious revels of Dionysus, and the seed of the goat song, or dithyramb, grew until it blossomed into a theatre.

At first, the poets made and recited the songs to the god, telling in verse the story of his life, or the story of one of the great Greek warriors. Young men were chosen to help the poet with singing and dancing. It became the custom for the singer and this chorus of dancers to act out together the story of the poem. The poet pretended to be the various gods and heroes of whom he told. He went pretty far toward turning from a reciter into an actor. Music was played as he chanted; the chorus danced and sang. The tragoedia was becoming a splendid entertainment as well as a religious festival.

Thespis was supposed to have been the first poet who stepped out of the chorus and devised a dialogue with its members to make his poem more vivid. He was an Icarian, and his first official performance is supposed to have taken place in 534 B. C. The fashion he set quickly moved to Athens. Here the festivals were celebrated in a crude natural theatre. The dancers and poet-actor performed on the flat ground at the foot of a hill. The spectators sat on the slope, which was finally lined with wooden benches. At Athens, as in other places, a prize was given yearly for the making of the best tragic poem. The custom probably came down from early days, when the poet was rewarded for his work by the gift of a goat, perhaps the very goat sacrificed in honour of the god.

Meanwhile a boy had been born who was to make a new thing of all tragedy. His name was Æschylus.

He was born in 525 B. C., at Eleusis, a little town twelve miles from Athens. Here a great hall of initiation had been built, where the Eleusinian mysteries were celebrated. There were also groves sacred to Demeter, goddess of the earth and growing grain. Here lived the priests and priestesses of the goddess. To

Eleusis came noble Athenians to pray and make sacrifice and join in sacred celebrations.

Little Æschylus saw white-robed processions pass, bearing wreaths and incense, and chanting hymns. He saw the priests and priestesses file through the stately trees at dawn or sunset, or stand bowing by torchlit altars at night. He saw dances, and men and women marching to the groves and temples to take part in the Eleusinian "mysteries"—secret religious rites known only to certain worshippers. All through the poetry that Æschylus wrote later run a beauty and solemnity that may be a reflection of things he heard and saw as a boy.

But Æschylus was also preparing for a more active life. Like other Athenians of good family, he was taught to bear armour and fight. Soon the Persians under Darius landed at Marathon near Athens—kings and satraps, and swordsmen and slaves, rich in coloured cloaks and gilded armour, bent on overrunning rocky little Greece. Among the Athenians who went forth to oppose them were Æschylus and at least one of his brothers. Both fought well, and the brother died performing an act of great bravery. Æschylus was proud of being a soldier, and the Greeks say he wrote of himself the words that were carved on his tombstone. These tell nothing of the poems he wrote. They read:

Beneath this stone lies Æschylus, son of Euphorion, the Athenian . . . of his noble prowess the grove of Marathon can speak, and the long-haired Persian who knows it well.

Although the Persians were beaten at Marathon, they returned later, and Æschylus is supposed to have fought once more against them at Salamis.

Meanwhile, at the age of twenty-six, he had written a tragedy, and in 484 B. C., when he was forty-one, he won the tragedy prize. He was to win it twelve times more before he died.

Now, in writing tragedy, Æschylus did two things that greatly changed the celebrations. Up to this time, as we have seen, there had not been what we know as plays. There were only the single actor and the chorus. Nothing much could happen in the orchestra while this was the custom. The actor could talk to the chorus, or he could recite his poem.

But Æschylus put on two actors, and was then able to make his poem an imitation of the actual happenings of the legends the Greeks knew. One character could tell the story by talking to another, messengers could bring news. Kings could quarrel, prophets could warn foolish warriors. With the two actors and the chorus it was possible to make almost any story live again in speech and action before men's very eyes.

The second gift of Æschylus grew out of the first. With the new form of making a poem, he brought great skill as a poet. As this was fused with the acting out of the legends he retold, a new kind of poetry was born. In epic poetry, the listeners could hear *about* their heroes. In this new tragedy, they saw and listened *to* them.

The great Prometheus, chained in torment by Zeus because he had stolen fire from heaven for men, suffered his agony before their eyes and foretold to them the triumph he must win. Agamemnon, proud and sinful, came back from Troy in triumph to be murdered by his own wife.

These legends were serious stories, most of them unhappy or terrible. The Athenians, watching one of them lived out again, saw a warning against pride or cruelty or folly, or perhaps felt a likeness to misfortunes which they themselves had actually suffered. But pain was softened by the sound of flutes and lyre, the rhythm of dancers, the majesty of noble words. So there was a relief, a cleansing of the spirit, in watching this dream-like beauty and sorrow. As there is something healing in the shedding of tears for a loved one who has died, so in this new poetry the Athenians in an exalted manner found a relief from their fear of misfortune and their memories of pain in the sobbing "Woe! Woe!" of the chorus.

Of the more than ninety plays Æschylus is said to have written before he died at the age of seventy-one, we have only seven. Probably the greatest and most moving of his works is the terrible story, told in three plays, of Agamemnon's murder by Clytemnestra and Clytemnestra's death at the hands of her own son, Orestes. One distinguished modern poet has called it "the greatest spiritual work of the human mind." *The Persians*, another drama, is splendid in a different way. Cast in the form of a tragedy, it tells of the defeat of Xerxes and the Persian fleet at Salamis, 480 B. C. The scene is the Persian court, the heroine is Atossa, the Persian queen. Yet, though her sorrow is told with understanding and sympathy, the play was a celebration for the Athenians as well as a representation of grief. The ringing description of the battle, given by the messenger to the queen, is a triumphant hymn for the victory that meant life and freedom to Athens:

Then sounded the voice of the trumpet, with syllabled fire,
Troubling their line. Commands were shouted. The measured
Sweep of oars smote the ocean. Their ships each one
Clearly took shape before us. The right wing loomed
Foremost, well-ordered; after it galley on galley
Swept proudly, and as they approached us a thundering shout
Stormed at our ears: "O sons of the Greeks, advance!
Free now your native land, set free your children,
Your wives, and the temples of your fathers' gods,
The tombs of your ancestors—now you fight for them all!"
Swift from our decks there arose a responsive clamour—
A babel of Persian speech. There was no time now.
Bronze-beaked and swift, fiercely dashed ship on ship;
First with its stroke was a ship of Hellas that sheared
From a Phœnician galley her figurehead;
Locked then was foe with his foe in the fury of fight!
At first the torrent of Persian vessels sustained
The shock, but when the multitude of our galleys
Jammed in the rocky narrows, and none could help
His fellow, but each with bronze beak tore the other—
Shivered then were their oars, and the cunning Greeks

Hemmed them about and smote them on every side.
The hulls of our ships rolled over, the sea was hidden
With wreckage and slaughtered men; the shores and the reefs
Were choked with our dead. With wild oars went in flight
Each ship unfoundered of our Barbarian fleet.

Now, after Salamis, the Athenians celebrated their deliverance from the Persian ships. A procession of young men danced through the streets chanting of the victory. Their leader was a youth of fifteen named Sophocles, chosen for his grace and beauty. And when, eight years later, Æschylus's drama *The Persians* was enacted, Sophocles must already have been making verses and dreaming of the tragedy prize.

To win this meant skill as a poet, skill as a deviser of dramatic story, a genius for writing music and arranging the dances. The poet was the creator of all these things—words, story, gestures, and melody. It seems incredible to us now that more than one man with the genius Æschylus showed should have lived in a city of about one hundred thousand people—or in all of Greece. Yet, four years after *The Persians* was first acted, Sophocles won the tragedy prize, and for all the music and power of Æschylus, men have been disputing ever since as to which of these two writers of tragedy was the greater.

Their work was different. Æschylus, in telling the great hero stories, made human sorrow majestic, but chiefly celebrated the power and justice of the gods. The gods as he made them were nobler than Homer's gods—who had loved men and quarrelled with one another, and punished mortals at times in mere petulance. To Æschylus, Zeus and his companions were just though fearful. They were much like the Jehovah of the Jewish prophets, then being written of in another tongue and land, in stories and psalms that were to become the Old Testament of the Christian Bible. Æschylus, too, was a prophet in voice and religious zeal. Like the utterances of Isaiah and Elijah, his dramas were more like great songs than are the plays we commonly know. Less attention was paid to the story and

more to the emotions of woe and fear and reverence which the
poet wished to sing.

Sophocles brought a different mood to tragedy. He had been
born in time to see the triumph of Athens over the Persians,
and the great splendour and prosperity it enjoyed under the
leadership of his friend Pericles. He felt the power of the gods
almost as much as Æschylus, but he also felt much more than
Æschylus the power and glory of men.

> Marvels are many, but none
> More marvellous than man!

he makes the chorus exclaim in his tragedy *Antigone*. Then
follows a remarkable song of what man has accomplished:

> He that rideth the white sea
> Sped by the angry south wind,
> Pushing his path through waves
> That curl their tongues to engulf him.
> And Earth, the oldest of gods
> The unwearied, the everlasting,
> He harries—turning her soil
> With ploughs that are drawn by horses—
> Furrowing to and fro
> Forever, from year to year!

He traps birds and fishes and beasts in his nets, and, even
more—

> Speech hath he taught to himself
> And thought, wind-winged, and the mood
> That is moulder of law. He hath flown
> From the arrows of frost, when the cold
> Hard sky is a comfortless roor;
> From the rush of the arrows of rain
> He escapes; he hath cunning for all.

The poetry of Sophocles throbs with this exhilaration over
human achievement, the exhilaration of life in Athens that was
the pride and delight of the Athenian crowds.

The result of this was to make the men and women of Sophocles's tragedies more important and the tragic stories more

complicated. Æschylus had brought in two actors instead of one. Sophocles added a third. Accepting the power of the gods, he suggested that their will was hard to know and difficult to follow, and that at times there was something admirable in the pride they punished. Ajax, for instance, scorned the help of Athena, confident in his own strength and bravery. He goes mad and perishes for his audacity and self-confidence, but there is a greatness in his defiance.

In *Antigone* it is impossible not to admire the unfortunate heroine. Polyneices, the brother of Antigone, had come to capture Thebes, his own city. His brother Eteocles led out an army to oppose him, and the young princes died in battle with each other. Creon, their uncle, then became ruler of Thebes. He forbade anyone to bury the body of Polyneices, whom he called the enemy of the town. But Antigone went out and buried the body. When she was brought before Creon to explain why she had broken his law, she declared that the burial of a brother's body was an unwritten obligation laid upon her by the gods. What force was there in Creon's commands if they were against heavenly will? She could not obey what he had decreed:

> For not from the lips of Zeus such edicts were uttered,
> And never Justice, that men have enthroned with the gods
> Set these ways for the dealing of men with men.
> Nor had I dreamed that thou with thy mortal breath
> Wouldst challenge the sure, the unwritten word of immortals.
> Not to-day was it fashioned, nor yesterday,
> Deathless it stands; no man can say its beginning.
> The law of men may be broken—I dared not dishonour
> The word of the gods, inviting the anger of heaven!

Creon does not agree with her. The law, he declares, is sacred and must be obeyed. Antigone has broken it; she shall be walled up in a niche of rock, there to die. Creon's own son and wife beg him to alter his decision. Creon sends them away in anger. Finally, the prophet Tiresias warns him:

Think thou upon this, my son: it is common to men
To err; but he who hath erred and hath fallen on evil,
Neither rash is he nor unblest if humbly he seeketh
Healing, and holds no more to a stubborn purpose.
Self-will is pride, corruption of spirit. Be wise:
Yield then to the dead, defame not a breathless body.

Creon is persuaded. He goes forth and buries Polyneices, but
when he returns to release Antigone he finds that she and his
son and his wife have all destroyed themselves. He had not
seen clearly in his difficult situation the will of the gods.

Sophocles set forth in such tragedies the glory of man and his
danger. He shows how even admirable and virtuous men and
women can be destroyed by Fate. He does not blame the gods:
let men accept the beauty and splendour of life and let them
accept its peril also. His plays, made with a grave symmetry
and beauty, leave us, despite the calamity they display, with a
sense of serenity. It is a noble feeling, rejoicing in the good of
life, accepting its evil.

But now a poet came who was not so ready to accept it.
Euripides, born sixteen years later than Sophocles, was troubled
and daring and rebellious. The story runs that his father had
him trained to be an athlete. If this was so, he was soon more
interested in his mind than in his body. He left running and
discus throwing to be a painter, and seems to have listened
much to the talk of philosophers. Many of them had flocked
to the marble courts and elegant talk and poetry of Athens—
great thinkers like Anaxagoras and Protagoras and Prodicus.
It was their business to understand life, and they went asking
questions about the ideas and ways of men, about the nature
of the gods.

This questioning about life passed into the plays of Euripides.
Sophocles had shown that even the way of just men could lead
where chance and cruelty and injustice stalked them like savage
beasts. Euripides saw this, and more. To him the Greek gods,
as the legends pictured them, were often abominable. In some
of his dramas he showed their wicked use of power. In a similar

way he looked at war and saw its inhumanity. His tragedy
The Trojan Women is a terrible picture of the pain and sorrow
that follow after most battles, falling on countries like a dark,
choking cloud of shame and grief. His *Medea* reveals the sympathy he had for women, doomed to bear children in pain, to be
the toys and slaves of men.

Medea, the legend runs, had fallen in love with the hero Jason.
She helped him subdue the fire-breathing bulls and carry off
the golden fleece from Colchis, and fled with him. For his safety
and glory, she used the magic she understood, sometimes
wickedly. In his tragedy, Euripides shows her when Jason has
begun to tire of her. The hero proposes to send her and her
children away and wed another woman. In the legend, this was
supposed to serve Medea well enough, but Euripides lets his
heroine speak for herself. Her terrible words leave Jason not
quite so much a hero as he was generally supposed to be:

> Tell me then, where shall I go?
> Back to the house of my father, the house I betrayed
> When I fled love-maddened with thee? Shall I seek out the daughters
> Of Pelias, stained with the blood of a parent I tricked them
> To slay? So deed by deed I could tell out my story.
> Once I was loved in the land of my birth, but to-day
> My name is a curse. And the friends that were shelter in trouble,
> That merited most of my kindness—for thee I have turned them
> To foes . . . and behold! a reward for the curse of my service:
> Crowned with joy, I was blessed among maids of Hellas;
> Thee I won, the longed-for, the brave, world-splendid
> Hero and lover, who watches me now go banished,
> Thrust with my children to wander alone, unpitied,
> Hearing a mockery under the festal torches:
> "Where go the babes of the bridegroom to beg their bread
> Exiled, and she the woman who stinted of nothing
> To save him?"
> O Zeus, shall gold in the mart bear clearly
> Thy sign, by which is sifted the good from the base,
> And no mark show on the face of a man, proclaiming
> Before too late, the lie that is hiding beneath it?

Such speeches come often in Euripides's plays. He questioned
all pretense and mock heroism. He championed fiercely what

he regarded as the truth. His new ideas disturbed the Athenians, Of course, what he said was exciting, and a few citizens idolized this daring poet who made them think and wonder about everything on earth and in heaven. But the more conservative men of the town were alarmed. To them Euripides was a kind of Bolshevik (if they had known that word!). They feared that his criticism of the gods would make men irreligious, that his hate of war would cool the spirit of the Athenian soldiers, that his ideas about women would disrupt the home. They thought he ought to be exiled or clapped into prison.

The witty Aristophanes ridiculed Euripides bitterly. Aristophanes was a writer of comedies—humorous plays which gave the Athenians a lighter form of entertainment than the tragedies. He kept up his war on the author of *Medea* and *The Trojan Women* even after Euripides had died. A scene in his comedy *The Frogs* shows Æschylus and Euripides having a poetic contest in the underworld. Æschylus complains that it is not a fair competition. He has none of his plays with him, for they are all still on earth above, where men love them, but the plays of Euripides have all perished with their author, and Euripides has them with him, to quote from as he likes!

This distrust of Euripides and propaganda against him probably explain why he won only five tragedy prizes with the ninety-two serious plays he is supposed to have written.

Yet, if the Athenians distrusted him, they were also fascinated by him. They were undoubtedly fascinated by the traits they feared—his audacious exposure of shame, and his pity for the weak. However, he brought other gifts to tragedy besides these.

For one thing, he was a great musician. He made his choruses less a part of his tragedies, and more like a harmonious decorative element. Many scholars feel that this injured tragedy as Æschylus and Sophocles had made it. Yet Euripides made songs for his dancers which were sweeter and lovelier than the grand hymn-like harmonies of Æschylus. The poet-scholar Gilbert

Murray has caught the flowing beauty of such songs, though he has changed the metre of the Greek and uses the rhyme Euripides never used, and introduces many ideas not in the Greek. Cries the chorus in *Hippolytus*:

> Could I take me to some cavern for my hiding
> In the hilltops where the Sun scarce hath trod;
> Or a cloud make the home of mine abiding,
> As a bird among the bird groves of God!

Euripides was also a master of saying simply what he wished to say, and the better to make his plays clear to the Athenian farmers and mechanics, he invented the prologue. This was a speech by a god or hero, explaining what the play was going to show. In the plays themselves, he devised complicated plots, more ingenious and surprising than the slow and inexorable happenings of earlier tragedy.

Euripides also did more with love than his great rivals had done. Æschylus has put his attention on more solemn things. "No one knows of a woman in love in any play of mine," he says in Aristophanes's comedy *The Frogs*. Sophocles was not so austere—there is a splendid song on the power of love toward the end of *Antigone*. But Euripides made a great deal more than Sophocles of the love of men and women and its part in tragedy, and makers of plays have followed his example ever since.

Perhaps his greatest gift was the development of character. He paid more attention than Æschylus or Sophocles to his people, making them human, natural, living. Such interest led him to show the struggles men and women had with their own desires. Æschylus and Sophocles had invented the struggle between gods and men and between men and men. Euripides first staged the struggle of a man against himself.

All this interested the Athenians. Doubtless, they thought Euripides queer and "radical." They laughed with Aristophanes at his too melodious music and his romantic study and library in a sea cave on the island of Salamis. Still, they sang his songs on the streets, and Plutarch says that they were partly persuaded to make a truce with Sparta (the Peace of Nicias) by the praise of peace in Euripides's tragedy *Erectheus*. He was honoured outside of Athens also. When the Athenian expedition against the Sicilian city of Syracuse failed, and many Athenian soldiers were captured, the Syracusans freed all who could recite Euripides!

And in the end Athens had still greater cause to be glad that Euripides had made tragedies for them. Soon after he had gone in his old age to die at the strange court of the Macedonian king among the wild northern hills, Athens was captured by the Spartans and their allies. The leaders of the victorious army, the story goes, had decided to tear down the walls of the city and sell its people into slavery. "We'll make a sheep pasture of it," they said. Then they heard someone singing in the street:

O child of Agamemnon
I have come, Electra, to thy home in the wild!

The words of Euripides rang out, words about a Lacedæmonian king and his daughter. Tears filled the eyes of the leaders as they thought of their Sparta and its heroes and of the great Athenian poet who had woven both into music. They talked no more of destroying his city. Athens was saved by the singer she had feared.

III

Æschylus, Sophocles, Euripides. Their work was done in a single city of a hundred thousand people. Between the birth of the first and the death of the last not one hundred and twenty-five years elapsed. Yet out of their work came impulses that have throbbed in poetry and music and drama through all the years after, and are throbbing now.

All plays written in poetry—the French tragedies of Racine and the English tragedies of Shakespeare, for instance—are the descendants of the dramatic verse Æschylus created. They use not only the mechanics of drama which the Greeks developed, but the mood of high, terrible sorrow which was born of the tragic poems.

All plays written in prose—the plays we usually hear to-day —owe Æschylus and Sophocles and Euripides almost as much. These prose plays use the pattern the poets made, and often they seek for the effect one or the other of them produced. New York has recently applauded an American drama built of three New England tragedies and inspired by the Agamemnon-Electra-Orestes story, holding audiences from four in the afternoon until the edge of midnight.

But the tragedies of Athens did more than father our plays. They gave us music, too. The great spectacle the Greeks knew split in half and gave Shakespeare and Racine and Ibsen one part of itself and Verdi and Wagner and Puccini the other. Before the footlights of any grand opera, the dances and choruses of two thousand nine hundred years ago live still in an altered form.

This is a meagre outline of the influence of these tragedy writers on the world. To fill in the outline would take the rest of the book. Yet much is said if we say that for the moods of tragedy in their purest form we still go to Æschylus and his companions. We go to Æschylus himself for tragic power. We go to Sophocles for tragedy of inevitable things—the serenely terrible quality of plays like *Œdipus the King* and *Antigone.* We go to Euripides for the tragedy of pity, the tragedy of protest, the tragedy of men struggling against themselves.

For the Athenian poets who invented plays saw very deep into human souls—as deep, apparently, as the end of time. We say they are "modern." We mean merely that they understood the terror and grief of men and showed us how these could be blended with beauty. No one since has blended better than they, though one poet has written greater poetry.

CHAPTER VII

THE ROMANS: HORACE AND VIRGIL

I

The Greek poets made their songs in little city-states that could be snuffed out like so many candles, and often were. So, though these pigmy democracies and oligarchies thrust back Xerxes of Persia and his million men, all of them yielded at last to the spearmen of Alexander the Great of Macedon. And when Alexander had died and his empire broke up and the Greeks talked about freedom, and fought and plotted, the iron-hearted legions of Rome soon clanked out of the west. The Romans routed the quarrelling Greeks, killed the last king of Macedon, shipped women and children by thousands to be slaves in Rome, and left the others to pay taxes to greedy governors.

Poets sing best to free peoples, and when freedom died in Greece the making of great poetry died, too. But the poetry already made still lived on. The Romans read it, and their young men yearned to write like Homer and Sappho and Sophocles, and soon the homely poetry of the early Romans swelled into gay or grave music that was to cheer and teach and exalt the world for two thousand years after the first words of it were written.

II

One of the makers of this music was born about sixty-five years before Christ, in a humble family, in Venusia, a little Italian town on the eastern slope of the Apennines. The boy was named Quintus Horatius Flaccus, and we know him now as Horace.

The father of Horace had ambitions for his child. He himself had begun life as a slave, and though he became free and a respectable property owner, he was never rich. But he was only the more eager that his son should have what he had lacked. He had never learned to write—well, young Horace should. The father found teachers for him at first in Venusia. Then he got the daring idea that his boy should be taught, not in a rude provincial town, but at Rome, where the best teachers in Italy could be hired.

Even Rome was not good enough for Horace. Perhaps the young student sighed as one of his noble friends left for Athens to study poetry and philosophy. Perhaps the blunt father said: "Would you go there, too, my son?" and then, "Good. Let it be so." In any case, Horace was soon in the city where Simonides and Sophocles had sung, and where the great philosophers Socrates and Plato had taught, polishing off his ability to think and talk, to make verses, and bear himself courteously and calmly among other men.

But his college course was never finished. In the midst of it there came the news that the great Cæsar had been stabbed to death in the Campus Martius at Rome. The students were excited. Brutus, they learned, had led a conspiracy against Cæsar, because Cæsar was a tyrant. Now Brutus came through Greece, fighting Cæsar's friends, so he said, to keep Liberty alive in the world. Hurrah! Horace, with others, quit his books. He enlisted in Brutus's army. He fought at Philippi against young Octavius Cæsar and Mark Antony until Brutus was beaten and fell on his sword, and Horace and the rest of the army fled or were killed or captured. Soon afterward, Horace's father died. Octavius was busy just then parcelling out the estates of his enemies among those who had fought for him. The lands of Horace were among his gifts, and the young man found himself penniless.

But Octavius also declared forgiveness to his enemies, and Horace could return to Rome. He got a job as clerk of the quæstor—a position not unlike that of an office worker in our Treasury Department at Washington to-day. In his spare time he wrote verses.

And now he became acquainted with a young man named Virgil. Virgil, too, had started making poetry. He introduced Horace to the rich Mæcenas, a close friend and adviser of Octavius Cæsar and a patron of many poets. If Mæcenas lived in America to-day, he would have five automobiles to ride in, sail to France for a holiday, direct corporations, and collect books.

Mæcenas was a lover of feasts and company. He found in Horace a young dog who had a merry wit to season wine and good food. A poet, too. Perhaps it was not exactly as Horace himself had put it:

> Fretted in spirit, of my wings bereft,
> And robbed of everything my father left,
> Want looked me in the eye, so then and there
> I took to scribbling verse in sheer despair.

Still, the young man made laughing, reckless verses, and his art struck sparks as it "hit off" Mæcenas and his friends very much as it does in the four lines above.

This being a poet was the chance Horace thrived on. For to know and go with the Roman four hundred and to make witty verses for them seemed what he was made for. It was a kind of journalistic work, much like running a lively newspaper column in New York or London to-day. Of course, there was still no promise of a newspaper in the world, but the Roman patricians, merry at their banquets, listened greedily to each

scrap of polished humour thrown out to them by the poet-wit.
They tossed it about until it was better known than any printing press could have made it.

We sometimes have a poor opinion of poetry written for
banquets and ceremonies. This is because such poetry is often
done badly when it is done at all. But Horace took time to do it
well, and brought a fine art to it. Seeing the loves and faults and
failures and vanities of men about him, he made brief verse all
golden with music, swift as an arrow with truth and wit. It
came out sparkling, warm. It put the life men knew into dancing, dramatic rhythm. It showed the meaning of what men did,
and the fun or absurdity of it. Sometimes such poetry hurt.
Horace, poor among the insolent rich, proud among the vulgar,
loving virtue among the greedy and unscrupulous, got his revenge on the world that hurt him. He said later of himself:

> In youth's lusty Maytime
> The barbs of my passion at random I'd chuck,
> And, rushing head foremost into hot rhyme,
> I cared not at whom or how fiercely I struck.

So we see him cut the whip of his poetry at fools:

> In avoiding a vice fools run to extremities:
> Maltinus waddles with his robe like a sheik's;
> There's a Beau Brummel wears his, if you please,
> Tucked up to his waist. Rufillus reeks
> Like a silly scent-box; and, phagh! will you note,
> That fellow Gargonius smells like a goat.

or hold up to ridicule the "lounge lizards" of the day:

> But you, Demetrius, and Tigellius, you
> Go whine before the sofas of your few
> Pupils in petticoats as you're wont to do.

Probably Mæcenas and his guests didn't object to Horace's
sharpness. The crowd will always laugh at the other fellow. And
they were forced, too, to admire the beauty as well as the
satiric edge of this verse. Then they must also have liked

Horace's gayer poems to certain ladies—charming, sly, half-wicked, or light and airy. There was Lydia who—but let us get at the spirit of Horace's own spoofing:

> Zounds, Lydia, 'tis a shame, it is,
> So to burn up poor Sybaris!
> Have a heart, you cat, or, sooth,
> You'll soon have worms devour the youth!

And Phyllis seems to have been quite as attractive. "F. P. A." has put her into our own verse, keeping very close to Horace's unrhymed metre, and catching, in racy American words, the swing and the point of it:

> Phyllis, I've a keg of fine fermented grapejuice,
> Alban wine that's been nine years in the cellar.
> Ivy chaplets? Sure. Also, in the garden,
> > Plenty of parsley.
>
> See my little shack—why, you'd hardly know it.
> All the rooms are swept, Sunday-like and shiny;
> Flowers all around, altar simply famished—
> > Hungry for lamb stew.
>
> Neighbours all are coming over to the party,
> All the busy boys, all the giggling girlies,
> Whiffs of certain things wafted from the kitchen—
> > Simply delicious.
>
> Oh, of course. You ask why the fancy fireworks,
> Why the awning out, why the stylish doings.
> Well, I'll tell you why.   It's Mæcenas' birthday—
> > 13th of April.
>
> .   .   .   .
>
> If these few remarks, rather aptly chosen,
> Make a hit with you, come, don't make me jealous.
> Let me sing you songs of my own composing.
> > Oh, come on over!

Mæcenas listened to much of such poetry. The gay picture galleries of girls, the sharp arrows pointed for frauds and rascals, pleased him to his very heart. He perceived, like soberer modern

critics, the greatness of the writer who could make humour so
keen and musical and true. He saw to it that Horace's life was
made pleasant. He presented him with a farm in the Sabine
country near Rome. Here the poet retired at times to live as a
gentleman farmer, making his love poetry of ladies who mattered little to him in exquisite lines that mattered much, poking
fun at his friends in verse, poking fun at himself.

That much of his humour was just, even if sharp, is proved
by the fact that he had many friends of many occupations. And
as he grew older, the lashing violence of his earlier poetry disappeared. His later satires are more generous, though no less
spirited. Clean and charitable and sympathetic, spiced with
raillery, they rebuke without offending. He himself felt

> Compelled to touch a friend's defect
> With finger merciful, and fond respect;
> Even as a father's love will gently hint
> His urchin's eyes are roguish—if they squint;
> Or if the child be short and flat and thick
> As Sisyphus the dwarf, he'll call him "chick!"
>
> .   .   .   .
>
> So, should one friend betray too tight a fist,
> We'll speak of him as an economist;
>
> .   .   .   .
>
> Another wags too loose a tongue and tart,
> Let's blame it on his blunt and honest heart!

This quieter and mellower Horace has an infinite charm and
variety. Now he will have an anecdote to tell in verse, now it
is a little essay that he packs into his terse rhythms; now
proverbs dance by us; now there is a deft, shrewd stroke at a
human weakness as Horace has discovered it in some man or
woman whom all Rome must have known.

Horace wrote also of the joys of the simple life. In fact, few
have written so charmingly of it before or since. He sat among
his grapes and books, he dreamed under dark trees beside singing water, and celebrated the riches of the spirit at peace with

the world. Let others hunt for power, chase chimæras, worry
about beauty and pleasure—

> For me, the poet's ivy is very heaven:
> Me the cool woods wet with the dewy even,
> Where Nymphs and Satyrs frolic now shut in
> From the polluted rabble and their din,
> So let Euterpe's breath revive my reed
> And Polyhymnia string my lute at need.
> Oh, write me with the lyric choir, and I
> With my proud head shall bump against the sky!

Yes, he preferred simplicity to confusion, serene liberty to all the
luxurious vexations of the soul that lay waiting for men in Rome.

Yet to Rome he would return. After too much of peace he
would hustle off to banquet with Mæcenas, to play ball with
him the next day, perhaps, puffing furiously all the time (for
he was getting older and fatter now), carefully combing his
scant pepper and salt hair over his bald spot. Ah, he knew the
joke on himself. He makes his blunt valet, Davus, point out that
all his chatter about the charms of rural life and single blessedness is mostly fol-de-rol, and that, like the friends he derides, he
is a fickle fellow himself:

> When you are running around in Rome,
> You pull a heavy sigh for home;
> When in the country, you must cry
> The city's virtues to the sky.
> If no one asks you out to dine,
> Oh, then a beef stew is divine!
> You step out on strict orders only—
> It is so thrilling to be lonely;
> And gulping bumpers is a bore
> You edge away from more and more.
> But just let Sir Mæcenas send
> Command for you to meet some friend;
> Although the summons come so slow
> The lamps are being lighted, "Ho!
> Where's my hair oil? Look sharp!" you shout,
> "Great guns! Is there nobody about?
> Are you all deaf?" And in a flurry
> At the whole household, off you hurry.

And of course he could not help but fly off. In Rome lay that fascinating mob, humanity. A faker or a bore was waiting to be pinned with an epithet. Rich Alphieus, the miser, would come to be watched and studied and put into a poem. In fact, the whole city would come. If we read those mellow, glittering satires, we can indeed make a journey with the poet through the streets of the great town. Let us read and see it live again.

We have started. We are strolling by the loungers along the Via Sacra. On the Campus Martius we can watch the handsome young Hebrus putting his horse through his paces. We see games of quoits and tennis. We see the fops with their noses in the air, with their imitation of Greek manners, their absurd lispings. On the Via Appia the cocotte Barine swishes past us in her chariot. She is dressed like a queen, and her eyes are bewitchingly busy. The men gape. Young Pompilius forgets the wife he has just wedded as he stares after this naughty girl. Mrs. Pompilius bites her lovely lips and rushes home to loneliness and tears. And what ho! Here stalks Barrus, the ugliest mongrel in Rome, oiled and perfumed to the gizzard, one vast substantial grin. The girls giggle and wink as he goes by. And as we live there passes by us now the great hunter Gargilius. He is off again for the Hercynian forests, ringed about with an army of servants, rattling a very arsenal of arms. How much do you suppose he paid for the last boar he brought back?

Ah, well, it is dark now—time to return to our lodgings. Stray pigs and mad curs in the narrow streets, beggars to bother us, and a longer climb than we like before we are snug in our rooms!

No, we will not go to the show to-morrow. We had too much of it yesterday. There was that actor fellow who gave in to strong wine and snored in the middle of the performance! Let the bleachers shout at him. Let them have their spectacles and music. Give them bears and boxers, camelopards and elephants, and let them see

Whole fleets of ships in long procession pass
And captive ivory follow captive brass.

But to-morrow evening we shall dine out. Of course, Mæcenas
will come in as usual, bearing heavily on his two henchmen,
the buffoons and makers of small talk who will amuse him and
all the parasites and friends he feasts like a king. If there is
trouble in Spain, if he has got wind of a plot against Augustus,
he will frown darkly. Varius, the doleful playwright, will go on
punning. Sad authors do that. Young Sybaris will think of his
Lydia and sigh like a draughty furnace. Merciful heavens, grant
that we get away from the tipsy table before that Piso person
with his incurable literary aspirations can whisper more of his
spavined elegiacs or clinch that appointment for us to hear the
first half-dozen books of his eternal epic!

How cool the night air on the Fabrician bridge! What a
pack of knaves Mæcenas can collect. Sharp there! that man with
the mantle over his head, one foot poised on the bridge railing, is
about to leap into the Tiber! What an idiot to drown himself on
such a night! And in such a muddy stream! This will never do.
We arrest his cloak. We lecture him on the evils of speculations,
Jewish pawnbrokers, and the jaundiced Tiber. We empty our
person of all the sesterces we possess, quote a maxim, get him
home, and put him to bed. When next we meet the old repro-
bate, he will have acquired a great beard and established a
school in the latest garden variety of philosophy for pious old
ladies. He, in his turn, will read the riot act to us on every
conceivable shortcoming with which we are even faintly soiled.
He will hand us his pasteboard, mutter the hope that we may
commend him to Mæcenas and get him some pupils, and leave
us to wonder why we were ever so mad and foolish as to pluck
the bluenose from that sweet clear river.

Come, let us away from all this immense and fantastic hive
of the city! Back to the Sabine Farm and the silver fountain of
Bandusia. Back to the lentils and the olives and the leisurely
flagons!

> No Persian prettiness for me,
> My boy! I hate your garlands plaited
> With linden bark; leave on the tree
> Winter's rose where it droops belated.
> Twist me plain myrtle; do not quibble:
> It fits your brows as you serve and mine
> It graces as I sit and bibble
> Beneath the thick-leaved myrtle vine.

Perhaps the naughty Phryne will blow in, or Neæra with her Sapphic lute—if she has got over her sulks. Perhaps some lovely Chloe or Lalage. But these fascinatingly doubtful ladies are hothouse orchids. No danger. This is a strictly stag affair, thank you. Ho hum! the night draws on apace. To sleep, to sleep!

So—we have gone through some of Horace's poetry, getting as well as we could the gay picture of it. And as we read we can see why its very froth is immortal. There is a kind of eternal quality in some laughter, and Horace has it. In his songs of varied pattern—translated into English rhyme because rhyme, though he never used it, seems to help us capture the spirit of the verse—he stored wisdom and luminous peace and ridicule and fun and that half-sad thing, humour. And always he has made them in some way beautiful, in all ways human. He has held beside them, too, the image of the true deed or conduct that was ever in his mind. Not preaching truth—often laughing at it or with it, but always aware of it. Perhaps this, at the bottom of Horace's skill and humour and human kindness, has helped men read him for almost two thousand years. This with the rest of him has made great writers love him and imitate him. Petrarch, Voltaire, Nietzsche, Shakespeare, Ben Jonson, Milton, Pope, Byron—these are only a few who have remembered Horace as they wrote. And even to-day it will be a strange week when some poet does not translate him or sing of him in London or Paris or New York.

III

In the year 1930 the good citizens of Mantua will declare a holiday to all the world. There will be pride and music among the Mantuans. If you will stop any man, woman, child, or dog in the streets of that ancient Italian city, on the fifteenth day of October in that year, and ask, "Why this bustle and wagging of tails?" you will very likely be greeted with a smile, compounded of pity, pride, and contempt. And it will serve you right. For not to know that this is the celebration of the two thousandth anniversary of the birth of the greatest of Mantuans, Publius Vergilius Maro, will be like not knowing who chopped down a certain cherry tree, or who was born in a certain house in the town of Stratford-on-Avon.

Some say that before Virgil was born, seventy years before Christ, his mother Magia dreamed a marvellous dream of her son's greatness. That may be only a legend. So may be the tale that a poplar tree sprang up at once miraculously on the spot of his nativity. But if these stories are incredible, so is Virgil. Something quite as wonderful as dreams and poplar trees ought to have happened in connection with his birth.

Mantua is in northern Italy, then Cis-Alpine Gaul, and about Virgil's birthplace many Gauls still lived. Some scholars think Virgil was partly Gaul himself, and thus related by blood to modern peoples like the French and Irish. His father was supposed to have started life as a servant; if this was so, he gradually made his way up in life until he was at last a gentleman farmer. Like Horace's father, he wanted a good education for his son and took him to school at Cremona not far away. The great Julius Cæsar was governor of Nearer and Farther Gaul (France) then, and was busy fighting in the far north of his provinces. Cremona was his great recruiting station. Virgil may have seen Cæsar there, coming down into Italy between campaigns—at any rate, he always admired him in later years as men often do their boyhood heroes. He may have seen the legions gathering and marching off under their eagle standards to battle in Belgium and that new foggy island of Britain. Perhaps the whole story Cæsar told later in his *Gallic Wars* came to the boy Virgil at Cremona in news and dispatches and the sight of soldiers going and returning.

When Virgil was fifteen, he put on the toga, more to a Roman boy than first long trousers, and left for Milan to finish what we would call his "prep" school work. How long he stayed in Milan we are not sure; but very likely he went to Rome as early as 53 B. C., learning pompous orations under the tutor who instructed Octavius and Mark Antony. What Virgil thought of the stuff, we can see from his farewell to rhetoric:

> Out on ye, paint pots of the school, whose prose
> Periods reek, though not of Attic rose!
> Ye silly tinkling cymbals whose dull breath
> Drivels the poor young fellows to their death!

But like Horace, Virgil was possibly drawn from his studies into battle. The struggle, then at its height, was between Cæsar and Pompey. Certainly, his pitiful pictures of the dead on the battlefields of Pharsalia could well have been made by one who had fought under the triumphant standards of Cæsar. It is possible also that he saw rather stormy service on the Adriatic Sea with Mark Antony. There are signs that some detested bully of an officer made camp life, none too pleasant at best, quite unendurable for the poet who was never blessed with vigorous health. And the winter of 49 B. C., severe enough to leave even Cæsar shaken, may well have shattered Virgil. At any rate, if he served for a time, he returned soon to his books. From the outset, his heart could but little rejoice in the struggle which was making brother fight brother and draining Italy of her best blood.

After his withdrawal from the war, some contend, Virgil made a single and unsuccessful appearance as lawyer before the Roman court of law. This is of considerable interest when we reflect that the orators in his great poem, the *Æneid*, are all fluent but dreary fellows. We hear of him in Rome, a tall, dark, gaunt man, suffering much in his stomach, throat, and head, sometimes spitting blood; in food and drink most cautious —even at the abundant board of his patron Mæcenas, to whom, with such happy results, he had presented his friend Horace. Like Horace, he, too, seems to have lost his lands in the wars, but the poems he had now begun to write made him known and honoured, and other lands were given to him, so that he had enough money to live comfortably. Some scholars detect in one of Horace's satires a reference to Virgil as he might have been just then—a person with a rural haircut, an ungraceful toga, and untied shoelaces. However, it is equally possible that Horace had himself in mind. It was just the sort of thing he liked to do—caricaturing his whimsies and his hayseed locks and his flapping coat.

We can picture the two poets on a now famous journey they took with Mæcenas, going to Brundisium. There are Horace with his black eyewash (a lotion for his weak eyes), and Virgil with his black headache, both of them snoring while Mæcenas and his company hopped about after the tennis balls. And there was a voyage to Athens which Horace celebrated in another poem. But the two followed their separate ways. Both had a passion for philosophy and a passion for the country in common, but each took his solitude and often his social life in his own fashion.

The first poems Virgil wrote were about the earth and the farmers and the shepherds and the simple things of their life. These poems he called Eclogues. They took the outward form of the pastorals of Theocritus and the other Greek poets of the Alexandrian school. In them Virgil sang the radiance of the seasons, the tenderness of Italian landscapes, the charm of Italian friendships. All of April and the delicate tintings of the wild flowers and the glossy-leafed orchards and his own deep love of home and his tranquil memories and his longing for peace in a troubled world and the melancholy beauty of love— all these things went into the Eclogues. They were different from the Greek pastorals (aside from language)—using the beauty of the earth only as an introduction to a romantic understanding of the larger life beyond the glades and meadows. And with what exquisitely chosen phrases, with what fullness and rhythm and force the new poet sang! Rhyme Virgil never used, and his metre was different from ours, but something of the colour and spirit and tenderness of his verse may come in these lines about an aged shepherd:

> Happy old man! So will your land be yours and enough
> Though the marsh streak the pastures with slime and flinty stuff
> Be everywhere. Still no alien fodder will touch your little
> Tottering ewes, and no contagion. Oh, happy, here the brittle
> Hedge whose willow-blossoms, browsed by Hybla's bees,
> Will whisper you to sleep; there the sweet mysteries
> Of water, the streams you know so well, the sacred springs;
> From here, under that tall stone's curve, the dresser sings
> Out into the air—while your hoarse wood-pigeons and white doves
> Will go on murmuring the inconsolable alto of their loves.

The Eclogues were soon the rage in Rome. They were sung in the theatres, according to an Alexandrian fashion then in vogue, and were thus the unprinted "best sellers" of the day. Horace, congratulating his friend, said that the muses had granted him tenderness and refined wit. Sweet indeed was the pastoral pipe Virgil blew upon, and its music charmed the heart.

The years that followed the Eclogues were devoted to reading, travelling, observing, and brooding. Virgil had become more and more sober—even more sad. Rome was full of suspicion, plots, and selfishness. Though the Eclogues had scored big hits, and though Mæcenas wanted to keep him at Rome and gave him a villa in his own gardens on the Esquiline Hill, the city was not for him. It appealed to his imagination, but only because he thought of an older and more shadowy Rome—the city of heroes. And in order to dream of that, he went back to his own garden villa near Naples.

When the Georgics, his next poems, were finished, there was more in them than the lyrical celebration of labour in the fields. There was more even than the intoxication of April, the brotherhood of plants, animals, and men. Virgil's heavy heart, his fears for the future of his city, also went into the Georgics. Few pictures convey the feeling of horror and passion which convulsed Italy at the assassination of Julius Cæsar as indelibly as that silhouetted in bitter black at the close of the first Georgic. All nature mourns: the sun hides his golden head in a veil of darkness.

But everything was a prelude to Virgil's greatest work, a work for which he had been preparing himself these many years. It had been his earliest ambition to compose an heroic poem on the traditions and the glories of the Roman people. Taking the epics of Homer as a model, using even some of Homer's scenes and characters, he wished to sing of the birth and future of Rome. The Emperor Augustus had repeatedly urged him to the task. Once, when absent on a campaign, he wrote Virgil a half-playful, half-threatening letter demanding the first draft, or if not that, then any single passage of this poem about Æneas, the founder of Rome. And the poet would reply to his imperial patron, imploring time, time, more time to mould his ideas into perfect form—and, in the same breath, lamenting the hugeness and great range of them and expressing an abrupt desire to burn the book.

We can sympathize with both the Emperor and his poet—especially with the poet. For Virgil had in mind a magnificent, a tremendous thing. He wanted to sing of the age of heroes, but make what he wrote stir the blood of living men. The story was to be of Æneas, but of later Rome, too, and it was to tell also the very meaning of life.

Partly, this was to be done by making the olden hero suggest the hero Virgil knew himself. Virgil had never forgotten a cer-

tain holiday in September, 46 B.C., when Julius Cæsar celebrated
his four triumphs—over Gaul, Egypt, Pontus, and Africa. Such
plunder, gold, chariots, captives, men had never seen. The
gorgeous athletic games Virgil had remembered and put into
the fifth book of the Æneid. And there was that marvellous moment when Cæsar dedicated the Temple of Venus Genetrix,
Venus the Birth-Giver. By doing this he seemed to say, "I am
descended from the goddess." Then, soon after, he had put a
statue of himself among the gods on the Capitoline Hill. To
young Virgil this purple pomp and daring ceremony had been
an inspiration. Perhaps the plot of the Æneid flashed vaguely
but blindingly into his mind and soul as Cæsar's golden chariot
swept through the clouds of flowers and trumpet blasts.

So Cæsar is sometimes Æneas. When the Trojan lingers at
Carthage making love to Dido, it is hard not to believe that
Virgil remembers how the great Julius stayed in Egypt in 47
B.C., flirting with the bewitching young Cleopatra, instead of
coming back to Rome and his great work there. And young
Octavius peers through the disguise of little Ascanius, while he
appears later in Æneas's vision of the future as the great emperor who should bring peace and a golden age to the world.
And through all this glorification of Rome and Rome's Cæsar
and his successor, the ruler of the earth, ran a telling of what
man's place and use and hopes in life should be.

Yes, it was a tremendous and difficult poem, and as it stands
now, wanting much that Virgil wished to do to it, it lacks harmony. The third book seems to have been written before the
first. There are things in some parts of the poem that do not
fit with things in other parts of it. Virgil, dying after a sea
voyage he vainly took in search of health, begged his friends to
destroy the poem. They were gloriously wise and did not, but
we can see that it was not finished, and how Virgil, the perfect
artist, writhed at the thought that anyone might read his great
dream before it was written true.

But how great a dream it is even as we have it! Nobody

tells better the delight there is in discovering Virgil for the first time than George Moore, a living Irish writer, in his *Héloïse and Abélard*. In limpid prose he relates how in the middle ages the young lovely Héloïse, spending a vacation from her convent in the house of her uncle, a learned and devout man, is by him brought to the beauty of the Mantuan. Her uncle had put his books away, for he expected his niece to be a mere frivolous girl. When he found she knew Latin, he was delighted and told her of Virgil:

"Never to have read Virgil. O Héloïse, what joy awaits thee! Eclogues! Æneid! Georgics! At which end wilt thou begin? With the story of Dido, doubtless."

Then he went out of the room, leaving her alone with the great poet. She read of Æneas, the Trojan, flying from burning Troy, of his wanderings over the seas as he hunted for the new city the gods bade him found. She read of the Cyclops, of his cavern home, as described to Æneas by one of the sailors of Odysseus. Odysseus, it will be remembered, had escaped from the Cyclops cave by ramming out the monster's one eye with a burning pine tree:

It is a den of gore and orgies, deep, dark, monstrous;
Its lord stretches to heaven and strikes the terrified stars. . . .
The flesh of wretched men and their black blood are his rations.
These eyes beheld two bodies, comrades caught by his huge hand,
As, in the midst of his cave, he threw back his horrible tresses,
Saw them brained against granite, the floor splashed swimming with blood—
Saw the warm joints quivering under his tusks and his talons.

She read also of Queen Dido at Carthage who loved Æneas. Héloïse saw, as she read Virgil, that life had a purpose—all life. And she saw it had beauty she had never dreamed of. After reading, one day she stood at the window:

She stood for a long time looking at the landscape before her, wondering at the leaves. One after another the leaves, faded, discoloured, detached themselves from the stems, fluttered and fell into the stream and were borne away. And turning her eyes from the willows to the fields, she noticed how quiet and reposeful they were, as if weary and glad to dream a little while before the white oxen came forth again to turn them into tilth, preparing them for the sower who would come after the plough. "The death of the year," she said, "just as Virgil described it a thousand years gone by. A year dies every year and is born again, and that forever and ever." Her eyes followed the clouds, bringing as they passed over the sun a little dimness that she welcomed, and while admiring the fields she asked herself how it was that she had never before perceived how beautiful they were, though she had been looking at them ever since she had returned from Argenteuil, the same fields under different aspects and signs, always beautiful under dark skies or somnolent blue. . . .

"How beautiful," she said, "is the dark cloud now at poise over the next parish, drenching the ploughman there, and in a few minutes it will drench that other in the field yonder bending over the stilts as the white oxen fare to the headland slowly step by step, so slowly that it seems they will never reach it. The same white oxen that we read of in Virgil are before me now, the same oxen, their sides showing against the tilth; and were I to go down to the river I would find among the willows the swarm of bees about which he wrote, murmuring in and out of a hollow tree.

"If it had not been for Virgil I should only have known the story of the world as told in the relations of martyrdoms and miracles, and have seen the world only in relics of the saints. But he unsealed my eyes, and by night and day the skies and seas will be beautiful to me, and along the coasts that the galleys drove against in their flight from smoking Troy I shall see wreckage and Dido, the unfortunate Queen whose lover the gods raped from her, Æneas having been chosen by them for their fateful purpose." The smoke from the pyre trailing over the sea in the wake of the departing galleys appeared to her, and she fell to thinking that greater than the gift of vision was Virgil's revelation of human love, love of woman for man and man for woman; and the story with all its sorrow seemed to her so beautiful that she would have changed places with Dido or with Æneas, for on leaving Dido his heart, too, was wrung, but he had obeyed the gods and founded Rome. . . . "Beauty was Virgil's theme always," she said, "and he taught us by drawing our attention to what is beautiful, and his art was to make things beautiful in themselves more beautiful by selection and exquisite refinements of language. Nothing of the world's beauty seems to have escaped him," she continued, picking up the book again; "he raised all things to a higher level, even the gods, for the gods of his day were perhaps not as beautiful as he made them, nor the men and women, though it would grieve me to find myself thinking that they were less august than he painted them to us. Even the insects he raises out of their lowly instincts and includes them in divinity."

We can turn, as Héloïse may have done often, to the tenderly toned Eclogues, dew-washed, as fresh to-day as a spring morning hundreds and hundreds of years ago:

You, Tityrus, piping under the covert of the shadowing beech
Upon your thin pipe study the woodland speech;
While we exiles are quitting our country's borders, the lilies
Of our love, you, Tityrus, in cool repose can teach
Tree and rock the charms of your Amaryllis.

Like Héloïse, we can find ourselves recollecting verses out of
Virgil's Georgics as we contemplate the pageant of summer:

What makes a cornfield shine;
What star favours the furrow,
The wedlock of elm and vine;
The oxen and the kine,
Their care and breed; how borrow
For all the frugal, fine
Commonwealth of bees
From our rich lore—of these
I build the singing line.

These Georgics Virgil wrote as a protest against the luxury
and greed and vice that he saw growing on Rome, and as a call
for men to forget the terrible wars they had endured, and re-
build suffering Italy. It was his intent, proudly and lyrically,
to teach the nobility of labour in the fields, to show the strength
that could be derived from closeness to nature and the bliss
which living near to the soil gave to the soul. He wished to contrast the simplicity, safety, and sanity of such a life with the
luxury and sickness of the world. He wished to link up the ideal
of a lifetime of rough labour with the splendours of Italy and the
grandeurs of Rome. We thrill to his purpose and his poem still.

Virgil can come to us in an even richer way, if we go out to
him. He can mix in our lives and become part of what we feel
and remember. He can be something to call upon when we need
examples of courage to sustain us against sorrow. He can help
us when we are threatened, when we are defeated. He can give
us examples of the comradeship and love that can be between
father and son who have known great grief together and the
loss of those whom they cherished, and much treasure. He can
show the examples of the men who follow a leader through sad-

ness and treacheries and disputes over desperate seas and in hostile lands. He can tell us how a man can obey, as Æneas did, a great divine will that calls him away from pleasures though the heart mutiny and red lips and white hands plead with him to stay longer and eat of the drowsy lotus and forget again.

Let us hear Virgil speak in his fashion. Here is a call for you when your courage is low or gone—these ringing words of Æneas to his exhausted men after a savage storm:

> Comrades! for comrades we are, no strangers to hardships already;
> Hearts that have felt deeper wounds! Of these too Heaven will heal us!
> Why, men, you have even looked on Scylla in her delirium!
> Heard those rock-rousing yells and tested the crags of the Cyclops!
> Come, call your spirits back, and banish your dark forebodings—
> Who knows but some day this we shall also remember with gladness.

And if you thrill to the colour and din of battle, here is an instant etched in blood and lightning:

> There, at the very gate, looms Pyrrhus in violent splendour,
> Gleaming with spear and sword and with all the glitter of steel!
> Even as against the daylight a serpent gorged upon dead stuff
> Whom winter had kept clammy and bloated under the ground,
> Now, his skin sloughed, renewed now, in the confident beauty of April,
> Rears his breast erect and twists his glittering meshes
> Towering to the sun, and flashes in his mouth his tongue, the three-forked,
> With him gigantic Periphas and Automedon, his arms-bearer,
> Once the charioteer of Achilles, with him the ax-men of Scyros
> Press to the ramparts and heave red fire-balls up to the roof-top,
> Himself in the thick of the foremost, a two-edged ax in his right hand,
> Splinters the stubborn portal and the copper-sheathed valves from their hinges:
> Crack! See!—Now he has hacked out a plank and plunged to the oak's heart
> Till in the middle a window gapes. . . .

One could go on quoting such ringing lines, and other lines softer and more golden, all wrought with marvellous smoothness, carrying a glorious sound and glorious meanings. We could follow Virgil down through the ages to tell how Dante, the Italian poet, hailed him as Master, and Chaucer, the first great writer of English verse. We could show how he gave the art

and meaning of poetry to Shakespeare and Milton, and how
Lord Tennyson sang on the nineteen hundredth anniversary
of Virgil's death:

Roman Virgil, thou that singest Ilion's lofty temples robed in fire,
Ilion falling, Rome arising, wars, and filial faith, and Dido's pyre;
Landscape-lover, lord of language more than he that sang the Works and Days,
All the chosen coin of fancy flashing out from many a golden phrase;
Thou that singest wheat and woodland, tilth and vineyard, hive and horse
    and herd;
All the charm of all the Muses often flowering in a lonely word;
. . . Thou that seëst Universal Nature moved by Universal Mind,
Thou majestic in thy sadness at the doubtful doom of human kind;
Light among the vanish'd ages; star that gildest yet this phantom shore;
Golden branch amid the shadows, kings and realms that pass to rise no more;
. . . I salute thee, Mantovano, I that loved thee since my day began,
Wielder of the stateliest measure ever moulded by the lips of man.

I V

So we pass from Horace and Virgil. There were other poets
in Rome—Lucretius, Catullus, Ovid, Terence, Seneca: Horace
and Virgil were the greatest. They made Roman laughter immortal, Roman wisdom, Roman beauty. Some people, remembering how the Romans conquered and punished and taxed the
world, call them hard and cold and dry of beauty. But Horace
and Virgil live to-day to tell other things of some Romans. We
read them still and know there was other power than the power
of the sword in the Roman world.

CHAPTER VIII

THE POETRY OF HEROES AND DRAGONS

There was poetry written in Rome and Greece after Virgil and Horace died, but it was not great poetry. Rome had conquered Greece, and now luxury conquered Rome. Feasts and circuses and parades and idle love making—these made up the life that poets had to write about. Soon the Barbarians from the north came pouring into Gaul, Iberia, and Italy, killing and destroying. By the time they came, in the Fifth Century after Christ, there was no valuable poetry being made.

In fact, the next great poetry of the Western world was produced by the very Barbarians the decadent Romans feared and despised.

These Barbarians were not so barbarous as they were once supposed to be. Of course, they came to plunder the Romans of their cattle and gold and jewels. Naturally, anyone who sets fire to your house and shakes an ax at you while he demands your money looks barbarous. And the Romans wrote of the Goths and Vandals and Visigoths as if they were wild, savage, and ignorant people.

But they were not so bad as they looked. It is true they

79

sacked Rome and overran Spain and Africa and smashed what was left of the great Roman Empire. Still, the empire was ready to be smashed, and the Barbarians, after breaking it, soon helped to patch it up again and defend it from other Barbarians. And the life that these Teutonic peoples lived in their own lands (as we find it described in their poems and stories) was in many ways a noble one.

It was apparently a life not unlike that of the Greeks of Homer's time. The chiefs or kings built great halls or castles out of rough-hewn timber. Their people hunted, fished, raised cattle and grain, wove cloth, wrought goblets, wagons, boats, musical instruments. They held meetings, established laws, played chess and—made poetry.

We don't know when they began to write their first great poems. The first of their poems we have found shows that they must have known how to make poetry for a long time. And this poem was probably written in the Seventh Century after Christ.

It is in one sense an English poem. The epic of *Beowulf* was probably first made on the shores of the Baltic Sea, in Denmark or southern Sweden. It tells of people who lived in these places between 550 and 600 A. D. But apparently the tribes who made the poem came with the Angles, Saxons, and Jutes to conquer Britain, and it was in Britain or England between 800 and 900 A. D. that someone finally wrote *Beowulf* down. So it was written down in the Old English or Anglo-Saxon tongue, and came to be, not only the first English poem we have, but also the first poem we have from the Teutonic peoples.

It tells the story of Beowulf, a prince and warrior of the Geats. His people probably lived in southern Sweden. Beowulf came to the country of Hrothgar, King of the Danes. He had heard that a great monster called Grendel had been killing the people there. Grendel was in the habit of coming to the king's hall and seizing a number of men and making off to dine on them in his lair in the dark forest.

Beowulf went into the hall and slept there, and when Grendel appeared, the hero seized him by the arm. The beast knew at once that someone of great strength had gripped him, and he was afraid and tried to run away. But Beowulf held him, and finally Grendel, threshing vainly in this terrible grip, had to tear off his own arm to escape. He fled to his lair and died there.

But hardly had the Danes begun to celebrate their deliverance when his mother came back to avenge him. She killed one of King Hrothgar's bravest men, and the king was in despair. But Beowulf said: "Do not mourn. Avenging our friends is better than weeping too much for them. Let us hunt out this fiend. I promise you she shall not escape—no, not in any wood or dark mountain chasm, nor on the floor of the sea itself."

So they set out for the home of the monsters:

A land of wolf-slopes	and windy headlands,
Wildered fen ways;	there the fierce torrent
Shadowed by misty	mountain shoulders
Dashes downward	dark under earth.
Thence a mile's measure	lies the mere,
Fast overhung	by frost-rimed forests:
Ringed is the water	with roots of trees.
There may a watcher	spy a night wonder
Fire on the flood.	No gray grandfather,
None mothered of woman	knows the place.

Here the hero found the monster. He dived after her into the dark water and came up under the mountain into a cave. There he fought with her and killed her. Then there was great feasting in King Hrothgar's hall, and ale drinking and songs of heroes.

Beowulf was written in what is called alliterative verse. Alliteration is a musical sound made by using close together important words or syllables beginning with the same sound. Each line of this alliterative poetry was divided into two parts, as can be seen in the verses quoted above. The sound to be repeated throughout each line was usually used twice in the first half and once in the second. In the line

Dashes downward   dark under earth

it is the "d" sound that is used. These sounds gave the lines their character, and probably the poet emphasized the alliterating syllables as he said them. In between, the rhythm could vary a great deal; in fact, almost as the poet wished.

Alliterative poetry was the poetry of most of the Northern peoples. We see it in the *Lay of Hildebrand*, the earliest German poem we have, and in the Scandinavian poetry. Gradually, it became mixed with rhyme, and finally the old swinging lines of *Beowulf* and similar poems disappeared. Still, it lasted in England until 700 years after *Beowulf* was written, and to-day our poets still use alliteration.

Between the first great Northern poem and the next important poetry that was written in Europe, there is a gap of several hundred years. During this time, much had been happening. The Barbarians had conquered France, Italy, Spain, and England. They had settled down and learned how to do and make many new things. They became Christians, too, and the old chiefs and kings were now knights, fighting for the Church and their ladies, and trying, if not always successfully, to be just, courteous, and kind. Hundreds of thousands of them went on the crusades to capture the Holy Land from the Turks and Saracens. Some came back with jewelled swords and silken cloth, with tales of spices and Syrian fruits, elephants, Greek palaces, Arabian horses.

And this new life soon turned into new poetry. In the southern part of France, poets writing in the Provençal or southern French language began to make songs of war and spring and love. Theirs was a beautiful land, with green fields running down to blue seas, and in the south, hanging in the sunny air, the snow-capped peaks of the Alps or the Pyrenees. Here even the knights became poets, calling themselves troubadours. They told tales in verse and made songs to mock their enemies. But for the most part they sang of the ladies they loved. Love, they said, made poetry. One of them wrote:

What marvel if my song excel
The songs of others? I who pay
More homage unto love than they
From him have grace to sing so well!

Each troubadour strove to sing better than all the others, so that he might thus win glory for his lady. From the hymns of the priests or the old street ballads they had picked up the craft of rhyming, and one thing they did was to use rhyme in new strange ways. Whether they became skilled in poetry from knowing something of the old Roman poets, or heard the poems of the Arabs, who had conquered Spain, or whether they taught themselves, it was a new poetry they made, lovelier than any of the Northern alliterative poems.

Unfortunately, we have only fragments of their verse. With the gay singing of the troubadours went a gay life. Their religion, too, was a little different from that of their neighbours in France and Italy. The French King and the Pope did not like them, and finally there was a crusade against the country of the troubadours. The singer knights were defeated, and fled or died in battle, and there was an end to the great Provençal poetry. The new lords of the land destroyed the books and castles of those they had conquered, and only here and there a few poems have survived in rare manuscripts to show us what the troubadours had done.

But the poets of southern France had put new life into poets in other countries. In Germany the troubadour spirit sprang up among the knights, and the songs of the minnesingers were made. In the north of France jongleurs, priests, knights, and even kings made poems. A lady, Marie de France, was a famous poet. Richard the Lion-Hearted, King of England, was a singer of love and a lover of singing.

There is a story of how he once got out of prison by means of a song. Richard had gone on a crusade, and when he came back, he was shipwrecked and had to pass through the country of his enemy, Duke Leopold of Austria. He was captured and imprisoned in the castle of Dürenstein, on the Danube River, and no one knew where he was. Many thought he had died.

Then the story says that Richard's minstrel, Blondel, went through Germany and Austria singing outside all the castles a song that King Richard knew. When he came to Dürenstein he sang the first verse of the song. Then he heard King Richard down in the castle prison singing the second. And—according to the story—this is how King Richard was found and later set free.

But the short songs or lyrics of this time meant less to the people than the poetry of their heroes.

Spring and love were pleasant things to make poetry about, but heroes were more important. Unfortunately, the people of those days had many perils to fear. Wild beasts killed their sheep and cattle. Robbers lurked in the woods to attack them if they went travelling. Anyone might have a bad neighbour who would steal from him or quarrel with him. The great nobles fought with one another, and kings fought against kings. Then there were pirates at sea, and to the south the infidel Turks and Arabs.

So bravery and strength and good faith meant saving men's homes and lives. And each town and province and country gloried in its champions, while there was nothing finer a boy could dream of than becoming a great knight. And, as Americans like to hear of how Daniel Boone led the way across the Alleghanies into Kentucky, how Frémont made a path to California, how Lincoln's courage, common sense, and patience saved the Union, and how Roosevelt fought to make the workers of the land better off and the ways of doing business fairer for everyone, so the people of these older days liked to hear the stories of their heroes. And the poets sang what the people wanted them to. They made long poems or lays of brave knights that made old fighters live their younger days again and boys long for great adventures.

The greatest of the hero poems of the French is *The Song of*

Roland. Roland was the nephew of Charlemagne, the great emperor of the Franks who ruled France and Germany. After fighting for seven years in Spain against King Marsilla and the Saracens, Charlemagne made peace and started back to France. Count Roland commanded the rearguard, which came along after the main army. At Ronceveaux he was attacked by a great army of Saracens, who had been persuaded to fall on him by the false Count Ganelon, Charlemagne's brother-in-law. The poem tells how Roland's friend Oliver begged him by the oath of their friendship to sound his horn Olifant, so that Charlemagne would know the rearguard was in peril. But Roland would not, crying out that such would be a coward's way. So he and his knights fought the great army of Saracens and finally scattered it. Then another host appeared. Roland sounded his horn now. Thirty leagues away the Emperor heard it. Twice it sounded, and twice he wanted to turn back, but each time Ganelon said with a sneer: "Why should we turn back? Who would dare to attack the great Roland?" But a third time the far voice of Olifant reached the ear of Charlemagne. Then the Emperor would no longer listen to Ganelon. He faced the great army about, and footmen, and knights and princes hurried gladly but fearfully to deliver their hero:

> High are the peaks, monstrous and dark; and deep
> Are the valleys, and the streams lash down the steep
> Cliffs; and the voices of the bugles sweep
> From front to rear—to Olifant they leap
> Replying, and the Emperor spurs his steed,
> The Franks run crying—none but in his speed
> Weeps and laments and prays to God to heed—
> Keep Roland safe from King Marsilla's hate,
> Until they come—and storming in one great
> Surge, smite the cursèd foe, and devastate!
> In vain they pray, the battle will not wait,
> They were slow to hear and turn. They come too late.

Then the song tells how at length Roland's army was cut down man by man, and how Oliver died, and even Roland at last was fatally wounded, and how he knew he would die and tried to break his great sword Durendal on the rocks so that the Saracens could not get it, and how Durendal split the rocks, but would not break, and finally Roland lay down on it and died praying, and how Charlemagne found his body and went back to Spain and avenged his death on the Saracens, punishing the traitor Ganelon who had caused Roland's death.

The Germans also had a great epic—the *Nibelungenlied*. This was an old story, known also to the Scandinavians, who made tales and poetry of their own about it. The *Nibelungenlied* is the song of the Nibelungs, or people of the mist. The poem says:

> We hear in olden story many marvels told
> Of heroes great in glory, of mighty deeds and bold.
> Of folk in feast delighting, of weeping and of woe,
> Of gallant fighters fighting, now if you listen
> you may the wonder know.

And it goes on to tell of Siegfried, of the dragon he killed and the hoard of gold he got, of how he won the fair Kriemhild and helped Gunther her brother to win Brunhild, the warrior-queen. It tells of the quarrel between Kriemhild and Brunhild, and how Brunhild persuaded Gunther and his uncle Hagen to kill the great Siegfried by treachery, and how they were later killed by Kriemhild.

There were also hero poems of the British king, Arthur. The French sang of him, and then the English. Arthur was a king who lived in and near what is now Wales and fought against the Angles and Jutes and Saxons. That was hundreds of years before there were knights as the French and English knew them. But the mediæval poets told how King Arthur was a great and good king, and how he had at his city Camelot a Round Table at which he sat with his knights, and how Launcelot and Gawain and Percival and Tristram and other of King Arthur's warriors did great deeds. Then there was Merlin the wizard, and there was also Queen Guinevere, King Arthur's wife, who fell in love with Launcelot. And in the Arthurian legends appeared Modred, King Arthur's own nephew, who rebelled against him and finally killed him, and was killed himself. All these stories made a great group of poems for English poets, though it was left for the English poet, Tennyson, six hundred years later, to bring them all together and write of them so that we can read them to-day.

The poetry of heroes and their deeds was not great poetry as the Iliad and Odyssey and the Æneid were great poems. It was not so well made as the great Greek and Roman epics. But the poems are great stories. They taught the people of the Middle Ages how to live nobly, how to be courageous, how to be faithful to friends, how to die for their Christ or their king. They told of great love, of sin and repentance and holiness.

And there has been enough in these old poems to keep the world telling or reading them ever since. Perhaps most of the stories were only half true. Maybe Roland was killed in a skirmish with a few of the wild robber Basques of the Pyrenees instead of the Saracens. Maybe Siegfried never killed a dragon. Maybe Arthur was just a chief of the Britons who beat back the Angles and Jutes for a while, and never had any knights or any round table.

Still, even we to-day live nobler lives because the poets wrote of these men. In New York and London and Paris and Berlin we see the operas Richard Wagner wrote of Siegfried and Parsifal and Tristram fifty years ago. We read in the schools, in the poetry Tennyson made, of the nobleness of Arthur and the sad love story of Guinevere and-Launcelot. We still talk of the great friendship of Roland and Oliver. We write the stories of the hero poems in prose for boys and girls to read. We make new poems of them.

For the heroes of the days of knights and dragons, as their poets tell about them, had a courage worth knowing still. We don't find so much of it in these days of machinery, and when we find it, it isn't so exciting to read about. Siegfried and Tristram and Roland and Launcelot are interesting and even useful to us, though armour is worn only in museums and the last dragon was killed more than a thousand years ago.

CHAPTER IX

THE POET OF HEAVEN AND HELL

I

In the spring of 1274, Folco Portinari, an influential citizen of Florence, Italy, announced to his friends that he would celebrate his family *festa*. Nine-year-old Dante Alighieri heard it much talked about, and, like other boys, tagged along after his father. There were a number of children who had done likewise, anticipating left-over sweets, minstrels, pageants, magicians, jugglers, tumblers, and the races, both on foot and on horseback.

Dante, a slender boy with great dark serious eyes and pale olive skin, standing quietly apart, suddenly saw Portinari's little daughter Beatrice. On his intense mind, the first impression of Beatrice was indelibly engraved.

Her dress on that day . . . was of a most noble colour, a subdued and goodly crimson, girdled and adorned in such sort as best suited to her very tender age. . . . Her features were most delicate and perfectly proportioned, and, in addition to their beauty, full of such pure loveliness that many thought her almost an angel.

Dante's boyish heart and soul were completely taken with her. Though, as Boccaccio, a contemporary, tells us, "he gave himself . . . not to youthful lust and indolence . . . but to continued study," and though he never spoke a word to Beatrice, he could not forget her. He eyed her furtively, but often, from a distance. He himself records:

I, in my boyhood, often went seeking her, and saw her of such noble and praiseworthy deportment, that truly of her might be said that word of the poet Homer, "She seems not a daughter of mortal man, but of God."

Nine years later, that second event occurred which was Dante's dedication to poetry.

Beatrice, "clothed in purest white, between two gentle ladies who were of greater age," passed by him on the street, and

turned her eyes toward that place where I stood very timidly; and by ineffable courtesy, . . . saluted me with such virtue that it seemed to me then that I saw all the bounds of bliss. . . . Since it was the first time that her words came to my ears, I took in such sweetness, that, as it were, intoxicated, I turned away from the folk; and betaking myself to the solitude of my own chamber, I sat down to think of this most courteous lady.

And not only to think of her; he sealed the golden day with a sonnet. For Dante, like almost every young Florentine gentleman, turned naturally to verse. All Italy was turning to it. The poetry of southern France had died when the troubadours had been scattered. But the troubadours had fled southward. Their songs of love flavoured arguments about philosophy at the University of Bologna, and ran like quicksilver down into Sicily. The very religion of the time was quickened with song. Saint Francis of Assisi, in his own joyous and impassioned music, a *jongleur* of the Lord, hailed his "brother sun" and "sister moon and the stars," his "brother wind" and "brother fire." "The Little Flowers" of Francis, the "Canticle of the Sun," break with their keen cry and cordial rhythm through the church drone.

But the first important artist is Guido Guinicelli of Bologna, whom Dante later hailed. He isolated the sonnet, breaking it off from the canzone, a highly wrought and intricate lyrical business. He brought into Italian poetry that new style which gives to the eyes and the heart and the soul separate voices with which to speak together. The poets of Provence had prayed to a Christ with the ears of Pan and the appetites of Bacchus. They were naïve. They used their minds to invent novelties of *manner*. In Dante's Tuscany the poets applied those novelties to the *matter* of verse.

The sonnet Dante wrote that day of his lady's salutation began,

> To every heart which the sweet pain doth move,

and ended with a sigh. Sighs were the fashion. The poet Guido Cavalcanti had set the song mood of the hour, telling how his lady

> . . with her leadeth love so no man hath
> The might to speak, but sigheth, every one.

Cavalcanti, first a friend, then an enemy of Dante, was older than the lover of Beatrice, and the leading spirit of the young men's love cult in Florence. He wrote beautiful *ballate*, or much-rhymed love ballads, that weave on nimble feet. Many of his lines are intense and poignant with adoration of his beloved:

> Not even so much of virtue in me resides
> To comprehend, woe's me!
> The blossom of her surpassing purity!

Dante openly acknowledges his debt to Cavalcanti, whose phrases fired the poet in him, They fired other young Florentines also. One of them, Guido Orlandi, wrote a sonnet-letter to the greater Guido, an elegant and fashionable gesture. The poem suggests, incidentally, how much the English writers of Queen Elizabeth's time took from these Italian writers. No sonnet could be more Elizabethan in spirit than this playful epistle, dispatched all of three hundred years before sonnet-sighing agitated the ladies of London:

Whence moveth Love and whence hath he his birth,
What is his proper stead, wherein he dwelleth?
Is he substaunce, mishap, or memory's mirth,
A dart of eyes or heart's desire that welleth?
And whence proceeds his madness or his state?
Is he a flame that doth devour in rages,
Or is he food? I ask you to relate
How, when and whom his cruel whim encages?
What is this Love, I ask: hath he a face,
Hath he a form by self, or others' feature?
Is this Love life, or is he Death's cold peace?
Whoso serveth him should know his nature.
I ask thee, Guido, this (though not in malice),
Since thou art called "familiar" at his palace.

The sonnet celebrating the greeting that Beatrice had given him was only the beginning of many poems which Dante, like these other Tuscan poets, wrote about his lady. We know them now as the *Vita Nuova*, or *New Life*. They make a little ivory testament of his youth. But even in these lyrics of a heart exceedingly timid, sensitive, bookish, and dreamy, there shines the intensity that was later to shake the world. Now it quivers in a fine spiritual radiance that suffers like something alive if you try to pull the text apart. Now it is reflected in the fierce reality of Love—that "Lord of Terrible Aspect." It was this high and passionate spirit that lifted Dante above his contemporaries and made him sum up and render half sublime the poetry of these elegant lovers.

There is something a little grotesque and terrible about his exquisite devotion. Poor Beatrice must have been bewildered by this hawk-beaked, owl-eyed zealot who grew pale gazing at her in church and dreaming of her at night. She must have been amazed by his intricate devotion to the number nine. This mysterious adoration at a distance, all very nice and poetic, was probably not so thrilling. No wonder she once mocked his confusion when he trembled at the sudden sight of her, and sometimes withheld her salutation when she passed him on the street!

Not that such cruelties shook Dante's faith in his lady. It was after all better that she should be remote and inaccessible. He could continue to write his despair and passionate faithfulness. In fact, it was once when she had particularly troubled him with her disfavour that he turned so resolutely to praising her that in his enthusiasm his "sweet new style" was born. Indeed, he succeeded in discarding all artificiality in the canzone beginning:

> My Lady looks so pure, so gentle when
> She yields to anyone her mild salute,
> That the tongue trembles and is rendered mute,
> And the eyes, fain to see, are dazzled then.

In this sonnet he adopted a *nuova rima*, or new rhyme scheme, the sort of thing young poets delight in doing. His audacious experiment won recognition in Florence and brought fame to Dante. He followed it with the fragrant flower of Italian lyrical poetry:

> My Lady carries love deep in her eyes:
> Whatsoever she looks upon is made
> Fairer; she walks—and will all eyes persuade;
> She smiles—and the beholder's heart will rise,
> And his unhappy face fall, and his sighs,
> And his heart's evil will confess its shade,
> Hate turn to love, pride in the dust be laid.
> O Ladies, lend your praises to my prize:
> Humility and hope beneath her spell
> Are nurtured marvellously in the mind;
> And whoso sees is purged of many guiles;
> Her look when she a very little smiles
> May not be spoken, nor in thought confined,
> So new it is, so sweet a miracle.

The death of Beatrice's father brought two more sonnets for her sorrow.

Frail and worn with his intense love, the young Dante fell ill, and upon the ninth day, he reflected: "It needs must be that the most gentle Beatrice will some day die." In this fancy the sun grew dark, the stars sombre, the birds fell dead out of the sky, and there were great earthquakes. He beheld the dead body of his lady whose aspect of humility seemed to say: "Now do I behold the beginning of peace." After, when he had recovered, he recorded this vision in the finest of his youthful poems, the one beginning:

> A lady pitiful and very young,
> Exceeding rich in human sympathies,
> Stood by what time I cried on Death's decrees,
> And at the whirling words that moved my tongue,
> And at the liquid look within mine eyes
> She was sore frighted. . . .

Not long after this, the dream of Beatrice's death came true, and the poems of the *New Life* drew to an end. For Dante determined not to write of his lady's passing. He gathered together the verses he had composed and wove them into a continuous story of his love—jewels of intense and brilliant poetry on the thread of a prose narrative. The whole was completed in 1295, when Dante was twenty-nine. It was dedicated to Guido Cavalcanti, the "familiar" at Love's palace.

II

All this has been the story of Dante the poet-lover, and properly so. Love and poetry filled much of his life. Yet we must not think of him solely as a love-sick young anchorite. Though he had time for dreams and sighing and sonnets, he had also a zest for all the manly exercises of the time. Many passages in the great poem he was to write show how he had flung his javelin at the wild boar, and loosed the falcon from his wrist. He knew the ways of cavalry:

> Often have I seen squadrons shift their places,
> Dash to the dark assault, then quick retreat,
> Or suddenly scatter over the outstretched spaces:
> Thy plains, Arezzo, often have I seen
> Swept fiercely by the light horse on swift feet;
> At tilts and tourneys have I often been

> With bells and bugles making shrill alarms,
> With drums and signals throbbing from some tower,
> Native or alien, summoning to arms!

He was a soldier, a merrymaker, an ambassador. We hear of him fighting in the great battle of Campaldino, in which he was wounded. Later, he joined with his gallant fellow poets and took part in the revelries celebrating the victory for Florence. For such as he

formed bands and companies of gentle youths clad in new raiment, and raised new pavilions covered with cloth and silk and with wooden walls, in divers parts of the city; and likewise there were bands of women and maidens going through the city dancing in ordered fashion, and ladies two by two, with instruments, and with garlands of flowers on their heads, continuing in pastimes and joyance and at feasts and banquets.

He was active also in the political life of Florence. There were two parties struggling for the control of the city. Dante, when his party was in power, held office and had a strong voice in deciding what should be done. He was intense here, as in his love and poetry, and very egotistical. Once, the story runs, when there was talk of sending an embassy from the city, he exclaimed: "If I go, who will stay; if I stay, who will go?" Dante belonged to an old aristocratic family, hated the new rich of the city, and had no doubt of his own fitness to rule.

It was probably this good opinion of himself which helped to make his enemies hate him, and brought it about that, when they got control of Florence during one of his absences from the city, they had him sentenced to exile beyond the borders of Tuscany, for two years. This was later made a life sentence with something like a price on Dante's head. There is a record in the archives of Florence to this day, dooming Messer Dante, when, as, and if caught, to be burnt alive, a charming method which he was to visit upon his enemies, poetically speaking, with interest. Another document of considerable value is a letter from Dante to the Florentine magistrates in reply to a proposal that he might return on apologizing and paying a fine. The fine he could not pay if he would, the apology he would not pay if he could. "If I cannot return," retorted this haughty Tuscan, "without calling myself guilty, I will never return."

In the ten years between Beatrice's death and the beginning of his exile, Dante remained faithful to his lady. It is true that he married Gemma di Manuetto Donati, of a distinguished family, and that she bore him four children. But she was only his wife! Dante's love for Beatrice was ideal, and therefore permitted his practical existence to go the usual way. However, there was one episode that seems to have been really menacing. It is said that one day the young Dante lifted his great sad eyes to a window and saw a gentle lady looking at him with compassion and pity. He wrote several sonnets to her, and the new love seemed sweet until one day he imagined he saw the glorified Beatrice in those crimson robes she wore when first he saw her, and straightway his heart was freed from the sympathetic lady of the window.

At the end of the *New Life* Dante records how

... a wonderful vision appeared to me, in which I saw things which made me resolve to speak no more of this blessed one, until I could more worthily treat of her, and to attain to this, I study to the utmost of my power, as she truly knows. So that, if it shall please Him through whom all things live, that my life be prolonged for some years, I hope to say of her what has never been said of any woman.

Other ladies besides the lady at the window came briefly into his life, but the vision of Beatrice and his determination to celebrate her in a great epic never dimmed. This epic gradually took shape as the *Divine Comedy*, his imaginary journey through Hell, Purgatory, and Heaven. He invented for it the famous *terza rima*, or "three-rhyme," of which specimens can be read in this chapter. As he studied at various universities—Bologna, Padua, Paris, perhaps even Oxford—he brooded upon the poem. It grew, also, as he wandered from patron to patron, a tolerated guest, learning "how hard is the path" of the exile, while his wife was learning elsewhere the difficulty of managing existence for herself and the poet's four children.

Dante was not an easy guest for those whom he visited. Poor, proud, earnest, and exiled, with black moods and brown humors, he was hardly the sort of man to conciliate men. Petrarch tells of him, that, being at Can della Scala's castle one day, as milord stood with his courtiers roaring mirthfully at one of his buffoons, he addressed himself to Dante, saying: "Is it not strange now, that this poor fool should do so much to amuse us, whilst you, a wise man, sit there day after day, and have nothing to amuse us with at all?" To which the poet answered, sharply, perhaps a little wearily, "No, it is not strange. You are to recollect the proverb, 'Like to Like'!"

Nobody's lackey, this exile, with his sarcasms and his sorrows. So he ate the food of this or that patron, took offence at a word or gesture, reserved a warm place in his *Inferno* for the unfortunate offender, and departed abruptly.

Dante, during the time when he was writing in exile the *Divina Commedia*, 1314–1321,

... was of moderate height, and, after reaching maturity, was accustomed to walk somewhat bowed, with a slow and gentle pace, clad always in such sober dress as befitted his ripe years. His face was long, his nose aquiline, and his eyes rather large than small. His jaws were large, and the lower lip protruded beyond the upper. His complexion was dark, his hair and beard thick, black, and curled, and his expression ever melancholy and thoughtful.

And one day in Verona, when everyone knew of his work, especially the *Inferno*, as he was going by a doorway where several women sat embroidering and gossiping, one said softly, but distinctly enough for Dante to hear,

"Do you see that man who goes down into hell and returns when he pleases, and brings back tidings of them that are below?"

Another crossed herself quickly and whispered, again loud enough for the poet's ear, "You must indeed say true. Do you not see how his beard is crisped and his colour darkened by the heat and smoke down there?"

In Ravenna, his last refuge and residence Dante, taught

rhetoric in the vernacular. For he had exalted the Italian tongue
and given it preference to Latin; indeed, writing his great poem
in the vulgar tongue, the voice of Tuscany, that "soft bastard
Latin." His income from tutoring gave him a small independence. Two of his children were with him, and in serenity and
peace of mind, the *Paradiso* was written. On September 13
or 14, 1321, he died of fever, weakened by a fruitless journey
to Venice in behalf of his host, and exhausted by that book,
"which has made me lean many years." He was fifty-six years
old, not yet really old, though old in the world's grief. He died
broken-hearted, some say, but that grim, bloody, beautiful book
out of his heart's sickness was finished. A century after his
death, the Florentines begged back the poet's body. The people
of Ravenna refused, remembering his epitaph: "Here am I,
Dante, laid—shut out from my native shores!"

III

The *Divine Comedy* begins as Dante finds himself at dusk
in a dense forest that shuts out the light of the stars. Through
this dense forest, dark with allegorical beasts of hideous visage,
he is led by Virgil, whom he hails as his master and his authority, "Thou glory and light of all other poets," into and out
of Hell to the top of Purgatory where Virgil hands him over to
another guide for the journey through Paradise.

It is the custom to talk about Dante's Hell and forget the
Purgatory and the Paradise. And that, in spite of the poet's
own warning: "But to tell of the *good* which I found, I will speak
also of the other things." It is because Dante passes through the
horror and pain of Hell to the eternal bliss of Heaven that he
calls his great itinerary a comedy—and a divine one. In other
words, the Hell is merely a necessary prelude, the first black
movement of a gigantic symphony by which the last is in contrast made more radiant.

Down into a cone-shaped pit, from one narrow circle to

another still narrower circle, nine all told, the air increasingly dark and dangerous, we enter Hell, or the general state of man controlled by his appetites. We stand first, beneath the starless atmosphere, with those who were neither fit for Hell nor Heaven, lacking both the energy to sin and the strength to refrain.

Next we proceed with Dante under Virgil's direction to the ferry of Charon, Hell's official boatman, with his hoary beard and his demon shape and his red eyes, who strikes the lagging victim with his oar:

> As the leaves fall
> First one and then another, till the bough
> Honours the earth with its autumnal pall,
> Even so the evil brood of Adam throw
> Themselves from the shore. . . .

In a swoon, Dante is ferried across the "livid marsh" to another place, "not sad with torment, but with shadows only." Here he meets with the Big Four among poets, besides Virgil, as his time and he ranked them—first Sovran Homer; next, Horace the satirist; third, Ovid; and last, Lucan. These nod to him as to a guest. Virgil smiles. Nor is that all. They nominate him sixth in their company! The election is carried unanimously. There is no dissenting voice! Dante counts the ballots!

To one side, walking with grave steps apart, he then sees the ancient heroes, and his heart leaps within him, mighty warriors like Æneas and Hector; Cæsar, falcon-eyed; Brutus, who drove the Tarquin from Rome; and lonely Saladin. And, higher still, he beholds the philosophers, Aristotle holding his Olympian court with Plato and Socrates and the other great knowers.

Then the four poets leave Dante alone with Virgil, and "out from the mild air" they move "to a place where there is no shining." Here Minos, the sin-weigher, gnashing horribly and beating his tail around, is lord and judge. It is a "dolorous hospice," a region "where all light is hushed," and "there is a

bellowing as of the sea in tempest, of a storm that never rests."
Whirling and lashing, the infernal blast smites the spirits of
such as were victims of their passions; and

> As trumpeting their melancholy song
> The cranes upon their wings with wide alarm
> Wheel in a wedged and agitated throng,
> So I beheld the ghosts in a wailing swarm
> Who fluttered towards us swiftly, being swept
> By the terrific pulses of the storm.

And here he sees Cleopatra, Helen, Achilles, "whose last battle
was for love," the knights and paladins and ladies who died for
love. Then come two who float "so light upon the wind." In
the name of love he accosts them, and lo, "as one that speaketh
and weepeth," Francesca da Rimini tells of her guilt with her
lover Paolo. It is a story that breaks the heart even now as we
read it, so simple and tender and terrible in its tenderness and
its tragedy, a story well known to Italians of that day, a sort
of headline feature in the yellow journalism of Dante's time.
Dante, overcome with pity, as she finishes her tale, falls "like
a dead body to the ground."

Then come new torments, through the circle of the glutton-
ous, who twist in mire under a steady storm of hail, snow, and
discoloured water while Cerberus, three-throated, with his talons
tears their limbs piecemeal, and the circle of the greedy and
the wasteful (Dante had somehow got into financial difficulties
in Florence, piling up a debt which he never paid, and he must
have been a little nervous here), to the circles of the wrathful
and sullen, sunken in the ooze of their sullenness.

Across their pool Dante and Virgil come to the circular City
of Dis, which hangs over the pit of the Inferno, livid, walled
with apparent iron, the minarets throbbing with a vermilion
glow like a furnace. It is the place of fallen angels and blood-
stained furies formed like women. Belted with greenest hydras
these are, that roll their coils, with serpents and horned cerastes
writhing and hissing instead of hair and binding their savage

temples. The guardian demons of this dreadful city refuse to let the poets in, but their "fatal going" is not to be gainsaid. They see a thousand spirits fleeing as frogs from a snake run pell-mell through the water till each squats on the bottom. In the city itself Dante looks upon a spectacle of horror, for he sees the arch-heretics burned in hot tombs, through the lifted lids of which issue grievous moans.

Out of one of these flaming coffins towers up the most commanding figure of the entire Comedy, Farinata degli Uberti, who, when the council voted to destroy Florence, "defended her with open face." He, scornful, as if "he held Hell in huge contempt," stretches his tortured length out of the fiery tomb to dispute with his political enemy. Thus exposed for a vivid interval in that red glare of Hell, he remains unforgettably superb.

Uberti is only one of the innumerable enemies whom Dante planted in his nine hells. Dante never forgot anything and, as far as we have been able to discover, never forgave anything. Perhaps he could not help it; perhaps it was part of the passionate process of self-absorption and self-perfection which worked in him continually, making him at last the wisest and the saddest of men—and the loneliest.

At any rate, he became the unrivalled connoisseur of torture, an expert in pain, a master in exquisite combinations of torment. Hell was paved with his enemies. It was a literary revenge, but it soothed his soul. No man ever hated so inclusively and satisfyingly as this great exponent of divine love. A grim fellow, our Dante, with a rather charming sense of humour. He had once broken a font in the Church of St. John the Baptist at Florence in order to rescue a child that had been playing near by and fallen in. His enemies put a malicious interpretation upon the act. So, since that rankled in his memory and his "hard mind" let nothing ever go, and he had a refined sense of the ridiculous, lo and behold, that font crops up in the third gulf of his Hell as a "livid stone" wherein he gives these same slanderers a perpetual Turkish bath, their legs kicking out of the fiery holes, flame gliding from heel to point of their soles!

But if Dante had a ghastly sort of humour, why so had the great prophets of the Old Testament, and for the same reason and with the same purpose. In both cases, it has enriched the world with poetry of the noblest, if most terrifying, quality. It grips the imagination like Greek tragedy. It searches out the heart, washes the soul with pity and terror even while it fascinates the mind. Dante gives some traitor's shoulders a wrench in Hell's furnace that time can never iron out. Intensely visual, fiery, emphatic, narrow, prejudiced with the prejudices of his age and his own life, he seizes the entrails of a vision, etches it with merciless and rapid economy in scarlet lightning. Plutus, the blustering giant, at Virgil's rebuke, collapses "as the sails sag, the mast being suddenly snapt"; Sordello has a "baked face." And yet in the midst of all this horror, the story of Francesca of Rimini instantly shines like a lily in Hell's jaws. No man who is incapable of severity is capable of pity. Here is the severity of a god, the pity of an angel.

After leaving Uberti, the poets descend into thicker stench. Dante sees Judas, and the later Brutus, and Cassius, eternally fixed in ice, the doom of the traitorous heart. We pass by another figure, that of Caponæus, a lesser Farinata, but admirable in his defiance, "though Jove outweary his smith," standing in sand under a terrible rain that

> shook in a soft slow fall
> Dilated flakes of fire, as flakes of snow
> On the Alpine peaks when the wind is not heard.

This repulsively fascinating pageant, boiling beneath the reek of the lurid air, over rivers of blood, guarded by monsters borrowed from the myths of Greece and Rome, and, if possible, rendered more monstrous, is, in effect, the symbol of the mediæval world's ignorance, violence, and filth as Dante felt it.

But we pass to better things. We ascend to see again the

stars in "that second realm," as Dante names Purgatory, "where the human spirit is purged and becomes worthy to go up to Heaven." Perhaps the characters are less arresting, less interesting than those in the Inferno. Perhaps Dante explains too much (though Heaven knows he argued enough in Hell). But, for sheer poetry, the description of the Earthly Paradise in the final six cantos is as fine as anything in the whole book.

And now, having drunk of Lethe waters, Dante, reborn, comes back "pure and ready to climb to the stars." They have worked to the mountain top of Purgatory. Virgil's duties as guide, as intellectual and moral counsellor, are at an end. Beatrice, who represents Christian wisdom as opposed to the pagan wisdom of Virgil, soon takes the Mantuan's place. This gives Dante a gorgeous opportunity to air his obsession, that is, to lecture about obscure points of Church doctrine from a pulpit. Of course, no man has ever had such a positive genius for explanation. We may resent his cocksureness about everything under the sun. But those in the audience who have brain enough are captivated by his masterly discourses, and the rest of us have the thrill of our lives looking at the pictures he throws on his immense screen.

We may regard the *Paradiso* as the last chapter of Dante's own Book of Job—with this difference, that Dante triumphs by justifying himself to God politically and personally—with God applauding with great enthusiasm. Being more or less a solitary egotist who, if the stories about him be true, repulsed rather than sought human contacts, creating within himself by his internal intensity and phenomenal memory an amazing universe wherein he sat enthroned with Beatrice, it is small wonder that Paradise gives the poet a grand ovation.

Everybody turns out the moment Dante and Beatrice arrive. The Emperor Justinian delivers himself of a lecture covering the history of Rome from Constantine to Dante, not omitting some nasty little digs at Charles II, King of Naples, whom Dante loathed with special emphasis. Soon one of Dante's adorations has the floor and recites the first line of an early poem by Dante, observing that all the spirits in the Heaven of Venus love Dante very much. Then the theologians dance around Dante and Beatrice, now and then letting out musical sounds. When they stop, Thomas Aquinas points out among the dancers at least a dozen of the greatest of the Church Fathers like Boethius and King Solomon. He delivers two lengthy lectures expounding Dante's views on something or other. The saints are impressed. It is as though we were present at a Heavenly Convention where all the Presidents from Washington to Lincoln make speeches backing up some defeated and forlorn politician against his successful enemies. With sacred music during intermissions, to be sure, and considerable dancing!

But having said all this, there remains the transcendent luminosity and music of the *Paradiso*. Dante's conception resounds with angelic voices; the very light throbs melodiously. Never before had poet imagined such radiant beauty. The words are saturated with it. We ascend and "a cloud envelops us, shining dense, firm and polished, like sun-smitten diamond." The human eyes cannot bear so much light, all ecstatic pearl and intolerable white glory. The verses with their triple hooks of silver catch hold of each other, each lifting the next until the senses drown and we reel like drunken men in the final terrific vision of the Divine Rose.

That final vision of blessedness decides the *Divine Comedy*. It vindicates the horrors of Dante's Hell and the ingenuities of his Purgatory. It is the whole poem's reason. It throws a golden thread back to the very bottom of Hell's last abyss. It steadies the foot that stumbles and strengthens the heart that falters on the long and perilous journey. For the *Divine Comedy* is a poem of repentance, a diary of redemption through love. Were this not so, the poem, for all its magnificent passages, would be merely one more graphic record of a violent era, one more sublime nightmare. But Dante's supreme conviction that no experience, however degrading—and he wrote from the bitter memory and remorse of his own—can keep a man down, that, guided by Love, he can reach the stars from the dark forest in his heart's hell—this it is that endows the *Divine Comedy* with a vitality which makes it live to us and in us, a reality which we can feel in ourselves and understand.

CHAPTER X

PETRARCH AND HIS LAURA

I

Six hundred years ago, in French Avignon, lovely city of the Popes, on the sixth of April at precisely six o'clock in the morning, a young Italian twenty-three years old, kneeling in the church of Sainte Claire, bowed his dark head and made a vow —a vow wherein he determined to renounce all worldly temptations and delights, yielding himself wholly to the service of our Lord.

He lifted his head, his black eyes eloquent with consecration —but they were interrupted. Something got in the way— something that seemed strangely a part of his dream, melting into the colour of his radiant revery, questioning his renunciation delicately, with no sense of intrusion.

It consisted of two golden braids twisted about a tiny head like a diadem. Was it a woman indeed? Could it possibly be flesh and blood authentic to the senses? Or was it not some angelic vision, perhaps a spirit that had floated in while he was making up his mind about the world, and men and women, and—

Suddenly, through the smoky cold of the church a single

ray of sunlight dizzied in and trembled upon the glorious head. "By my troth, 'tis a dream indeed!" sighed the sad young man aloud. And just then the dream got to its feet, and an older companion who was no dream at all got up, too.

Still on his knees, the dazed young man saw for the first time the mantle that the Lady of the Golden Hair drew a little closer about her. It was green like April and sprinkled with violets. He saw also the very slender throat, the small forehead, the delicate face. The entire congregation was standing. He, alone on his knees, continued to regard with adoration this new deity. She turned and looked—at him! Oh, heart, be still! Such a look, mingled at once of indignation and pity, with something of laughter and recognition in her eyes. Holy Mother, those eyes! They were blue, sheer larkspur-blue! No, they were deep dark violets after rain! Or turquoise, maybe! At any rate, they were incredible. He felt himself "smitten for life with human love." He tottered to his feet, swaying toward the door like a drunken sailor. He thought he heard the silver mockery of her laughter. An image of her was already burned into his soul— an image that was to haunt a hundred sonnets:

> The incandescent skin, the loveliest eyes
> That ever flamed, and that incredible hair
> Whereto the sun's own gold could not compare;
> The laugh, the voice that by a swift surprise
> Ambushed the listener with silver cries;
> The little moon-stained feet that softer were
> Than silence, and that body woven of air
> Conceived under the ribs of Paradise—

An instant he dallied at the door, unsure of his feet, of his hands. Then he lurched out into the fog and clatter of the early morning. A little petal of cool wind fell on his face.

Suddenly, he remembered his hat, a recent purchase, black velvet with a silver plume. He was rather proud of that hat, especially the plume. He turned back to fetch it. But those eyes! It would be like facing God twice!

He stood shuddering in the door. The verger, the ageing official caretaker of the church, approached.

"My hat, good Stephano, I left it—just this side of the fair lady."

He pressed silver into the clammy palm. The man vanished, croaking a little. The excited young Italian was certain he would never find the lady.

"She is an apparition, I know. Something that I, and I alone, have gazed upon. Like Saul on the Road to Damascus when the vision smote him full in the face and blinded him to earthly things. Like——"

The verger was handing him his hat.

"And the lady—you—you know her name?"

"Oh, she, the lovely lady with the golden hair? That is the Lady Laura de Sade."

"Of course, of course! How stupid of me!" said the sad, mad, glad young man very absent-mindedly, and, digging into a leathern pouch pocket that was slung from a belt beneath his cloak, he took out a fistful of silver and poured it into the astonished palm. And with that he flew down the street like a crazy man.

So much for vows the most austere. Of what avail were they against golden hair six hundred years ago? Of what avail to-day? But we know whom the golden hair belonged to. We shall know more in time. We do not, however, know who our so sad, so excited young Italian is. Perhaps the verger can tell us.

"His name is Petrarch—Messer Francis Petrarch. Such a proud, quiet, gentle-speaking person, so tall and well-formed and . . ."

The old man's voice rubs to a whisper.

"These eyes have seen many a matron of high degree languish and sigh for one glance from that dark oval face. And they gabble like so many geese about their poetic souls and their religious yearnings! Bah, I know them."

We interrupt the outburst against the ladies.

"Now, Stephano, very likely you are right. But tell us further of this Messer Pe—Pete—this devil with the dames of Avignon."

"Well, good sirs, I have heard the holy Abbé himself talk of this same Messer Petrarch. One day I overheard the blessed Father in the refectory. He was speaking of someone just arrived from Florence with a letter from none other than the Cardinal Colonna himself, wherein that illustrious prince of the Church did with much affection commend to our Abbé this young Messer Petrarch, saying that he was of an ancient and worthy family of Florence which had fallen upon evil days through the political mishaps of the young man's father."

"But, come, Stephano, you stray like an untethered sheep. To the point."

The verger's old eyes pucker up aggrievedly.

"I *shall* to the point. Let me see, where was I? Oh, yes. As I was saying, the father of this same Messer Petrarch was a lawyer of some note before his exile. Whereupon he wandered from place to place, now up, now down, a soldier of misfortune."

The verger stopped to chuckle at his cleverness. But we were impatient. He pressed on.

"Be that as it may, hither comes his father and his sorely tried mother (an excellent lady, I have heard tell) with her little brood, after living like Arabs in half a dozen towns and cities. Matters were on the mend. Our curious young friend was persuaded to go to Montpellier and study the law. For the Cardinal in his epistle spoke with the greatest admiration of Messer Petrarch's learning, saying that he was a born student with a raging hunger for books. Why, he can discourse in Latin as well as in Italian, and knows a thing or two of Greek. Learning is meat to him. He has flown through schools and monasteries at Pisa, Bologna, Rome, and Venice, not to mention Montpellier and our own Avignon. Just as you have seen him go flying into the street a moment since. Ha! Ha! He is a rare bird, I warrant you. Would you believe it, sirs, this Messer Petrarch, young as he is, can dispute with the most profound scholars. Faith, they can teach him nothing and they know it. I am told that he has his Cicero and Seneca, his Livy and his Virgil by heart! Think of it, good sirs, and only twenty-three! Ah, when I was young——"

"Yes, yes, Stephano, we know all about that. When you were young, you were wondrously acquainted with—ah—books."

Stephano cackled. He nudged us in the ribs mischievously. He was pleased.

"Well, well, I have my secrets. But as to the young man, it is rumoured that the father of this same young Solomon, visiting his son after some months had passed at Montpellier, discovered on his table a mound of books concerned with rhetoric and poetry and such contrivances of the Devil. Now, you know, the young scapegrace should have been deep in his law. And so the parent, in a towering passion, flung the books into the fire. And now, sirs, mark you what happened. The lad, chancing to come into the room at this moment, raised such a cry that his beloved Virgil and his Cicero were snatched from the flames. But the other books perished, I know not what number, and, the legend goes, much original manuscript of no mean excellence.

"Ah, he is a proud fellow, is this young Messer Petrarch, never satisfied. He was not even satisfied, I have heard, with his family name, Petracco, changing it when he was a mere lad of fifteen to Petrarch. It may be, as some would have it, that he called himself Petrarch with Plutarch in mind. Or it may be, as he himself has said, that he did this strange thing for the sake of euphony. Though I, for my part, if you ask me, gentlemen, can see no benefit to euphony in it. But as to the parents of this young man, the mother of whom he was so fond was gathered to her eternal rest when Messer Petrarch was but twenty years old. His father joined her two years later. May their souls rest in peace." The verger crossed himself vigorously. "I, too, shall soon——"

"Not now, Stephano, not now. Your time is not yet come. At any rate, you cannot die on our hands in the midst of your excellent story.

The aged narrator revived immediately. "Bless you, sirs, I shall go on. Being young, the death of his parents did not altogether crush our friend. Indeed, he managed to compose a poem wherein, I have been told, he solaced himself with the reflection that their souls were at last safe in Paradise and they need no longer wander in exile. Then he took minor orders in the Church and became some sort of assistant to the secretary of one of the Cardinals, I forget which one. Those who knew him at the time say that he was a melancholy self-willed fellow who knew too much. No, it is not good to know too much. It makes a man unhappy. I have never been unhappy. I remember——"

"But, good Stephano, what of this young Messer Petrarch's passion for books that you speak of? And what is he doing in Avignon?"

"Concerning this passion for books, I can inform you readily. Wherever he has been, and he has been in divers places, Paris, Belgium, Germany, Switzerland, everywhere he goes about digging up old Latin manuscripts, translating them or transcribing them, as the case may be. Because of his insatiable hunger for knowledge, he has said, whenever, as he travelled on foot or on horse, he espied in the distance some old monastery, he would instantly turn aside and press toward it, always hoping to discover some of the classical treasures for which he was searching. I have heard him recount that, when he reached Liége in Belgium, having been told that many books were to be found there, he stopped, and begging his friends to wait for him, unearthed two orations of Cicero, of which he copied one, and a friend the other. He said, with pardonable pride, that, by means of him, Italy has received them both.

"He has indeed enriched not only his beloved Italy (for whom he labours thus night and day, greatly to the hurt of his eyes, I fear), but France and England as well. Nay, is not the whole of Europe thereby given a new birth of intellectual curiosity and vigour? And he has often worked under difficulties. He has told me that when he was copying the orations of Cicero in Liége, ink was as scarce as the devil and what there was of it was as yellow as saffron. But, alas, I am sore afraid that this morning's business has lost him forever to these labours." The old verger sighed and muttered something about "golden hair" and the "devil."

We hastened to console him. "But if, as you insist, this toil of discovery and salvaging the sunken jewels of antiquity is such an overmastering passion with him, surely a pair of gold braids and blue eyes will not turn him aside. 'Tis but a passing fancy. 'Twill blow over, and that soon."

The old man shook his head dubiously. "Truly I hope so. All the same, it is the devil's work, I tell you."

"Nay, nay, be not alarmed, good Stephano, this will wear off. But you persist in avoiding our question, namely, what is Messer Petrarch doing in Avignon? 'Tis a simple question enough."

"Ah, sirs, not so simple. Perhaps he whacked the Italian lawyers too hard for their frauds and their follies. Perhaps the physicians hounded him. For I have heard him speak with scorn of the pill-men and blood-letters as the greediest set of rascals in Christendom, who prey on the ignorant and superstitious public that is all too ready to swallow everything. Perhaps he is here because of the sad state of affairs in Italy. What with civil wars and political dissensions, with assassinations and jealousies, and with the nobles and commoners of his own Florence doing their utmost to kill each other off as speedily as possible, Avignon is not an unwholesome place for him to be.

"For, let me tell you, this Messer Petrarch is a burning Italian patriot. He is always urging the rival states to bury their private quarrels and unite to restore the grandeur of their country. Though he is a Republican in his principles, he is will-

ing to see them unite under an Emperor, if this be necessary.
Than all else dearer to him, he declares, is the public good,
dearer is Rome, dearer is Italy! Still, if you ask me, I am inclined to the opinion that he is here because of that book hunger
and that lust for seeing things, which drive him like a fever from
place to place.

"But, ah me, our young friend is tripped neatly this time.
He has not in him, I fear, the stuff recluses are made of, for all
his vows and protestations to the contrary. He never wearied,
he told the Abbè, of solitary places, dark forests, secret nooks.
And he would not look at another woman as long as he lives,
save only his mother in Heaven!"

"Vex not yourself, good Stephano, there can no harm come
of it——"

"Hm, I am not so sure of that. There is the noble lady's
husband, for one thing—and a more morose, hard-headed, un-
romantic husband than this same Messer Hugh de Sade never
drew breath. And a jealous old hawk, too, though a more faithful and pure wife lives not in all Provence, nor a more devoted
mother. I have no great love for Messer Hugh. Nevertheless, I
cannot quite blame him his jealousy, albeit he suffer it without
reason. After all, she is only nineteen years of age, beautiful,
and, as you have observed by the antics of our young friend
at mass this morning, quite capable of turning a man's head."

"But surely you do not believe that this infatuation of the
moment will be permitted to go very far. She does not seem
to be the sort of lady to encourage it. And then there is her
husband."

The verger made a swift impatient gesture of contempt.

"Ah, that husband again! It is true he sends a duenna about
with her, that being the custom. But he has nothing to fear, I
warrant you. This lovely Laura with her golden hair and her
guileless eyes carries in her bosom the constant seed of virtue.
She can inspire in our handsome young poet only the loftiest of
passions. For he is none of your swagger gentry that dash about

with their blood up. He is too fine a fellow and a Christian gentleman withal. Of course, they will meet—in discretion—and under auspices the most unimpeachable. And I dare say Messer Petrarch, his eyes brilliant with a fine frenzy, will walk the streets all night by the moon composing verses in his head, and present himself at the church door, a haggard spectacle, knocking the porter out of his slumbers."

We laughed. "But come, come, good Stephano, surely, if matters take such a turn, 'twill be a rare morsel for your tongue."

The verger's face fell and his palms protested. "Ah, good sirs, you do me wrong. I am no eavesdropper. I do not tattle. I cannot help hearing certain things."

"There, we meant nothing. 'Twas but a jest." The verger shook his head and sighed and would not be consoled. We had insulted an artist. There was no remedy in words. We left, however, with his promise of more news within the next few days singing in our ears.

But, as it turned out, we needed not the verger so soon.

The Lady Laura accepted the daily poems which Messer Petrarch dispatched to her by way of the duenna. As the old verger had foretold, the church at early mass proved most convenient for the passing of little pieces of parchment which might on occasion be dropped from a cloak as though by accident. The duenna was in her element. She enjoyed a situation which made her important, nay, essential.

About a week had elapsed when one day, toward dusk, the verger presented himself at our lodgings, all out of breath, his shrewd old eyes dancing with ill-suppressed eagerness. After he had somewhat recovered his composure, aided by a generous glass of Burgundy, he cleared his throat, rubbed his hands, and made a strange birdlike chirping sound. "Ah, sirs, I have such news for you, such news!"

The little wizened-up eyes glittered. The hands rubbed more furiously than ever.

"Ah, gentlemen, first there is the husband. Only yesterday Messer Hugh, having become considerably annoyed by the gossips, sent a request couched in the most respectful terms to our young poet friend that he cease his attentions to his wife. Whereupon our Messer Petrarch, nothing daunted, replies with another sonnet, distributed throughout the town, as fervent as the last, to the effect that his love for the Lady Laura was as sacred as his love for the Madonna."

The old man cackled. He had been watching us narrowly, and the effect of his disclosure was not altogether unflattering to his narrative skill.

"But, good Stephano, you amaze us. We were not aware that gossip had passed over into scandal. You do not mean to imply——"

The old verger could hardly sit still. "Nay, nay, I imply nothing. The lovers have met only at church or upon the street. That much I can vouch for. Moreover, if these eyes mistake not, Messer Petrarch's passion is pure and high, too. And the Lady Laura is not the woman to permit liberties. This morning, after mass, when I was arranging the prayer cushions, I found——"

He reached inside his rusty cloak and drew forth a crumpled strip of parchment. He smoothed it out as well as he could on the table and said, "Read."

We read, "Messer Petrarch, remember my good name and protect it."

We looked up at the old man, whose mouth was wide open as though he were still forming the words. We were a little disappointed.

"Is that all?" we said.

Like a sleight-of-hand performer who keeps his best trick up his sleeve to the last, he ran his little thin tongue over his lips and eyed the Burgundy. We filled up his glass. He gulped it down. Then he extracted from his person another sheet of parchment, as badly crumpled as the first. He spread it out before us and got up from the table to pace the room with his long brown hands working behind his back. We read:

> O rich and happy flowers forever apart
> On which my pensive Lady puts her heel!
> O golden acres privileged to feel
> Her phrase, her footprint pressed upon your heart!
> Trees silver green with April's earliest art;
> Pale passionate violets; dark grove that can steal
> Only so much of sun as may reveal
> Your swarthy steeples in a radiant dart!
> O comely landscape! O translucent stream
> Mirroring her pure face, her intense eyes
> And seizing all alive their bluest beam!
> I envy you your crystal burglaries!
> No rock, however cold, but with my theme
> Shall henceforth kindle and consume in sighs!

For a full moment there was silence. Then the old verger, unable to hold himself in any longer, cried out, "What say you to that! Is it not a gem! Such passion! Such art! If I were a woman——"

II

But we must leave the verger and finish our story as best we can from archive, history, and poems. Messer Petrarch continued to suffer as a lover must and to write exquisite sonnets as a poet should. All these sonnets were written in the tightly knitted form followed in this chapter: the stately octave with its two rhymes echoing the theme from line to line; and the sestet, or final six verses, weaving through various patterns to a decision. Dante and others had already used this sonnet scheme. Petrarch, with his art and passion, fixed it as a literary habit and glory. It persists to-day in many languages as the chief sonnet design.

But the making of many sonnets often wears down the maker. Petrarch's friend Colonna, alarmed for his health, offered him a bishopric or some other position which might absorb his energies. The lovesick poet refused politely. Colonna then had himself transferred to Lombes and appointed Messer Petrarch his secretary. The two friends set out on a six-hundred-mile journey, surrounded by a shining cavalcade of carriages and retainers. Honours were showered upon them wherever they went. Petrarch's patron hoped that the change of scene, the sight of new places, the thrill of making addresses in public, the various cities, schools, and monasteries which they visited in their roundabout passage would gradually wean him away from his passion.

Messer Petrarch kept a diary of all he saw and did. He remained in Lombes for something like two years. His spirits revived. But his poetry died within him. Nobody in Lombes gave a thought to poetry. The Lady Laura passed into a sweet memory. Still, the young secretary found himself, when he was off guard, yearning for Avignon, for its excitement, its music, its art, its society. Moreover, he was determined to convince himself that he was master of his passion.

He returned to Avignon. He saw Laura on the street. There was that same terrific stare of recognition. As she went by, his knees trembled beneath him, havoc was in his heart, and a fiery weakness. He leaned against a pillar to keep from falling. That night he poured his soul out in a sonnet. Love had conquered:

O straying steps! O blind and busy dreams!
O constant memory! O keen desire!
O passion strong! Heart weak with its own fire!
O eyes, not eyes, but salt and living streams!
O laurel boughs whose fluent garland seems
Guerdon enough to which lords may aspire!
O haunted life! Mirage I must admire
Or wallow else in little sluggard schemes!
O glamorous face, where Love has hoarded well
His lash and spur to prick the heart and move
The mind at will; nor heart nor mind to spare!
O spirits consumed with love, if yet you dwell
Upon this earth, and you, great Ghosts of Love,
Pause and observe my passion, my despair!

Bitterly he confessed the truth to himself—a difficult defeat for his proud nature. Laura's love was of her life a thing apart; it was Messer Petrarch's whole existence. Sick in body and soul, he was ordered by his physician to the country. For ten years, in the romantic solitude of the valley of Vaucluse, fifteen miles from Avignon, he sought refuge in his dreams and his sonnets. He must have seen Laura, though not so often or so intimately as the sonnets suggest. He found a feeble escape from his unbearable love in some other woman who gave him a son and a daughter.

On the 8th of April, 1341, a solemn procession followed a blare of trumpets up the Capitoline Hill in Rome. Young boys in scarlet marched before six citizens in green, each decked with a laurel crown, while Messer Petrarch stepped in their midst, garmented in one of the King's own regal robes. Windows and balconies were crowded with lovely ladies dressed as for a festival. The streets were heaped with flowers of every colour. Perfumed waters were sprinkled upon the poet and his escort. The highest senator of the land removed the laurel wreath from his own head and placed it upon that of Petrarch. Then the proclamation was read aloud to the multitude, wherein was conferred on the poet "by the authority of King Robert and of the Roman Senate and people at Rome and elsewhere the privilege to read, to dispute, to explain ancient books, to make new ones, and to wear a crown, according to his choice, either of laurel, beech, or myrtle, as well as the poetic habit." Poets, then as now, sometimes wore queer costumes.

About this time, the Lady Laura was threatened with blindness. But the beautiful blue eyes recovered, and it flattered the poet, who, oddly enough, managed to get the same trouble with his eyes, to fancy that he had taken the affliction away from his beloved. This was in 1346, and, soon after, Petrarch took his final farewell of the lady—there must have been quite a few farewells before this one—to go to Rome and throw himself into political affairs. Throughout his life he had worked to please the Pope to this end. For he was not wanting in vanity.

This last farewell was a rather melancholy business. Laura, in a robe unadorned either with pearls or the happy colours she was wont to wear, sat in silence. She did not sing as the poet had often heard her do. Those lovely eyes were sad. It was all over.

Petrarch travelled from Rome to the north of Italy. He was in Verona when the news came to him that Laura, in her fortieth year, had succumbed to the plague. His grief convulsed him. He knew that he was hers forever, even as he believed that she was his. On the margin of his *Virgil* he wrote: "This convinces me that I have nothing now left worth living for, since the strongest cord of my life is broken."

III

But there was still much poetry—in fact, his best poetry— to live for. Petrarch did not lose Laura in her death. Instead, he called her back as he had seen her in her most radiant moments, and left her shining eternally in his lines.

In these sonnets, poured out of an immortal grief, he recalls her face:

> Alas! that face, the misted stare, the way
> She had of carrying her tiny head!
> And oh, her voice, the vivid things it said
> That track me down and eat my heart away!

He writes of her house, the garden walks, his own anguish as he stands

> At the cruel mercy of these haunted walls.

He writes the pity of her death:

> You have outraged, O Death, the sweetest face
> That ever I knew, and drowned the deepest eyes;
> Forcing the seals and shattering the device
> Of a fair soul locked in a golden case.

He makes a tender sonnet to a friend who had just died, beg-ging him:

> O Friend, when to the Love Queen's star
> You come—Guittone, Cino, Dante greet,
> And our Francesco, and all that holy are;
> But, meeting Laura in the lilied street,
> Kiss only the jewelled wheel-rim of her car.

He tells how Laura has taken his heart with her, so that

> Not Sirius in a savage violet sky
> Throbbing, nor white sails on a violet sea,
> Nor glittering knights riding through greenery,
> Nor long-eyed stags that dizzily flash by,
> Nor tidings that could make a dead man cry,
> Nor Love apparelled in royal melody,

could ever stir him again. He cries out to her as he sees her aloft in Heaven:

> O loveliest novice, God's new kerchiefed nun,
> A beggar at the feast grows faint! O feed
> Me, miserable and human—O my dear!

Indeed, he looks forward to the time when he shall be sum-moned to join her, and sends a sonnet on an embassy of grief:

> Go, grief-bewildered Sonnet, kneel and knock
> On the grim slab that locks all I held dear,
> Calling her by her name. Heaven may hear,
> Where she in sooth is, though the stone may mock;
> Say to her that I sicken of life, the shock
> Of loss being greater now than I can bear;
> Gathering her black roses I see clear
> Her candid footprints in the tragic rock.
> Singing of her incessantly I wander;
> Of her alive, her dead, I sing to men.
> Tell her I wait where she knows, being fain
> To see her. Oh, when she shall draw me yonder,
> Touch me immortal, then, my Sonnet, then
> Shall we not be on fire with bliss—and pain?

One more sonnet, in which the whole agony of bereavement is packed into fourteen lines, will leave nothing to be quoted here from this poetry and its pain:

Where is that forehead and the gemmed headdress
That turned my gaze forever from vile things,
And the brows arched like two thin little wings,
Those planet eyes that searched my wilderness,
That curved white face where thought and mood confess
Unveiled their colour? Oh, in what air now sings
The silver progress of her words that wrings
The heart with rapture? Words the angels guess,
Perhaps. That wit, grace, ardour, glory, all
Are gone. And you, my heart of grievous lead,
Must lie so heavy in her small hand pressed!
Oh, in some street to feel her shadow fall
Just once—the shadow of her casual head—
Across the hunger of this hollow breast!

Petrarch survived Laura by twenty-six years; while her husband, seven months after her death, no whit daunted by the ten children Laura had bequeathed to him, married again.

The tale of Messer Petrarch approaches its end. On the 18th of June, 1374, his servants, coming into his room, found their master dead, his head resting on a book. He was buried in his red satin robe, and sixteen doctors carried the coffin into the little parish church at Arqua.

Thus passed from the earthly scene Francesco Petrarch, poet, lover, traveller, translator, intimate of the great ancients, friend of princes and popes and kings, diplomat as well, ambassador to a troubled world from the serene and illustrious dead, the most learned man in Europe of his time, the chief agent of the Renaissance, the first modern.

As a poet, we know him and love him, principally, if not exclusively, for his sonnets to Laura alive and Laura dead, sonnets which occupied him from his twenty-third to his seventieth year, the greatest love sonnets ever written by any poet in any language. Though he was much influenced by his great fellow-Tuscan Dante, using metaphors and symbols which abound in the poet of Beatrice, yet he was intensely different. His songs

and his sonnets took the ideas and images which were current
in the love language of the time and drenched them in the music
of his own passionate sincerity. He is, therefore, warmer than
Dante, though not as forbiddingly wise; less aloof, though not
less lofty; more lovable, more accessible, more human in his
strength and his weakness. We admire Dante. We adore Petrarch. Dante blew the trumpets of the Tuscan tongue from the
bottom of Hell to the top of Heaven. Petrarch, easing his heart
in the same melodious tongue, was concerned, not with any
moral message, but only with the little bittersweet private Hell
inside of him where Laura was not, and only with that particular part of a Heaven which Laura made by her being there.

The first sonnets in the English language were inspired by
Petrarch. His poems—canzoni and idyls he wrote also—
coloured the greatest period of English poetry, the Elizabethan,
and his sonnets were an inspiration for John Milton in the century that followed. Indeed, so indelibly did he make the sonnet
his messenger to English poets that, to this very day, we speak
of the Petrarchan sonnet and regard it as our finest sonnet form.
And on the twenty-first day of April of 1927, Avignon com-
memorated that other day in another April six hundred years
ago, when a young Italian poet, kneeling in a damp church early
in the morning, saw a lady whose hair was knitted gold and
whose mantle was green and violet-sprinkled. On the site where
that young man, smitten with human love, sang in sorrow and
solitude, a marble tablet will henceforth say to pilgrims: "Here
Petrarch sang of Laura of Provence and gave back to the world
the treasure of classical literature."

> That April—and that morning! Holy hour!
> How cold the flags! The early air how cold!
> The candles in their sconces fogged with gold!
> The candlewicks pulled sideways to a flower!
> And there the young Italian prayed for power
> To shut his heart, to point it up, to hold
> It straight for Heaven: so he kneeled, so told
> His mother's ghost in her unearthly tower.

O Avignon! O little golden head!
The braids that twisted candleflame between
The young Italian and the words he said!
O violet-sprinkled cloak she wore, as green
As April—on that morning! . . . She is dead
Six hundred years. . . . This April is as keen.

For deynte of the newe somerys sake
I bad hem strowe flouris on my bed

CHAPTER XI

PEGASUS IN ENGLAND

I

Early in A.D. 1373 a young Englishman came riding through northern Italy. He was the envoy of the King of England, with business in Pisa, Genoa, and Florence. He was gone from England on his mission for eleven months.

The record tells us these things and these only. It is a pity we don't know more. Perhaps it is this journey to Italy from which we must trace the beginning of modern English poetry!

For Geoffrey Chaucer, the King of England's envoy, was also Geoffrey Chaucer the poet. And it is probable that not Bellerophon himself, astride Pegasus, was more amazed and excited than this young Englishman on his palfrey by what he found in the Italy of Petrarch and Boccaccio.

If we go back to England and to Chaucer's life there, we can understand why this was so. England had been kind enough to Chaucer. He was only the son of a wine merchant when he was born in London in 1340, but by money or influence he had got a place at court. He served as a page to the wife of the Duke of Clarence, a son of King Edward III. Later, he went to France with the English army and was captured by the French. In these early years, he learned to read and write (not easy things to do in those days) and to speak French well. Such accomplishments made him useful to princes and great nobles. Probably the good humour and charm that later warmed his poetry may also have helped him to prosper serving the King and the King's sons.

At court young Chaucer had begun to write poems. It is thought that five long poems of his and some short ones were composed before he went to Italy. Probably there were many others. All of these early verses show the influence of the French poets. The Norman kings of England and many of the nobles still spoke French almost as well as they did English. Rondels and ballades and the rhymed romances of France and Germany had gone far toward driving out old English alliterative verse. Chaucer fell in with the fashion of the court, and it is not surprising that one of the poems of which he was most proud was a translation of the French chivalric epic, *The Romance of the Rose*.

Chaucer learned a great deal from French poetry. It had a grace and smoothness that English poetry lacked. These qualities show themselves in Chaucer's early poems. We can see how he wrote just before he went to Italy by reading *The Book of the Duchess*. This is a poem he composed in 1369 on the death of Blanche, the wife of John of Gaunt, Duke of Lancaster, the King's fourth son. John of Gaunt was now Chaucer's master and patron. The Duke of Clarence, in whose castle he had first served, had died.

In *The Book of the Duchess* Chaucer tells how he dreamed a dream in which he was awakened

> By little birds—a goodly number—
> That had shaken me from out my slumber
> With noise and sweetness of their song.

He dreamed that they sat on the roof of his house—

And sang—each one in his own way,
The sweetest concert, the most gay
That men could ever hear, I trow.
For some sang high and some sang low
Yet all their song made one accord.

And after that he got up and went out, and heard horns and
saw horses and men and dogs go by. He walked along after the
hunt until it disappeared. Then a little dog came up to him.

It came toward me just as though
It knew me—crept along so low,
Held down its head and joined its ears,
And laid back smoothly all its hairs.

The dog led him down a flowery green path into a wood where
great trees stood ten or twelve paces apart, and in the gloom
he saw a noble young man dressed all in black. The young man
told him how his wife had been stolen from him. He described
how beautiful she was, how lovely were her eyes, how

Her throat, as I have memory,
Seemed a round tower of ivory,

and how at times when she talked and laughed with her friends
she was so joyous

That she was like a torch—so bright
That every man may take its light
And yet it never shines the less!

Then Chaucer asked, "Where is she?" The young man answered, "She is dead," and Chaucer knew that Death had
stolen her. The men and dogs come back now from the hunt
and the young man joined them and disappeared.

This was Chaucer's way of describing John of Gaunt his
master and the Duchess his mistress who had died. The poem
has kept the memory of this lady for us through five hundred
years. It still keeps for us, too, the bird songs, the music of horns,
the flowers, and the green forests in which the Duchess Blanche
walked once, and now would not walk any more. It shows the

idyllic life Chaucer knew about court, and it also shows that he could write exquisite poetry. The Italians did not have to teach him that.

But there was much they could teach him. For Italy had begun to blossom with tall cathedrals, statues in bronze and marble, bright paintings, music, and ships of coloured sails bound for Greece, Arabia, and India. And in its shops there were books, books, lettered by hand (for printing was yet to be invented in Europe) with initials and borders of red and blue and gold and bearing names at which Geoffrey Chaucer must have looked with his eyes wide open, and sometimes his mouth, too.

For here were Latin manuscripts of Cicero, Virgil, Boëthius, Statius, some of them writers as renowned and little known in England as Sappho is with us to-day. And here in Italian were the poems of Dante, Petrarch, and Boccaccio, new singers who, men said, had written like second Homers or Virgils.

Perhaps Chaucer actually saw Boccaccio. Perhaps the ageing Italian, who had by this time begun to regret some of the gay tales he had written, said to his visitor: "Young man, leave off rhyming and write soberly for the glory of God." Or perhaps meeting Boccaccio fired Chaucer with new ambition. One modern poet, Walter Savage Landor, pictures Chaucer, Boccaccio, and Petrarch talking together, and in the conversation he has Chaucer say:

I will attempt to show Englishmen what Italians are; how much deeper in thought, intenser in feeling, and richer in imagination, than ever formerly: and I will try whether we cannot raise poetry under our fogs, and merriment among our marshes.

II

Whether or not he may have said anything like this, it was very like what he actually did. It is certain that he brought back with him many books, Latin and Italian, and about six years after he returned to England from this first trip to Italy he wrote *Troilus and Cressida*, a long romance in rhyme of two lovers in Troy during the Trojan War. Later, he composed *The Parliament of Birds, The House of Fame,* and *The Legend of Good Women.* All showed the results of his Latin and Italian reading.

For in these poems he broke away from the graceful but artificial style of the French lyrics and romances, and wrote more directly and naturally. It is true that he often used the stories and even translated the words of the foreign writers he had been reading, but he made them his own. *Troilus and Cressida* has 2,583 lines out of 8,239, translated from Boccaccio, and Chaucer uses one of Petrarch's sonnets as a song. But the poem is very different from Boccaccio's *Filostrato,* from which it was taken. The people are different and the poetry is different. Here Chaucer makes a hero and a heroine and a "villain" we cannot forget, and here and in the other poems of this period his humour flashes out in full force for the first time. There are also beautiful descriptions and tender lyrical passages. Chaucer had brought the winged horse of the Italians to England, but he made it soar with a new sweep of wings and into regions that were unknown to Dante and Petrarch.

It is surprising that Chaucer was able to go forward writing better and better poetry, for he must have had to do at night most of what he did.

In the daytime, he was busy serving the Duke of Lancaster or the King. He was married, too. We know only this, and that his wife's name was Philippa and that he had at least one child.

Chaucer's everyday work was rather important. He had charge of collecting duty or customs on all the wool, skins, and leather passing in and out of the port of London. Later he had charge of petty customs—or miscellaneous goods—as well. He was paid well for this, and he had several pensions. He got money for managing estates and acting as the King's representative abroad. He went to Flanders, France, and a second time to Italy on such business. In 1386, he was elected to Parliament as knight of the shire of Kent.

All this made him very much what one of our government

officials would be to-day, and something, too, like a successful
business man. Probably we have a glimpse of the life he led
when he tells in *The Legend of Good Women* (written about 1385)
how one night in May—

> Home to my house full swiftly then I sped,
> And in a little arbour there I bade
> My servants have my couch that evening made
> Where, new embanked, the turf was freshly mown,
> And ordered also that the bed be strown
> With flowers for the new-born summer's sake.

Here we see the prosperous man of affairs ordering his servants about, and here we see the poet celebrating the arrival of
summer. Imagine the servants bustling about to obey their
master, and then whispering to the cook when they went to
the kitchen for supper:

"He had us put his bed in the arbour and throw flowers all
over it!"

III. THE CANTERBURY PILGRIMS

And now Chaucer began the greatest of all his poems. He
started work on *The Canterbury Tales*.

In this he was to do one thing he had not as yet accomplished:
he was to write of the world of everyday men, of all England.

To be sure, in all his poems we catch glimpses of the life he
lived. But what he had written up to 1387 had been about love,
ancient wars, dreams, or ideas. He had paid little attention to
the real world. In England there had been a great plague that
had killed off a third of the people; the working classes had revolted against the King; preachers, like Wycliffe, were creating
religious excitement, soldiers were going to France to fight great
battles. But Chaucer wrote nothing of these things.

Now in *The Canterbury Tales* he turned to the real world,
and we have a vivid picture of living men and women.

The Canterbury Tales are made up of a number of stories told
by a group of twenty-nine pilgrims going on a pilgrimage to

Canterbury, then the religious centre of England. The stories are told to pass the time away. They are all different, for one is told by a knight, another by a merchant, another by a housewife, another by a prioress, another by a shipman, etc. There are altogether twenty-four tales. Originally, Chaucer intended to write one hundred and sixteen, four for each pilgrim, but in what has come down to us we have all we need to know of the people who lived in Chaucer's England—their dress, their talk, their ideas.

The Canterbury Tales are full of humour, of excitement, of beautiful poetry.

When the knight tells his story, we hear of Palamon and Arcite, imprisoned in a tower, and both falling in love with the Princess Emily who walks in the garden below. We follow them through many adventures to the great tournament in which they fight to see which shall marry her.

When the pardoner entertains the pilgrims, we go into a tavern and hear the rough talk of loafers and drunkards, and see how three rascals set off to hunt for Death and kill him, and what became of this peculiar quest.

The nun's priest tells the quaint story of Chanticleer the cock, and Pertelote his lady, and Reynard the wicked fox—a tale full of sly laughter and amusing excitement.

The *Tales*, with the many other poems Chaucer wrote, had an important effect on poetry in England and on England itself.

For one thing, they made other poets write better. Good poetry had been written in English before Chaucer came and while he was writing—snatches of ballads, and poems like *Sir Gawain and the Green Knight*, *The Pearl*, Langland's *Piers Plowman*. But Chaucer's poetry was greater in what it attempted to do than were any of these, and more finished as verse. Also, it brought in new forms like the rhyme royal, in which *Troilus* had been written, and the heroic couplet, of which there are examples below, and in which a number of *The Canterbury Tales* were composed.

Chaucer also did a great service for those who read or heard of poetry. His poems could not be printed—they were copied by hand. But thousands on thousands must have heard them, for the tales of Chaucer told in verse were read much as novels are to-day. These people, most of whom had only heard of Homer and Virgil and Horace, now had something in English which showed them what great poetry could be.

Finally, Chaucer helped to create the language we use to-day. When he began to write, there were English dialects, but there was no English language. He took the dialect spoken near London and wrote so well in it that it became the speech other writers wrote in, and then the language of all educated people.

Unfortunately, it has changed a great deal in six hundred years, and if we want to read Chaucer to-day, we first ought to study Middle English, his language. The poetry quoted in this chapter is "modernized." If it were printed as Chaucer wrote it, few readers of this book could read it properly, and the meaning would often be lost. Yet many people foolishly try to read Chaucer without a knowledge of the words he used, and complain because they think he wrote crude, uneven lines and bad rhymes.

Of course, this is silly. Chaucer was a careful scholar and a great artist, and knew inside out the craft of writing poetry. He could make lovely and tender pictures. There is the lady Emily whom Palamon and Arcite saw walking in the garden:

> Her yellow hair was braided in a tress
> Behind her back, a yard long, I should guess;
> And in the garden as the sun uprose,
> She wandered up and down, and there she chose
> And gathered, now of white and now of red,
> Flowers to make a garland for her head,
> And like an angel heavenly she sang.

He could write quite as well poetry that was sombre, as of the forest

> Of trees all knotty, gnarled, barren, old,
> With trunks shorn off and hideous to behold,

Through which there ran a rumble and a sough
As though a storm should shatter every bough

He was a master of sly jokes and kindly humour. He tells of the pardoner with pardons "all hot from Rome," and of the dainty prioress who spoke excellent French

After the school of Stratford on the Bowe;
The French they speak in France she didn't know.

Nobody ever wrote conversation in verse so well as Chaucer. We get the very tone of voice of his characters. And he knew what was in their hearts and minds, too; nobody but Shakespeare has ever made such real people as this oldest of great English poets.

And although we ought to study Chaucer's language if we want to enjoy his poetry fully, the stories he told, and the people he made, the dance of his metre and the shrewd truth of what he said have lived out the centuries and are still with us. Chaucer will never be forgotten while there is an English language to remind us with many of his phrases that he helped to make it; or humour to make us recall how he laughed tenderly at men and women; or a springtime to make us remember how he loved the first warm weather.

While Chaucer was writing *The Canterbury Tales*, things were not going so smoothly for him at court as they had been. His patron John of Gaunt went to Spain, and Chaucer lost his offices and some of his pension money. John of Gaunt came back and things went better, but after his death, Henry of Bolingbroke, his son, had trouble with King Richard II. Finally, there was war, and King Richard was put in prison and the son of Chaucer's old patron became King Henry IV.

Apparently Chaucer had been having a rough time of it while the fighting was going on. Still, he was the same cheerful poet who had rollicked through his many tales in rhyme, and he sat down and wrote a poem to the new king. He called it

THE COMPLAINT OF CHAUCER TO HIS EMPTY PURSE

To you, my purse, and to no other wight,
Complain I—for you are my lady dear;
I am so sorry now that you are light,—
For truly, unless you make me heavy cheer
I had as lief be laid upon my bier;
Wherefore unto your mercy thus I cry:
Be heavy for me again or else I die!

Vouchsafe me, purse, this day—ere it be night—
That I from you the blissful sound may hear—
Or see your colour like the sun's own light,
That of yellowness has never had a peer!
You are my life, the star by which I steer,
The queen of comfort and good company:
Be heavy for me again or else I die!

Now purse, my worldly saviour, my life's light,
If you'll not be my banker, as I fear,
At least deliver me by your sovereign might
Out of this town, for I am shaved as near
As any friar; and yet, since you are here,
Once more I pray unto your courtesy:
Be heavy for me again or else I die!

ENVOY (TO KING HENRY IV)

O conqueror of Brutus' Albion!
Whom now free vote and royal blood have won
True kingship: unto you this song I send;
And you, that all misfortune can amend,
Give mind to what I pray, and have it done!

The King had it done. He doubled Chaucer's pension. The ageing poet (for Chaucer was now almost sixty) could now look forward to a time free from worry and rich in writing. But this was not to be, for in October, 1400, he died. It was left to other and later English poets to ride the winged horse that Chaucer had brought to England from Italy.

CHAPTER XII

THE BALLAD-MAKERS

After Chaucer's death no great poet made poetry in England for one hundred and seventy-nine years.

There were poets who imitated Chaucer. Thomas Occleve and John Lydgate wrote elaborate moral allegories in verse, and long stories of Rome and Troy. They wrote in the metres and stanzas Chaucer had made at home in English poetry, but they wrote badly. It is chiefly because no one else of consequence was writing then that we remember them at all.

Perhaps there might have been better poets if the times had been better for poetry. Unhappily, it was a discouraging period for any writer. The King and the nobles had at last left off using French and the gayety and polish of the troubadours had faded from the court. English, now the language of all Englishmen, was changing. It was difficult to write well in a tongue that was one thing one year and something else the next. Perhaps it was also a task to make poetry in the midst of Henry V's conquest of France and the Wars of the Roses that devastated England after Henry's death. Young men of the kind that wrote sonnets and lyrics a hundred years later were probably routing the French at Agincourt or dying at Barnet Moors with Warwick the King-maker.

Yet in this time when there was no great poet in England there was great poetry. All over England itself and throughout the lowlands of Scotland it was a living thing. We do not know any man who made a line of it. None of the poems was written down until years after they were first made. All are in language very simple and often crude. Yet they are great in art and great in what they have done for prose and verse written in English since 1500. If one man had given us all the ballads that took their final shape during the fourteen and early fifteen hundreds, we would set him beside Chaucer and Wordsworth and Milton as one of the mighty poets of the language.

These ballads are poems of a very definite kind, different from all others in English. They always tell a story. They are all, as was pointed out above, by unknown authors. They were made to be sung to tunes. They were all passed on by word of mouth for a number of generations, changing sometimes only a little, sometimes much, as different people sang them. They were never "literary." No court poets composed them, no harpers or minstrels. They were made and sung among the common folk away from courts and cities and books.

There has been quarrelling among scholars as to just how the ballads were made, and how long ago. Some believe the habit of ballad-making was older in English than poems like *Beowulf*. There are no ballad manuscripts dating back to that period; in fact, except for one fragment which may or may not be a ballad, none is older than the Thirteenth Century, if as old. Yet quite probably ballad-making was very old. For these poems of the people seem to have been made by groups of men and women singing together, and the custom may have gone back farther than any written English.

Perhaps the ballads were sung for country dancing. Many of them are made in four-line stanzas. The first and third lines are a couplet, and the second and fourth are chorus lines or refrains which all the crowd could sing:

"She's gi'en to him a gay gold ring
With a hey lillelu and a how lo lan,
Wi' seven bright diamonds set therein,
And the birk and the broom blows bonnie."

As a group of people talked and danced, they may have put into such form the stories of love and war which they knew. It was much like the making of early chants and songs. Someone who had a quick tongue would sing out a line:

"As lang's these diamonds keep their hue,"

and the crowd would sing a refrain:

"With a hey lillelu and a how lo lan."

Then the first singer, or perhaps another in the group, would match the first line:

"Ye'll know I am a lover true,"

leaving the others to finish off the stanza with the chorus:

"And the birk and the broom blows bonnie."

Thus, gradually, the whole story would be told. Undoubtedly, some of these simple singers were poets. However, they didn't think of themselves as composing poetry. They knew they were good at helping to make ballads. About the castle fires or on the green in spring they were spurred on to make songs with the others—songs that were good to sing and that kept old tales and memories alive. The ballads came out of the daily lives, the singing spirit, and the deep feelings of people. That is why they are so much more genuine than most of the songs of the minstrels, who had little, if anything, to do with making ballads and who went the rounds of towns and castles performing for their living and not chiefly to express their emotions.

The ballads told a great variety of stories. There were jovial ballads of the greenwood. These described how

> In summer when the shawes [groves] be sheen
>   And leaves be large and long,
> It is full merry in fair forest
>   To hear the fowlès' [birds'] song:
>
> To see the deer draw to the dale,
>   And leave the hillès hee [high]
> And shadow them in the leaves green,
>   Under the greenwood tree.

They sang the adventures of Robin Hood and Little John in and about Sherwood Forest, and how merry a life they lived until at last the great outlaw and archer was betrayed and died, saying:

> But lay a green sod under my head,
>   And another at my feet;
> And lay my bent bow at my side,
>   Which was my music sweet.

Other ballads were darker and sterner. Some told of weird and magic things—mermaids wooing knights to their death, ghosts coming at marriages, demons stealing away with unfortunate ladies. One lady goes aboard her lover's ship to fly away with him:

> She set her foot upon the ship,
>   No mariners could she behold;
> But the sails were o' the taffetie,
>   And the masts of beaten gold.

Alas! it is the Evil One himself who has lured her away, and at last he grows to enormous size:

> He strack the top-mast wi' his hand,
>   The fore-mast wi' his knee;
> And he brake that gallant ship in twain,
>   And sank her in the sea.

Other ballads tell of sorcerers, of harps strung with the hair of perished princesses that would sing the story of their deaths. Much like wild fairy tales they are, but with a deeper sense of human love and pain. They were the song tales of a rude land

where storms and winds seemed to be full of more than earthly
powers, and men and magic mingled terribly together.

There were ballads of lovers true and false—girls who dressed
as pages and followed their sweethearts, knights who sailed back
across the sea in time to save their loves from marrying detested
suitors—or arrived just too late to prevent them, but not too
late to carry them off. There were ballads made of the Bible
stories. Finally, there were poems of border raids and sea voyages and battles. One of the simplest and finest of all the ballads
is that about Sir Patrick Spens. He was sent out to sea by the
Scotch king in the storm season of the year, to carry to Norway
a company of lords who bore a message for the Norwegian king.
Sir Patrick suspects that his enemies have been at work. He
cries:

> O wha is this has done this deed,
>   This ill deed done to me,
> To send me out this time o' year,
>   To sail upon the sea!

But he will not disobey the King's order. He mans his ship and
pushes out with the gay noblemen. Then, says the ballad:

> O lang, lang may the ladies sit,
>   Wi' their fans into their hand,
> Or e'er they see Sir Patrick Spens
>   Come sailing to the strand.
>
> Half o'er, half o'er to Aberdour
>   'Tis fifty fathom deep,
> And there lies guid Sir Patrick Spens,
>   Wi' the Scots lords at his feet!

Ballads like *Kinmount Willie* and the *Battle of Otterburne* tell
of border wars, and ring with daring and courage, with generosity between foemen. Says the great Percy to the dying
Douglas:

> To have sav'd thy life I'd have parted with
>   My lands for yearès three,
> For a better man of heart nor of hand
>   Was not in the north countree.

Written in the plain, crude speech of common folk, these poems lay for hundreds of years half neglected. Men sang them and loved them, but did not think they were great poetry. Yet as they were sung from hall to hall, from cottage to cottage, some of them were changed until they became marvellous expressions of simple terror or sorrow or courage. The ballads the people loved were those that were plain and direct and exciting and full of deep feeling. Many ballads that were not wholly of this character at first were made so to suit the people who sang them. Some of the poems told their stories with a fearful briefness. Lord Randal comes back from hunting, and his mother asks him four questions. Where has he been?

> I hae been to the wild wood; mother,
>   make my bed soon,
> For I'm weary wi' hunting, and fain
>   wald lie doon.

Where did he eat?

> I dined wi' my true love; mother,
>   make my bed soon,
> For I'm weary wi' hunting, and fain
>   wald lie doon.

What did he eat with his lady?

> I got eels boiled in broo [broth]; mother,
>   make my bed soon,
> For I'm weary wi' hunting, and fain
>   wald lie doon.

Where are the bloodhounds that went out with him?

> O they swell'd and they died; mother,
>   make my bed soon,
> For I'm weary wi' hunting, and fain
>   wald lie doon.

And so we have the story of how a lady poisoned her lover; just the terrible outline to be filled in as we can guess it.

It was a great art, singing these tales so simply and in so few words. But sometimes the words were also wonderful themselves. Sometimes they had a kind of beauty about them that is the beauty of a picture only:

> And we will sail the sea sae green
>   Unto some far countrie;
> Or we'll sail to some bonny isle,
>   Stands lonely midst the sea.

Again, they may give the bold talk of the people of the time, like the boasting of the angry Scotch nobleman, Lord Buccleuch, when he hears the English have captured Kinmount Willie and taken him to Carlisle Castle.

> O were there war between the lands,
>   As well I wot that there is nane,
> I would slight Carlisle castell high,
>   Though it were builded of marble stane.
>
> I would set that castle in a low
>   And slocken it wi' English blood,
> There's never a man in Cumberland
>   Should ken where Carlisle castell stood.

But the words of ballads are best remembered for the way in which they tell great emotion in a few lines. There is little written so wistfully pitiful as the cry of Lady Margaret at the grave of her knight, Clerk Saunders:

> Is there ony room at your head, Saunders?
>   Is there ony room at your feet?
> Or ony room at your side, Saunders,
>   Where fain, fain, I wad sleep?

And there is cruel Barbara Allen, who felt she had killed her lover with coldness, and pined away herself:

> O mother, mother, make my bed,
>   O make it soft and narrow;
> Since my love died for me to-day,
>   I'll die for him to-morrow.

The habit of making folk ballads began to die in the early Sixteenth Century. Good roads and printing presses and the wealth of growing England and Scotland broke up the loneliness of the countryside. People did not have to depend so much on themselves for their amusement. They had books and the travelling player folk and news from the cities. Ballads of a sort were made by poets of the town, who rhymed about the latest scandals, and sent out sheets to be sold like sensational newspapers to-day. The country folk kept their old songs in memory. They made no new ones like them.

But men and poets had been stirred by the ballads. The spirit of these rude poems got into Shakespeare's songs and lines of Milton's poems. Here and there, gentlemen wrote down the ballads they knew and loved. From some of these manuscripts the ballad poems were finally gathered together. Bishop Percy printed the first great collection in 1765, calling it *Reliques of English Poetry*. Walter Scott added another group in his *Minstrelsy of the Scottish Border*, published in 1802: an American scholar, Professor Child, discovered a number of unknown ballads when he brought all the true ballad poetry together.

Since their appearance in book form in the middle 1700's, the ballads have had an influence on the poetry of almost all poets writing afterward. Their swinging stanzas, their direct style (telling much while omitting much) come to us in so many echoes that we forget how often we hear them. Those long years when there was no great poet in England are memorable for the great poetry of poets whose names are unknown to us—and unknowable.

CHAPTER XIII

QUEEN ELIZABETH'S POETS

I

All this time the more finished poetry that Chaucer had kindled in England had been flickering along like a flame about to die.

England did not seem to be ready for it. Chaucer had put into English verse some of the fire of the Renaissance, the renascence or new birth of learning and ideas and life which he had seen in Italy. But Lydgate and Occleve did not know what to do with such magic. Lydgate had been to Italy, but certainly he had lacked the eyes and soul to see what Chaucer saw. And in England there was as yet no Renaissance. What could a solemn versifier do in such a troubled land, with men-at-arms tramping and burning and shouting all over the country, scaring poets like Lydgate into monasteries!

But soon it was not necessary for poets to go to Italy. Italy began to come to England. Scholars brought rare manuscripts of Greek and Latin to the universities. Soon young men of twenty at Cambridge and Oxford were learning more of Virgil and Homer, of Sophocles and Horace, than Chaucer had known.

They talked with contempt of the Latin Bible, the Vulgate, and read the New Testament in the original Greek.

While they were revelling in their new learning, William Caxton brought the first printing press to England. Near Winchester, in 1477, he struck off his first book. There was now no more need of stupid scribes copying by hand. Book after book could be born by the mere setting of paper against type. A hundred could be had now where one had been difficult to get before. What wonder if books flooded England? Virgil and Horace became texts for schoolboys. Travellers brought French volumes from France (for printing had begun in Europe even before Caxton brought it to England), and Petrarch and Boccaccio from Italy. The Bible was translated and printed. The beauty of poetry and the inspiration of the Holy Word were set out like a glittering feast. The great nobles whose fathers had looked on writing and reading as priests' work declaimed the Æneid and fashioned love lyrics. Lusty Henry VIII, rich king of a thriving kingdom, lover of sports and paintings and revelries, made songs and wrote a tract defending the Pope against the reformer Luther, and set his daughters to reading Greek.

All this was a kind of poetry itself. Men breathed the beauty of Virgil and the great Italian singers and longed to make a lasting kind of song in English. They did not think of the rough, unprinted ballads as poetry. They knew Chaucer and relished his tales, but their English was already different from his, and he seemed quaint and unmusical to them. They wanted the polished cadences and harmonious wisdom of Greece and Rome, the colour of Florence and Milan and farther India. They wanted the wonder of the new Indies of the West, later to be known as America, that had loomed up across oceans to make the earth shoot out into unsuspected distances and incredible adventure.

II

In 1579 this poetry seemed to have come. That year saw the publication of *The Shepherd's Calendar*. The author of the book did not give his name, but gradually it became known about court that it was a young man named Edmund Spenser who had written the most important book of poetry since Chaucer.

There had been signs of new song before. Sir Thomas Wyatt had been to Spain and read Petrarch and written graceful love songs showing that he knew Chaucer also. He could edge his singing with bitterness:

> With serving still
> This have I won:
> For my goodwill
> To be undone.
>
> And for redress
> Of all my pain,
> Disdainfulness
> I have again.

He and the young Earl of Surrey (beheaded at thirty by the suspicious king) had brought the fourteen-line sonnet of Petrarch to England. And in all their poetry they had escaped from the stiff and solemn verse of Lydgate, and the crabbed if livelier verse of the later poet, John Skelton. Their songs had a charm and gallantry that had been lacking in England since the maker of *The Canterbury Tales* had stopped writing.

But Spenser in his *Shepherd's Calendar* succeeded in doing fully what Surrey and Wyatt had only half done. He had written poetry in English that, in promise at least, might be likened to Petrarch's or even Virgil's.

For the literary gentlemen and ladies of London, much of its merit lay in the scholarly nature of the *Calendar*. It took the ancient pastoral form and presented twelve "æglogues" or pastoral episodes, one for each month of the year. These were modelled on the work of Theocritus and Virgil, on the pastoral writers of Renaissance Italy, Mantuan and Petrarch, and on the poems of the French poet Marot. Glittering with allusions to gods, nymphs, dryads, satyrs, and myths, now telling the

woes of love-lorn shepherds, now discussing in learned allegory
the art of poetry or the state of religion in modern England, the
Calendar filled the English scholars and nobles with delight.
English pastorals had been attempted before, but none had
been successful. The best of those theretofore composed were
crude, like the name of the man who had written them—Googe.
Spenser, on the other hand, had made a poem that could be
set beside the pastorals of Greek and Latin and Italian.

Chief among the shepherds whom Spenser portrayed was
Colin Clout. The "glosse" or notes which were given after each
"æglogue" in explanation of its meaning, stated that Colin was
Spenser himself, and that the shepherd Tityrus was Chaucer.
So it is important to hear Colin cry in the June "æglogue":

> The god of Shepherds, Tityrus, is dead,
> Who taught me, homely as I can, to make [compose],

and to hear him say later that he learned his songs of Tityrus.
For this explains a great deal. It shows that Spenser had taken
the best music in his own language and enriched it with what
he could gather from great poets of other languages. He blended
the freshness and life of Chaucer with the sweetness of Virgil.
In the process he gave something all his own. We cannot be
surprised that the ladies and gentlemen of London praised his
grave descriptions of winter with its

> . . . naked trees, whose shady leaves are lost
> Wherein the birds were wont to build their bower.

Nor is it a wonder that they loved the sad "complaints" of the
shepherds—the quaint fancy, for instance, of the love-sad swain
who praised the nightingale because she was always sad like
him:

> That blessed bird, that spends her time of sleep
> In songs and plaintive pleas.

And who could fail to delight in the rollicking song of the shepherds Willie and Perigot about the fair lass Bonnibeli:

PERIGOT: A chaplet on her head she wore,
WILLIE: Hey, ho, chapelet!
PERIGOT: Of sweet violets therein was store,
WILLIE: She sweeter than the violet.
PERIGOT: My sheep did leave their wonted food,
WILLIE: Hey, ho, silly sheep!
PERIGOT: And gazed on her as they were wood [crazy]
WILLIE: Wood as he that did them keep!

In five of the eclogues, as we have said, Spenser was writing of events or conditions in England. Three are devoted to religion—showing a serious, moral quality in the poet which was to be important in all his work. In another he praised Henry VIII's daughter Elizabeth, now Queen of England:

> Of fair Eliza be your silver song,
>   That blessed wight:
> The flowre of virgins, may she flourish long
>   In princely plight.

Queen Elizabeth was worth singing about. Her island kingdom was at peace and very prosperous. Her father, King Henry, had broken free of the Pope of Rome and made a separate Church of England with himself at the head of it. Elizabeth inherited the power he had acquired. With it she inherited lands and money, much of it taken from the priests Henry had thrust out of England. Her merchants were sending ships to the bazaars of India and the markets of Marco Polo's China: they were pushing through ice to Russian Archangel, hunting whales for precious oil and ambergris, pillaging off the Barbary coast. Her great city of London was growing proud and populous, with white linen, tapestries, silver and gold dishes. Through its muddy, ill-drained streets splashed splendidly appointed horses, and processions of cooks and pastrymen went following trumpeters, bearing roasts and pies to York House or Durham Palace or Somerset House—many-turreted and gabled piles, with coloured oriel windows and blazoned coats of arms and statuary and Italian gardens behind the walls, and steps going down through lawns to the Thames River. A rich land, a great land, with marvellous coloured silken and embroidered clothing. A land of ladies with painted faces and dyed hair, waving feather fans and carrying elegant mirrors at their girdles:

> With silken coats, and caps, and golden rings,
> With ruffs, and cuffs, and farthingales, and things;
> With scarfs and fans, and double change of bravery,
> With amber bracelets, beads, and all this knavery.

A land, too, of greater learning and scholarship, of men more intoxicated with ideas and song than Chaucer had dared to dream of in John of Gaunt's castle. The books came faster and more splendid. Philosophy and romance were getting translated from old and new tongues. Scholars chatted and wrote in Latin. Plays, first made by monks for the delight and instruction of simple folk, were produced elegantly at court, and at fine inns fitted up for players—the first London theatres.

Elizabeth, by the grace of God, queen of all this and infinitely more—of course young Edmund Spenser would sing of her. He was dazzled with the glory and gold of her kingdom, and hoped for enough gold to win glory himself. Of a gentleman's family, he had been poor all his life, pushing up through school and university on scholarships. After university, he had found service in London. Sir Philip Sidney, himself a poet, had read and applauded his verses and got him an irregular post with the great Earl of Leicester. Spenser hoped for a more settled office of some kind to bring him "ordinary wages."

The poems did not change this hope. They brought him a little money, but the readers of even the best verse were few and there was no protection by law against printers who chose to "pirate" poems or entire volumes—that is, to copy them and sell them without paying the author a penny. In fact, after 1579, poor Spenser, as he himself wrote a friend, "was minded for a while to have intermitted the uttering [publishing] of my writings; leaste, by overmuch cloying their [his patrons'] noble ears, I should gather a contempt of myself." So he worked hard at being a man of affairs, hoping to get a modest fortune and become a gentleman, thus winning leisure to write. There were no more books from him for eleven years.

Those years were years of adventure in a rough, strange land. Spenser got a regular position at last as secretary to Arthur, Lord Grey, the new Queen's Deputy in Ireland. How he went there and saw the English fight with Irish rebels and Spaniards, and massacre both of them by the hundred, how he got 3,000 acres of the rebels' land and built a castle and tried to be an English gentleman among the hostile Irish is a story we know little of. Spenser found it hard. He quarrelled with his Irish neighbours and pined for London, and bitterly resented being set down among a rude people who spoke no English. Of course, it was harder on the Irish than on Spenser, but the poet was not the first or the last Englishman to overlook their point of view.

Despite his distracting activity in an unsettled land, Spenser had not forgotten that he was a poet. Before he left England for Ireland, he had written other poems than *The Shepherd's Calendar*. Most of them were done when he was younger and were poorer poetry than his first published verse. But he had also begun about 1580 a poem of great length which he hoped to make into a great English epic.

The Faery Queen, even more than *The Shepherd's Calendar*, brought the glamour of the classics and the green land and lusty spirit of England, the wonder of the Renaissance and the religious feeling of the Reformation together.

It was to be a moral poem. Spenser was not, like many of the men and women of the Sixteenth Century, a religious fanatic, but a spirit of reverence and piety was in him. Like his age, he loved the parade of men and deeds and gay garments, and, like his age, he thought at times much of how the flesh would wither at last, and the soul go to be judged by God. So he made his great new poem a poem that was to improve the world. "The general end of all the books is to fashion a gentleman or noble person in vertuous and gentle discipline."

But this was to be done by a story. The reader was to be taken back to the time of King Arthur, greatest of romantic British kings. And he was to be led to the court of the Faery Queen, who represented, in allegory, Queen Elizabeth. There were to be twelve books in which various knights went forth from the court of the Queen to do adventures, and each knight represented one of the twelve virtues enumerated by Aristotle. In the adventures were to shine the wisdom and moral philosophy of the ancient Greeks and Romans, the religious fervour of Christianity, the bravery and faith of chivalry, the love of lovely colour and form and sound that had revived with the Renaissance. Indeed, the poem Spenser probably had most in mind to equal or excel was the Renaissance epic of the Italian poet Ariosto—*Orlando Furioso*. This, like *The Faery Queen*, was full of moral teaching and gorgeous knights and strange adventures.

For the writing of his poem, Spenser invented a new stanza. He did not find any of Chaucer's stanzas sufficiently stately for his purpose. He took one of these and added a last line to it— making it nine lines instead of eight. In this final line were two extra syllables, which gave a rolling, sonorous effect. But the beginning of *The Faery Queen* itself will show the now famous "Spenserian stanza":

> A gentle knight was pricking on the plain,
> Yclad in mightie arms and silver shield,
> Wherein old dints of deep wounds did remain,
> The cruel marks of many a bloody field;
> Yet arms till that time did he never wield;
> His angry steed did chide his foaming bit,
> As much disdaining to the curb to yield;
> Full jolly knight he seemed, and fair did sit,
> *As one for knightly jousts and fierce encounters fit.*

[The italics show the extra line which Spenser added.]

For the first ten years of his troubled life in Ireland Spenser wrought at *The Faery Queen*. Between helping Lord Grey and establishing his castle and quarrelling with his neighbours, he wrote the first three of the twelve books he planned to compose. He must have been greatly discouraged. Already England was forgetting *The Shepherd's Calendar* and the half-known poet who made it. Then, in the summer of 1589, Sir Walter Raleigh, soldier, verse-maker, favourite of Queen Elizabeth, visited Spenser at Kilcolman. Spenser showed him the beginning of the great poem.

"Why, man," Raleigh seems to have said, "this is the very truth and magic of poetry. You cannot keep it here among bogs and savages. There's nothing for it but you must go to London and the Queen. Once she hears these verses, and hear them, by my faith, she shall—you are done with Ireland forever."

Spenser went to London with Raleigh. He prepared to publish the beginning of his poem. Raleigh took him to the Queen, and the great Elizabeth listened to the poem made in her honour, and praised it and promised honour and money to the poet. The first three books of *The Faery Queen* were published. They confessed that Spenser had been the author of *The Shepherd's Calendar*. The nobles and scholars of London, still remembering this work, hailed Spenser now as the greatest of all English poets.

But how much bread will praise buy? The money and offices Spenser hoped for never came. After a year of bitter hanging about court, he took ship to Ireland again. In his poem *Colin Cloute's Come Home Again* he wrote of the shame of suing for favour at the court in London to no purpose, while a passage in his *Mother Hubbard's Tale* (1591) opens the poet's wretched heart to us. The poem was probably written ten years earlier than its publication. But the passage applies well to Spenser's later experience, and was almost certainly written and inserted in 1590:

> Full little knowest thou, that hast not tried,
> What hell it is, in suing long to bide:
> To lose good days, that might be better spent;
> To waste long nights in pensive discontent;
> To speed to-day, to be put back to-morrow;
> To feed on hope, to pine with fear and sorrow;

To have thy Prince's grace, yet want her Peers',
To have thy asking, yet wait many years;
To fret thy soul with crosses and with cares;
To eat thy heart through comfortless despairs;
To fawn, to crouch, to wait, to ride, to run,
To spend, to give, to want, to be undone.
Unhappy wight, born to disastrous end,
That doth his life in so long tendance spend!

But Spenser was to have a taste of happiness. After his return from England, he fell in love and married and wrote eighty sonnets which he called *Amoretti* (love-songs) and two lovely marriage hymns, the *Prothalamion* and *Epithalamion*, to his wife. He returned to London in 1595 and published his new poems, and three more books of *The Faery Queen*. He lived on in Ireland for several years more and seemed about to prosper. But hardly had he been appointed Sheriff of Cork, when the Irish rose against their English masters. Spenser's castle was burned, and he fled with his family, one of his four children perishing, it is said, in the flames of his house. Apparently broken in spirit, he came to England with dispatches. A few months later, he died there. Ben Jonson said: "He died for lack of bread in King Street, and refused twenty pieces sent to him by my Lord of Essex, saying he had no time to spend them." Perhaps this exaggerates Spenser's misery. At any rate, he was buried with great honour. The Earl of Essex took charge of the funeral and prepared a tomb for the poet in Westminster Abbey, the burial place of England's distinguished men. Poets threw elegies into his grave, with the pens that wrote them. The Queen bade a monument to be made for Spenser, though even in death the neglect and ill luck of his life followed him, and he never got it. English poets mourned his passing. When the remaining unpublished cantos of *The Faery Queen*, completing eight of the twelve books he had planned, appeared in 1609, the dead poet gained fresh honour.

When Spenser died, the English thought him the greatest of their poets, and they had cause to praise him. He had caught the buoyant beauty of the new life in England. When he came, there was no English poetry with a noble style, save the already unreadable Chaucer. Spenser gathered the freshness of Chaucer, the dignity of Virgil, the elaborate colour of Petrarch and Ariosto, and blended them all into a poetic language that was firm and musical and lovely. He found men asking if they should not give up rhyme and try to write like the ancients. He took old English metres and stanzas and showed that these could be handled superbly. He made happy experiments with new rhyme schemes and refrains, and in his epic he used a stanza form entirely his own which reflected the embroidered, half-chivalric beauty of the Renaissance world. The "Spenserian stanza" has been used since by other poets in the making of great English poetry. After Spenser, poets have never doubted that English was a fit language for great poems.

All this gave an impulse of golden life to English poetry. It gave the great poetry of the past new life, and it showed the shining path for English poetry of the future. It was much more than skilful—the beauty of Spenser was fresh in his own day and remains fresh in ours. He first of all in English gave what poets like Shakespeare and Milton and Keats have given since—the loveliness of exquisite phrases and lines in which the sound of words blends perfectly with the picture or story.

So we can lose ourselves still in the slow music of his marriage hymn, filled with his own delight in his bride, who is so lovely as she stands blushing before the priest

> That even the angels that continually
> About the sacred altar do remaine,
> Forget their service and about her fly,
> Oft peeping in her face, that seems more fayre
> The more they on it stare.

We can see her led to the bridal couch—

> Lay her in lilies and in violets,
> And silken curtains over her display,
> And odoured sheetes, and Arras coverlets.

We can turn to pictures from *The Faery Queen* such as delighted
Keats:

> They bring their wines from Greece and Araby,
> And dainty spices fetch'd from furthest Ind,

or

> A goodly lady clad in scarlet red
> Purfled with gold and pearl and rich assay.

As Sir Guyon stands in the Cave of Error we can see how

> His glistering armour made
> A little glooming light, much like a shade.

More ambitious and extended are passages like the description
of the entrance of the Cave of Despair, very much like a passage in Chaucer quoted earlier in this book:

> And all about old stocks and stubs of trees,
> Whereon nor fruit nor leaf was even seen,
> Did hang upon the ragged rocky knees;
> On which had many wretches hangèd been,
> Whose carcasses were scattered in the green,
> And thrown about the cliffs.

His description of Venus shows how the voluptuous richness
or Renaissance life had become a part of his poetry:

> Right in the midst the Goddess' self did stand
> Upon an altar of some costly mass,
> Whose substance was uneath to understand
>   [could scarcely be recognized]:
> For neither precious stone, nor dureful brass,
> Nor shining gold, nor mould'ring clay it was;
> But much more rare and precious to esteem,
> Pure in aspect, and like to christal glass,
> Yet glass was not, if one did rightly deem;
> But, being faire and brickle, likest glass did seeme.
> . . . .
> And all about her neck and shoulders flew
> A flock of little loves, and sports, and joys,
> With nimble wings of gold and purple hue;
> Whose shapes seem'd not like to terrestrial boys,

But like to Angels playing heavenly toys,
The whilst their eldest brother was away,
Cupid their eldest brother; he enjoys
The wide kingdom of love with lordly sway,
And to his law compels all creatures to obey.

It is true that few will read Spenser's great unfinished epic
now. Fewer will seriously study its moral lessons, woven in a
massive tapestry of allegory and symbol, the truth peeping
out from behind the golden clang of knightly combat and
the embroidered beauty of description. But *The Faery Queen*
seemed to Elizabethan England to be full of deep meaning.
England wanted to be taught the secret of life, the truth of
Christianity. It wanted to have woven beauty also—colour and
music and dance. Spenser tried to give it both. He was most
interested in the moral of his poetry, but wrote best when he
forgot it. We tire of his dreamy allegorical story to-day. Probably this is because the ideal of modesty and purity Spenser set
forth is no longer new to us. Spenser was really what we would
call a Victorian. His virtuous point of view was fresh and rare
in Elizabeth's court, and pleased sober-minded men. As to those
not so religious as Spenser himself, the great bulk and slow
music of *The Faery Queen* amazed and enchanted them. It lent
a dignity to all the poetry about it, like a gorgeous cathedral
towering over a town.

Looking at *The Faery Queen*, Englishmen were proud of
English poetry. And the poets of England sang with clearer
and finer voices because of the music that breathed through
its massive arches and broke against the coloured pictures of
its tall windows.

III

There was no other epic in Queen Elizabeth's time like *The
Faery Queen*, but there was a vast volume of other poetry.
If "Elizabethan poetry" is mentioned to-day, most people
will think of other verse than Spenser's. Spenser's poetry was

sweet and grave and slow. Many of the other poems of his time were sweet and gay and fantastically lively. Certainly they seem more human to us than Spenser, and more delightful for everyday music.

It would be impossible to tell in detail of the many Elizabethan poets. We should choose with difficulty among men like the gallant Sir Philip Sidney with his silver sonnets and his romantic death in battle; Sir Walter Raleigh, courtier and explorer and prisoner; the wild and little-known play-writers like Heywood and Dekker; Lodge, Nash, Greene; the scholarly Ben Jonson; passionate Marlowe, murdered at thirty. Some of these can be spoken of with Shakespeare in the next chapter. Like Shakespeare, some were chiefly makers of dramas, but all were also writers of songs, and some, like Jonson and Marlowe, of serious poems. Then there is Chapman, who translated the Iliad from Greek into English, and Donne, the poet who wrote exquisite poems for a few years and then fell to preaching.

Fortunately, most of these poets have a common spirit. They reflect the ever-growing exuberance of England. This had been rising since *The Shepherd's Calendar* appeared. The defeat of the Spanish Armada in 1588 had given all England a new pride. Sea captains were bringing new riches stolen from Spanish galleons. Gallants of the court were tasting new delights like tobacco from America and spices and fineries from the Far East. Most other Elizabethan poets reflect this more than Spenser. These writers, too, carried on in a new way the work Spenser had begun of making the English language elastic and easy-flowing for the uses of poetry. They had no great ideas to express. They sang of love, death, ambition, virtue—all very simply. Often they took the sentiments they expressed from Latin and Greek and Italian writers, changing them very little. Except in their sonnets, they hardly talked about themselves at all. But they explored like adventurers all the trickeries and surprises of words, all the fine ways of saying things already known. And they did this with a delight and capering grace that make us go to them still to renew ourselves in their abounding life. Dekker's song to Content shows the contagious spirit of this poetry:

> Art thou poor, yet hast thou golden slumbers?
> O sweet content!
> Art thou rich, yet is thy mind perplexèd?
> O punishment!
> Dost thou laugh to see how fools are vexèd
> To add to golden numbers, golden numbers?
> O sweet content, O sweet, O sweet content!
> Work apace, apace, apace;
> Honest labour bears a lovely face;
> Then hey nonny nonny, hey nonny nonny!

The hunting for "quaint conceits" and odd rhyme schemes of Elizabethan love poetry is in these stanzas of Davison:

> How often have my sighs declared my anguish
> Wherein I daily languish;
> Yet doth she still procure it.
> Heart, let her go, for I cannot endure it.
> Say, shall she go?
> Oh no, no, no, no, no!
> She gave the wound, and she alone must cure it.
>
> But if the love that hath, and still doth burn me
> No love at length return me,
> Out of my thoughts I'll set her.
> Heart, let her go; O heart, I pray thee, let her!
> Say, shall she go?
> Oh no, no, no, no, no!
> Fixed in the heart, how can the heart forget her?

Some of Shakespeare's songs are the supreme expression of this lightness and grace. There is

> HARK! HARK! THE LARK
>
> Hark! hark! the lark at heaven's gate sings,
> And Phœbus 'gins arise,
> His steeds to water at those springs
> On chaliced flowers that lies;
> And winking Mary-buds begin to ope their golden eyes:
> With everything that pretty is, my lady sweet, arise;
> Arise, arise.

Ben Jonson was less light, but made biting satires on fools and fops and villains, and knew how to play with words even in more serious poems. In his *Epitaph on Elizabeth, L. H.* he does this:

> Underneath this stone doth lie
> As much beauty as could die;
> Which in life did harbour give
> To more virtue than doth live.

But with the lighter poetry went the love for beauty Spenser had celebrated, and the understanding of the briefness of life and the darkness of death. Jonson could burst into poetry glowing white, as in his praise of poets themselves:

> Who heaved Heracles
> Unto the stars, or the Tyndarides?
> Who lifted Jason's Argo to the sky,
> Who set bright Ariadne's throne so high,
> Who made a lamp of Berenice's hair
> And lifted Cassiopea in her chair
> But only poets, rapt with rage divine?

Donne wrote quaintly of death:

> Thou'rt slave to fate, chance, kings, and desperate men,
> And doth with poison, war, and sickness dwell;
> And poppy or charms can make us sleep as well
> And better than thy stroke; why swell'st thou then?
> One short sleep past, we wake eternally,
> And Death shall be no more: Death, thou shalt die!

This is the ending of one of Donne's sonnets. It is a sonnet different in form from Petrarch's. It has fourteen lines, but they are merely three quatrains, each with its own rhymes, and one couplet at the end. Elizabethan writers invented it, and used it so often that it is called the "Elizabethan sonnet." Shakespeare's sonnet on his despair shows the form and the splendour of poetry it could achieve:

> When in disgrace with fortune and men's eyes,
> I all alone beweep my outcast state,
> And trouble deaf heaven with my bootless cries,
> And look upon myself, and curse my fate,

Wishing me like to one more rich in hope,
Featur'd like him, like him with friends possess'd,
Desiring this man's art, and that man's scope,
With what I most enjoy contented least;
Yet in these thoughts myself almost despising,
Haply I think on thee,—and then my state,
Like to the lark at break of day arising
From sullen earth, sings hymns at heaven's gate;
    For thy sweet love remembered such wealth brings
    That then I scorn to change my state with kings.

The beauty and life of Elizabethan poetry could be poured out in page on page. The stories in verse which Shakespeare and Marlowe and Drayton and others wrought have passages we still read and remember. Jonson's epigrams and Chapman's translations, the many sonnets of Sidney and Drayton and Constable and Shakespeare delight thousands of readers to-day.

Yet the poetry of the time seems to us now to group itself around the poetic plays which were written between 1585 and 1620. These round out and help to explain the other verse. And they in turn can be explained and exemplified almost wholly in the work of a single writer, the greatest that has ever made words into poetry.

CHAPTER XIV

WILL SHAKESPEARE

"... What a piece of work is man! how noble in reason! how infinite in faculty! in form and moving how express and admirable! in action how like an angel! in apprehension how like a god! ..."

Hamlet, Act. II, Sc. ii.

I

It is near three o'clock on a summer's afternoon. From the roof of the theatre a flag flies, telling Londoners that a play will be played that day. The drums beat. The trumpets bellow. Inside the building the spectators wait for the parting of the curtains.

Some of them are in the balconies, where benches rise tier on tier as in theatres of to-day. Some are in the pit or yard, standing: apprentices and mechanics and grooms—all who could not pay enough to get a seat. The stage juts out among them, and on the sides of it sit young nobles and gentlemen, pulling their pipes, ogling the girls that sell oranges, playing with elegant conversation. The mob in the yard munch apples, gamble, crack nuts, hurl banter and orange peel at the gallants above.

A third blast of the trumpet. Gravely a player steps from behind the curtain screening the rear of the stage. He is the

Prologue. Clad in black velvet mantle and flowing wig decked with a laurel wreath, he comes forward on the long front portion of the stage, and bows. He promises the audience that

> We'll lead you to the stately tent of War,
> Where you shall hear the Scythian Tamburlaine
> Threat'ning the world with high astounding terms
> And scourging kingdoms with his conquering sword.

Necks are thrust forward. The gallants stop smoking. There is a fine, full-throated energy in that verse. Who is this fellow "Christopher Marlowe," advertised in the playbills? One of these new play-writers that the actor troupes have been hiring —wits from the university? Ha! Let him air what he learned of Seneca. Why shouldn't there be some stuff in London to match Euripides?

They are about to have something like that. The curtain rises. The simple stage, bare of scenery as we know it, takes them to Persia. Now they are in the palace of the weak king Mycetes. Now they see him overthrown in battle by his brother Cosroe. They see the robber-shepherd, Tamburlaine, a captain in the rebel hosts. But now that he has helped Cosroe win the crown, a mighty and audacious thought comes to him. Listen to the fellow as he talks to his men:

> TAMBURLAINE
> And ride in triumph through Persepolis!
> Is it not brave to be a king, Techelles?
> Usumcasane and Theridamas,
> Is it not passing brave to be a king,
> And ride in triumph through Persepolis?
>
> TECHELLES
> O my Lord, 'tis sweet and full of pomp.
>
> USUMCASANE
> To be a king, is half to be a god.
>
> THERIDAMAS
> A god is not so glorious as a king:
> I think the pleasure they enjoy in heaven
> Cannot compare with kingly joys in earth.

To wear a crown enchased with pearl and gold,
Whose virtues carry with it life and death,
To ask, and have; command, and be obeyed;
When looks breed love, with looks to gain the prize—
Such power attractive shines in princes' eyes.

TAMBURLAINE
Why, say, Theridamas, wilt thou *be* a king?

THERIDAMAS
Nay, though I praise it, I can live without it.

TAMBURLAINE
What says my other friends, will you be kings?

TECHELLES
Aye, if I could—with all my heart, my Lord! . . .

TAMBURLAINE
Why then, [Techelles,] shall we wish for aught
The world affords in greatest novelty,
And rest attemptless, faint and destitute?
Methinks we should not: I am strongly moved,
That if I should desire the Persian Crown,
I could attain it with a wondrous ease—

So the actors declaim the high-sounding lines. This is the new poetry the play-makers invented only a few years before. Unrhymed it is—what was later to be called "blank verse." What a ring and power it gives to this tale of the world-toppling Tamburlaine! The applause rocks the balconies. This is a play for you! This is noble shouting that goes to the head like strong drink, and makes you beat palm on palm. The whole town thirsts for more of it. And what a draft of golden words and mimic action it shall have during the next thirty years!

II

But not chiefly from the poet who created *Tamburlaine* and first made great poetry for English actors to utter. Poor Kit Marlowe! He set the tone for noble dramatic poetry in London, but he did not live to write much of it. His *Doctor Faustus* (the story of the German philosopher who sold his soul to the devil) had its splendid lines. Those two about Helen of Troy:

Was this the face that launch'd a thousand ships
And burnt the topless towers of Ilium?

His *Jew of Malta*, as we shall see, inspired another, greater play. His *Edward II* promised new life and power to dramas made from history. But, at thirty, hot-spirited Marlowe had words about a few pence with one in a tavern, and a dagger thrust dispatched him from London and life, his poetry for the most part unwritten.

Fortunately, a greater poet had already appeared to finish what Marlowe had begun. When *Edward II* was being applauded, William Shakespeare had probably written his *Comedy of Errors* and was composing a modish play called *Love's Labour's Lost*, soon to be the rage in London.

Shakespeare had been born in the little town of Stratford-on-Avon, in Warwickshire, a hundred miles northwest of London. The town lay in a country as lovely as any in England, with forests and singing streams and " pastures with their green mantles so embroidered with flowers [as a writer of the time says] that it seemed another Eden."

All the flowers have been listed and the houses and meadows and castles in the vicinity explored by Shakespeare scholars during the last hundred years, but on April 21, 22, or 23, 1564, not a single Ph.D. was prowling about the beautiful Stratford landscape. Only quiet townfolk were excited over the birth of a son on one of these days to John Shakespeare, glove maker, tanner, dealer in wool and grain.

John Shakespeare was a rising young man. He had wed the lovely Mary Arden, of a family of gentlefolk-farmers, not long before. As time went on, he was to acquire several houses in Stratford, become High Bailiff of the town (a kind of Mayor), and apply for a coat of arms. Still, his son William, as he grew, was only a boy among other traders' and farmers' sons. He attended the excellent grammar school of the town, cracked jests with his merry-natured father, laughed at the queer village drapers and butchers and idlers he was later to put into plays, swam, and roamed through the country

> With shadowy forests, and with champaigns rich'd,
> With plenteous rivers, and wide-skirted meads.

He got a fair knowledge of Latin at the grammar school, but he got a better knowledge of the earth and simple men. He saw

> . . . the morn in russet mantle clad,
> Walk o'er the dew of yon high eastern hill.

He saw the

> . . . winking Mary-buds begin
> To ope their golden eyes.

He knew and loved

> . . . daffodils
> That come before the swallow dares, and take
> The winds of March with beauty, violets dim,
> But sweeter than the lids of Juno's eyes
> Or Cytherea's breath.

He saw deer in forest glades, heard huntsmen's songs, watched hounds pursuing the hare. If the legend is true, he crept into the woods of a certain nobleman, when he was in his 'teens, and brought down a buck with his own arrow. He saw my Lord of Leicester's castle, Kenilworth. There, in Shakespeare's twelfth year, a stupendous celebration was made in honour of Queen Elizabeth's visit to the castle, and perhaps Will Shakespeare came from Stratford, only ten miles away as the crow flies. Perhaps the boy took in the pomp, the silver music, the cloaks of many colours, the Arab horses, and the Queen herself, clad in pearls and satin and gold, and entering the gates to the voices of terrible cannon.

At Kenilworth, too, he may have caught a glimpse of the players preparing to act a play for Her Majesty. Certainly, he knew the plays of the trade guilds. These were much as they had been when the priests had first encouraged the artisans to make them hundreds of years before. The trade folk came yearly, rolling on their wagons into Coventry not far away, to give their "mysteries." Shakespeare never forgot the Herod of Jewry with scarlet gauntlets and blazing crown who thundered about, knocking the nearest spectators on the head with his club. "What a Herod of Jewry is this!" he says in *The Merry Wives of Windsor*.

Then, while his father was still High Bailiff, the Queen's Own Players, the best who acted, visited Stratford, and the Earl of Worcester's Players—almost as good. London companies these were, skilled at making men laugh and stirring them to wonder or tears with stories of clowns and temptations and kings.

Will Shakespeare could have seen these, and all through the plays he made later are what seem to be echoes and memories of such spectacles. Doubtless the Bailiff's boy with wide, serious face, framed in auburn hair, watched the London actors spellbound. Doubtless, like many boys, he longed to be off to London with them, perhaps to play before the Queen.

But that was a dream. He stayed at his school, toiling from gray morn until late afternoon, reading Æsop's *Fables* in Latin, Virgil's *Eclogues*, the story-poems of Ovid, perhaps Horace and Cicero. He knew the English Bible well. It was the Geneva translation, much like the King James's, and sometimes called the "Breeches Bible," because of the breeches Adam and Eve, according to the translators, made for themselves in the Garden. As the boy grew older, he may have borrowed English books from the teacher or the vicar. There were always sermons to be had. There may have been English poetry—Chaucer or Lydgate. Perhaps there were chronicles like Froissart's, and even a romance or two.

In his early 'teens Will seems to have left school to serve in his father's shop. John Shakespeare, after some years of prosperity, was in hard straits. At eighteen, the records show us, the boy married a woman eight years older than himself. Concerning this time come the tales of his shooting the deer of Sir Thomas Lucy, and writing a mocking poem about the noble-man. Was he making songs and verses? Did he, as some think, teach school for a while? Did he devour what books he could, and remember with growing restlessness the marvellous make-believe of the players? Did he take a plot from a Latin comedy of Plautus and write around it a play of his own? Did he come from Stratford to London already a poet, having taught himself much of what the craft of writing was, because by nature he had been gifted supremely among all men for the setting to-gether of words?

III

These questions are so many guesses. Yet what we know seems to prove something. Shakespeare is first heard of in Lon-don in 1592, but in a way to suggest that he had come several years before. And in 1592 he is acting and writing with skill. We can imagine him bringing his play to an actor-manager. We can imagine a shrewd glance at the sturdy young man with a merry eye, at the verses, showing talent, if not, in the form they had then, a fitness for the stage. Here was a fellow who might act and write both. Why not put him to work?

At any rate, in 1592 he is at work. He is playing, and he is retouching old plays. Even Shakespeare did not burst on the Elizabethan theatre like a miracle. He was a 'prentice at first, trying to imitate the latest sensational success, working over other people's writing with a businesslike modesty.

What else could he do? He may have come to London know-ing much of writing, but he had to digest the wonder of the city before he could use his power. There were the mobs, eager to gaze at the bloody sport of bear-baiting, or to throng to a hanging or beheading. They were eager for sentiment, too, for preposterous romance, for the noise of cannon and the clash of armed men. The city was thronging also with gentlemen and sailors, with eloquent preachers and severe scholars, some of them talking of the mystery of life, of Ovid and Euripides, some gossiping of cities of gold and fountains of eternal youth, some discussing superstitions and sciences, holiness and damnation and gay Italian romance. There were the theatres themselves with tallow-smelling properties and tawdry tinsel and curtains and flowers. There were the plot mongers ready to furnish drama by the yard, and the poet-playwrights that young Shakespeare must measure his strength with.

All afire these were with the new excitement of words. Their imaginations were young eagles staring at the sun, hounds unleashed on their first hunt, seven-day colts exulting in their sinews. They sang in coloured jets of music, giddy with trickery of words and exuberance of life and the fertility of great imaginations.

If poetry were in a man, such a town would light it. But the first thing was to get success. Plays were needed that were in the mode. The town was wild, for instance, over "tragedies of blood" like Thomas Kyd's *The Spanish Tragedy*. Revenges and murders on the stage packed the theatres as certain trials pack our courtrooms to-day. We can imagine the manager of Shakespeare's company saying to the new actor-writer from Stratford:

"Killing and howling, lad—these be the fashion. We must have noise and fury or starve else. Here—what can you make of this? 'Tis a nightmare of a play that George Peele mounted but could not master. I think the jade threw him. Bridle her and run a course if ye can."

And Shakespeare took the terrible *Titus Andronicus* and shaped it to draw a crowd.

Scholars agree, too, that he worked on three plays about Henry VI which appeared in the early 1590's. These, too, were in a fashion of the hour, historical drama. One of them had probably been started by Marlowe before he left off writing for Shakespeare's company (some months before Shakespeare joined it). The history of England had been a good source for plays from 1583 on, and now a new enjoyment of it was setting in. The three plays on Henry VI and the Wars of the Roses which Shakespeare now fashioned were to gain immediate popularity.

Yet even in this work of patching and sewing together, the poet was no ordinary apprentice. He learned from Kyd and Marlowe, but it was more what to do than how to do it. Marlowe must have shown him not a little about the music of poetry, but Shakespeare had that music in him. What Marlowe did mostly was to show him that there was room for great imagination on the stage. In a similar way, John Lyly, in his comedies, had made drama of elegant phrasing and witty songs and comic characters. And the ability to do that was in Shakespeare also. The first play he did entirely by himself shows how easily he took up Marlowe's trick of playing with golden verse and Lyly's of toying with elegance and wit. The opening of *Love's Labour's Lost* is touched with rhetorical music as proud as Marlowe's:

> Let fame, that all hunt after in their lives,
> Live register'd upon our brazen tombs.

But in a few lines elegant puns and similes and light love sonnets are tumbling over themselves, graceful and easy and very different from the "high astounding terms" of *Tamburlaine*. And there are two songs, one of spring

> When daisies pied and violets blue
> And lady-smocks all silver-white
> And cuckoo-buds of yellow hue
> Do paint the meadows with delight,

and the other of the colder, darker months

> When icicles hang by the wall,
> And Dick the shepherd blows his nail,
> And Tom bears logs into the hall,
> And milk comes frozen home in pail.

These and much else in this comedy are still delightful. The plot, telling of a king and his three nobles who swore to live for three years with their books and shun ladies the while (which of course they did not do), is no stronger than a kitten. It was the first and last plot made mostly by Shakespeare himself. But the play has human zest and poetic ability so easy and spontaneous that few who enjoyed its wit and liveliness saw how promising of greatness it was.

IV

Early in 1593, soon after *Love's Labour's Lost* is supposed to have been produced before Queen Elizabeth, the plague was raging in London. The theatres were closed by law. There was no play-acting by the Thames for two years.

Some of the players fled into the provinces to seek a miserable living there until the disease should wear itself out. But Shakespeare stayed in London. What he was doing soon became apparent. On April 18, 1593, he entered in the Stationers' Register a long narrative poem entitled *Venus and Adonis*.

This was Shakespeare's attempt to live by writing "pure literature." Plays, in the opinion of the Elizabethans, were not fully literary. Making them was a trade, and the poet was paid more as a newspaper writer is to-day—by the proceeds from the business he helped to create. A poet, on the other hand, could make little from anything he could *sell*. He was supposed to be supported by a patron. And to be so supported was Shakespeare's hope. He dedicated *Venus and Adonis* to the young Earl of Southampton, looking for approval and money to follow if the Earl was pleased.

Shakespeare's judgment was good. Southampton was fond of love poetry. Well, Shakespeare had taken the Goddess of Love herself for his heroine. Following the old legend, he told how she saw the beautiful youth Adonis going to the hunt:

Hunting he lov'd, but love he laughed to scorn,

and at once began to woo him. But Southampton also relished, like many men of the day, a rich ornamental style. Well, the poem is the very pattern of it. The stanzas are lily-sweet with the persuasive words of Venus. They are decorated like a fabulous tapestry with the beauty of meadows, groves, lithe horses, huntsmen and horns and hounds. Nothing is too slight or too exciting for elegance. When Adonis speaks, we hear that

> Once more the ruby-coloured portal open'd
> Which to his speech did honey passage yield.

When dawn comes, it marches in with a noble burst of fancy:

> Lo! here the gentle lark, weary of rest,
> From his moist cabinet mounts up on high,
> And wakes the morning, from whose silver breast
> The sun ariseth in his majesty.

And when unhappy Adonis lies dead, slain by the tusk of the wild boar, his white body

> With purple tears, that his wound wept, was drench'd;
> No flower was nigh, no grass, herb, leaf or weed,
> But stole his blood and seem'd with him to bleed.

Such poetry pleased Southampton, and he showed his pleasure generously. Shakespeare speaks, in dedicating his second poem to the Earl, of "the warrant I have of your honourable disposition." Under Southampton's patronage he wrote for the two years the theatres were closed, and *Venus and Adonis* and *The Rape of Lucrece* were hailed by men of letters as "mellifluous" and "honey-tongued."

At this time, Shakespeare must also have begun to write his sonnets. In 1591 Sir Philip Sidney had taken London by storm with a sonnet sequence of more than one hundred poems, all on the story of his love for the lovely "Stella," who in real life was Penelope Devereux. The poets at once gathered to the making of sonnets like a drove of bees after honey in a newly discovered garden. There were sonnets to "Delia" and "Diana" and "Parthenope" and "Phillis" and "Celia," and Spenser's *Amoretti* was a part of this frenzy. Shakespeare composed a sonnet sequence, perhaps two. We have 144 of his sonnets. There are sonnets about a friend, not a woman, but a beautiful young man whom the poet loves. There are sonnets also to a dark, dark lady, who, in the sonnets at least, fascinated the poet and then abandoned him for the beautiful young man.

These sonnets are like most Elizabethan sonnets in form— three quatrains and a couplet—but they surpass all sonnets in their range of emotion and poetical skill. At times they are sweet and simple with tender admiration:

> How sweet and lovely dost thou make the shame,
> Which, like a canker in the fragrant rose,
> Doth spot the beauty of thy budding name!
> O! in what sweets dost thou thy sins enclose.
> That tongue that tells the story of thy days,
> Making lascivious comments on thy sport,
> Cannot dispraise but in a kind of praise;
> Naming thy name blesses an ill report!

Again there is a fine boldness of imagination:

> Devouring Time, blunt thou the lion's paws,
> And make the earth devour her own sweet brood;
> Pluck the keen teeth from the fierce tiger's jaws,
> And burn the long-liv'd phœnix in her blood. . . .
> But I forbid thee one most heinous crime:
> O! carve not with thy hours my love's fair brow.

Again, there is desperation:

> Then hate me when thou wilt; if ever, now;
> Now, when the world is bent my deeds to cross,
> Join with the spite of fortune, make me bow,
> And do not drop in for an after-loss.

There is gentle sadness. There are grave words on world-weariness and age, as in the sonnet beginning

> Tir'd with all these, for restful death I cry,

or that other, perhaps the greatest of them all:

> That time of year thou may'st in me behold
> When yellow leaves, or none, or few, do hang
> Upon those boughs which shake against the cold,
> Bare ruin'd choirs, where late the sweet birds sang.

All lovers turn to these sonnets for delight and sympathy, and words from them have made the titles of dozens of books. They were not printed until 1608, because the people about whom any sonnets were written in the 1590's were supposedly real. It would not be decent to expose them to public gaze! However, Shakespeare's sonnets were passed about among his friends, for we have mention of them.

Whether the lovely young man was real, whether the dark lady was more than a dream on paper, nobody has proved. Scholars have tried often enough to tag both of them, but they are still mysteries.

We can say only thus much: there was deep reality in the poems where these people live. The poet who made the boy and the lady immortal with his writing knew love and pride and shame, bitterness and sorrow and quiet resignation. Perhaps, during his early thirties, Shakespeare lived his own tragedy. Perhaps he drew from this the knowledge of the human pain he was to sing about later. Certainly, in the sonnets, he shows this knowledge, and with it the poetic power which he was to turn now into the theatre once more.

v

For, late in 1594, he was again an actor and playwright. Perhaps he found it uncertain, depending on my Lord of Southampton for bread. Perhaps the players, anxious to have plays from him, made offers too good for him to refuse. We know he was now paid a full salary as actor in the new Lord Chamberlain's company, was part owner in a theatre, and was rewarded also as a playwright. Actors of that day did well when busy, and this threefold income was much more than any patron would offer.

Shakespeare's years of "pure poetry" had doubtless been years of reading also. His easy use of words and ideas and history indicate that he must have devoured books at all times, but when free from acting and play-making he must have found more time than ever before for a kind of debauch in poetry and romance and history. He returned to the theatre with a new fund of stories and ideas. His first plays he had patched up from old dramas of others, his *Love's Labour's Lost* had been much his own invention. *The Comedy of Errors* was an echo from his schoolbook reading. But with 1594 he begins to tap richer treasuries. The plot of his first new play, *The Two Gentlemen of Verona*, came from a Spanish romance, *Diana*, which Shakespeare apparently read in a French translation. He made the acquaintance of North's English version of Plutarch's *Lives*—biographies of the great Greeks and Romans. One of the best of his new plays came from an Italian story, and this had not been translated. These facts are interesting because they suggest that Shakespeare knew French, and possibly Italian, as well as Latin and—as Ben Jonson put it later—"less Greek." Despite his lack of a university education, he had apparently taught himself well, drawing widely and wisely upon the things he needed in the making of plays and verse.

Of the poetic dramas which Shakespeare wrote in the next five years (1594–1599) many form a group dealing with English history. Englishmen were interested in England. After all the disturbances since the Normans had conquered her—French Wars, Scotch Wars, civil wars—the land was one at last. The great Spanish Armada had been scattered in 1588 by English storms and English seamen. English pride walked the land like a lion. There was a great Queen and a great English spirit and a great relish for hearing about England.

As we have seen, Shakespeare had been successful with his plays about the Wars of the Roses (*Henry VI*, Parts I, II, and

III), and he now took up the story of England again where he had left off. *Richard III* made London playgoers dizzy with excitement. Young Burbage, the actor, became known all over the land for the line Richard cried on the battlefield when he was fighting ferociously and vainly for his life:

> A horse! A horse! My kingdom for a horse.

Then came *Richard II* and *King John*, *Henry IV*, Part I; and *Henry IV*, Part II. Finally, *Henry V* completed a series that told the story of England for the greater part of a hundred and twenty-five years. From King John to Henry VII was actually almost two hundred and seventy-five years, but the plays did not cover the entire period. However, no poet ever sang a story in drama like this. It was an epic, yet more living and actual than an epic.

In these poetic historical tragedies the great Shakespeare emerges. Marlowe in *Edward II* had shown that, by taking a chief character and weaving the events of history around it, something more than a chronicle could be made of "chronicle plays." Shakespeare carried forward what Marlowe had begun. He made character and history and poetry blend into one unified story.

> Oh, how the audience
> Were ravish'd! With what wonder they went thence!

cries a writer of the time with reference to the later *Julius Cæsar*, a play also taken from history. The groundlings and gallants were quite as excited over *Richard II* and *Richard III*. This latter tragedy, with its fascinating and malignant hero, ran as a Broadway success only a few years ago. Something inside us stirs greatly still to its poetry and that of its companion plays.

We find in them the grand style Marlowe had set, bass-voiced music that we can boom with as much joy as Burbage:

Now is the winter of our discontent
Made glorious summer by this sun of York;
Now all the clouds that lour'd upon our house
In the deep bosom of the ocean buried.

The ecstatic praise of England, put in the mouth of old John of Gaunt, is as fresh to-day as ever:

This other Eden, demi-paradise,
This fortress built by Nature for herself
Against infection and the hand of war,
This happy breed of men, this little world,
This precious stone set in a silver sea
. . . This blessed plot, this earth, this realm, this England!

This is pride in country, the patriotic love of the peace and beauty of a land. There is poetry also of fierce war patriotism, voiced most marvellously as Henry V voices it on the battlefield in his famous speech:

Once more unto the breach, dear friends, once more;
Or close the wall up with our English dead!

Such lines set English audiences afire in the 1590's, and they wake fire in our hearts now.

Yet if we wish to get a full view of the poet who was uttering such verse, we should turn also to other plays that came from his pen during the same period. In *A Midsummer Night's Dream* and *Romeo and Juliet* his genius shone with a jewel-like variety of light that the steel-clashing atmosphere of his historical war plays did not permit.

We have seen that he could write in his plays poetry that rang mightily like Marlowe's or burst forth with a freshness like Chaucer's and a gay energy Chaucer never quite had. This was a wholly new thing. There had been humorous poets and serious poets, but no great poet had been able to turn from solemn beauty or dark horror to sunny, rollicking mirth. Shakespeare had done this, though in plays like *Henry VI* and *Love's Labour's Lost* he had done neither tragedy nor comedy supremely well. Now he did both supremely well.

Of course, in accomplishing this, he had done much more than write marvellous poetry. He had grown in the understanding and expressing of the men and women he put into his plays, and he had grown in the art of play-making. The two ran together. So in *A Midsummer Night's Dream* he took a fanciful jumble of characters and a crazy-quilt of a plot and made a comedy of it that somehow held together and blended into one story all beauty and laughter. And in *Romeo and Juliet* he took two lovers whose families were bitter enemies, and sang the rapture of a youthful love that shone with lyric brightness against the darkness and death that it led to. Both plays range from fun through laughter and passion and exquisite beauty, and *Romeo and Juliet* carries us on to fear and tragic courage and high sorrow. The poetry has the same range. One minute we are listening to the happy description of Queen Mab going in her tiny carriage

> Athwart men's noses as they lie asleep:

A little later we see Romeo, hidden in the garden of his enemy Capulet's house, gazing on Juliet as she stands in the balcony, and murmuring:

>   thou art
> As glorious to this night, being o'er my head,
> As is a wingèd messenger of heaven
> Unto the white upturnèd wond'ring eyes
> Of mortals.

And still later we see him again as he stands beside the sleeping Juliet and thinks her dead and speaks the very ecstasy of grief:

>   O my love! my wife!
> Death, that hath suck'd the honey of thy breath,
> Hath had no power yet upon thy beauty:
> Thou art not conquer'd; beauty's ensign yet
> Is crimson in thy lips and in thy cheeks. . . .
> Why art thou yet so fair? Shall I believe
> That unsubstantial Death is amorous,
> And that the lean abhorrèd monster keeps
> Thee here in dark to be thy paramour?
> For fear of that I still will stay with thee,

And never from this palace of dim night
Depart again: here, here will I remain
With worms that are thy chambermaids; O! here
Will I set up my everlasting rest,
And shake the yoke of inauspicious stars
From this world-wearied flesh.

In *A Midsummer Night's Dream* there is poetry of a still different kind. Less of humanity and more of pure beauty it is,
whether it talks of ladies

Chanting faint hymns to the cold fruitless moon,

or tells how

The course of true love never did run smooth,

or sports with the fairies

By pavèd fountain, or by rushy brook
Or in the beachèd margent of the sea.

In such drama Shakespeare reached a rich expression, though
not his highest expression, of the marvellous variety of poetry
which no other poet achieved. It was always true poetry because
it was true to the shifting human emotions he already understood so widely. But it was also true because of its music. In
this verse of his early thirties we see a poet intoxicated with the
magic of words. Already the largest and most amazing vocabu-
lary ever used by any man is set out before us. And they are
words used artfully by one who was responsive to their sound
as well as their sense. Pontifical words they can be, or steel-
edged, or rumbling, or fantastic. They can fling classical names
about with a gorgeous abandon, even in the midst of common
talk. Says the strutting rogue, Captain Pistol:

Shall pack-horses,
And hollow pamper'd jades of Asia,
Which cannot go but thirty miles a day,
Compare with Cæsars, and with Cannibals
And Trojan Greeks?

Yet it is doubtful how much the Elizabethans realized the greatness of these plays as poetry. Though with those mentioned had come *The Merchant of Venice* with its great character of Shylock (drawn after Barabas in Marlowe's *Jew of Malta*), and *Julius Cæsar*, full of fine poetic oratory, the idea of play poetry as great poetry was still new. It was not yet accepted that dramatic verse might excel verse like Chaucer's *Canterbury Tales* or Spenser's *Faery Queen*. For one thing, the players guarded the manuscripts, and the tragedies and comedies appeared in print only when someone succeeded in stealing them, or when their popularity was pretty well over. Then, the very poetic miracles Shakespeare was performing were also brought about in a way to obscure themselves. His men and women were too real. The gallant Mercutio charmed the audience and they thought of him and not of his lines. Poetry made the malignant Richard Crookback real, and the poetry he uttered was less important than the man. This was true only in part; there was admiration for Shakespeare's verse, and it grew steadily. But in 1599 his own world was too close to him and liked him too well to see how big he was.

VI

It is doubtful if Shakespeare himself knew his full size as a poet. Probably he guessed he was bigger than his fellows thought: he had too deep an understanding of men not to understand much of himself. But he, like his audiences, got other things than poetic satisfaction from his plays.

He was pleasantly aware that they went famously as plays, and, after all, they were written to be acted and make money. He was aware that they gave him the honour of being the greatest playwright in London. As an actor and a writer and a theatre owner he got enough income to buy and remake a big house at Stratford, and to purchase other properties. He had been let into the society of gentlemen and nobles, he drank canary with poets. There were great times at the Mermaid, as the poet-playwright, Francis Beaumont, wrote later:

> What things have we seen
> Done at the Mermaid! heard words that have been
> So nimble, and so full of subtile flame,
> As if that every one from whence they came
> Had meant to put his whole wit in a jest,
> And had resolved to live a fool the rest
> Of his dull life.

Then in 1598 Shakespeare had secured in his father's name a coat of arms, and could now write "Gent." after his name.

These were rewards that might make him care the less as to whether poetic plays could be as good poetry as poems. At any rate, the plays had served him well in a number of ways.

In 1599, Shakespeare's company opened their new theatre, the Globe. It was an event for the actors. It was also the beginning of a new period for Shakespeare. He was fully grown now. In the three comedies that were his next plays, there is all his early wit and buoyancy, and there is an ease of style and a sureness of play structure that he had not attained in most of the comedies and tragedies of the 1590's. And from these he went on to the writing of his greatest tragedies—*Hamlet*, *Lear*, *Othello*, and *Macbeth*, and a fifth tragedy, *Antony and Cleopatra*, which some think quite their equal.

These plays are, on the whole, Shakespeare's greatest. It is true that the poetry of a comedy like *A Midsummer Night's Dream* is finer in passages than anything in *Twelfth Night* or *As You Like It*. On the other hand, the latter plays are shaped more skilfully. And the great tragedies of the early 1600's are more powerful than anything Shakespeare had done before.

Indeed, it is when we throw them into any argument about the quality of Shakespeare that we find there is nothing to be said against crowning him as supreme among poets.

For *Macbeth* and *Hamlet* and *Lear* show a new quality in

Shakespeare, rounding him out and completing him as no other poet has been completed. In his earlier tragedy Shakespeare had set forth all the agony of beauty dying, as in *Romeo and Juliet;* all the grave awe of brave spirits passing, as in *Julius Cæsar;* all the grim inevitability of a villain going at last to his just end, as in *Richard III.* But he had never touched with Sophocles and Æschylus the terrible or horrible depths and heights of pain. Now he did so. In *Macbeth* we see a great captain, kinsman to the King of Scotland. On a blasted heath three witches stay him to tell him: "Thou shalt be king hereafter." Immediately he thinks: "For me to be king, my cousin Duncan must die." And we see how this suggestion

> Whose horrid image doth unfix my hair
> And make my seated heart knock at my ribs,

goads him on to evil. King Duncan comes to Macbeth's castle. Macbeth and his wife plot to slay him, though, as Macbeth himself says,

> This Duncan
> Hath borne his faculties so meek, hath been
> So clear in his great office, that his virtues
> Will plead like angels trumpet-tongu'd against
> The deep damnation of his taking-off.

But the deed is done, and the soul of Macbeth, once a brave and honourable soul, is pledged to blood. He is horrified at what he has done. He cries:

> Will all great Neptune's ocean wash this blood
> Clean from my hand? No, this my hand will rather
> The multitudinous seas incarnadine,
> Making the green one red.

But there is no taking back his deed. He seizes the throne, and to protect himself he goes on killing those he fears are his enemies.

> I am in blood
> Stepp'd in so far, that, should I wade no more,
> Returning were as tedious as go o'er!

So he pushes on in his desperate course, till at last he is feared and hated throughout the land, and Duncan's son dares to invade Scotland. He hems Macbeth in his castle, Lady Macbeth dies half mad with the murders that trouble her soul. The tyrant himself goes out to die in battle, muttering about life:

> Out, out, brief candle!
> Life's but a walking shadow, a poor player
> That struts and frets his hour upon the stage,
> And then is heard no more; it is a tale
> Told by an idiot, full of sound and fury
> Signifying nothing.

The story of King Lear, of an aged father brought to madness and death by the ingratitude of his daughters, drives like *Macbeth* along the wind-swept heights of tragedy.

In *Hamlet*, a drama of revenge and indecision, many find Shakespeare's greatest tragic poetry. Hamlet's father has died suddenly. His brother Claudius has become king. He has married Hamlet's own mother with a suspicious swiftness. This is before the play opens. Then on the castle battlements we see with Hamlet how the grave

> Hath op'd his ponderous and marble jaws

to let the ghost of the murdered king appear to his son, bidding him

> Revenge his foul and most unnatural murder.

How Hamlet promises, how he becomes unsure later if it was a demon who talked with him or a genuine ghost, how he tests his uncle, how he feigns madness, dreams of seeking by suicide

> The undiscover'd country from whose bourn
> No traveller returns

is a fascinating story of a man's struggle with his own mind. In the course of it, Hamlet accidentally kills the father of his love, Ophelia, and we forget all else in pity for her madness and the death she meets by drowning where

A willow grows aslant a brook
That shows his hoar leaves in the glassy stream.

And there is greater pity for Hamlet himself, winning his revenge at last, but perishing of a poisoned rapier.

Such tragedy is as high as any in mood, and perhaps surpasses all other tragedy in poetry. Yet, in measuring Shakespeare as a poet, we must remember that he not only wrote *Macbeth* and *Hamlet*, but wrote also of Romeo, of Oberon, of bragging Falstaff, and of absurd Malvolio. No other poet is great in tragedy and great in comedy also.

And we must remember, too, that the poet's office is one of understanding. Of all poets Shakespeare understands most fully. He understands so well, for instance, that he never takes sides with his characters. His greatest villain, Iago, does a hideous thing, yet Iago is set before us not as worse than he is, but as exactly what he is. We are horrified by what he does, but we see why he did it. The same truth goes into Shakespeare's laughter. Just as in tragic understanding he excels Sophocles and Æschylus, so in comic understanding he excels Aristophanes and Molière and his own friend Ben Jonson, the greatest of English comedy writers down to Bernard Shaw. Yet though he does not take sides, he tells us fully of the life he describes. So our notions of nonsense and folly, of jealousy and romance, of evil ambitions and the ingratitude of children are seen through the wisdom we find in Shakespeare's poetry. And because of this he is not only a great poet in comedy and in tragedy; he is supreme in both.

VII

All the while he was writing these plays and several others of lesser note, Shakespeare was a man living among men in London and Stratford.

He was more prosperous than ever. Queen Elizabeth had died, and her cousin James of Scotland had come to rule on the Thames. King James was fond of plays. He took the Chamberlain's men, as Shakespeare's company was called, under his own protection, renaming them the King's Men. He made Shakespeare and others grooms of the Royal Chamber. He gave them special grants of cloth and money. It is estimated from very reliable sources that Shakespeare was receiving from his acting, his writing, the properties he owned, and the special performances he helped to give, a yearly sum of almost £400. In purchasing value of our money, this was a large income. One scholar estimates that Shakespeare during his most prosperous period received what would correspond to $30,000 a year to-day. At any rate, Shakespeare had the comforts and luxuries of life which men with such an income have to-day. He visited Stratford increasingly, often staying at the house of Mrs. Hall, his witty daughter Susanna.

It may be because he had become so prosperous that he retired permanently from London and play-making about 1612. It may be that his health was poor. At any rate, his last complete play was finished in 1611, and the little work he did after this was in helping younger playwrights with plays for the King's Men.

We hear of *Henry VIII* being billed at the Globe in June, 1613, as the work of "Mr. John Fletcher and Mr. William Shakespeare, Gent." But at the first performance a cannon fired in the first act set the theatre afire, "consuming within less than an hour the whole house to the ground." It was as if Fate had set a final piece of fireworks for the poet. After this, we know of nothing that he helped to write or wrote himself.

The Vicar of Stratford tells of how Ben Jonson and Michael Drayton passed through Stratford, and "had a merry meeting" with Shakespeare, "and, it seems, drank too hard, for Shakespeare died of a fever there contracted." This may be legend instead of truth; it is the only report we have of his dying. He was buried the twenty-fifth of April, making it possible that he passed away on the same day of the year that he was born. But we know exactly neither the date of his birth nor that of his death.

He died prosperous and loved and honoured. How greatly his friends among the actors and poets esteemed him is shown in the complete edition of his works published by two of his fellow players, Heminges and Condell, in 1623. This Folio Edition is a careful effort to put into a book all of Shakespeare's work in its best form. In the volume, too, is a portrait. A bad one, some contend, but Ben Jonson says in a little verse:

> This figure that thou here see'st put
> It was for gentle Shakespeare cut;
> Wherein the graver had a strife
> With nature to outdo the life.

So we may conclude that the gentleman with high forehead growing bald; large, quiet eyes, and broad face with small moustache and the ghost of a Van Dyke beard was not unlike the actor and theatre owner, the solid citizen of Stratford, the maker of Falstaff and Hamlet.

Ben Jonson wrote more than these lines about Shakespeare's picture. He wrote an immortal poem in addition about "My Beloved, the Author, Mr. William Shakespeare, and What He Hath Left Us."

Ben, as we have said elsewhere, was a scholar, and the unscholarly ways of Shakespeare were not always to his liking. He tells in his prose writings how some friends of the Globe playwright boasted that Shakespeare "had never blotted a line." Jonson says, "I would he had blotted a thousand!" What, then, did he think of Shakespeare as a whole? Was the Stratford poet merely a gifted fellow with too little education and too much laziness—a jewel needing polish? His commemorative poem tells another story:

> Soul of the age!
> The applause! delight! the wonder of our stage!
> My Shakespeare, rise! I will not lodge thee by
> Chaucer, or Spenser, or bid Beaumont lie
> A little further to make thee a room:
> Thou art a monument without a tomb,

And art alive still while thy book doth live,
And we have wits to read, and praise to give. . .
And though thou hadst small Latin and less Greek,
From thence to honour thee I would not seek
For names, but call forth thund'ring Æschylus,
Euripides, and Sophocles to us,
Paccuvius, Accius, him of Cordova dead,
To life again to hear thy buskin tread
And shake a stage: or, when thy socks were on,
Leave thee alone for the comparison
Of all that insolent Greece or haughty Rome
Sent forth, or since did from their ashes come.

Here was the first estimate of Shakespeare by one able to estimate him well. It has been said that Jonson was merely giving a customary praise to one dead, exaggerating greatly his own actual opinion. This is improbable. Careful reading shows that his remarks are precise, not vague. The very words "applause," "delight," "wonder" are accurate. Spenser, the greatest of English poets, is set below Shakespeare, even "out of his class," and Jonson's own beloved classic poets are no more than equals. Jonson meant what he said.

Of course, the world agrees with him now. The Eighteenth Century patronized Shakespeare, though it conceded him a very high place. With the Nineteenth Century came that idolatry which lovers of poetry feel now to be just. Shakespeare conquered England anew; he strode into Germany and is to-day known and loved there quite as well as in Great Britain or America; he forced a reluctant acknowledgment of his supreme genius from France. To-day there is no sign that his fame will lessen. His marvellous phrases are part of everyday English speech, his plays help us to know and judge life, his men and women dwell with us as people of our own time. The poet Browning puts him down as the great *human* creator—less than divine, yet close to divine in his ability to build with golden words that world of his own in which shines the supreme humour of Malvolio and Falstaff, the matchless tragic poetry of Lear, Hamlet, and Macbeth.

CHAPTER XV

MILTON AND HIS ANGELS

I

In the year 1608 in London and on Bread Street, John Milton, the Poet of Paradise, was born. In the same year, and in the same London, Shakespeare, the Poet of the World, was publishing *Antony and Cleopatra*, a play about people who would never have been let into paradise if Milton had had anything to say about it.

It is strange that Shakespeare, born in a village remote from the world's hubbub, should have put so much of the stir of human courage, weakness, laughter, and passion into what he wrote, and that Milton, born on Bread Street in the city's din, should sing little of the bread-getting world, but of devils and angels instead, of unworldly meditations and ecstasies. But often the sons of ministers want to be actors, and farm boys dream of the black smoke of ferry boats. And Milton, London born and reared, was from the first reaching for intangible things alien to the hurry and grime of the town about him.

His home life encouraged him to do this. John Milton the elder was a prosperous scrivener—a kind of real-estate lawyer

—but though he was successful at making money, his soul was not in it. Independent and severe at times (he was disowned by his father because he forsook the Roman Catholic faith to become a Protestant), he had a deep interest in books and music. He put young John into the excellent St. Paul's School, and in addition hired a special tutor for him. He himself composed music, and he taught the boy to play on the organ and to love its majestic harmonies. The scrivener wrote poetry also. A little of his verse still survives to suggest where his son may first have got a notion of rhyme and metre.

At St. Paul's School Milton took to learning as most boys do to spinning tops. We hear of him even at the age of twelve studying through midnight into the early morning, to the injury of his eyes. He drank in also his father's spirit of independence, and perhaps his Presbyterian tutor, Edward Young, fed in him a kind of fierce passion for freedom as well as for knowledge. When he went to Christ's College, Cambridge, at the age of seventeen, he had a slight body and a delicately chiselled face framed in soft hair falling about his shoulders. "The lady of Christ's," some are said to have called him. Yet in the apparently fragile boy were steel and fire. He quarrelled with his tutor and was punished for "indocility" and—to judge by what he wrote later—already had ideas of his own on education. He was fond of active physical exercise also. Until his eyes began to fail him, he was an excellent fencer. In later years, in a tract denouncing English schools, he advocated walking, horseback riding, wrestling, fencing, and military manœuvres as a part of the regular work in an ideal institution!

Milton resided at Cambridge for seven years, still studying, to the injury of his weak eyes, making Latin poetry, writing verse in English. Then, after taking his A. M. degree, he retired to his father's country residence at Horton, less than twenty miles from London.

Here he was to stay for more than five years. John Milton the elder had given up his business and was living in this quiet, lovely place within sight of Windsor Castle. He was disappointed that his son had not gone into the Church. Young Milton himself had hoped to do so, but gradually he had come to resent what he thought were the show and oppressive forms to which an Anglican minister must submit. "He who would take orders must write himself a slave," he declared. It was probably the same resentment of formalism and thirst for greater freedom which the older Milton had felt when he left the Roman faith. At any rate, the father did not blame his son for giving up the Church. And he seems to have been satisfied with the decision Milton now made to devote himself to the writing of poetry.

I I

It was a natural decision. At fifteen, Milton had put a number of psalms into English verse. From his intense study of the classics he had caught a love for the rolling music of Virgil, the severe beauty of Greek. This showed in the Latin poetry he wrote, and it took shape in the remarkable hymn, *On the Morning of Christ's Nativity*, written when he was twenty-one. The firm deep tones of this poem, its colour, as of a beautiful church window, its leaping imagination, showed Milton's genius. The language gave a promise of a definiteness and beauty closer to classical poetry than anything written in English. The description of the heavenly music at the birth of Jesus gives this remarkable quality of life and graven beauty blended in one:

> For if such holy song
> Enwrap our fancy long,
>   Time will run back, and fetch the age of gold,
> And speckl'd Vanity
> Will sicken soon and die,
>   And leprous Sin will melt from earthly mould,
> And Hell itself will pass away,
> And leave her dolorous mansions to the peering day.

Such verses had undoubtedly brought praise to Milton from the few who read them. The poem may have been printed privately; some of his Latin poems were printed in 1628, and an *Epitaph on the Marchioness of Winchester*, showing a skill in more courtly verse. And in 1632, when the second Folio edition of Shakespeare's plays appeared, an unsigned poem of sixteen lines was included in memory of the great dramatist:

> What needs my Shakespeare for his honour'd bones,
> The labour of an age in pilèd stones,
> Or that his hallow'd relics should be hid
> Under a star-ypointing Pyramid?
> Dear son of memory, great heir of fame,
> What need'st thou such weak witness of thy name?
> Thou in our wonder and astonishment
> Hast built thyself a live-long monument.

So, for eight lines more, ran one of the most splendid tributes to Shakespeare, written in 1630 by Milton. The poem proved that, although he had shown an unusual ability to put spiritual feeling into verse, he was human enough to be a lover of life and the theatre as well as a lover of God.

During his years in the country, Milton, though he had finally decided to write poetry, seems to have done more reading than writing. He pondered on Homer and Euripides, on Horace, Ovid, Dante, Petrarch. He studied Shakespeare and Jonson and Spenser. He walked much, listening to the farmer whistle at the plough, hearing the milkmaid sing, seeing

> Meadows trim, with daisies pied,
> Shallow brooks and rivers wide;

wandering in woods of pine and oak, where he could

> Hide me from day's garish eye,
> While the bee with honied thigh
> That at her flowery work doth sing,
> And the waters murmuring
> . . . Entice the dewy-feather'd sleep.

Also he was asking himself now what a poet should be, and gradually shaping an answer to his own question. The Puritans and their idea of life greatly influenced him. Originally getting their name because they were people who wanted to "purify" the Church of England of its show and "Popery," this religious group had come to take a similar attitude toward the rest of life. They were shocked at the extravagance of the court, the wickedness of the theatres, the drinking and roistering of young men. They were for purifying these things as well as the Church. They wanted to purify the government, too, by getting more liberty and power for the people, and they were to be the backbone of the Parliamentary party when Parliament struggled with the foolish and unhappy Charles I.

Milton was puritanical himself in his love for simplicity and independence and reverence, but he was also a poet. He saw the charm and beauty of much that the Puritans detested. He had lived at college with gentlemen. He had enjoyed Shakespeare's plays. He loved good wine in moderation. He loved music. He enjoyed seeing the grace of dancing, he liked beautiful garments, and rich church windows, and the laughter of wits and lovely women. He was pondering now on whether a man must choose between the sober or Puritan life and the gayer life of the court gentlemen, or cavaliers—and—if the choice must be made— what it would be.

Two poems which he wrote in 1635 show his doubt; *L'Allegro* (Italian for "The gay or cheerful man") and *Il Penseroso* (Milton's incorrect spelling for "the sober-minded man") set forth different moods. There is the jocund daytime mood of *L'Allegro*, ushered in with the lark's silver-throated salute, full of shepherds' dancing, stories, feasting, good company, and plays in the city at the day's end. And there is the twilight mood of *Il Penseroso*, a mood of books, trim gardens, nightingales—of meditations in

> The studious cloister's pale,
> . . . .
> With antique pillars massy proof,
> And storied windows richly dight,
> Casting a dim religious light.

Of the two moods, Milton wrote better and apparently with more feeling of the sober one. Yet he could not let the other go. Soon after writing *L'Allegro* and *Il Penseroso* he composed a lyrical drama or "mask." And in *Comus*, the title of this pageant of song and dance and simple story, he sang again of sober virtue, and again showed that gayety and beauty appealed to him. His out-of-doors drama (produced in the gardens of the Earl of Bridgewater) told of a beautiful young lady who strays from her brothers in an enchanted forest. An evil spirit in human shape tries to carry her off but cannot because of her purity. The lady struggles through the dark woods in fear and danger, but her goodness protects her from "Malice" and "Sorcery" and "Mischief." And at the end, when she has found her brothers again, the Heavenly Spirit who has helped her cries:

> Mortals, that would follow me,
> Love virtue; she alone is free:
> She can teach ye how to climb
> Higher than the sphery chime;
> Or, if virtue feeble were,
> Heaven itself would stoop to her.

So purity prevails. But music and dancing and the moon prevail also. That is why, in spite of its preachiness, *Comus* is sometimes a happy pagan affair:

> Meanwhile, welcome joy and feas⁺
> Midnight shout and revelry,
> Tipsy dance, and jollity.
> Braid your locks with rosy twine,
> Dropping odours, dropping wine.
> Rigour now is gone to bed;
> And Advice with scrupulous head,
> Strict Age, and sour Severity,
> With their grave saws in slumber lie.

In *Lycidas*, his next poem, there is none of this mellow dancing poetry. Mourning the death of his college friend, Edward

King, Milton is grave and sad. It is true that the best part of the poem is the magnificent opening, rolling in stately reminiscence of classical poetry, showing a power and beauty that would have told men, had they listened, that another great poet had come:

> Yet once more, O ye laurels, and once more
> Ye myrtles brown, with ivy never sere,
> I come to pluck your berries harsh and crude,
> And with forc'd fingers rude,
> Shatter your leaves before the mellowing year.

But if this is un-Puritanical, the poem grows very severe and moral before its end. For Milton turns from lamenting his friend to denouncing the lazy and corrupt ministers of the day. Though he had not reconciled Puritanism and beauty, Milton showed in this poem a decisive sympathy with the purifiers.

This—the writing of *Lycidas*—was in 1637, and the great Civil War was only a few years away. Parliament had been quarrelling with the King, becoming more and more angry with him because he wanted to rule by himself. The King and his followers, in their turn, were equally excited and indignant. With Parliament stood the simpler, more sober Englishmen, and of these the reforming Puritans were most eager. With the King were the gay nobles, the rich churchmen, the devil-may-care soldiers. The sober-minded man and the gay-hearted man— the two whom Milton had sung in his poems—stood ready to struggle for power.

But the struggle did not seem as near as it was, and in 1639 Milton, tired of his almost six years of country solitude, left for a journey of fifteen months on the continent of Europe. He passed through Paris and into Italy. He met the astronomer Galileo, visited Venice, attended a concert in a Cardinal's palace, wrote sonnets in Italian to a Lady of Bologna. But news from England broke in on his pleasure. War seemed about to begin—perhaps would begin before he could return. "I considered it base that, while my countrymen were fighting at home for liberty, I should be travelling abroad for intellectual culture," he wrote later.

So back to England. The war had not begun, and Milton began to tutor his two young nephews. How, about this time, he married the daughter of a cavalier, how Mary Powell left on a visit to her father a month after the marriage and refused to return—all this is an exciting and rather scandalous story showing how a man may be a scholar and a poet and still find it difficult to manage a wife.

It is rather more than likely that Milton was a hard person to get along with. Certainly, the austerity of his character, even as a very young man, was not calculated to warm any woman's heart. Least of all would it heat that of his first wife, a bride of seventeen summers, Royalist into the bargain. Little Mary Powell must have found the stiff routine of her husband's house too much for her. And Milton, now almost thirty-five, was more than twice her age. She missed the hilarity of her father's spacious establishment; the nephews quartered with her husband as his pupils were often beaten and bawling. Even a "pretty garden house" in one of the quietest streets in all of London could hardly make up for the lack of social animation. Mrs. Milton was undoubtedly discouraged. We can hardly blame the lady whose husband, during the honeymoon, could calmly pen a pamphlet on divorce!

Meanwhile, the war broke out, and Milton began the writing of tracts in defense of the Parliamentary side and against the King. As the war went on, his importance increased. He became what we should call the head of government publicity. Publicity was a more learned business then than it is now, and the office Milton finally came to hold was called Latin Secretary of the Commonwealth. It was a busy and exciting position, including correspondence with foreign nations and the writing of pamphlets explaining government policy. It paid him a salary worth about $5,000 of our money to-day.

The armies of Parliament finally triumphed and captured Charles I, and the unfortunate King was beheaded. Cromwell, the leading Parliamentary general, became the ruler of an English republic—Protector of the Commonwealth. Meanwhile, Milton's wife had begged to return to him, and he took her back and protected her family. She bore him three daughters and died in 1652. Milton, toiling at night at his writing for the Commonwealth, wore out his weak eyes at last and went completely blind. He married twice afterward, never seeing his third wife. Cromwell died, the Commonwealth crumbled, and the Cavaliers brought back the kingdom and triumphed in 1660 with the crowning of Charles II, the son of the beheaded King. Milton was lucky to be pardoned. He lost much of his property and retired with his blindness to a proud and bitter seclusion at Bunhill Fields, near London. Here he lived in seclusion, loving to walk in the garden he could not see, perhaps being very severe with his wife and daughters (though with himself also), and turning once more to the often-interrupted delight and labour of making poetry.

III

He had written little poetry during the troubled years of the great Civil War. In 1645, he had gathered together his early verses and published them. Since then a few sonnets made the sum of all he had found time to do. Yet never, in fury of Civil War or in personal anguish, had he ceased to think of himself as a poet, and a great one!

We can see now that the work he had already done was great, but in his own day few saw it. The poems had been kept in manuscript for years, then printed in the midst of civil war. Poetry readers were few, and they did not perceive that this verse was melodious like Spenser's but more powerful; that, if less human than Shakespeare's, it had a finish (partly the result of Milton's wide scholarship) different from the poetry of *Macbeth* and *Hamlet*, and never achieved before in English.

But Milton did not worry about the world's opinion of his work. He did not worry about his poverty, his fifty-odd years, his blindness. He did not enjoy his afflictions. Perhaps he lost the spontaneity and charm which in earlier years seem to have modified his rather severe disposition. Still, he accepted what— as he would have put it—Heaven had given him. As to his poems, he knew those he had done were good, and he knew there was better work still to come from him. He set himself to produce it. Among all the great spirits of history, few shine out greater than Milton during these dark hours of his life. Thrust for almost twenty years from the work he loved, struck to the dust at the end with the loss of public position and property and sight, his soul rose like a giant to the task he had set himself.

For years he had known in a general way what he wanted to do. Even in his years of reading at Horton he had the ambition to write a great epic poem. Doubtless, he knew that he had already made a style closer than anything in English to the majestic rolling music of Virgil. He had thought of King Arthur as a hero. Later, probably from Old English poetry and the Bible, he got the idea of a poem on the Fall of Man. An epic by the great Dutch poet, Vondel, published in 1656, may have helped him to make his story. And what a story it was! Milton took the unrhymed blank verse used heretofore only for plays, and made it into the metre for an epic. He told in this new and vital poetry (enriching it with experience from his wide classical reading, his travels, his religious feeling), how some of the angels revolted against God. He told how, after terrific battle, they were

> Hurled headlong flaming from th' ethereal sky
> With hideous ruin and combustion down
> To bottomless perdition, there to dwell
> In adamantine chains and penal fire
> Who durst defy th' Omnipotent to arms.

He told how God created the Earth, and man and woman, and how Satan, leader of the fallen angels, made his way through fire and chaos to the new world. He told how in the shape of a serpent Satan tempted Eve, and how the first man and woman lost the paradise in which they had dwelled happily.

This was a story the whole Christian world knew. It was especially a story that meant much to Puritans. Setting forth the coming of evil and the first sin and the purpose of God toward man, it voiced the reverent Puritan spirit. It flashed, too, the Puritan passion for freedom, though Milton, on account of the story, had to put this passion in the breast of Satan and thus make Satan the most interesting character in this poem of *Paradise Lost*. But, and this is perhaps the most important thing of all, this poem permitted the puritan in Milton to triumph without any loss of the love of colour and beauty. For here were magnificent things to write of. There was Hell—

> A dungeon horrible, on all sides round
> As one great furnace flam'd, yet from those flames
> No light, but rather darkness visible
> Serv'd only to discover sights of woe,
> Regions of sorrow, doleful shades where peace
> And rest can never dwell, hope never comes
> That comes to all; but torture without end
> Still urges, and a fiery deluge, fed
> With ever-burning sulphur unconsumed.

There was Chaos—that lay between Hell and Earth:

> A dark
> Illimitable ocean without bound,
> ... The womb of nature and perhaps her grave;

There were Heaven and Earth, as Satan, flying among the stars, saw them from afar—Heaven

> With opal towers and battlements adorn'd
> Of living sapphire, once his native seat;
> And fast by, hanging in a golden chain,
> This pendant world, in bigness as a star
> Of the smallest magnitude close by the moon.

In such a poem the great puritan and the great poet, different though they were, could sing together. And Milton sang. True, he could not see to write. He mourns the loss of sight in a majestic passage:

> Thus with the year
> Seasons return, but not to me returns
> Day, or the sweet approach of ev'n or morn,
> Or sight of vernal bloom, or summer's rose,
> Or flocks, or herds, or human face divine;
> But cloud instead, and ever-during dark
> Surrounds me.

However, he saw with the eyes of his imagination:

> So much the rather thou, celestial Light
> Shine inward, and the mind through all her powers
> Irradiate; there plant eyes, all mist from thence
> Purge and disperse, that I may see and tell
> Of things invisible to mortal sight.

So he sat writing his poem inwardly, and reciting it to his daughters. There is a famous painting by the Hungarian Munkácsy in the New York Public Library which shows the poet as he had been described by someone who visited him at this time. Dressed in black, seated in an armchair in a room with dark green velvet hangings, his fine silver hair falling over his shoulders, his staring eyes still a brilliant blue, he keeps his ears open to the voices of demons and archangels, and his lips pronouncing for half-awed, half-impatient girls the words that should "justify the ways of God to men."

Paradise Lost is a long book, and so is its companion epic, *Paradise Regained*. There are many dreary pages in both— heavenly harangues and never-ending sermons. Adam is too often a good puritan family man. He smiles "with superior love" on Eve's "submissive charms," and lectures her on her conduct. And even Eve herself talks sometimes like a windy doctor of divinity. The visiting angel Michael, though immortal and unfleshly, eats like a farmhand. The Serpent argues like a lawyer. Heaven is filled with heavy conversation, and Hell, too—though the weary talk sometimes seems fit enough there as a part of the eternal punishment that all the inhabitants must suffer.

But there is more in *Paradise Lost* than solemn speeches. There are movement and colour and tremendous passionate feeling. There is music like a chorus of tall angels and a cathedral organ heard in a dream. There is an imagination that bursts like a tireless rocket upward from earth to search stars and spaces. It was in Milton to reach out for the eternal, and he had taken a story that let him reach as far as he would. The result is poetry that in majesty, grandeur, and exaltation stands alone. Only Dante comes close to its soaring, intense power. The words have multitudinous reverberations. They coil in sonorous involutions, twisting like snakes and lashing over from line to line. And again each syllable is a blow, or the flash and roar of a gun.

All this makes *Paradise Lost* a great poem. The epic set a style for noble poetry. Since its time blank verse has been used for many great poems outside of drama, and Milton's music has been a school for later writers—some of them, like Keats and Shelley and Tennyson, great ones.

But its marvellous musical quality grows partly from its greatness of spirit. Milton, in telling this story of devils, angels, men, and God, expressed, better than anyone else before him or since, something noble and eternal in the human soul. It is not enough to call *Paradise Lost* the only great epic in English. It is not even enough to call it one of the greatest of Christian epics. It is more than these. It is the great puritan epic.

The truth is that all the world, in some of its moods, is puritan. It reaches out for sober and high things, for the utmost height of the spirit. In the puritan mood the whole world must find satisfaction in *Paradise Lost*. All of us must become intoxicated with the spiritual harmonies and aspiration of Milton. Satan with his

> unconquerable will,
> And study of revenge, immortal hate,
> And courage never to submit or yield,

stirs us to reluctant admiration. We thrill at the gates of Hell:

> Three folds were brass,
> Three iron, three of adamantine rock,
> Impenetrable, impaled with circling fire,
> Yet unconsumed.

We hover in mid air, with the greatest of the fallen angels, looking at the earth, and plunge through space as he

> throws
> His flight precipitant, and winds with ease
> Through the pure marble air his oblique way
> Amongst innumerable stars.

We hear the thunder of armies warring in Heaven, we taste the peace of Paradise, the pain of its loss.

From such an experience we take into our own lives some of the majesty, the music, the eternity of Milton's aspiration, his sure faith. It does not matter whether or not we believe his story—much of it he himself knew was imagination. If we accept the march and grandeur of his spirit we must ourselves move through life with firmer steps, with spirits more aroused, more noble.

IV

It took the world a long time to discover the greatness of *Paradise Lost*. Only 1,300 copies of the book were sold in the first year and a half, and 3,000 in ten years. But its place in the lives of men grew more important with time. Milton got only £10 for the poem, but poets and men have paid him high in remembrance since, and a manuscript of *Comus* was sold for $81,500 not long ago. This is much to pay for a few words, but words are precious when they are those of a man who expressed better than all other men the exalted spiritual mood that we treasure still, though we are not puritans. Milton would doubtless have been glad to know that, to the minds of poetry lovers, he had wrought well, but when he died in 1674 it was not with any sense of a wasted life. He knew he had done his work. His last creation had been the poetic tragedy *Samson Agonistes*. This told in nobly fashioned blank verse and unrhymed choruses in irregular lines, resembling the Greek, the story of the Bible hero—blind like Milton, like Milton living among his enemies, like him invincible in spirit. The words Milton speaks at the end of the drama over the dead wrestler might have been uttered of himself:

> Nothing is here for tears, nothing to wail,
> Or knock the breast; no weakness, no contempt,
> Dispraise, or blame; nothing but well and fair,
> And what may quiet us in a death so noble.

CHAPTER XVI

POETRY BECOMES SENSIBLE

I

Even before Milton died poets began to talk of entirely re-forming English poetry. They decided that it would never amount to much unless it could be civilized. And the way to civilize it, they said, was to make it like the French poetry of the time, smooth and regular in form, and reasonable and restrained in the expression of feeling.

Shakespeare and Chaucer, some of them asserted, showed how poetry should *not* be written. They admitted that Shakespeare had been a poet of genius, but they found him uncouth, like a naturally intelligent person who has had only a few years at school. They were sure that the Greeks and the Romans would have been shocked at the lack of polish and correctness in Shakespeare's poetry.

They feared that the Greeks and Romans would not have been satisfied even with the more learned and regular poems of John Milton. It was clear to them that a new kind of poetry ought to be made that would be polished and sensible, like the talk of well-educated ladies and gentlemen of exquisite manners.

Among these poets was one who soon became very successful. John Dryden developed a poetic style that pleased the other poets and pleased people in general. His poetry was hailed as the new poetry everyone had been looking for.

Dryden wrote for the most part in a form that had been used for hundreds of years—the heroic couplet. The heroic couplet had been a favourite of Chaucer's, who had employed it in a number of *The Canterbury Tales*. Shakespeare and other Elizabethan poets had written poetry in this form.

But Dryden made the couplet smoother and used it to a greater extent than any other poet had done before him. He wrote entire plays in it. He used it for short poems. He composed satirical poems in couplets dealing with political or literary subjects.

Dryden made the heroic couplet so popular that he himself and almost everyone else soon came to believe it was the best of forms for all important poems. Dryden was sure that Milton's *Paradise Lost* would be better in couplets than in blank verse, and he asked Milton if he might dramatize the poem in rhyme.

"Aye, you may tag my verses," said Milton, who was old and blind and grimly amused by the proposal. And Dryden "tagged" the verses in his play *The State of Innocence and the Fall of Man*.

All this seems a little amusing to us now, but Dryden's glittering couplets suited people in England in the late 1600's. There was a gay king and a gay court. Fine manners and wit and knowledge of the world were rated high. People were tired of killing one another for politics and religion, as the Cavaliers and Puritans had been doing through the long Civil War. They thought common sense was an excellent thing. They liked it in everyday life, and when Dryden offered them common sense in poetry they liked it there, too.

Dryden was a great poet, but he was unable to finish the work of making poetry sensible. When he died in 1700 he had made more than a good start, but a great deal remained to be done if English poetry were to be entirely made over.

II

Soon a young man appeared who began to carry the work forward. His name was Alexander Pope.

Like some others who have accomplished a great deal, Pope's prospects for poetry or anything else seemed at first to be rather poor. For one thing, he was a Roman Catholic. The Roman Catholics had few rights in England in 1700. They could not vote or hold office. Their children could not go to the regular public schools. Other people looked on them with suspicion.

So, while young Pope's father had done well enough as a linen draper to retire from business and live comfortably in the country near London, he had difficulty in giving his son an education.

Again, Alexander Pope had a small, frail, twisted body. All his life he had delicate health. He suffered from headaches and indigestion, and for many years before his death could not get up or dress or get to bed alone.

But Pope did not worry about his disadvantages. He could not find a good school or good tutors, so he taught himself. At twelve he was already reading poetry and writing verses.

He admired Dryden's poetry above that of all others. There is a story that a friend of Pope's who knew Dryden took the boy to Will's Coffee House in London where Dryden dined, and introduced him to the old poet.

"Mr. Dryden, I would present my young friend Master Pope. He admires your writings and hopes to follow where you have led. He hath already written excellent verses for a lad of his age."

So it might have been said.

And perhaps the great poet took a pinch of snuff and shook little Pope's hand and asked to see some of his poetry. Dryden was a kind man, though he could write sharp things about his enemies.

Such a meeting with Dryden must have strengthened Pope's

desire to be a poet. But he was even more impressed by what one of his friends said.

"There is one way left of excelling in poetry," said this friend. "For, though we have had several great poets, we have never had any great poet who was correct. If you would succeed, make correctness your study and aim."

Pope found in these words the plan of the writing he hoped to do.

From the first, he followed this plan with success. The verse he wrote in his 'teens was remarkably smooth and easy-flowing. When he was not yet twenty he composed his *Pastorals*. Meanwhile, he had made the acquaintance of literary men in London, and they read these verses in manuscript. Pope had followed the tradition of Theocritus, Virgil, and Spenser, writing of country scenes and country people. But he had written in the new couplet, smooth and balanced and pointed. All praised the finish of his verse, and in 1709, when he was only twenty-one, he published the poems.

Immediately he became known, but when he produced *An Essay on Criticism*, in 1711, he quickly took his place as the most brilliant and promising of the successors of Dryden. "Here is a new master of the couplet!" his admirers exclaimed.

It is worth while looking for a moment at the poem that excited such attention. Perhaps it shows to us to-day better than any other poem exactly what Dryden and Pope tried to do, and why people admired their work.

To begin with, the plan of *An Essay on Criticism* would, to our notion, fit a magazine article better than a piece of verse. Pope sets out to discuss critics, and especially those who write about new books, saying whether these are good or bad and why. He tells about the difficulties of being a critic, the mistakes critics make, and how they might do better. Throughout the poem he explains and argues, and it is his logic, his graceful phrasing, and his wit that we admire.

People say now: "Why put such ideas into poetry?"

The answer is, you can put them into poetry or into prose, just as you please. Perhaps we get into habits about such matters. We read editorials in verse when we read Walt Mason, and the clever verse of F. P. A. and other newspaper "columnists" is often playfully argumentative. It is more difficult to explain or argue in verse than in prose, and perhaps harder to read such explanations or arguments. But if you *like* verse there is no reason why you shouldn't like an argument in poetic form more than you like it in prose form. The rhythm and rhyme give a pleasure in themselves. Pope wrote in *An Essay on Criticism*

> 'Tis with our judgments as our watches, none
> Go just alike, yet each believes his own.

And again:

> A little learning is a dangerous thing,
> Drink deep, or taste not the Pierian spring;

and

> Some praise at morning what they blame at night
> And always think the last opinion right.

In each case he had a point to make, and he probably made it better in rhyme and metre than he could have made it in prose. We repeat these couplets to-day because they express so well what we know to be the truth. Others besides Pope had put the same ideas into prose, but their words have been forgotten while Pope's rhymes have been remembered.

There is something in the way Pope's couplets are written that makes them hard to forget. We like to notice contrasts and differences. A dwarf and a seven-footer side by side attract our attention. Pope realized the effectiveness of contrast, and many of his verses show how he worked to secure it.

> Hope springs eternal   in the human breast
> Man never is   but always to be blest.

In the first half of the first line of this couplet he talks about hope and eternity. In the second half, he brings into contrast with this the human body, which, unlike Hope, is something you can touch; and unlike eternal things, does not last long. In the second line there is the sharp difference between what we are and what we hope to be.

Pope was a master at setting forth differences of this kind. His couplets were unsurpassed for the precision and point with which they expressed ideas. It is easy to understand how those who loved logic and wit admired this sort of poetry.

III

An Essay on Criticism was soon followed by *The Rape of the Lock*.

This is the most imaginative of Pope's poems. It was written to patch up a quarrel. A nobleman had playfully cut a lock of hair from a lady's head, and the lady had become so angry that she would have nothing to do with him or his family. Pope heard about the affair. He thought it a silly thing to quarrel over. He decided to write a poem describing the incident as if it were a great event and making both the lord and lady laugh over the absurdity of the whole episode.

So he made a mock epic in rhyme. Unfortunately, the lady did not like to have everyone talking about her, and so was displeased that Pope had written *The Rape of the Lock*. However, the public liked it, and the poem is still interesting, though the actual lord and lady have been forgotten.

The Rape of the Lock shows that if Pope had been born at a different time he might have written more imaginative poetry. He let his fancy loose in this story, and wrote with delicacy and charm. For instance, there is the description of the lady's dressing table with the various things ladies used (and still use) to make themselves beautiful:

This casket India's glowing gems unlocks,
And all Arabia breathes from yonder box,
The tortoise and the elephant unite,
Transformed to combs, the speckled, and the white.
Here files of pins extend their shining rows,
Puffs, powders, patches, bibles, billets-doux.

The Rape of the Lock made Pope the foremost poet in England. He was known now and honoured by all the great literary men of the day. He became a friend of Addison, then one of the editors of the *Spectator*, a poet himself, and a kind of king of the literary world. Pope wrote a prologue for Addison's play, *Cato*. A little later he got acquainted with Swift, the author of *Gulliver's Travels*.

And now an important idea came to Pope. He decided to translate the Iliad of Homer into English rhymed couplets. Swift encouraged him. Swift was now very powerful with those who were in charge of the government. He had helped them to get their positions by his writing, and they were afraid he might help turn them out if they displeased him. So it was a great thing for Pope when Dean Swift bustled about among the rich noblemen saying to them:

"Gentlemen, the best poet in England is Mr. Pope, a Papist. He hath begun a translation of Homer into English verse, and there is nothing for it but I must have all your subscriptions. The author will not begin to print 'til I have a thousand guineas for him."

Swift got the guineas. In fact, when the great translation was published in 1715, Pope had closer to five thousand guineas, and altogether made £5,320 from the Iliad. The Odyssey brought in another large sum, and it is estimated Homer paid Pope altogether £9,000, or about $45,000—which in those days was probably worth at least $150,000 of our money to-day.

No poet had ever been paid like this. Pope himself, for all his previous writing, had got but £150. Poets in those days still depended on patrons—noblemen willing to give money in return for having poems dedicated to them. Pope was the first poet to make a fortune from his own writings, and years later he could write

> But (thanks to Homer) [I can] live and thrive
> Indebted to no prince or peer alive

I V

But now things began to go less happily for Pope. For one thing, his cleverness had made him enemies. Sometimes this was merely jealousy. Sometimes he said sharp things, as in *An Essay on Criticism*, which poets and critics did not like. He displeased Addison by writing a pamphlet about Dennis, a critic who had found fault with Addison's *Cato*. Later, Addison encouraged another poet to translate Homer, and Pope thought this was done by Addison in jealousy, and the two were never good friends again. And later still, in 1725, Pope brought out an edition of Shakespeare's plays, and made a number of mistakes (for he knew little about Shakespeare) and these were pointed out by scholars and other poets. Also, Pope had written silly letters to several women, and one of them had laughed at him and helped write pamphlets ridiculing his pride and his crooked body.

Now, it was one of the advantages of sensible poetry (as Pope thought, at least) that you could use it for argument and quarrelling. And for some years Pope spent a great deal of his time trying to make ridiculous the critics and poets who had said or done things that he disliked.

He wrote one poem called *The Dunciad*. This was another mock epic. It told a story about the goddess Dullness and the various writers who gathered at her court to sing her praise in stupid poems. These writers were none other than those who had criticized Pope unfavourably. Everyone rushed to read what the great Pope had written about his enemies, and laughed, and thought Pope greater than ever. But many of the things Pope had written were unjust, and many of those he had made fun of published pamphlets and poems attacking him, so that he never heard the last of their complaints.

He continued writing against them in many of his *Moral Epistles* and *Satires*. He said it was a noble task to expose fools and bores (as he always thought his enemies), and was proud of his satiric poems.

> Yes, I am proud; I must be proud to see
> Men not afraid of God, afraid of me:
> Safe from the bar, the pulpit, and the throne,
> Yet touched and shamed by ridicule alone.

Still, the Pope of *The Dunciad* and the *Satires* is often like a small boy pulling off the legs of flies or throwing mud at someone who has hit him.

But Pope had another side to his nature. He loved his mother, he was kind to poor people, he loved his many friends. At Twickenham he had a house and a few acres of ground. Here he made a garden, and a tunnel under the road that separated one part of his garden from the other. He called the tunnel a grotto, and in it he planted ferns, herbs, and flowers, and put many kinds of shells. He loved to sit in the grotto or under the trees with his friends, talking about poetry and people and the meaning of life. Perhaps many of the unjust and irritating things he did were really a result of his being sick. Certainly, Pope wanted to be noble. Even though we know now that he was sometimes deceitful (as in pretending he did not want to get his letters published while he was plotting all the time to bring about their publication), it is easy to believe he deceived himself as well as other people and meant to do right.

v

His *Essay on Man* showed his anxiety to accomplish something serious. This poem, the first part of which was published in 1732, was another example of what common sense led Pope to do. He thought that if one could reason in poetry, one could write philosophy in it. The *Essay on Man* is philosophy. It has many descriptive passages which Pope's readers in the 1730's admired, and it puts many ideas into rhyme in a graceful way. It was harder to read than his other poems, but on this very account people had a great respect for it. It seemed to leave nothing to be done in the way of making poetry sensible.

And, in fact, Pope had succeeded thoroughly in making poetry a common-sense affair. With Dryden, he had established it as a means of expressing opinions. He had made smoothness more important than beauty, reason more important than imagination. No one had ever brought poetry and common sense together so successfully. And the age that honoured common sense honoured Pope. When he died in 1744 he was considered the greatest of living poets and one of the greatest of all poets.

To-day we do not think so highly of his work. We are inclined to believe that the fashion Pope set in poetry smothered the genius of writers like Thomas Gray, remembered for his finely wrought and noble poem, *Elegy Written in a Country Churchyard*. Some people in Pope's own time suspected this. It was not long after his death before they began to suggest that perhaps Pope had made poetry so sensible that it was really no longer poetry. By 1800 other poets were rescuing poetry from common sense, and it has never been wholly sensible since.

Perhaps it could be. Perhaps we could, if we wished, have poetry like Pope's and more imaginative poetry as well. But the two are so different that, when one is in fashion, the other is usually out. Pope's kind of poetry, though it had its day for one hundred and fifty years, is out of fashion now.

Yet, when we catch ourselves saying day by day a number of things Pope said, we realize that there must have been something in a writer who, like Shakespeare, has helped us build our very language. We admire Pope's skill and sanity. And when poets of to-day let their imaginations run away with them, there are those who think of Pope and wish he were living now to write poetry that would be different and—sensible.

CHAPTER XVII

THE POETS OF NATURE

I

Although Pope made the poetry of common sense fashionable, there were many readers of verse in England and Europe who were not satisfied with common sense. Certain poets, too, wanted something less rational and more exciting. A little ashamed of themselves, writers like Young and James Thomson and Collins wrote blank verse and Spenserian stanzas and unrhymed odes modelled on the Greek. They made most of their poetry rather formal because that was the kind of poetry they were expected to produce. But we can see now that, like boys tired of school, they wanted to escape from the little cage of the heroic couplet, and its well-behaved ideas, and do something more spontaneous. Thomas Gray, careful scholar though he was, yearned for freedom, too, and his great poem, *Elegy Written in a Country Churchyard* (1751), sings the beauty and honour of toil and proclaims of the artificial world of powdered wigs and ceremony that

> The boast of heraldry, the pomp of pow'r,
>   And all that beauty, all that wealth e'er gave,
> Await alike the inevitable hour.
>   The paths of glory lead but to the grave.

But this *Elegy*, grand and moving though it is, had no hot human sympathy behind it. It was rather a highly polished series of grave reflections on death by a sick, disappointed, and lonely scholar. Gray wrote also of old Irish and Norse myths. He and the few others who shared his restlessness sought in sombre contemplation of nature or in the mysterious pageantry of the imagination an escape from common things and ordinary feelings.

Meanwhile, Jean Jacques Rousseau, writing in France, had a great effect on the ideas of the people, and on poetry and other writings throughout Europe. He had been a sensitive boy. He felt ill at ease under the severe discipline of the schools, and under the mechanical manners of the time which he believed were crushing out the individualities of men and making everyone inhuman and artificial. Gradually, he became certain that the rules and customs and many of the institutions of men were foolish and harmful because they interfered with the joyous, inspired feelings that, he thought, were natural to human beings. If men would trust less to reason and more to instinct, to nature, to the heart, they would be better and happier, declared Rousseau. Spontaneous thoughts and actions were good, manufactured thoughts and the manufactured business of society were bad. He wrote in his *Confessions*:

I was so tired of fine rooms, fountains, artificial groves and flower beds, and the still more tiresome people who displayed all these; . . . with pamphlets, card-playing, music, silly jokes, insipid mincing airs, great suppers, that whenever I spied a poor hawthorn copse, a hedge, a farmstead, a meadow or . . . heard from a distance the rude refrain of the shepherd's songs, I used to wish at the devil the whole tale of rouge and furbelows.

Many men and women in England read such words and agreed with them. In fact, the first English novelist, Samuel Richardson, had already turned to the natural feelings of humble men and women in his emotional story *Pamela*, which, though it stretched out to the crack of doom, was much wept over, and, in consequence, enjoyed. Later, wild romances of the time of armour and castles and supernatural happenings began to be written and read and shivered over with delight. In fact, haunted ruins and mournful soliloquies and ghost-wailings became quite the rage. In 1764, Bishop Percy added fuel to the romantic fire by publishing a great collection of old ballads called *Reliques of Ancient English Poetry*. Here and there Scotch and English poets began to write in the simple ballad style that had been popular with the people in the Fourteenth and Fifteenth centuries. Men were talking also of changes in government and inventing machines like the steam engine to do the work that had once been done by hand. There was a feeling of unrest, a great hope of change. In life and poetry, men were asking for something warmer and more exciting and miraculous than common sense.

II

This yearning and unrest came to a farmer boy driving his plough through the dark soil of Ayrshire, Scotland. Reading a book by candlelight as he bent over his porridge at night, or toiling by day in the fields, Robert Burns found words singing in his head to rude ballad tunes.

They came in spite of everything that might have stopped them.

For William "Burness" had worked hard and won little. He and his two sons had ploughed and planted and harvested and barely managed to make a living. Young Robert had got what learning he had after his day's work was over, or in rare months at school. But he had organized debating clubs and gone to country dancing school and read the poems of Scotch poets like Ramsay and Ferguson. After his father died, he and his brother Gilbert took a new farm and decided to study farming and get the best of the tough land and the bad weather.

But Robert couldn't get away from rhyme and metre. He got a book to make notes on farming. However, as Gilbert told

later, he wrote little in it about digging and planting. He put
down his odd thoughts instead. He scribbled:

> O why the deuce should I repine,
> And be an ill foreboder?
> I'm twenty-three, and five-foot nine,—
> I'll go and be a sodger.

And as he and Gilbert weeded their garden or ploughed or drained
fields, Robert recited witty rhymes in Scotch dialect spoofing
ministers in the neighbouring towns. Or in a more serious mood
he may have repeated lines he had made about a girl he had
fallen in love with, lines fresh and tender as opening leaves:

> O Mary, canst thou wreck his peace,
> Wha for thy sake wad gladly die?
> Or canst thou break that heart of his,
> Whase only faut is loving thee?
> If love for love thou wilt na gie,
> At least be pity to me shown!
> A thought ungentle canna be
> The thought o' Mary Morison.

Gilbert praised these verses. He and Robert thought they
might be printed in a magazine. Robert copied off one of the
poems he had made and gave it to a friend. It was a satiric,
fun-poking thing about two preachers.

"I can't guess who is the author o' it," said Burns slyly, "but
for myself I think it's clever."

So did his friend. The poem was too good to keep and was
passed about. Others came after it. Hamilton, Burns's landlord,
was a writer himself, and another writer, Aiken, had a fine
way of reciting poetry. They soon had all the shire talking about
Burns, the ploughboys for the most part praising him and
laughing with him, and the ministers wondering what they
could do to quiet him.

But, in the meantime, the farm work had gone badly, and
Burns had been getting into trouble. Strong and handsome,
warm-hearted and alive to beauty, he had continually fallen in

love during the years of his hard-working youth. And finally he had met Jean Armour and wanted to marry her.

But Jean's father wanted nothing to do with this wild poet. He refused to give his consent. When at last Jean became a mother, Burns was in danger of going to jail. One of his friends got a position for him as assistant manager of a plantation in Jamaica, and he decided to go there, but he had no money to pay his passage. It occurred to him that, if he got together some of the poems he had written, perhaps the people who knew of them would buy copies and he could earn his way across the ocean. Hamilton and Aiken were enthusiastic about the idea, and got so many promises that the printer was soon busy. When the poems appeared, those copies of the book which had not been paid for already were quickly sold. Gentlemen and ladies discovered them and were delighted with them, and ploughboys and maidservants went without shoes and bonnets to get the poems.

Burns was now ready to sail for Jamaica, but just as he was leaving home a letter came from Edinburgh, the capital and literary centre of Scotland. It was written by Dr. Blacklock, a blind poet and a man of wealth and influence, who had received a copy of Burns's book. He urged Burns to come to Edinburgh and arrange for a new edition of the poems.

Burns gave up the Jamaica plan, went to Edinburgh, and remained in one hospitable house or another for sixteen months. In Scotland's capital he was feasted and fussed over with the most extraordinary enthusiasm.

The ladies and gentlemen quoted his lyrics. They marvelled at his love-songs, yearning with the simple but fervid ring of

> O, my luve is like a red, red rose,
> That's newly sprung in June;
> O, my luve is like the melodie
> That's sweetly play'd in tune,

and sighing to the sadness of

> Ae fond kiss, and then we sever!

They laughed at the sharp stabs of Burns's satiric verse, and shed tears over the lines to a field mouse:

> Wee, sleekit, cow'rin', tim'rous beastie,
> O, what a panic's in thy breastie!
> Thou need na start awa sae hasty,
>   Wi' bickering brattle!
> I wad be laith to rin an' chase thee,
>   Wi' murd'ring pattle!
>
> I'm truly sorry man's dominion
> Has broken Nature's social union,
> An' justifies that ill opinion,
>   Which makes thee startle
> At me, thy poor, earth-born companion,
>   An' fellow-mortal!
>
>   .   .   .   .
>
> Still thou art blest, compared wi' me!
> The present only toucheth thee:
> But och! I backward cast my e'e
>   On prospects drear!
> An' forward, tho' I canna see,
>   I guess an' fear!

Burns's appearance and personality also helped to make him a sensation. Here was a farmer boy. Handsome, awkward enough to be interesting, skilful in glowing argument or flattery or tender compliment, he startled the gentlemen of the city and thrilled the ladies. He seemed a living proof of what Rousseau had said—that truth and poetry were found among simple men. The troubadour in homespun became the lion of the season.

The gay, slightly eccentric, slightly literary Duchess of Gordon displayed him to her fashionable set. "The town is at present agog with the Ploughman Poet," wrote one ecstatic lady to a friend. Through function upon function, private and public, he moved triumphantly. There were food and wine of excellent savour, speeches, applause. It was Mr. Burns here, Brother Burns there. He was greeted with flutters and exclamations from the "How interesting!" females, hailed by the Grand

Lodge of Scotland as "Caledonia's Bard," and in short was marvelled at everywhere. By this time, his rough homespun had been cast off for a suit of buff and blue, with buckskin breeches, his muddy brogans for the latest top boots. He carried the vivacious Duchess already mentioned completely off her feet—by her own confession. He sat for painters. And no wonder the ladies always loved him. How could they help it, when he threw up his black shaggy head, straightened up his heavy shoulders rounded from toil, his dark eyes flashing, his mouth mobile and fluent with the graces of conversation. He could be charmingly vivacious, and he could be superbly eloquent when his wrath was aroused by instances of tyranny or injustice. Then his eyes glowed like coals of fire. Sometimes he startled his hosts with his spontaneous wrath. At a private breakfast, for example, he called a clergyman who had unjustly attacked his beloved Gray's *Elegy* a "damned blockhead!"

It is not hard to understand how the priests and professors, a small, narrow-minded group in the main, must have been shocked by this big-boned, black-browed visitor who, still fresh from the ploughtail, settled questions of scholarship with authority, refused to flatter them by noticing their flattery, laughed the wits down, agitated the bosoms of habitually reserved ladies with his talk and his accents of natural pathos, and, to cap his insolence, was known to consort with company which they turned up their cultured noses at, putting the merry bucks of Edinburgh into a roar with his gibes at *them*. And while we rather chuckle with the poet, we cannot help feeling that it might have been better for his health and person, if not for his poetry, had he avoided the tavern and the boon companions.

But, for the time, all went happily and prosperously for him. Though he pretended to resent being exhibited as a kind of literary freak, he spoke in the Preface of the first Edinburgh Edition (1797) of the plough and his "wild, artless notes." And the lords and gentlemen of the Caledonia Hunt, to whom he dedicated the book, and other fashionables of Edinburgh, sub-

scribed for his poems and read them. Being a ploughboy was very
profitable during this brief season of popularity. We could wish
that Burns, who was willing to take the benefits of it, could
have been less touchy about it.

However, it must be granted him that, though he enjoyed
the posing and the lip service, he was aware himself that the
curiosity of the town would die, that the select circles would
no longer buzz in his ears, that carriages would pass him by and
hand-clapping and excitement cease. So we find him writing to
a friend on the 15th of January, 1787: "You are afraid I shall
grow intoxicated with my prosperity as a poet. Alas! Madam,
I know myself and the world too well. . . . I am willing to believe
that my abilities deserved some notice; . . . but . . . to be
dragged forth to the full glare of learned and polite conversation,
with all my imperfections of awkward rusticity, and crude
unpolished ideas, on my head—I . . . tremble for the con-
sequences. . . . But . . . you will bear me witness, that when my
bubble of fame was at its highest, I stood unintoxicated with
the inebriating cup in my hand, looking forward with rueful
resolve."

There was another kind of intoxication of which he par-
took, however, too freely. What the boors of Ayrshire had failed
to do to the sturdy son of William Burness, the bucks of Edinburgh did. He had been but a few months in the capital when,
accustomed by his talents to be the cock of the company, he
turned from the lifted eyebrows and the frowns of the drawing
room to the freedom and the hearty bravos of the inn table.
By talk he had first distinguished himself among his fellow
peasants. By talk he would continue his triumph. He saw the
writing on the wall. He was doomed to go back. His heart was
heavy and bitter. Without a practical aim in life, too fond of
congenial conversation and the pleasures of applause, he could
not resist the cup. No man was ever more the victim of his
friends and himself.

On the 23d of April, 1787, he wrote:

I leave Edinburgh in the course of ten days or a fortnight. I shall return to my rural shades, in all likelihood never more to quit them. . . .

The second edition of his poems had come out in March, with few new poems, as might be expected, and sold to no less than fifteen hundred subscribers, many of whom paid more than the shop price of the book.

Burns had now quite a sum of money. He wished to visit some of the places rich in Scottish history and romance. He erected a decent stone over the neglected grave of his predecessor in wretchedness and poetry, Robert Ferguson, then quit the city, travelled on horseback through the southern border and the spots celebrated by the old minstrels whom he had loved from infancy, and came back again to the plough.

The rest of the poet's life does not make happy reading. In 1788 he leased a farm in Dumfriesshire, married Jean Armour, and enjoyed one of his few quiet and contented years. In 1789, driven by an increasing family, he applied for and gained an appointment as exciseman or district inspector of goods liable to a tax. He began drinking heavily. His health failed. His spirits fell. Bouts of drunkenness were followed by orgies of remorse. He was miserable and sang marvellously. He tried to pull himself together. In his last letter, dated July 18, 1796, he writes:

I returned from sea-bathing quarters to-day, and my medical friends would almost persuade me that I am better; but I think and feel that my strength is so gone that the disorder will prove fatal to me.

Three days later he becomes delirious. The children are called for and stand around the bed. His last word is a curse on some law agent who had sent for money. It is the twenty-first day of July, 1796. Robert Burns is dead. He is buried on the twenty-fifth with local honours, the volunteers fire three volleys over the poet's grave, and his wife gives birth to a son on the day of the funeral.

III

Burns had made his songs for a brief ten years. He had written no epic, and all his best verse was in a dialect strange to English readers. Yet he died leaving poetry a different thing from what it had been when he found it.

To some extent, this was because he took poetry away from fine houses and fine people. Gray in his famous *Elegy* had got as far as writing about humble folk who had been safely laid beneath their tombstones. Burns wrote about them as they lived. In *The Cotter's Saturday Night* he described a simple peasant family, drawing from his own father the picture of the farmer returning after his day's toil:

> At length his lonely cot appears in view,
> Beneath the shelter of an agèd tree;
> Th' expectant wee-things, toddlin, stacher through
> To meet their Dad, wi' flichterin noise an' glee.
> His wee bit ingle, blinkin bonilie,
> His clean hearth-stane, his thrifty wifie's smile,
> The lisping infant prattling on his knee,
> Does a' his weary kiaugh and care beguile,
> An' makes him quite forget his labour an' his toil.

In *Tam o' Shanter* he went much farther and sang a rollicking tale of the tipsy cronies, gathered round the blazing ingle of the tavern, and piping up their catches, forgetful of the storm outside and the wife who waits at home

> Nursing her wrath to keep it warm.

Even dumb animals got his attention. He told in *The Death and Dying Words of Poor Mailie* the dolorous tale of his only pet ewe. He offers a New Year morning salutation to the Auld Farmer's Auld Mare, Maggie. He made immortal poetry about a field mouse, and a louse on a lady's bonnet inspired the lines known now by all the world:

> O wad some power the giftie gie us
> To see oursels as ithers see us!

Such writing was an immense service to poetry. It opened the doors of the pretty prison in which poetry readers had been held for a hundred years and sent them out among the hardships and hopes and loves of the poor. It came to many in Scotland and England like a fulfillment of the hopes and prophecies of Rousseau. It was also in harmony with the hopes the French Revolution had stirred everywhere in 1789. Burns himself undoubtedly rejoiced to see France reaching for liberty. He was keenly aware of the wrongs of the poor, crying that

> Man's inhumanity to man
> Makes countless thousands mourn,

and he wrote a song rejoicing in the dignity of poverty and honest labour which has become a kind of *Marseillaise* of democracy:

> A prince can mak a belted knight,
> A marquis, duke, an' a' that;
> But an honest man's aboon his might,
> Guid faith, he mauna fa' [make] that!
> For a' that, an' a' that,
> Their dignities, an' a' that,
> The pith o' sense, an' pride o' worth,
> Are higher rank than a' that.

But Burns was bigger than any cause. He was bigger than a love of liberty, or the love of his native Scotland, which he put into a very flame of song in an imaginary address of Robert Bruce to the Scotch army before the Battle of Bannockburn:

> Scots, wha hae wi' Wallace bled,
> Scots, wham Bruce has aften led,
> Welcome to your gory bed,
> Or to victorie.

For Burns had what was even greater than his reach for freedom or his patriotism—he had an understanding heart. This showed in his poetry about common men and animals. It showed in his humour, softening the sting of his keen satire and flavouring his rollicking fun with pity and tenderness, as only Chaucer and Shakespeare among the other great poets have been able to do. His sympathy is full and rich also in his love-songs, making these the tenderest, as they are the most natural, in English poetry. What can be more touching for anguish of simple sadness than the lament of the forsaken lass:

> Ye flowery banks o' bonnie Doon,
>   How can ye blume sae fair?
> How can ye chant, ye little birds,
>   And I sae fu' o' care!

And what can surpass the words of the aged Scotch wife to her lifelong mate:

> "John Anderson, my jo, John,
>   We clamb the hill' thegither,
> And mony a canty day, John,
>   We've had wi' ane anither:
> Now we maun totter down, John,
>   But hand in hand we'll go,
> And sleep thegither at the foot,
>   John Anderson, my jo."

These songs were sung by one who knew poverty and toil under the open sky, and they have the sun and wind and the lilt of folk ballads in them. Burns was human to the core, and had his faults, but these have enriched rather than marred his poetry. Being often weak, he knew how to be charitable toward his fellow men. He had kindling intelligence that darted out in sharp, haunting truth. He had humility. He had tenderness and humour. So, where Milton is severe, Burns is friendly as the sun. Where Wordsworth is solemn, Burns is full of abounding joy. And while Byron's satire is brilliant but rarely humorous, and while poets like Shelley and Keats and Tennyson move in a region of glamour where a smile is a criminal offense, Burns blends beauty and satire, pain and humour, and produces the most human of fine poetry. He knows the pathos of little things, and finds a key in this to the humanity of big things. He struggles, like many of us, with emotions that are stronger than his resolutions, and becomes the maker of human melodies that are like proverbs of the emotions.

IV

While Burns was giving a new birth to spontaneous poetry in Scotland, poetry in England was also making ready for change. Even before Burns's time, in fact, in the late 1760's, a boy in the town of Bristol had dreamed dreams of chivalry and romance. Thomas Chatterton studied such old writers and old manuscripts as he could lay his hands on. He wrote ballads and songs in quaint English and printed them on old parchment he found in a Bristol church, and deceived not a few gentlemen into thinking they were genuine poetry hundreds of years old. Then, in his eighteenth year, he went to London seeking his fortune as a writer, and after a brief, vain struggle for success, ended with his own hands his marvellous life. His verse was extraordinary for a boy's, but his story and his poetry alike were at the time only an unnoticed flare of genius.

In the early 1780's a gentleman in the late forties by the name of William Cowper lifted a quiet voice different from Dr. Samuel Johnson's or Oliver Goldsmith's, or any other follower of Pope. Cowper had a sense for simple language, he loved nature, he wrote ballads. The romantic spirit was in him, but he was not quite young enough to do great things with it. He was rather solemn in tone; in fact, was always fighting off a melancholy that at times made him insane. Though he wrote a great deal of admirable poetry, he helped only a little, and indirectly, to swing poetry away from common sense.

Soon after Cowper began to write, two friends of a young engraver, William Blake, printed privately and in loose-leaf form his *Poetical Sketches*. In a Preface one of them wrote that the poems were "the production of an untutored youth, commenced in his twelfth year, and occasionally resumed by the author until his twentieth year." Since then, the Preface continued, Blake had been busy with his profession, and had had no time for verse. They apologized that he had not revised his *Sketches* and made them better.

Nevertheless, the poems were written with a strange and magical simplicity. They showed no likeness to common-sense poetry at all. There was something in them like Elizabethan verse, and perhaps more that was like the Fourteenth and Fifteenth Century ballads that had been published eighteen years earlier by Bishop Percy. But poems like this Song were in the main more like William Blake than anything else:

> How sweet I roam'd from field to field
> And tasted all the summer's pride,
> Till I the prince of love beheld
> Who in the sunny beams did glide!
>
> He show'd me lilies for my hair
> And blushing roses for my brow;
> He led me through his gardens fair
> Where all his golden pleasures grow.
>
> With sweet May dews my wings were wet,
> And Phœbus fir'd my vocal rage;
> He caught me in his silken net,
> And shut me in his golden cage.
>
> He loves to sit and hear me sing,
> Then laughing, sports and plays with me;
> Then stretches out my golden wing,
> And mocks my loss of liberty.

This is a strange poem, though a beautiful one, and the little book was mysteriously charged with this almost unearthly simplicity. Yet it was entirely natural poetry for Blake to write. He had been a strange boy. Perhaps he got a wild visionary strain from his Irish grandfather. Perhaps it throve on the discussions of Swedenborg and the New Church he heard at nights as a boy in the shop of his father, a draper or hosier. At any rate, when still very small, he had seen a tree full of angels, their wings spangling the boughs. Later, he had seen angels walking in a field. When he went for a time to art school, not only angels but all the great figures of the Bible came before him, so clearly that he could use them for models. Later, still apprenticed to an engraver, he was sent to Westminster Abbey to copy certain designs, and there Christ and His Apostles visited the young apprentice. A boy with such an unusual imagination might well write unusual poetry.

Blake did not get less imaginative as he grew older. He married a dark, handsome girl named Catherine Boucher, the unlettered daughter of a market gardener. She, like Blake, was of a simple, almost childlike nature. She believed in all his visions and lived with him in poverty, serving as a model for his drawings, keeping house, helping him to make engravings and colour illuminated books. To those who visited them, the two seemed a strange couple. On one occasion Catherine remarked, "You know, dear, the first time you saw God was when you were four years old, and He put His head to the window and set you a-screaming." Another time a caller found them sitting in the summer house like Adam and Eve in the Garden. The caller was most frightfully embarrassed, but was assured by Blake that they were "only Adam and Eve."

Blake and Catherine lived by what Blake made from his engraving, but there was as little as possible of commercial work in the house. The poet-artist turned instead to meditating, to engraving and illustrating his own books of poems, to making pictures, such as his designs for Dante and for Blair's *The Grave*, which were glorious poems themselves.

The first of his hand-made books, coming six years after *Poetical Sketches*, was *Songs of Innocence* (1789). Sweet and clear as the voices of children are the poems of this volume. Indeed, Blake tells in his Introduction how

> Piping down the valleys wild,
> Piping songs of pleasant glee,
> On a cloud I saw a child,

and how the child said to him,

> "Piper, sit thee down and write
> In a book, that all may read,"
> So he vanished from my sight,
> And I plucked a hollow reed,
>
> And I made a rural pen,
> And I stained the water clear
> And I wrote my happy songs
> Every child may joy to hear.

In this volume was the poem to the lamb:

> Little lamb, who made thee?
> Dost thou know who made thee?
> Gave thee life, and bade thee feed
> By the stream and o'er the mead;
> Gave thee clothing of delight,
> Softest clothing woolly, bright;
> Gave thee such a tender voice,
> Making all the vales rejoice?
> Little lamb, who made thee?
> Dost thou know who made thee?

In a later volume, *Songs of Experience* (1794), Blake wrote the fearful yet fascinating lines on the tiger:

> Tiger! Tiger! burning bright,
> In the forests of the night,
> What immortal hand or eye
> Could frame thy fearful symmetry?

including the cry:

> Did He who made the lamb make thee?

v

Songs of Innocence, if properly published, might have made a deep impression on England. It was a book of a startling simplicity that Rousseau would have loved. It was full of reverence and a keen delight in nature and a spontaneous quality which was at the opposite end of the world from the carefully balanced couplets that Pope had fashioned.

But Blake had made and printed and published the book himself, and it had little circulation. A few rare spirits saw and read it. Blake found his way into a small group of literati who met at a Mrs. Mathew's house, and there he recited and sang his poems. Later he met William Godwin, the philosopher, and Shelley and Keats and other writers. However, he had already begun the making of stranger books of poetry that half-frightened even the poets. *The Book of Thel*, *The Ghost of Abel*, *The Marriage of Heaven and Hell*, *Jerusalem*—these were fearful productions. Some scholars have found marvellous meanings in them, some a great deal of moonshine. Blake himself thought them full of truth and prophecy. He said they were created by someone in eternity who spoke the words which he wrote down, sometimes against his will. But Blake lived in a world of imagination, with a ladder of angels reaching from the heavens to his cottage, and

> With happiness stretched across the hills
> In a cloud that dewy sweetness distils;
> With a blue sky spread over with wings,
> And a wild sun that mounts and sings;
> With trees and fields full of fairy-elves
> And little devils who fight with themselves.
> . . . .
> With angels planted in hawthorn bowers
> And God himself in the passing hours.

He called the world of ordinary men the Vegetable world.

> Imagination is the real and eternal world of which this vegetable universe is but a faint shadow and in which we shall live in our eternal or imaginative bodies when these vegetable mortal bodies are no more.

It may be that all of this was a part of Blake's poetic wisdom —that he had the secret of life, that he sometimes stammered like a celestial being vainly trying to talk our language; and sometimes, as in his simpler poems, made part of his message understood. Certainly, he himself found joy in life. When the sun rose, he declared he saw "an innumerable company of the heavenly host, crying, 'Holy—holy—holy is the Lord God Almighty.'"

Yet, whether Blake was marvellously sane or marvellously mad, he was too different from his time to be immediately accepted. So, though he was an enthusiastic revolutionist and wore a red Liberty cap in London, though he had an ardent tenderness for nature and her creatures that made him cry—

> A Robin-Redbreast in a cage
> Puts all heaven in a rage,

he had no popular effect on poetry. He was thought half-mad or wholly so, and only a few read his poems. He did have an effect, finally, on poets, but not until other singers had first done the work of pushing Pope aside and making simplicity and emotion and romance fashionable in verse.

Yet it must not be forgotten that Blake was the first among the poets of the late seventeen hundreds to make poems startlingly simple, beautiful, and natural. It must not be forgotten that he was the first to turn back to poetic magic and capture it. And while he has never been a popular poet, he is accepted now as one of the fascinating and mysterious figures of poetry. Perhaps in his madness or his great sanity he walked close to truth. At any rate, his drawings and poems are priceless to-day, and scholars still search for the meaning of his extraordinary life.

CHAPTER XVIII

THE POETS OF NATURE (*Continued*)

I

One day in November, 1791, while the French Revolution was raging through debates and plots and bloody executions, a tall, raw-boned young Englishman sat in Paris among the ruins of the Bastille. For some time he looked about the deserted heaps of débris, apparently hunting for something. Then he picked up a fragment of stone and put it in his pocket, as if he would like to carry away a piece of the once-terrible prison which a Paris mob had pulled down two years before in the name of liberty.

But William Wordsworth really cared nothing about a souvenir from the Bastille. He had come to get a thrill that would match a picture made by his own imagination—a picture of the People sweeping in majestic fury to beat into dust forever the cruel power of kings. There was nothing like this among the junk piles of the almost forgotten prison, so he took the bit of stone because he had come for something and there seemed to be nothing else to take!

But why had young William Wordsworth come to France at all? France was a dangerous place. One might have supposed that a graduate of Cambridge University, with just enough money to support him for a few months, would have been getting into a lawyer's office or arranging for a commission on one of His Majesty's ships, or seeking a "living" as a clergyman. Wordsworth's uncles thought so. They had been waiting all summer to know what he wanted to do in life, and he had been idling about London unable to make up his mind. Now he had told them that he was going to France to learn French and later travel about Europe as the tutor for some wealthy young Englishman. Probably they liked this idea little enough, but at least it was better than loafing.

If the uncles could have known what young Wordsworth felt instead of what he said, they would have been even more dissatisfied with him than they were. For, though he may have persuaded himself that he wanted to learn French and be a tutor, he knew well that he cared no more for that plan than for being a lawyer or a sea captain or a minister. What he really wanted was to be a poet. The advantages of going to France were that he could study and write and put off a little longer being something he did not want to be.

Meanwhile, he might get some money. His father had managed the estate of the Earl of Lonsdale, and when John Wordsworth died, the Earl owed him £4,700. The Wordsworths had been trying to collect this money, but the crusty old nobleman would never pay up. At last they had sued him and hoped now for a judgment at any time. When the payment came, William would receive a fifth of it; and £940, or $4,700, in those days would have enabled him to write poetry for years.

Wordsworth already had ideas about the kind of poetry he wanted to write. He had been born in northern England among dark forested mountains and bright lakes. In *The Prelude*, a poem about his own life, he tells how he had tramped the hills trapping woodcocks, had climbed cliffs for ravens' eggs, or in winter had heard the din of skates and voices echoing until

> Smitten, the precipices rang aloud;
> The leafless trees and every icy crag
> Tinkled like iron; while far distant hills
> Into the tumult sent an alien sound
> Of melancholy not unnoticed, while the stars
> Eastward were sparkling clear and in the west
> The orange sky of evening died away.

He shot from the throng sometimes

> To cut across the reflex of a star
> That fled, and flying still before me, gleamed
> Upon the glassy plain.

At other seasons he had rowed across the lake water to some

> Island musical with birds
> That sang and ceased not,

or had lain reading in the summer shade of great trees, and in storms had stood

> Beneath some rock, listening to notes that are
> The ghostly language of the ancient earth
> Or make their dim abode in distant winds.

All these experiences had given Wordsworth a feeling of mingled companionship, joy, reverence, and love for the earth. This seems to have grown deeper because of the loss of his mother when he was eight years old, and the sudden death of his father five years later. Wordsworth did not greatly like his grandparents and uncles, who took charge of the five children. He seems to have turned from them to the hills and forests about him, and he felt afterward that the mountain-rimmed valleys were half teachers, half parents to him. Probably he liked to think this the more as he grew older and read Rousseau. For the Frenchmen proclaimed that they were happy and fortunate men who had Nature as a guide and friend and romantic counsellor.

The love for lakes and hills went with Wordsworth to Cambridge. Though he put on a wig and silk hose and studied geometry, he felt a little like an eagle in a cage. He thrilled at the sight of Milton's room, and he often looked out of his window at the statue of the great scientist Newton

> with his prim and silent face,
> The marble index of a mind forever
> Voyaging through strange seas of Thought, alone;

but when vacation came he rushed back to Grasmere to tramp the hills of the Lake Country by himself or with his sister Dorothy.

It was during his first two vacations from Cambridge that Wordsworth began to write poetry showing a quality all its own. *An Evening Walk* was cast in formal heroic couplets, but in its careful and reverent description of the end of a day there was an attitude toward the earth entirely new in poetry. Two of the lines run:

> And, fronting the bright west, yon oak entwines
> Its darkening boughs and leaves in stronger lines.

This was a memory. Wordsworth had actually noticed the vivid sunset light on a tree, and marvelled at the glory of flame and shadow. He was only fourteen then, but was so startled that he said to himself: "I have never read any poetry about things like that. I am going to write it myself."

And at seventeen he was already trying.

But *An Evening Walk* was a crude piece of work in 1789, full of a solemn stiffness that was to follow Wordsworth all his life. Even when finally printed in 1793 it was spotted with echoes of other poets and abstract personifications like Content and Impatience and Hope—bad habits of the poetry of common sense. By this time, Wordsworth was reaching out toward more than descriptions of scenery. His *Descriptive Sketches*, also published in 1793, were indeed descriptive, but they rang with stirring lines against tyranny. They had been written in 1790, after Wordsworth and his friend Jones had passed through France on their way to walk in the Alps. At Calais, and as they journeyed southward, they had breathed the atmosphere of exhilaration and hoped-for liberty that hung over the whole land. What wonder that young Wordsworth turned to France a year later when he himself longed for freedom and yearned to write great poetry. He had not forgotten Nature then, but he had remembered that in France men were abolishing old laws and cruelties, and trying to make a government founded on Reason and Brotherhood and Freedom and, therefore, they thought, in accord with Nature herself.

I I

Wordsworth did not stay long in Paris. He went southward to Orleans and then to Blois, and here he learned French and talked about the Revolution and fell in love.

To people in England, after Wordsworth had become famous, all this meant nothing. A few of them knew that he had been abroad in his youth, but thought his second visit to France a brief trip of little importance. Wordsworth himself, as he grew older, talked less and less about it. Yet in France be became a passionate believer in Democracy, and his love for Annette Vallon and his belief in the French people profoundly influenced his life for ten years.

It was an exciting time and an exciting place, and the young Englishman and the gay-spirited, generous daughter of a French surgeon seem to have been passionately devoted to each other. They planned to get married, and it seems to have been Wordsworth's hesitation and caution that prevented marriage. He had heard nothing about his money, and he feared what his uncles would say. Finally, he went back to England to see what he could do. This hesitation seems anything but admirable, and when Annette bore him a daughter, Caroline, Wordsworth must have realized how weak a part he

had acted. From Annette's letters to William and his sister
Dorothy we see that all three hoped that Annette could come
to England. But war suddenly broke out between France and
England, and there was no further chance of travelling or writing. Annette's letters were seized by the French police.

Though now frantic, Wordsworth could do nothing, and
gradually those exciting months in France, the woman who
spoke to him of love in a foreign language, and even the child
she had borne him, must have become half unreal. In 1802,
when he could finally go to France, neither he nor Annette
wished to marry. A birth certificate and two letters seized by
the French police prove that the story of their love was real.
The Wordsworths destroyed all other letters when the poet died
in 1850. No one in England but the family had heard of Caroline. No one had recognized her in the sonnet Wordsworth
wrote after walking on the beach at Calais one autumn evening
in 1802 with the child he was seeing then for the first time. It
was almost a hundred and twenty-five years after her birth
that scholars poked about among old documents and put the
story of William and Annette together, and the world knew at
last that Wordsworth had a French daughter.

III

All during the early 1790's Wordsworth seems to have been
tortured, as he should have been, with memories of his life in
France. In one poem, *Vaudracour and Julia*, he paints the
terrible picture of a young woman and her lover thrust apart,
as he was from Annette. The young woman, a mother like
Annette, dies, and the grieving hero finally goes crazy. Again we
see Wordsworth crying his indignation against his own country
for making war on the liberty-loving French. He had become a
passionate Republican during the months he spent abroad. He
wanted neither kings nor classes nor privileges. He seems to
have been a stiff-necked Radical, proud of his Republican
opinions.

"I disapprove of monarchical and aristocratical government, however modified," he wrote to a friend, "and privileged orders of every species. . . . Hence . . . I am not among the admirers of the British Constitution."

It was a natural time for him to sympathize with the poor and the oppressed, for he now had practically no money at all, and was visiting friends or going about Wales or England as a travelling companion to some of his former college associates.

He became still more sympathetic when he read a book by a new philosopher, William Godwin, called *An Inquiry Concerning Political Justice*. Godwin argued that the world was miserable because unjust laws and customs and institutions had come to control men instead of Reason. He urged people to abolish jails and armies and churches and live by Reason alone. Wordsworth agreed with him. He knew that the Revolutionists in France had crowned Reason as a goddess, and he was convinced that, if men had Freedom and used it to follow Reason, they would be happy.

"Throw aside your books on Chemistry," he told a young student, "and study Godwin on Necessity."

He tried to order his own life by logic. But as he sought to apply his theories to everyday existence, he became perplexed and disturbed. For instance, there was his love of Nature. It wasn't reasonable. He thought he ought to forget it. Yet to forget Nature seemed impossible, and often to behave in purely reasonable ways seemed ridiculous or cruel. Finally, as he says later,

> I lost
> All feeling of conviction, and, in fine,
> Sick, wearied out with contrarieties,
> Yielded up moral questions in despair.

It might have gone badly with Wordsworth then, and with poetry. But a sick friend he had been nursing died and left him £900, begging him to go and write poetry. And soon he and Dorothy had settled at Racedown, in Dorsetshire, back of the

city of Bristol. Here a change gradually took place in Wordsworth which led him to one of the great adventures in the poetry
of the world.

IV

When he came to Racedown, he had already broken free
from Eighteenth Century formality and artificiality. Two long
poems which he wrote about this time are simple and direct and
strong in language. He seems to have been reading Shakespeare
and Milton, Burns and Cowper. His trouble was no longer in his
ability to write well, but in his perplexed soul. His love for
Liberty and his love for Nature and his belief in Reason had
not merged together. *Guilt and Sorrow* and the poetic tragedy,
The Borderers, show that Wordsworth was depressed and
troubled.

However, day by day he became less troubled. Mail came
but once a week to the remote farmhouse at Racedown, and
gradually debates and wars and Godwin's philosophy seemed
less important than they had. Walking was the only exercise,
and Wordsworth walked. He saw the silver rain spin glittering
by the window and the moon wash the valleys blue-white. He
began to feel that he had been a little foolish about Reason.
And Dorothy was with him. Her delight in beauty, her belief in
him and love for him, he says later,

> Maintained for me a saving intercourse
> With my true self; for, though bedimmed and changed
> Much, as it seemed, I was no further changed
> Than as a clouded and a waning moon.
> She whispered still that brightness would return,
> She, in the midst of all, preserved me still
> A Poet, made me seek beneath that name,
> And that alone; my office upon earth.

Then, quite as important even as Dorothy and Nature, there
were the simple country folk he could watch working and suffering and enjoying themselves about him. He saw that they did

not live by Reason. In fact, many of their noblest deeds came from simple, unreasoning emotion. All this led him, not to despise his mind, but to become convinced that logic was perhaps less important than men's feelings in pointing the way to a better world.

And then—suddenly—Samuel Taylor Coleridge appeared. Philosopher, dreamer, and poet, he and his friend Robert Southey had planned a pantisocrasy, or government by everyone, on the banks of the Susquehanna River in America. It was a scheme by which a number of young ladies and gentlemen were to join together and each work a few hours a day. This, they believed, would give them the food and clothes they needed, and the rest of the time they could write or paint or talk.

Coleridge and Southey had gone so far with the idea as to find and marry the young ladies they required—then the dream of a pantisocrasy burst and evaporated. Coleridge lingered about Bristol, where he had met his wife, and soon he heard of the tall, odd young Wordsworth living off on a lonely country road back of town. He had read Wordsworth's *Descriptive Sketches* in 1793 and had thought then he saw a great poet emerging. Now he made Wordsworth's acquaintance and soon was dropping in at Racedown frequently. He heard Wordsworth read *Guilt and Sorrow* and praised its vividness and fidelity to Nature. After listening to *The Borderers*, he wrote to Cottle, a young printer in Bristol: "His drama is absolutely wonderful," and compared it with Shakespeare.

He went about declaring that Wordsworth was a genius, and when some of his friends laughed at his enthusiasm he cried: "He strides on so far before you that he dwindles in the distance!"

Such a visitor stirred Wordsworth with his electric praise, but he did more. He brought ideas about Reason and feeling and the meaning of life. Coleridge had read and pondered and argued over all the important philosophical writings in English.

He knew Godwin's work, and for a time had admired it. But now he agreed fully with Wordsworth that Reason was unsafe to trust as a supreme guide. His dark eyes flashing and his voice deep with his belief, he told Wordsworth that, while men should, of course, use their minds, there was a greater truth in their impulses and feelings. And when Wordsworth told Coleridge of his love for nature and the wisdom he was now finding in simple folk, Coleridge agreed with him again that it was probably in the hills and woods and the seemingly ignorant people who lived among them that poets ought to hunt for the meaning of life.

Out of such talking came at last Wordsworth's idea of what poetry ought to be and do, and both poets began to write under its influence. Gradually, the poems accumulated, poems startlingly different from the verse other poets were making. They appeared in a little book called *Lyrical Ballads*, printed first in Bristol in 1798.

In the second edition of this volume, Wordsworth explained in a prose preface exactly why he was writing as he did. Poetry, he said, had grown false and artificial, and he was seeking to make it simple and true and natural again.

One thing he had tried to do was to make poems in "language really used by men." The "capricious habits of expression" which the followers of Pope had adopted made a kind of poetry which few people could like or understand. Wordsworth wished to avoid language like the following:

> In vain for me the smiling mornings shine,
> And reddening Phœbus lifts his golden fire;
> The birds in vain their amorous descants join,
> Or cheerful fields resume their green attire.

Such words were about simple things like sunrises and birds and growing grass, but what was said had been hidden in a false finery of phrasing.

But Wordsworth wanted to do more than reform the language

of poetry. He wanted to reform also the artificiality of its soul. Poets, he said, were writing about trivial things—things having little relation to real life. He proposed to write about what men *felt*. Feeling, he said, was what mattered. And the simpler the feeling, the more easily it was understood and enjoyed, and the truer the poetry. So, he said, he had written about nature and about simple people. He hoped through doing this to make his poetry direct and widely understood. He proposed also to make it joyful poetry. Poets, gifted more than other men with imagination, should be able to feel more keenly than others. They would, of course, feel sorrow. But the proof of their being genuine poets would be their ability to make sorrow a part of a final happiness that their wisdom would help them teach to men.

These ideas were very close to Rousseau and the French Revolution. The importance of feeling, of nature and natural men, came from Rousseau. The sense of the importance of ordinary people came from the democratic notions Wordsworth had got in France. But, in poetry, all that Wordsworth had to say was new and startling.

Chatterton and Cowper, Burns and Blake had published verse that was simple and spontaneous, but the literary world still worshipped Pope. So there were many, like a critic in the *Edinburgh Review*, who said that labourers and old peasant women and idiot boys had no place in poetry, and that the *Lyrical Ballads* were ridiculous.

Wordsworth and Coleridge (and Wordsworth chiefly) were not a little responsible for this. They were sometimes enthusiastic to the point of being absurd. Wordsworth, Dorothy tells us in her journal, for weeks "tired himself with seeking an epithet for cuckoo." He had little sense of humour, and in his effort to be exact would write solemnly:

> Not five yards from the mountain path,
> The Thorn you on your left espy;
> And to the left, three yards beyond, *etc.*

There was not a little of such verse in *Lyrical Ballads*, and it explains why Wordsworth, in Lord Byron's phrase, became known to many as one

> Who, both by precept and example, shows
> That prose is verse, and verse is merely prose.

This dull, flat quality was indeed a very real characteristic in Wordsworth. It was part of the solemn egoism that prevented him from even wondering if it was right for Dorothy to give up a life of her own in order to serve him; and made him unable to tell his bad verse from his good.

But if many readers found Wordsworth ridiculous, there were others, mostly enthusiastic young men and women, who caught the bigness of his purpose, and fairly shouted with joy to see the challenge made by *Lyrical Ballads* to the formal poetry of Pope.

They read with delight the poems about Simon Lee and the idiot boy and poor Susan, and (in the 1800 edition) the lovely poems on *Lucy*, who was

> A violet by a mossy stone
> Half hidden from the eye!
> Fair as a star, when only one
> Is shining in the sky.

Such verse dealt in language as clear as clear water with everyday men and women. In the long narrative poem of *Michael* it became majestic as well as beautiful.

Others must have been more stirred by Coleridge's astonishing ballad, *The Rime of the Ancient Mariner*, a tale of the sailor who shot the sacred albatross and brought down on his ship the anger of the spirit protecting the bird, and on himself a still more terrible doom. This was one of four poems by Coleridge in the *Ballads* as they appeared in 1798. It was new, direct poetry, but it went back to the older medieval ballads for its form. It was a poem of romance and of mystery and the supernatural. Its magic descriptions of the seas where

> ... ice, mast high, came floating by,
> As green as emerald.

or where under a hot and copper sky the vessel hung for days,

> As idle as a painted ship
> Upon a painted ocean,

are as marvellous now as when Coleridge first wrote them. The dead men rising at night to pull on the ropes of the ship still haunt us. The water burning blue and green and white like a witch's oils has burned in the souls of men and women and of poet after poet since *Lyrical Ballads* gave the picture of it to the world.

Then there were the poems about Nature. In these Wordsworth wrote of the birds whose every motion was a "thrill of pleasure," of the leaves hopping about in the hailstorm

> As if with pipes and music rare
> Some Robin Good-Fellow were there,
> And all those leaves, in festive glee
> Were dancing to the minstrelsy.

In *Lines Composed a Few Miles Above Tintern Abbey* he became wholly serious and made a sonorous hymn to nature that has been on the lips and in the hearts of men ever since. He told in this poem how the hills and forest had healed him when he was weary, had given him moments of reverence and insight when

> with an eye made quiet by the power
> Of harmony, and the deep power of joy,
> We see into the life of things.

He told of how he had loved nature in his early manhood:

> The sounding cataract
> Haunted me like a passion: the tall rock,
> The mountain, and the deep and gloomy wood,
> Their colours and their forms were then to me
> An appetite; a feeling and a love.

He told how with years a deeper if quieter feeling had come:

> For I have learned
> To look on Nature, not as in the hour
> Of thoughtless youth; but hearing oftentimes
> The still, sad music of humanity,
> Nor harsh nor grating, though of ample power
> To chasten and subdue. And I have felt
> A presence that disturbs me with the joy
> Of elevated thoughts; a sense sublime
> Of something far more deeply interfused,
> Whose dwelling is the light of setting suns,
> And the round ocean and the living air,
> And the blue sky, and in the mind of man;
> A motion and a spirit, that impels
> All thinking things, all objects of all thought,
> And rolls through all things.

Such poetry was great in beauty and great in originality. It shows well the new poetic style Wordsworth had made—direct and simple even when there were difficult things to say, musical and rolling like Milton's but warmer and more natural. At the same time, it said something that had never before been expressed. It told men that the earth they lived on, with its beauty and power, was not only pleasing to look at, but a great force helping to mould human lives. It expressed in verse what Rousseau had said in prose, but more sanely and nobly.

Wordsworth was only beginning his work. Moving back to his old home, Grasmere, he settled in Dove Cottage, and for nine years wrote with the same power and insight that had made *Lyrical Ballads* one of the glorious books of literary history. Coleridge rented a house near by and was often at the Wordsworth home, talking with glowing eloquence far into the night, and leaving Wordsworth stirred and excited and eager to write the following day. Finally, in 1801, the Earl of Lonsdale died and his son paid the Wordsworths what had been owing them. Wordsworth then married his sister's friend, Mary Hutchinson. These years were rich in new comfort and happiness and poetry.

Many of the poems written in this period came out in 1807.

They surpassed the *Lyrical Ballads* in skill and power. There were poems of quiet simplicity, perhaps none so exquisite as *The Solitary Reaper* with its breathless description of a highland girl singing at her work in a mountain valley:

> No Nightingale did ever chaunt
> More welcome notes to weary bands
> Of travellers in some shady haunt,
> Among Arabian sands:
> A voice so thrilling ne'er was heard
> In spring-time from the Cuckoo-bird,
> Breaking the silence of the seas
> Among the farthest Hebrides.
>
> Will no one tell me what she sings?—
> Perhaps the plaintive numbers flow
> For old, unhappy, far-off things,
> And battles long ago;
> Or is it some more humble lay,
> Familiar matter of to-day?
> Some natural sorrow, loss, or pain,
> That had been, and may be again?

The sonnets Wordsworth published then were also among the great poems in English—that on Milton, for instance, with such lines as

> Thy soul was like a Star, and dwelt apart,

or *The World Is too Much with Us*, or the lines on London as seen from Westminster Bridge in the early morning all hushed and motionless:

> Dear God! the very houses seem asleep!

The *Ode on Intimations of Immortality from Recollections of Earliest Childhood* is a tremendous song proclaiming the closeness of childhood to true and eternal things, and the majestic rightness of our natural feelings, that lead us to

> the hour
> Of splendour in the grass, of glory in the flower.

These poems still shake our hearts with the mighty simplicity of their words. At the time they appeared, their power was not fully recognized, but, after their publication, the artificial style of the Eighteenth Century never was used again in important poetry, while the whole language of English poetry has become more direct and natural, like the language of Wordsworth.

V

In addition to the poems published in 1807, Wordsworth wrote a great deal of poetry during these years at Dove Cottage which was not published until later. *The Prelude*, the story of his own growth as a poet, was a long and great poem, with magnificent descriptions of nature and the French Revolution, which he left for publication after his death. Much of *The Excursion*, the longest of all his poems, was written during the nine years between 1798 and 1807. If Wordsworth had gone on to write for another nine years as he had been writing, it is difficult to say how high he would tower to-day among the poets of the world.

But he did not go on writing in this fashion. A change had come over him that affected everything he wrote. Though, during the forty-three years he was still to live, he produced thousands on thousands of lines, carefully and sometimes finely written, he made no more great poetry. In fact, everything he wrote during this long period of maturity and old age could be burned without hurting his reputation.

Why is this so?

The story is a long one if it is told fully. Here it must be put in a few words and most of it will be told if we say that with nature and his family Wordsworth lost the fire of his early years. He thought he believed in Liberty still. But he believed so much more in the quiet England he had come to love, in noble British gentlemen like Sir George Beaumont and Sir Walter Scott, that Liberty really did not matter to him. He got a government position as stamp distributor, carrying comfortable salary with little work. He became contented with his wife and children. Away from the stir of London and Paris (though he travelled about Europe at times) he thought less about transforming men with a new ecstasy. The dull, complacent egoism which had always been in him became the master of his soul. In 1810, he had a misunderstanding with Coleridge, and another excitement passed out of his life. Coleridge, it is true, was no longer the glorious enthusiast of 1798. He was no longer making fragments of beauty like *Christabel* and *Kubla Khan*, the latter of which some think the very magic of magic poetry. Yet, when he drew out of Wordsworth's life, Wordsworth sank back more easily into a contented, unpoetic world which he was willing to praise in uninspired verse. And somewhere between 1807 and 1812 the great poet in Wordsworth died forever.

Nobody in England knew about this. As was said earlier in the chapter, Wordsworth had kept unpublished many of his early poems. They appeared from time to time, and helped to make the world feel that he was growing in greatness. Wordsworth himself thought his latter poems quite as good as any he had done. Then, too, people were just beginning to understand the true value of the poems published in 1798 and 1807. As the years passed, the tremendous power of these sank into the minds and hearts of men, and Wordsworth got the honour that was his due. Pilgrims came to the Lake Country he had celebrated in his poems, and to his house at Rydal Mount, where he lived from 1813 until his death in 1850. In 1843, when his friend Robert Southey died, Wordsworth was made Poet Laureate of England. His final years were lived in a kind of sunset glow of popular admiration and reverence.

VI

Wordsworth deserved such honour well, and though the matter-of-fact complacency with which he received it is irritating, there is a satisfaction in knowing he enjoyed his just reward. He had been the leader among poets in freeing poetry from an artificial style. Burns had written simply, but in Scotch dialect; Cowper had been too quiet to make a stir; nobody had paid much attention to Chatterton or Blake. Wordsworth had sounded the trumpet blast against artificiality and written immortal poems in simple language. He had also stood forth to proclaim that the lives of humble men and women had poetry in them. Finally, he had expressed in poetry, in a sense he had discovered and revealed, the meaning of nature in the lives of modern men.

It is true that he had got much of his philosophy of nature from Rousseau and others, but this fact is not so important as some critics have thought. Rousseau *wrote* about nature, but Wordsworth *sang* of it. To-day we know *about* Rousseau; we *know Wordsworth*. And in his poems we find something different from what poets like Virgil, Chaucer, Shakespeare, and Milton give us. These earlier singers had used nature as a background. Wordsworth showed that it was more. Like Virgil and Shakespeare, he described the earth luminously, often more luminously than they did, because he described with greater interest and more accurately and fully. But he did far more than describe. He showed that the beauty and silence and sublimity of the earth could have a meaning, a rich use for men. To nature men could go for healing, for moments

> In which the burthen of the mystery,
> In which the heavy and the weary weight
> Of all this unintelligible world
> Is lightened.

They could go to her to be taught. They could find holiness and inspiration. Wordsworth thought of the lovely and terrible aspects of the outdoor world as giving the human soul a kind of pattern for the shaping of life—

> an obscure sense
> Of possible sublimity, whereto
> With growing faculties she doth aspire.

The calm of a twilight, the rush of a torrent—we yearn for the peace of the one, the energy of the other. Nature pours into us the thirst for life in its noblest forms.

In the early 1800's men grasped eagerly at such teaching. In former centuries, they had worked in the fields, and they absorbed the strength and peace of the earth and sky without thinking. Now they were crowding more and more into cities. The earth was less in their work-a-day lives. They needed her. Wordsworth's poems took them back to the field and cloud and refreshed and renewed them. His poems also taught them to go to nature themselves. We, who live in cities even more than people did a hundred years ago, visit the hills and the sea to-day with an understanding of them that Wordsworth was the first to give fully and beautifully. As we use Shakespeare wherever we talk with men and women, we use Wordsworth whenever we meditate on a sunset or walk a mountain trail.

Because he has done this for us Wordsworth is one of the mighty among poets. It does not matter that we must laugh at his complacent and solemn egoism. It does not matter that he finished his great work at forty and made many dry and dreary poems afterward. It does not matter that he grew timid and hypocritical and solemn. What matters is that, as a younger man, he knew human life, not only its joy and freedom, but its poverty, agony, and wrong, and sang of how pain could be healed and new strength and inspiration found in the grass beneath our feet and the sun above us.

CHAPTER XIX

"CHILDE HAROLD"

I

In 1807 there appeared in the bookshops of London a volume of poems called *Hours of Idleness*. It had been written by a young lord—George Gordon, Lord Byron. He was then nineteen years of age and was still at Cambridge University.

The *Edinburgh Review* had received a copy of the book. The *Edinburgh*, as we have seen in connection with Wordsworth, was one of the most important of the magazines that were then making a business of discussing newly published works of prose and poetry. It liked to print clever and amusing articles about these, even if being clever sometimes meant being unjust. A book by a young lord seemed a good thing to make fun of, and the *Edinburgh* made fun of Byron. It said: "The poesy of this young lord belongs to the class which neither God nor man are said to permit." After laughing at some of the poems, it advised Byron to "abandon poetry and turn his talents . . . and opportunities . . . to better account."

People read and laughed. Nobody took very seriously the young lord at college whose book had been ridiculed by one of the most powerful of the literary magazines.

But early in the spring of 1809 a new book of poetry by Byron appeared called *English Bards and Scotch Reviewers*. This was a satire in the manner of Pope. It jeered at the *Edinburgh* and at those who wrote reviews or criticisms for such magazines. Wrote Byron:

> A man must serve his time at every trade
> Save censure—Critics all are ready made.

To be a critic, he said, all that was necessary was a few stale jokes from *Joe Miller's Joke Book*, with "just enough of learning to misquote," and a willingness to invent faults where none existed.

> Fear not to lie, 'twill seem a sharper hit;
> Shrink not from blasphemy, 'twill pass for wit;
> Care not for feeling—pass your proper jest,
> And stand a critic, hated but caressed.

The poem did not stop with reviewers. It slashed out at the poets who were then writing:

> Nor know we when to spare, or where to strike,
> Our Bards and Censors are so much alike.

Little and great alike felt the jab of Byron's pen—Scott, Coleridge, and Wordsworth along with obscure writers. Praising a few, Byron mocked and denounced the greater part of them. Amazed and shocked by the daring of the poem and fascinated by its skill and wit, people gabbled and gossipped and rushed off to buy copies. And they asked, "Who is this mad devil called Byron, who has written the best satire since Pope?"

Who was he?

His father was "Mad Jack" Byron, a dashing spendthrift of a noble family who had married twice and run through the money both his wives had brought him. He died when Byron, who had been born in 1788, was three years old. "Mad Jack's" wife and son had very little to live on.

So the future Lord Byron was brought up in Aberdeen, Scotland, as a rather poor boy; spoiled and scolded by his mother and sometimes taunted by her and by others because he was lame in one foot. It was a great change for him when, at the age of ten, he suddenly inherited his granduncle's title and property. And, though things went well enough for him at school, where he swam and fought fist fights and played on the school cricket team, he arrived at Cambridge a rather unusual young man.

He had read widely in poetry and history and could behave charmingly if he wanted to. On the other hand, he was fat (although only of medium height he weighed 196 lbs.), he was very sensitive, he might fly into a passion over unimportant things, and he seemed to care for nobody's opinion of what he did.

This was the young man who had startled England with a poem. And before the English had time to learn more than a few of these things about him, in fact, a month or two after the publication of *English Bards and Scotch Reviewers*, Byron shot off on travels through Portugal, Spain, Greece, and Turkey. He did not come back for two years.

11

When he returned, he brought a new poem with him, and *Childe Harold's Pilgrimage* (Cantos I and II) was published early in 1812.

England went wild over it. "I awoke one morning and found myself famous," said Byron.

Reading the first two parts of *Childe Harold* to-day, some of us may wonder what was the matter with England. The poem tells about a young man who sailed away from his native country to forget a life of drinking and love-making in visiting Portugal, Spain, Greece, and Italy—about Byron, in fact. There is no story, but merely a series of descriptions of the places Childe Harold had seen, and his thoughts and feelings on seeing them.

But in 1812 this was exciting. There were no cables under the ocean then, no telegraph, no daily news service. Spain and Greece were far and strange to England, and Byron was a kind of elegant reporter, not unlike writers to-day who go capturing gorillas in Africa or hunting the eggs of dinosaurs in China.

And the poetry he wrote was a new, vivid kind of poetry, different from the dry heroic couplets of Pope and Goldsmith. He used the Spenserian stanza, with its flavour of romance and chivalry, and pictured dangerous cities, bullfights, Turkish chieftains, Spanish ladies. The readers of chivalric romances, the lovers of wild oceans and high mountain peaks and solitary hermit cells—all those who had begun to tire of Pope, at once found in this poem the kind of poetry they had wanted.

It is true that, before Byron commenced writing, the romantic poets had already begun to change the style. But Wordsworth and Coleridge and Blake seemed so odd or strange or crazy that most readers of poetry ignored them, or were doubtful about them. Burns and Scott were popular, but Burns wrote in the Scotch dialect, and Scott confined himself to ballads and tales. Singers like Moore and Campbell played with romantic ideas, yet still kept much of the Eighteenth Century manner.

Despite the earlier poets of nature, the spirit of the heroic couplet still seemed supreme.

But Byron wrote a romantic poetry that immediately shattered the spell of common sense, and brought nature and passion, melancholy and tears into fashion. Partly he did this by mingling common sense and romance. He had proved his skill in handling the heroic couplet, and the same skill showed sufficiently in *Childe Harold* so that many lovers of Pope and rational poetry were not offended. Yet *Childe Harold* and Byron's succeeding poems were romantic. They were romantic, not only in the scenes they described, the language they used, and the poetic forms in which they were cast, but also in the personal, intense feeling which Byron brought into them. For in these poems he sang of his own grief or hate or love. He sang also of his feeling toward the ancient cities he visited, the seas he sailed, the battlefields where he saw the signs of recent fighting, the news he heard of living men and nations. Under Byron's touch, poetry, that had begun to be remote and dull, suddenly became fresh, exciting, and important again.

And Byron himself became important. He was now remarkably handsome. By starving and dieting he had dropped from 196 to only 140 lbs. He had a beautifully shaped head with auburn curls; a fine, sensitive nose, mouth, and chin; and eyes that Coleridge called "the open portals of the sun." His savage and witty attack on the reviewers, the fact that he was a lord, his travels, and his proud bearing made him a romantic person. Sometimes ladies became so excited upon seeing him that they fainted away.

Byron went about in London society, now banqueting and drinking, and now starving himself to keep from getting fat. He talked with other poets, fell in and out of love with a number of ladies, and at night and in odd times generally wrote poetry. The short poems and romances that were done in this manner are not his best work, and when we think of how they were written, we can understand why.

Byron's love affairs were becoming particularly important in his life just now. He had always been attracted to women— although perhaps not so much as he pretended to be, for he loved to make people think he was worse than he was. And now it was especially easy for him to fall in love, for every woman in England was interested in him.

He passed from loving one lady to loving another—a practice he was to continue for years. It was probably in an effort to get away from love affairs that lasted only a few months and left him sad and bitter and made much trouble for others that Byron began the most unhappy of all his love affairs—his marriage.

We can see why he hoped to find peace and stability in this marriage. Anna Isabella Milbanke was a calm, quiet young lady. She was pretty, she was sensible, she was rich, she came of a good family. She must have been a welcome relief to Byron after the excited, babbling, gushing women he usually met.

But, as we can see now, the trouble was that Miss Milbanke, or Lady Byron, as she became, was a person of very firm habits and opinions, and these were the exact opposite of most of Byron's. And although she knew Byron had been wild, she apparently hoped to reform him. She thought that the turbulent poet would quiet down, change his opinions, improve his manners, and become like any ordinary husband while still remaining a passionate poet.

But tigers do not turn into tabby cats, and Byron remained— Byron. Once married, he did not like his wife's ideas and behaviour, and often he said so. It is certain he was rude and cruel to her.

One story is that she came into the room where he was writing and that, when she asked if she were disturbing him, he answered: "Yes, most damnably."

Finally, Lady Byron seems to have feared he was crazy, and when the doctors assured her he was not, she demanded a separation. This was arranged, and Lady Byron kept the little daughter that had recently been born to them. Byron wrote several indignant poems about the separation, which the newspapers got hold of, and he became very unpopular. In a short time he left England, saying he never wanted to come back. He never did.

III

This was in April, 1816. For eight years Byron wandered about Europe. In Switzerland he met Shelley, and the two remained friends until Shelley was drowned in 1821. Byron went from Switzerland to Venice, then to Ravenna, then to Pisa, then to Genoa.

All the time he was restless, often unhappy. Byron never forgot that he was a lord, and longed to do something besides write poems—to distinguish himself in politics or other practical affairs, to establish himself as the head of a great family. He brooded on being driven from England and on being separated from his little daughter.

Perhaps he put into his poetry what he felt unable to express in other ways. At any rate, while he was worrying about being nothing but a poet, he was composing his greatest poems. In Switzerland he wrote *The Prisoner of Chillon*, and finished *Childe Harold's Pilgrimage*. In Italy he wrote a number of plays in verse and the longest and greatest of all his poems, *Don Juan*.

What did Byron give the world in such poetry? He wrote well enough so that while he lived the world thought him the finest poet in English since Shakespeare. The great German Goethe praised him. In France, Italy, and Russia many people still think Byron one of the world's supreme singers.

Partly, he was thought so great because his poetry, as we have seen, was new and different. But there was more to Byron than novelty. While we now think poets like Milton, Wordsworth, and Keats greater than Byron, the poetry Byron wrote will be read for years to come.

This is chiefly because of what Byron was. We have seen how from his boyhood he was energetic and passionate. He was constantly getting into trouble because of his pride, his enthusiasm, and his anger. But trouble only made Byron more of a fighter. Whatever faults he had, he was never a coward. And because he suffered much and because he felt so quickly and keenly, he was able to write the better of grief and love and oppression and freedom.

His time was the time of the French Revolution. It was the time of the wars Napoleon fought with the other nations of Europe. People for centuries had obeyed kings. It was a good time for someone who liked to be free to write of freedom, and Byron wrote.

For instance, there was *The Prisoner of Chillon*. This is the story of a Swiss hunter put in prison because of his religious belief. Again, in the last two cantos of *Childe Harold*, Byron wrote about Napoleon and his thirst for power, of how men made slaves of themselves when they gathered in cities and worked in dark rooms and wronged and cheated one another. He wrote also of the splendid freedom of the mountain peaks and the ocean.

In *Don Juan* he told an exciting story, better for grown-ups than for children, of a young Spanish cavalier who had adventures in many lands. He made fun with odd rhymes and witty thrusts of the silly customs in various places, and of the silly things men did everywhere. But he wrote beautiful and stirring passages also. There is the shipwreck, the description of which begins:

> Then rose from sea to sky the wild farewell—
> Then shrieked the timid, and stood still the brave,—
> Then some leaped overboard with dreadful yell,
> As eager to anticipate their grave;
> And the sea yawned around her like a hell,
> And down she sucked with her the whirling wave,
> Like one who grapples with his enemy,
> And strives to strangle him before he die.

There is the picture of two lovers at twilight, pacing the shore beside high cliffs at sunset, under

> the rosy sky
> With one star sparkling through it like an eye.

Then there is the song of

> The Isles of Greece, the Isles of Greece,
> Where burning Sappho loved and sung,
> Where grew the arts of War and Peace,
> Where Delos rose, and Phœbus sprung!
> Eternal summer gilds them yet,
> But all, except their Sun, is set.

The mountains look on Marathon—
And Marathon looks on the sea;
And musing there an hour alone,
I dreamed that Greece might still be free;
For standing on the Persians' grave
I could not deem myself a slave.

This is noble poetry. The passion and the energy in it stir us still. While Byron was more careless than a great poet should be, and never wrote with the fusion of spirit and art that Keats and Wordsworth and Shakespeare have at their best, probably no poet ever wrote with more spirit than he did. Even when he is bitter and contemptuous, we feel the movement and bravery of his writing. It quickens our blood like the sound of the ocean or the taste of mountain air. Few can read Byron without a sense of becoming prouder, braver, and freer.

Meanwhile, Byron had gone on living in Italy. Here he met the Countess Guiccioli, and with her he lived for four years, more at peace than he had been. But he could not be satisfied with riding, swimming, talking, and writing poetry. He longed for something to do that should be different and—as he thought —more important.

And just then something came for him to do. The Greeks, who for centuries had been ruled by Turkey, began to fight for their independence. Byron decided to go to Greece, to give his money and time and perhaps his life to the country whose ancient art and literature he had loved and written about.

He gathered together what he could in the way of funds, sold his yacht, and fitted out a ship to take him to Greece. Here, after arriving, he tried to help the quarrelling Greeks organize an army and plan the war they were to fight.

He worked hard. The climate along the coast where he was staying was bad, and his health was poor. Probably he had feasted and starved and made love too much. Finally he became ill. His friends begged him to go back to Italy and rest but he refused. Perhaps he was merely too proud to leave Greece when he had just begun his work there. Perhaps he wanted a little to

die. Of course, he thought of dying on the battlefield. In a
poem he wrote not long before his death he says:

> Seek out—less often sought than found—
> A soldier's grave, for thee the best;
> Then look around, and choose thy ground,
> And take thy rest.

And soon he died. It was not on a battlefield, but in bed; not
of a bullet but of a fever; yet he died working courageously for
the freedom he had always loved, mourned by the Greeks, and
admired at last even by most of those who disliked him.

His body was brought back to England. Byron had declared
he never wanted to live in England again, but he loved his
country, and later he wrote that if he should be buried abroad
he thought his spirit would return to its native land. And—he
said—if his fame should die as quickly as it had come, and

> Oblivion bar
> My name from out the temple where the dead
> Are honoured by the Nations—let it be—
> And light the laurels on a loftier head!
> And be the Spartan's epitaph on me—
> "Sparta hath many a worthier son than he!"
> Meantime I seek no sympathies, nor need—
> The thorns which I have reaped are of the tree
> I planted,—they have torn me,—and I bleed:
> I should have known what fruit would spring from such a seed.

But the English brought back Byron's body to be buried
in England, and honoured him; and the world remembers him,
whatever were his faults, as a courageous spirit and a vivid poet.

CHAPTER XX

THE SUN TREADER

Sun treader, life and light be thine forever.
—ROBERT BROWNING.

I

Once upon a time—or, to be exact, about a hundred and eighteen years ago—there was a strangely slender youth with strangely thick and waving hair, who could be as beautiful as an angel, as courageous as an angry cat, and as wise as a witch. Now this youth was very unhappy. His father had packed him off to Eton School where there were other boys who played rough games and blacked each others' eyes, where the big boys made slaveys of the little boys, and where most of them had not the least fancy for strange upstanding hair and a girlish face and lovely blue eyes. They thought the owner of these looked too much like an angel. Then he would not play games, he would not fight, and, worst of all—he would not "fag." So the Eton boys tried to make him less angelic by taunting him and pelting him with mud.

It did not help the boy they tormented that he was an angel with pride and anger in him. It was of no use at all that, when the crowd left their games to jeer at him, his face went white and his blue eyes blazed with wrath, that his body shook with rage and his shrill voice rose like a wounded animal's as "Shelley! Mad Shelley!" rang across the Eton meadows. The only help was that, when the "Shelley-baiting" was over, he could wander off with a book under his arm, follow the stream back into the silence of quiet trees, and lie on the grass. Here he could open his book and read in the pages of *Political Justice*, by the new philosopher Godwin, how all the world would be very different from Eton if its armies and priests and lawyers and policemen could be abolished, and Reason and Love made the kings of the earth. And one day, after many hot tears, the boy vowed, as he put it later in poetry:

> I will be wise,
> And just, and free, and mild, if in me lies
> Such power; for I grow weary to behold
> The selfish and the strong still tyrannize
> Without reproach or check.

There was also consolation for Percy Bysshe Shelley when he came home on holiday to his rich father's house in Sussex. Here he was a most fearsome hero to his four sisters and his little brother. He filled them with delight and terror by telling them of the old Dragon and the Headless Spectre that lived in St. Leonard's wood near by. The locked room in the attic of the Shelley house was inhabited, he said, by a terrible old alchemist with a long beard, named Cornelius Agrippa. The little sisters shuddered, too, at the Great Old Snake, who, according to their older brother, was coiled in the garden pond. And how much more they shuddered when their brother told how he had made a ring on the ground at school, and pouring alcohol into a saucer had lighted it! He had stood inside the circle and cried "Demons of the air, and of fire——" until the Master saw him and asked, "What on earth are you doing, Shelley?" and was told: "Please, sir, I'm raising the devil!"

But there was something to make the young man unhappy at home, too. His mother and his father thought he was queer. Sir Timothy Shelley, Bart., Member of Parliament, was most disturbed about the peculiar ways of his son. The fact that Bysshe, as he called his heir, wrote romantic poems and novels disturbed him. So did the wild opinions that began to be heard from the youth. And the young man, in his turn, though he realized that his father was not a bad fellow at bottom, was terribly worried because Sir Timothy was so respectable. He was worried also about himself. *He* was in danger of becoming respectable. In a few years he would have a large income. And as he roamed through the Sussex woods dreaming of a world all glorified with Reason and Love, he would cry in anguish: "What shall I do? How am I going to tolerate receiving and spending £6,000 a year (which was then worth all of $100,000 of our money) in a world where the poor are starving and all rich people are abominations?"

It was a little better for the wild and unusual young man when, in 1810, at the age of eighteen, he entered Oxford University. For a few months, in fact, he revelled in reading the philosophers Locke and Hume and Voltaire. He talked much of these and of German philosophy and romance with his new friend Jefferson Hogg. But, alas! his ideas became more and more startling. He tried to express them in a novel, *St. Irvyne, or the Rosicrucian*, a mixture of Rousseau and romantic novels and Godwin, and got into an explosive argument with his father. His young cousin, Harriet Grove, to whom he was engaged, became alarmed and refused to have anything more to do with him.

"It is monstrous that I should not be allowed to express opinions which I have reached by the most logical of arguments," he declared in bewilderment.

In his desperation, he determined to shatter the intolerance of the world, so fearful of splendid ideas about Freedom. He wrote a little pamphlet called *On the Necessity of Atheism*, and in a few days was expelled from the university.

This was a sad thing for any young man, and it was especially sad for the son of a Member of Parliament with a sudden temper. Young Mr. Shelley was ordered to come home and be reformed, and when he indignantly refused, he was left to starve in London. But his sisters supported him secretly with their pin money. Through them, too, he met a lovely girl of sixteen named Harriet Westbrook. She was willing to listen as long as a young man with an angelic face and lovely hair and a baronet for a father cared to talk to her.

She in turn told him how she was often unhappy at home and school and thought of committing suicide. Shelley explained to her that this was most wrong and unreasonable. He talked to her about Liberty and Tolerance and Love. Harriet agreed with him that these were marvellous, and that there was something old-fashioned and smothering, if not downright wicked, about Churches and Government and Marriage. But soon she became particularly unhappy at home, and the two young people dashed off to Scotland and, in spite of Shelley's philosophizing about weddings, were married themselves!

For a time, marriage was a success. Though Harriet was the daughter of an innkeeper and had little "social background," she was lovely to look at. She was enthusiastic about her husband's intention to enlighten the world on Liberty and Tolerance and Morality. She did not mind it that Sir Timothy sent his son no money, for Shelley managed to borrow all he needed. The two children rambled through the Lake Region, where the poet Robert Southey (once a great radical) tried in a fatherly way to cure Percy of Atheism and Liberty, and cursed him when Shelley refused to be cured. There was a letter to the great Godwin, and discussion by correspondence of what a rich young man could do to reform the world. Then Shelley, getting enthusiastic, went to Ireland to work for Catholic Emancipation. He had written an address to the people of Ireland. He printed it and had it distributed throughout Dublin, and he and Harriet dropped copies from their hotel balcony on to the heads of passers-by in the street.

It was about this time that Shelley began to get his thoughts and feelings about government and poverty and toleration into a long poem. As we have seen, he had written poems before. Now, however, his sympathy and sense of the wrongs of the world and his desire to do something heroic swept him into a more ambitious effort—a fervid tale of a dream in which he told how

> The iron rod of penury still compels
> Her wretched slave to bow the knee to wealth,

and how

> All things are sold: the very light of heaven
> Is venal. . . . Even love is sold.

There was something about atheism and much about nobility, there was much also of stars and moons, lightning, wind—all in the spirit of this description of Queen Mab's chariot and its flight:

> The magic car moved on—
> From the celestial hoofs
> The atmosphere in flaming sparkles flew,
> And where the burning wheels
> Eddied above the mountain's loftiest peak,
> Was traced a line of lightning.

Queen Mab was dedicated to Harriet; with the cry:

> —thou wert my purer mind;
> Thou wert the inspiration of my song;
> Thine are these early wilding flowers
> Though garlanded by me.

Queen Mab was not on the whole very good poetry, but it was strange and breathless and intense. It had taken the wild spirit of romance and the spirit of freedom that was quite as wild, and hammered them into words that leaped and shone with vitality. Nobody but Shelley's friends read the poem, but it made Shelley realize that he wanted to write more and better poems.

Meanwhile, Harriet and Shelley had come back to England, and their baby, Ianthe, was born. And suddenly Harriet lost interest in Liberty and began to buy many new hats and dresses, and insisted that Shelley should become reconciled to his difficult father and get more money. When Shelley would not give up his principles to do this, she left him for a visit to her family, and, when he sought to talk to her, was hard and cold. During this time, Shelley had met Godwin, and he now fell in love with Godwin's daughter Mary, a lovely girl of sixteen, who saw that he was a genius and thought Harriet must be wicked and cruel.

"She only wants his money," said Mary.

Shelley believed Love was greater than Marriage, and he sent for Harriet and explained what had happened. He was sure she did not love him, and he on his part loved Mary.

"I want to be your best friend," he said very gently. "Mary and I will go and live together, and if you would like to join us, we will all be happy."

It was perfectly simple to Shelley. Harriet had a different idea. She wanted her husband back, and was sorry she had been cold and hard. But Shelley was soon off to France with Mary. He shocked Harriet and he shocked Godwin, who believed in the theory of free love but did not like to see it practised on his daughter. Shelley could not understand why Godwin could not approve his theories being carried out in real life, and why Harriet should object to his leaving her when he did not love her!

II

Much happened in the next two years. Harriet, discouraged and melancholy, finally committed suicide. Shelley wrote poetry and grieved over Harriet's death and married Mary. He tried to get the custody of the two children born to Harriet and him, but was pictured in court as immoral and an atheist. The Lord Chancellor finally refused Shelley's plea. He said:

This is a case in which a father has demonstrated that he must and does deem it to be a matter of duty to recommend opinions and habits . . . which the law calls upon me to consider as immoral and vicious . . . I cannot, therefore, in these conditions, entrust him with the guardianship of these children

This was on March 27, 1817. Shelley remained in England awhile, feeling like an outcast. He brooded over his misfortunes and began to fear that Mary's children (there were now two) might also be taken from him. Finally, in the spring of 1818, he went to Italy to live. He was never to return to England.

The poetry he had written during this time was important. First had come *Alastor*, composed in the spring of 1815. It was a different and much better poem than *Queen Mab*. The opening shows that Shelley had been reading Wordsworth and admiring the sublime calm of poems like *Tintern Abbey*. But the ecstasy of Shelley's lines was closer to the fervour of Coleridge than to the rather solid beauty of Wordsworth. It had also the intenser romantic feeling which his reading of novels and philosophy and his own darting imagination had supplied:

> Earth, ocean, air, beloved brotherhood!
> If our great Mother has imbued my soul
> With aught of natural piety to feel
> Your love, and recompense the boon with mine;
> If dewy morn, and odorous noon, and even,
> With sunset and its gorgeous ministers,
> And solemn midnight's tingling silentness;
> If autumn's hollow sighs in the sere wood,
> And winter robing with pure snow and crowns
> Of starry ice the gray grass and bare boughs;
> If spring's voluptuous pantings when she breathes
> Her first sweet kisses,—have been dear to me;
> If no bright bird, insect, or gentle beast
> I consciously have injured, but still loved
> And cherished these my kindred; then forgive
> This boast, beloved brethren, and withdraw
> No portion of your wonted favour now!

The story of *Alastor* is that of a "youth of uncorrupted feelings and adventurous genius" who goes forth on a quest for a vision—a woman—of divine beauty. It is to some extent an allegory of Shelley's own spiritual search:

> By solemn vision and bright silver dream
> His infancy was nurtured. Every sight
> And sound from the vast earth and ambient air

Sent to his heart its choicest impulses.
The fountains of divine philosophy
Fled not his thirsting lips, and all of great,
Or good, or lovely, which the sacred past
In truth or fable consecrates, he felt
And knew. When early youth had passed, he left
His cold fireside and alienated home
To seek strange truths in undiscovered lands.

How the youth wandered far, passing through Arabia and under

the ethereal cliffs
Of Caucasus, whose icy summits shone
Among the stars like sunlight,

and after an incredible voyage upon an incredible river died of too much devotion to his pale dream, tells us not a little of the poet's state of mind at the time he wrote. But aside from this, the story is nothing and the poetry all. For in the frosty, electric, gorgeous, ecstatic lines speaks the Sun Treader, under whose touch the spirit of romantic yearning and eager curiosity almost literally bursts into flaming words. The very night sparkles tremendously:

Evening came on;
The beams of sunset hung their rainbow hues
High 'mid the shifting domes of sheeted spray
That canopied his path o'er the waste deep;
Twilight, ascending slowly from the east,
Entwined in duskier wreaths her braided locks
O'er the fair front and radiant eyes of Day;
Night followed, clad with stars.

Again, there flashes

. . . the Spirit of Wind,
With lightning eyes, and eager breath, and feet
Disturbing not the drifted snow. . . .

The very silence is full of sharpness and suppressed energy, whether it takes shape as

A pool of treacherous and tremendous calm,

or in

> The cold white light of morning, the blue moon
> Low in the west, the clear and garish hills,
> The distinct valley and the vacant woods.

The Revolt of Islam, Shelley's next poem, was written in 1817, during his residence at Marlow, a town largely inhabited by poor lace-makers. Shelley was often busy giving them blankets and food, and his new work, a long symbolical tale in verse, resembled *Queen Mab* in its keen feeling for human wrong. Beautiful as were many of its Spenserian stanzas, the poem is not so fine as *Alastor*, nor so good as much that Shelley was still to do.

But by the time he had finished *The Revolt of Islam*, Shelley had grown in skill and understanding to a point where he was ready to do his best work. Few in England had read his verse or were to read it for many years. Shelley found this discouraging. "Nothing," he declared later, "is more difficult and unwelcome than to write without a confidence of finding readers." But while he was abroad in 1816 he had met Lord Byron, and became his fast friend. And in Italy, where he was to live, he found other Englishmen—admirers who saw his genius. One of them, Trelawney, tells a story that shows how, despite all the suffering Shelley had sustained in the preceding years, he still remained an idealistic, incredible child.

I was bathing one day in a deep pool in the Arno, and astonished the Poet by performing a series of aquatic gymnastics, which I had learnt from natives of the South Seas. On my coming out, whilst dressing, Shelley said, mournfully:

"Why can't I swim? It seems so very easy."

I answered, "Because you think you can't. If you determine, you will; take a header off this bank, and when you rise turn on your back, you will float like a duck; but you must reverse the arch in your spine, for it's now bent the wrong way."

He doffed his jacket and trousers, kicked off his shoes and socks, and plunged in; and there he lay stretched out on the bottom like a conger eel, not making the least effort to struggle or save himself. He would have been drowned if I had not instantly fished him out. When he recovered his breath, he said:

"I always find the bottom of the well, and they say Truth lies there. In another moment I should have found it, and you would have found an empty shell. It is an easy way of getting rid of the body."

Byron and Shelley got on well together, though they were very different. Both were poets of revolt, both were wealthy. Both loved solitude and rebellion. But Byron was a man of the world—now bitter, now sardonic, now gay, now black as a storm cloud. He loved the pure, lofty-minded, eerie beauty of Shelley's nature. Shelley admired Byron's courage and passion and knowledge of the world. He lectured "Childe Harold" on his love affairs, and Byron laughed at Shelley's idealism. He joked with him also on his gliding walk and wild gestures.

The story goes that Shelley was reading Goethe's *Faust* to Byron. In this great poetic drama, Mephistopheles the Tempter calls the original serpent of the Garden of Eden "My Aunt—the renowned Snake." Shelley was translating from the German, and kept saying over and over passages out of *Faust* (to infect Byron with moral ardour, as he hoped). When he reached that part about "My Aunt—the renowned Snake," Byron chuckled, "Then you are her nephew," and thereafter he would refer to Shelley as the Snake. And indeed the bright eyes, the lithe figure, the inaudible movements might well have supported, if they did not suggest, the simile. But perhaps Byron was the actual Snake.

III

In Italy, first near Venice in Byron's villa, later at Naples, later still in his permanent home at Leghorn, Shelley wrote the poetry by which he is chiefly remembered. He was never far from sorrow. First his daughter Clara died, later his son William. He cried in his *Stanzas Written in Dejection, Near Naples:*

> Alas! I have nor hope nor health,
>   Nor peace within nor calm around,
> Nor that content surpassing wealth
>   The sage in meditation found,

and asserted that

> I could lie down like a tired child,
>   And weep away the life of care
>   Which I have borne and yet must bear,
> Till death like sleep might steal on me,
>   And I might feel in the warm air
> My cheek grow cold, and hear the sea
> Breathe o'er my dying brain its last monotony.

It was not to be so long until the sea would grant his wish, but in the meantime he wrote exquisite poetry. There was the splendid *Prometheus Unbound*. This lyrical drama repeated the theme of *The Revolt of Islam*, but on a grander scale. Borrowing the story of the Fire-Giver from Greek tragedy, Shelley represents in Prometheus the passion of humanity, or the aspiring human mind, defying Jupiter, that despotic authority which keeps men in chains.

The first scene discovers Prometheus nailed to his

> . . . wall of eagle-baffling mountain,
>   Black, wintry, dead, unmeasured. . . .

It is night. He soliloquizes:

> The crawling glaciers pierce me with the spears
> Of their moon-freezing crystals; the bright chains
> Eat with their burning cold into my bones. . . .

And the Vulture:

> Heaven's wingèd hound, polluting from thy lips
> His beak in poison not his own, tears up
> My heart. . . .

But the hour of liberation is at hand. Asia, the Spirit of that unspeakable, unattainable ecstasy which Shelley always pursued, the "shadow of beauty unbeheld," is on her way to meet Prometheus. Jupiter is dethroned. Tyranny is dead. The shackles are stricken from Prometheus as he is united to Asia. In other words, the mind of man is joined in wedlock to his highest and holiest aspirations, and universal love

> ... folds over the world its healing wings.

Shelley poured so much of himself into this noble drama, so much of his personal sorrow and prophetic hope that the whole poem is his testament to the world. Again and again we see his thin face under the blowing wings of his hair, his sea-lit eyes darkened with the pain of Prometheus, that same pain which, the following year of 1821, should be renewed for the death of Keats in one of the greatest elegies in the language, the *Adonais:*

> See, on the silken fringe of his fair eyes
> A tear some Dream has loosened from his brain!
> Lost angel of a ruined Paradise!

Shelley knew Keats but little. Yet between Shelley and Keats, as between Shelley and Byron, a swift sympathy kindled in the brief correspondence which the two poets had. Keats perhaps saw less in Shelley than Shelley saw in him. In 1820 Shelley sent him a copy of his poetic tragedy, *The Cenci*, from Italy. Keats thought that it sometimes flowed too carelessly, and bade Shelley "load every rift with ore." This may have seemed presumptuous from a younger poet to an older, from the son of a livery-stable owner to the son of a baronet, but Shelley never seems to have resented the well-intended and just advice. He saw Keats's "transcendent genius," and put its immortal brightness into an immortal poem.

Men and women of flesh and blood in passionate action he touched once and once only in *The Cenci* (1820), a tragedy whose five acts were founded on an actual account of the horrors which ended with the fall of the House of Cenci at Rome in 1599. And yet Shelley said of what is probably the finest English tragedy since Shakespeare: "I don't think much of it. My object was to see how I could succeed in describing passions I have never felt."

A number of other poems, long and short, were being written by Shelley between 1818 and 1822. There were *The Witch of Atlas*, *Œdipus Tyrannus*, *Epipsychidion*, and his many lyrics. Some of these were published soon after they were written, others after Shelley's death. His passion for liberty and justice and love beats in many of them. And throughout there glows the incandescent poetical quality which was to be supremely Shelley's own.

It is difficult to describe this accurately, though any reader of Shelley can feel it. It is in one sense a kind of poetic ecstasy, an ability to make the brightest and swiftest beauty that any poet has ever made. Francis Thompson, himself a poet, has described this ecstatic side of Shelley:

The universe is his box of toys. He dabbles his fingers in the day-fall. He is gold-dusty with tumbling amidst the stars. He makes bright mischief with the moon. The meteors nuzzle their noses in his hand. He teases into growling the kennelled thunder, and laughs at the shaking of its fiery chain. He dances in and out of the gates of heaven; its floor is littered with his broken fancies. He runs wild over the fields of ether. He chases the rolling world. He gets between the feet of the horses of the sun. He stands in the lap of patient Nature, and twines her loosened tresses after a hundred wilful fashions, to see how she will look nicest in his song.

This is a glorious description, and true as far as it goes. Many have accepted it as the full picture of Shelley.

"Don't worry about his ideas," they say. "He had none of any importance. He was just a maker of deliciously beautiful music."

This is not only an exaggeration—it is untrue. Shelley was indeed an exquisite music maker. His verse is as sincere and spontaneous as a bird's rapture, and as careless. He mounts naturally, swiftly, liquidly with his own skylark, singing

In the golden lightning
Of the sunken sun,

mysterious in his

> Profuse strains of unpremeditated art.

He is the skylark of poets. It is true that he had no message of logic for the world. Yet to say that Shelley had no ideas or message is wholly to misunderstand him.

He was not a profound philosopher. But, aflame with imagination, he saw and felt human life keenly. And though he himself wrote, "Didactic poetry is my abhorrence," he wanted to express, and succeeded in expressing, the hatefulness of tyranny, the glory of freedom, the beauty of tenderness and tolerance. He has left pictures of wrong that prove him no "ineffectual angel." For instance, when a peaceable mass meeting on parliamentary reform at Manchester was charged by three hundred hussars in the fall of 1819, and six persons killed, he made in *The Mask of Anarchy* a fiery and compassionate outburst against the government and statesmen who could permit such cruel violence. Sometimes the lines are fiercely literal:

> I met Murder on the way—
> He had a mask like Castlereagh. . . .

Again, they outdo Dante in their hot glare of hatred:

> Very smooth he looked, yet grim;
> Seven bloodhounds followed him.
>
> All were fat; and well they might
> Be in admirable plight,
> For one by one, and two by two
> He tossed them human hearts to chew,
> Which from his wide cloak he drew.

This poetry has remained ever since its writing a searing cry of protest, stirring the hearts of thoughtful men and women against wanton violence. And a little poem found among Shelley's papers after his death is a lasting expression of hurt and protest against all injustice:

A DIRGE

Rough wind, that moanest loud
  Grief too sad for song;
Wild wind, when sullen cloud
  Knells all the night long;
Sad storm, whose tears are vain,
Bare woods whose branches strain,
Deep caves and dreary main,—
  Wail, for the world's wrong.

But Shelley's passion and ideas affected his poetry in a greater way than through the production of such particular poems of revolt. They had a greater influence than can be shown in any passages about liberty and religious freedom in other more general poems. They are chiefly important, not because they shine here and there as glorious propaganda, but because they are the heart that reddens the very blood stream of Shelley's verse, the dynamo that feeds it the electric energy which is only Shelley's. Shelley loved beauty, but he never would have made the intense beauty he achieved if it had not been for his insatiable hunger for right and freedom. He strikes off golden words that seem pure loveliness and truth. That simile, perhaps the greatest of all similes, for instance:

Life, like a dome of many-coloured glass,
Stains the white radiance of Eternity.

But in much of his best work the pulse of yearning for freedom is strong. The first lines of *Ode to the West Wind*, the greatest of all his lyrics, tingles with it:

O wild West Wind, thou breath of Autumn's being,
Thou, from whose unseen presence the leaves dead
Are driven, like ghosts from an enchanter fleeing,

Yellow, and black, and pale, and hectic red,
Pestilence-stricken multitudes: O thou,
Who chariotest to their dark wintry bed—

and all the magnificence which follows. For this invocation leads to the final cry:

> Drive my dead thoughts over the universe
> Like withered leaves to quicken a new birth!
> And, by the incantation of this verse,
>
> Scatter, as from an unextinguished hearth,
> Ashes and sparks, my words among mankind!
> Be through my lips to unawakened earth
>
> The trumpet of a prophecy! O Wind,
> If Winter comes, can Spring be far behind?

And although the great artistic ability of Shelley must not for a moment be forgotten, even in the poems where he seems to be sheer music or beauty the tumult of his intellectual eagerness persists. It is true that he literally thinks in metaphor, that at times he seems to have a lark in his heart and throat. Yet the dazzling light of his creative energy that makes his verse the swiftest of all poetry is always associated closely with his passion for freedom.

He sees the soaring skylark singing

> Till the world is wrought
> To sympathy with hopes and fears it heeded not.

Even in his music that is tired and tender the intensity of his nature gleams:

> Swiftly walk o'er the western wave,
> Spirit of Night!
> Out of the misty eastern cave,
> Where all the long and lone daylight
> Thou wovest dreams of joy and fear,
> Which make thee terrible and dear,—
> Swift be thy flight!
>
> Wrap thy form in a mantle gray,
> Star-inwrought!
> Blind with thine hair the eyes of Day;
> Kiss her until she be wearied out;
> Then wander o'er city, and sea, and land,
> Touching all with thine opiate wand—
> Come, long-sought!

"Swiftly walk," "terrible and dear," "swift be thy flight," "star-inwrought," "blind with thine hair the eyes of Day"— they are sparks from the restless spirit that would not be caged himself and tried to sing the world into a love of freedom.

And through the beauty of his poetry Shelley planted in the hearts of men a bright restlessness that still fires youth, urging it to some higher and purer endeavour.

IV

Shelley was happy with Mary. She understood him well, though she was often jealous of his idealistic friendships with numerous ladies and tried sometimes to tame his wildness. He wrote, he read Greek and Italian, he talked gloriously with friends. In the spring of 1822 he acquired a little sailboat which he named the *Ariel*. On July 8, 1822, he set off with his friend Williams to meet Leigh Hunt, who was due to arrive at Leghorn. There was a sudden storm—winds that lunged at a sea of lead, drops of rain that seemed the size of a man's fist, a black sky that cracked and let through crooked lightning. And after it— no trace of Shelley or the *Ariel*.

Two weeks later the shell of him, mutilated by fishes, was cast on the beach. Two books in the pockets of his clothes showed who he was. Perhaps in the black swirl of the storm, as he hurriedly shoved his beloved *Sophocles* into one pocket of his jacket and doubled back the unfinished page of Keats before ramming the volume into the other pocket—perhaps in that instant the breath of the Eternal whose strength he had called upon in his *Adonais* descended in a flash and seized him by the hair. Had he, who had looked for truth at the bottom of the well, found it at last? Was the search over and the high heart and its questionings fully answered, quieted like a child from whom the fever goes?

We only know that the wanderer ceased from wandering. His burning eyes explored no more the pyramids of books and piles of philosophy for a medicine that would heal the world. Over now, all over.

Or was it? There is a later scene. Trelawney and Byron and others come back to the beach to unearth and burn the hastily buried body. The funeral pyre is prepared. The strong Italian sunlight hammers on the tawny sand and the dark violet sea that is now calm enough for a boat of white paper. Beyond the greenish black pines are the snow-paved Apennines and the crystal cloud-fleeced sky. Such a day as Shelley would have loved. Silence in the knot of eager-eyed children. The soldiers dig an hour for the body. A mattock strikes with a dull thud on the skull. Byron shudders and remembers how Shelley, during a storm on Lake Leman, crossed his arms calmly. So like him. The body is washed with incense, oil, salt, and wine. The pyre is lighted. Its intense heat throbs like a pulse. At the end of three hours Shelley's heart defies the flames. Trelawney snatches it out of the furnace, badly burning his hand. Byron turns and swims fiercely away. Trelawney puts the ashes into a casket lined with black velvet. But—what has he kept with the ashes? Was there something that escaped? What hissed out of them with a sound as of wings? What is that swiftly diminishing speck in the sky—like *his* skylark?

> Higher still and higher
> From the earth thou springest
> Like a cloud of fire;
> The blue deep thou wingest,
> And singing still dost soar, and soaring ever singest.

CHAPTER XXI

"BEAUTY IS TRUTH, TRUTH BEAUTY"

I

On Christmas Eve in 1795, the horses stabled at the Swan and Hoop in London crunched their holiday oats and rubbed their noses on the worn mangers, while in the rooms above a mother held her first-born child to the lamplight and called the boy's father to see him smile—"smiling at seven weeks!" The hostlers below stairs looked forward to the time when little John Keats would take his first tottering steps holding on to a grimy hand. But little John Keats, when he did get to running around, must have created quite a rumpus, for he was a hot-tempered, irrepressible, and wilful child. Perhaps he was spoiled not a little, for his mother, whom he greatly resembled, adored him. John's mother was a passionate, gay, vivacious woman and John inherited her disposition but in a finer way.

Thomas Keats was head hostler of the Swan and Hoop. He was ambitious to get along in the world, and his common sense and competence were so noteworthy that Mr. Jennings, his father-in-law, left the business to him. The new owner prospered. John was packed off to school at Enfield, a little town about ten miles from London.

Thomas Keats came to a sudden end, falling from his horse and fracturing his skull. Mrs. Keats found herself helpless, and no doubt she was an appealing young widow, even if she did own a fine livery stable—for within a year she married a Mr. Rawlings. The marriage was unhappy, and Mrs. Rawlings left both the new husband and the livery stable, and with her children, who were now four—George, Tom, and Fanny had been born by that time—went to her mother's home.

At school, John was no prodigy in his studies, but he was a terror with his fists. His schoolfellows declared that "fighting was meat and drink to him" and that he had "a terrier-like resoluteness." He seemed destined to be anything but a poet. He would keep the boys pop-eyed with tall tales of a soldier-uncle on his mother's side of the family who was his hero. Or he would go for the usher who had boxed his brother Tom's ears. Of a keenly affectionate and morbidly sensitive disposition, he would often work himself sick with unfounded suspicions of his companions. They have testified that he was "always in extremes," now violent, now generous, "in passions of tears or outrageous fits of laughter." They liked the lad and admired his fiery pluck.

As for his mother, she idolized him, as he did her. When he came home for the holidays, she fell under the spell of his alternating moods of poetic depression and prankish merriment. And once, we hear, when Mrs. Keats was ill and quiet had been ordered, John found an old sword and, mounting guard in front of her door, would permit no one to pass!

Imagine, then, how a boy of fifteen, passionate in all things, susceptible beyond most to suffering, afflicted, in his own words, with "a horrid morbidity of temperament"—imagine how such a boy would recoil from the shock of death. We can understand what happened to Keats when, in 1810, his mother died. If he became more moody than ever, if he sulked and was inconsolable, hiding in a corner under the teacher's desk and spurning all comfort from teacher or friend, we can understand.

And we can understand all the more why, having suddenly and passionately discovered literature two years before, he should now turn in his despair to the glory and the forgetfulness that books could give. He read as intensely as he had fought and brooded. He translated Virgil's Æneid. He dipped into Shakespeare. Most important of all, though he knew no Greek, he found out a way to the golden myths of Greece through certain anthologies which he came upon in the school library. Gods, nymphs, and heroes took fire in him! When he left school in 1810, he had achieved the honour of winning a prize book— the *Dictionary of Merchandise!*

But he had achieved other "merchandise" far more essential to his work as a poet. For if ever anybody was doomed to be a poet and all poet, it was John Keats. And if ever that instinct by which genius smells out the food it most requires for its growth could be trusted, it was in the case of young Keats. But we must not forget his friend, the headmaster's son, Charles Cowden Clarke.

For it was he who helped Keats find himself, first in school and then out of it, after Keats had been apprenticed by his guardian to Mr. Hammond, surgeon at Edmonton. John had to run errands, clean the stable, help in the house, and hold the doctor's horse. But while the doctor was assisting some loud-lunged fellow into the world, John was daydreaming about last week's visit with the Clarkes (Enfield was only three or four miles away). Very likely he was murmuring some gorgeous passage out of the *Faery Queen* that he and Clarke had read aloud. For his friend had introduced Keats to the poetry of Spenser. This "discovery" of a new world of beauty in the one poet whose genius most richly answered his own was an event of the highest poetic significance. It determined that Keats should be a poet. His passionately romantic spirit went "ramping" through the luxurious poem "as a young horse would through a spring meadow." We have it on good authority that his first attempt at verse was an *Imitation of Spenser.* Another early effort with a

long proud name, *Specimen of an Induction to a Poem*, is full of
boyish delight in chivalry and armour and "large white plumes
dancing," and pays tribute to the master:

> Spenser! thy brows are archèd, open, kind,
> And come like a clear sunrise to my mind.

But we have forgotten Dr. Hammond's horse. We dare say
that horse has been pricking up his domestic ears in amazement
at the surgeon's young assistant mouthing

> Spenserian vowels that elope with ease.

And that assistant, doubtless, lost as he was in revery, had his
hand on the bridle of an altogether different horse, a horse with
wings who took him galloping among Olympian cities and cedar
groves and divinely beautiful creatures who did not look in the
least like Dr. Hammond.

At any rate, Dr. Hammond was not entirely pleased with his
assistant. He let Keats go. And so, at nineteen, we find the poet
finishing his last year in a London hospital. A fellow student,
recalling Keats at this time, tells us that

... his passion, if I may so call it, for poetry was soon manifested. He attended
lectures and went through the usual routine, but he had no desire to excel in
that pursuit. ... He was called by his fellow students "little Keats," being at
his full growth no more than five feet high. ... In a room, he was always at the
window, peering into space, so that the window-seat was spoken of by his
comrades as Keats's place. ... In the lecture room he seemed to sit apart and
to be absorbed in something else. ...

To the dumbfounding of his fellow students, Keats passed
his examinations in July, 1815, and got himself a certificate to
practise as an Apothecary in the Country. No doubt he rolled
many a luscious phrase on his tongue or even hummed a melody
of Mozart or Handel that Clarke had played for him when he
should have been engrossed in anatomy, and walked the hospital wards accompanied by his beloved Spenser or Chaucer

or Shakespeare or Milton. For though he had an apothecary's diploma, his energy and purpose were called elsewhere. "The other day," he informs Clarke, "during the lecture, there came a sunbeam into the room, and with it a whole troop of creatures floating in a ray; and I was off with them to Oberon and fairyland." And not only during a lecture, but even during an operation! "My last operation," says he, "was the opening of a man's temporal artery. I did it with the utmost nicety, but reflecting on what passed through my mind at the time, my dexterity seemed a miracle, and I never took up the lancet again."

A miracle indeed! Let us congratulate ourselves that *we* were not that man with the artery, dexterity or no dexterity. And let us congratulate ourselves in the name of all poetry lovers that this amazing young person turned to another kind of surgery, dropping the lancet for the quill. For this youth whose headlong eagerness, we remember, took him from battles to books which he devoured before, during, and after school hours at Enfield (going so far as to eat his meals from behind them!)—this same youth was now revelling in new friends like Leigh Hunt, discovering with Clarke old friends in Homer through the spirited translation by the Elizabethen poet Chapman, and—writing his own poetry! He was writing pretty much the sort of stuff all young poets write, verses *To Some Ladies* who had "elegant, pure, and aërial minds," verses to the same ladies *On Receiving a Curious Shell*, etc., verses *To Hope*, an ode, a *Hymn to Apollo*. He was writing poem letters to his friends or showing his latest poem to his brothers. We get a picture in a sonnet of Keats as he comes away from Hunt's little cottage, "brimful of the friendliness" he had found there, with Milton's Lycidas and Petrarch's Laura dwindling the miles back to London through the cool bleak air. We get a warming glimpse of Keats and Clarke sitting up through the night reading Chapman's Homer, and in the morning's post we glow with Clarke over that glorious sonnet, *On First Looking into Chapman's Homer*. And we feel with

Clarke concerning his poet friend as Keats felt on discovering Homer:

> . . . like some watcher of the skies
> When a new planet swims into his ken;
> Or like stout Cortez when with eagle eyes
> He star'd at the Pacific—and all his men
> Look'd at each other with a wild surmise—
> Silent, upon a peak in Darien.

Nor is ours "a wild surmise," as we shall see. For one day in 1817 we find a slim drab-coloured book with the back label declaring beyond a doubt "Keats's Poems Price 6s"—and we find this thin first volume, containing the short poems we have mentioned and a few others, becoming more and more drab with dust and neglect. The public and critics ignored it; ignored that joyous little cry of delight in nature, beginning "I stood tip-toe upon a little hill"; ignored that more important statement of his purpose as a poet in *Sleep and Poetry*. Perhaps the dedication to Leigh Hunt, who had been put in prison for certain unflattering remarks on the Prince of Wales, was to blame. To be sure, the slender book was not lacking in a lushness and sentimentality of phrase that went with youth. But there were darting accuracies of observation like

> A little noiseless noise among the leaves,
> Born of the very sigh that silence heaves

and

> . . . sweet peas, on tip-toe for a flight

and

> . . . the moon lifting her silver rim
> Above a cloud, and with a gradual swim
> Coming into the blue with all her light.

And there was that brave programme of his ideals as a poet in *Sleep and Poetry*, which he placed at the end of his book:

> O for ten years, that I may overwhelm
> Myself in poesy; so I may do the deed
> That my own soul has to itself decreed.
>
> . . . .
>
> First the realm I'll pass
> Of Flora, and old Pan: sleep in the grass,
> Feed upon apples red, and strawberries,
> And choose each pleasure that my fancy sees.

But this is only the first phase:

> And can I ever bid these joys farewell?
> Yes, I must pass them for a nobler life,
> Where I may find the agonies, the strife
> Of human hearts. . . .

He scorns the school of Pope:

> They sway'd about upon a rocking horse,
> And thought it Pegasus.

And yet, from this fervent championing of the imagination against artifice, he wanders off to versify the walls of his room. He burns with the conviction that he is a poet, that he has a mission. The hope of poems to come brings the blood to his head. But for the moment what he writes is rather the spontaneous outpouring of a nature overwrought with beauty than the curbed and critical work of an artist.

These poems, then, were hints of a strength that was gathering itself for a leap. A year later, 1818, Keats took that leap with his long narrative poem *Endymion*. And the *Quarterly* and *Blackwood's*, periodicals which hated Hunt's politics and his "Cockney school" of poets, pounced on Keats. They called him "a starved apothecary," "an amiable but infatuated bardling," bidding him back to his pots! We know now that the coarseness and cruelty of these attacks did not cause Keats's early death, though they may well have hastened it. Shelley was mistaken when he called the reviewers murderers. In spite of what Byron said about the author of *Endymion* being "snuffed out by an article," Keats was not snuffed out. There was too much fire and fight in him for that—and too much poetry. Of course, the romantic and sensitive young poet was hurt, terribly hurt. He would not have been a poet or Keats had he not felt the reviews bitterly. But, the first shock over, he showed the stuff there was in him. His power of rebound was great. He had a sense of humour, as his letters prove again and again. He knew the true from the false. He himself spoke of *Endymion* as "a feverish attempt rather than a deed accomplished." He wanted to fling it in the middle of the Sahara Desert.

> . . . I begin to get acquainted with my own strength and weakness [he said]. Praise or blame has but a momentary effect on the man whose love of beauty in the abstract makes him a severe critic of his own works. . . . It [*Endymion*] is as good as I had power to make it by myself. Had I . . . trembled over every page, it would not have been written; for it is not in my nature to fumble. I will write independently. I have written independently *without judgment*. I may write independently and *with judgment*, hereafter. The Genius of Poetry must work out its own salvation in a man. . . . In *Endymion* I leaped head-long into the sea, and thereby have become better acquainted with the sound-ings, the quicksands, and the rocks, than if I had stayed upon the green shore, and piped a silly pipe, and took tea and comfortable advice. I was never afraid of failure; for I would sooner fail than not be among the greatest.

This is what Keats believed. What he felt was different. Poetry was his very life's blood. He poured himself hot and throbbing into every poem he wrote. He had nothing of Words-worth's complacency. Even now, as we turn the pages of *Endymion*, they are still warm, with awareness of

> . . . a whispering blade
> Of grass, a wailful gnat, a bee bustling
> Down in the blue-bells. . . .

They vibrate to our fingers with the flush of his exquisite senses and the dance of his electrical nerves, dizzy and distraught with

> . . . visions all about my sight
> Of colours, wings, and bursts of spangly light;
> The which became more strange, and strange, and dim,
> And then were gulph'd in a tumultuous swim.

In these lines we touch the young poet's burning hand and feel, as Coleridge did, that there was death in that hand. And we know why Keats felt that he must do his work swiftly.

So *Endymion* remains alive and important. Aside from anything else, it is the most remarkable hugger-mugger of classical, medieval, and miscellaneous booty that ever a young poet emptied out of his head. It shows how fiercely he was foraging, how passionately Keats kept his contacts with glamorous books, people going and coming, clouds, flowers, trees, water, and moonlight. It is a young poet's adventure in the luxury of details. It is a boy's book in its chaos, its colour, its heat, its pedantry, its mistakes, and its rush. It is charged with that magic which, like marsh phosphor, plays over and under the surface and eludes capture. Most of all, it sets forth in its opening lines Keats's credo of poetic faith:

> A thing of beauty is a joy forever.

That credo he never modified. He simply added to it later:

> Beauty is truth, truth beauty.

II

Keats once exclaimed: "Oh, that something fortunate had ever happened to me or my brothers!" Ill fortune stalked relentlessly after the Keats boys: Tom, gentle and affectionate, died of tuberculosis in December, 1818; George was having a hard time in America, whither he had sailed with his bride; and John was alone in London. Keats's letters to his little sister whom he charges: "Now, Fanny, you must write soon—and write all you think about, never mind what—only let me have a good deal of your writing," are all full of the most engaging nonsense such as this tid-bit:

> I got to the stage half an hour before it set out and counted the buns and tarts in a Pastry-Cook's window and was just beginning with the Jellies.

And again our mouths water:

I should like now to promenade 'round your Gardens—apple-tasting—
pear-tasting—plum-sucking—apricot-nibbling—peach-scrunching—necta-
rine-sucking and melon-carving. I also have a great feeling for antiquated
cherries full of sugar cracks—and a white currant tree kept for company. I admire lolling on a lawn by a water-lilied pond to eat white currants and see
goldfish: and go to the Fair in the Evening if I'm good. There is not hope for
that—one is sure to get into some mess before evening.

Then this April foolery:

I hope you have a good store of double violets—I think they are the Princesses of flowers, and in a shower of rain, almost as fine as barley-sugar drops
are to a schoolboy's tongue.

In John Keats's need for intimate companionship, Charles
Brown invited him to share his half of a double house. Here, in
1819, John Keats met Fanny Brawne and loved Fanny Brawne,
and all emotions became intensified: things sweet became more
sweet and things bitter became more bitter.

Keats was an unhappy lover. He belonged to the romantic
Italian school of lovers, and here he was, living in the early
strait-laced Nineteenth Century, sick in body and soul, hopelessly in debt and out of pocket, with no prospects of being able
to set up housekeeping in the approved fashion.

Keats poured out the tumult and torment of his jealous
passion in *The Eve of St. Agnes* (1819). He should have been
able to slip out of the convention-bound century with Fanny
Brawne into the warm languors of the Medieval Age, where his
beloved, with

> . . . the poppied warmth of sleep oppress'd,

might sleep

> . . . an azure-lidded sleep,
> In blanched linen, smooth, and lavender'd,

and be thus

> Blissfully haven'd both from joy and pain;
> Clasp'd like a missal where swart Paynims pray,
> Blinded alike from sunshine and from rain,
> As though a rose should shut, and be a bud again;

and where he,

> Ethereal, flush'd, and like a throbbing star
> Seen mid the sapphire heaven's deep repose,

might melt into her dream

> . . . as the rose
> Blendeth its odour with the violet.

The Eve of St. Agnes is admittedly one of the great poems of romantic love. In it Keats could celebrate that hectic victory which the actual terms and conditions of his life and his love denied to him.

In a word, *The Eve of St. Agnes* is like a beautiful nightmare which a consumptive might feverishly dream and a poet poignantly remember. Much has been written of his literary reminiscences in this poem, his debt to Spenser and other poets. But there were other reminiscences, too: memories of poetic window shopping burned into the eyeballs of the mind, recollections of a tour of touch and taste and sight, all mixing strangely together so that touch was taste and the eye a nostril. His letters to his little sister Fanny scintillate like delicious diaries of inspection with these precious chunks and nuggets that would later, by that strange kidnapping kind of chemistry that only poets know, fill the golden dishes and wreathed baskets of Porphyro when he

> . . . from forth the closet brought a heap
> Of candied apple, quince, and plum, and gourd,
> With jellies soother than the creamy curd,
> And lucent syrops, tinct with cinnamon,
> Manna and dates, in argosy transferr'd
> From Fez; and spicèd dainties, every one,
> —From silken Samarcand to cedar'd Lebanon.

What a delightful indigestion we enjoy as we overeat at this banquet spread by Porphyro. And how unsteadily we tip-toe over the golden-fringed carpet into the corridor where "the long carpets rose along the gusty floor" and "the key turns, and the door upon its hinges groans." It is difficult to rouse ourselves from this vision—to come back from the Middle Ages to the Twentieth Century and lovers' rendezvous over guttering candles in Greenwich Village—with a banjo twanging and a sad tenor bleating about somebody's baby.

Perhaps there are compensations. We have been awakened to broader and deeper senses. We hear the silken rustle of tissue paper and we are acutely conscious of it. We see a light gleam through a coloured goblet of water casting a bright flower-like spot on the tablecloth, and something within us is glad. Even in the stone-clad city we see a shabby ailanthus tree embroidered with crystal fringes on a December day, or a skyscraper flung against "a dim silver twilight."

For Keats, poetry was the only compensation, a violent and exhausting one like a drug or a delirium, taking much, leaving "a burning forehead and a parching tongue" and a black sense of futility. This was the romantic abyss, the ghastly gap between desire and realization. But words were left, words that could be hurled like a glittering bridge across his immediate hell. When all else failed, there was always the desperate salve and serenity of words.

How did this young apothecary student come upon the magic of making over words? "What porridge had John Keats?" As a boy he was intoxicated with Spenser's epithet, "sea-shouldering whales." Throughout his letters we meet this enthusiasm for the phrase. Rarely does the idea as such excite him. He writes to a friend that he looks "upon fine phrases like a lover." This is in the truest poetic tradition. Not since Spenser and Marlowe and Shakespeare filled their spacious day with audacity and music did words walk with so luxuriant a tread. For Keats did give words an added lustre, they became more than words, they were sensations: he makes the word "jewel" not only sparkle with colour but radiate a soft warmth from the breast it lay upon; the silken flanks of a heifer "with garlands drest" is more than silky, it is odorous with the clover and lilies of the Golden Age. Words create illusions and Keats was fastidious and truthful in his devotion to beauty. Here are the opening lines of *Hyperion*, written in 1819, as we now have them:

> Deep in the shady sadness of a vale
> Far sunken from the healthy breath of morn,
> Far from the fiery noon, and eve's one star,
> Sat gray-haired Saturn, quiet as a stone,
> Still as the silence round about his lair;
> Forest on forest hung about his head
> Like cloud on cloud. No stir of air was there,
> Not so much life as on a summer's day
> Robs not one light seed from the feather'd grass,
> But where the dead leaf fell, there did it rest.

Keats has succeeded in creating the illusion of a lordlier reality than any out of our window. Every image is saturated with the truth of a terrible quiet, a peace of gigantic dimensions; nothing disturbs the brooding breathlessness, not a syllable out of kilter, not a metaphor out of key: "shady sadness of a vale," "eve's one star," "quiet as a stone," "still as the silence," "forest on forest . . . like cloud on cloud"—there, if ever, is the final wizardry of words.

Keats with Brown, seeking a quiet holiday in the country and hoping to find a library in Winchester, arrived there in August, 1819. He writes to his brother George how very still it is—only a cane patting down a side street—"excessively maiden-lady-like," he says, and "the knockers have a very staid, serious, nay, almost awful quietness about them. I never saw so quiet a collection of lions' and rams' heads. . . . I began a poem called *The Eve of St. Mark* quite in the spirit of town quietude. I think it will give you the sensation of walking about an old country town in a coolish evening. . . ." Let us quietly and sedately turn down a side street and follow the Sabbath bell clanging at ordered intervals through the damp air:

Upon a Sabbath-day it fell;
Twice holy was the Sabbath-bell,
That call'd the folk to evening prayer;
The city streets were clean and fair
From wholesome drench of April rains:
And, on the western window panes,
The chilly sunset faintly told
Of unmatur'd green valleys cold,
Of the green thorny bloomless hedge,
Of rivers new with spring-tide sedge,
Of primroses by shelter'd rills,
And daisies on the aguish hills.
Twice holy was the Sabbath-bell:
The silent streets were crowded well
With staid and pious companies,
Warm from their fire-side orat'ries;
And moving, with demurest air,
To even-song and vesper prayer.
Each archèd porch, and entry low,
Was fill'd with patient folk and slow,
With whispers hush, and shuffling feet,
While play'd the organ loud and sweet.

That, being perfection itself, not only requires no comment, but
baffles praise as well. To speak would jar the spell and tumble
the delicate evening like shattered pale rose.

This quality of immense quiet pervades the finer part of
Keats's poetry. It seems to soak through the texture of his
Odes like some drowsy syrup which would render his insistent
consciousness of sorrow and the mortality of things tolerable.

His friend, the sculptor Haydon, takes him one day in March,
1817, to see the Greek collection newly housed in the British
Museum, the famous Elgin marbles. And he cries out, sick with
their beauty:

My spirit is too weak—mortality
Weighs heavily on me like unwilling sleep,
And each imagin'd pinnacle and steep
Of godlike hardship, tells me I must die
Like a sick Eagle looking at the sky.

These were prophetic words—a prelude to pain and misery.
Even in the *Ode on a Grecian Urn* (May, 1819), the unflawed

crystallization of delight in beauty cannot quite conceal the personal envy, the too, too personal pang underneath:

> Bold lover, never, never canst thou kiss,
> Though winning near the goal—yet, do not grieve;
> She cannot fade, though thou hast not thy bliss,
> For ever wilt thou love, and she be fair!

In that other of the three melancholy odes, the *Ode to a Nightingale*, the sadness refuses to be shut down or bravely diminished. It is the whole poem. The fact that it is induced or called forth out of Keats by the bird's habitual song does not make his own misery any the less important. Miserable he was, and his condition merely found in the impersonal pain of the nightingale's music a sympathetic text for the pressure of personal illness and harassment and luxurious jealousy and weariness with the world. The origin of the poem is pathetically casual. He is living with his friend Charles Brown in that fateful double house. Let Brown tell it in his own way:

In the spring of 1819, a nightingale had built her nest near my house. Keats felt a tranquil and continual joy in her song; and one morning he took his chair from the breakfast table to the grass-plot under a plum-tree, where he sat for two or three hours. When he came into the house, I perceived he had some scraps of paper in his hand, and these he was quietly thrusting behind some books.

And these "scraps of paper" he "was quietly thrusting behind some books" were at once a creed, a testament, and a premonition. The intricately knitted lines are the heart's cry, the hunger of the lover's body, the yearning of intellectual and spiritual passion, the definite, though defiant, acceptance of the vast ephemeral fact that Beauty must die, that Joy has his hand forever at his lips in farewell, that Melancholy is the veiled Queen in the temple of Delight. Oh, to "fade away into the forest dim" with the secret little singer,

> Fade far away, dissolve, and quite forget
> What thou among the leaves hast never known,
> The weariness, the fever, and the fret
> Here, where men sit and hear each other groan;

> Where palsy shakes a few, sad, last gray hairs,
>   Where youth grows pale, and spectre-thin, and dies,
>   Where but to think is to be full of sorrow
> And leaden-eyed despairs;
>   Where Beauty cannot keep her lustrous eyes,
>   Or new Love pine at them beyond to-morrow.

We can almost count the hairs of palsied age in that series of drab monosyllables, "few, sad, last gray hairs"; we can see Keats watching in anguish the gradual wasting away of his brother Tom, who died of consumption in Keats's arms "where youth grows pale, and spectre-thin, and dies"; we can hear him frenziedly decline to think upon his state when "but to think is to be full of sorrow." Under the delicious influence of the nightingale's melody, he will fly

> —on the viewless wings of Poesy,
> Though the dull brain perplexes and retards. . . .

But the brain continues to interfere and question (for Keats had brain aplenty); the spell snaps as the last note of the bird's incantation dies out somewhere far off; he is brought back to earth and himself and his private agony with a shock—and we with him.

Though not for long. Keats, being excitably constituted as he was, could be drenched and scorched at the same moment. Sentimental he is always; but there is nothing halfway or luke-warmish about him. He tells us that "with a great poet the sense of beauty overcomes every other consideration, or rather obliterates all consideration." He tells Fanny Brawne that, without her beauty, he could never have loved her. "The glitter of the sea," says Haydon, "makes his nature tremble." He is the supreme surgeon of the senses. He is an epicure of the soul's finer palate. The taste of claret puts him in a rapture—even a stubble field stirs him.

Keats is writing from Winchester to his friend Reynolds in the early autumn of 1819:

How beautiful the season is now. . . . I never liked stubble fields so much as now—aye better than the chilly green of the Spring. Somehow, a stubble field looks warm—in the same way that some pictures look warm. This struck me so much in my Sunday's walk that I composed upon it.

There, in a nutshell, is the actual impression, the raw fact of a stubble field—not so raw, however, for a young man to whom a stubble field could *look warm !* And this is what that same young man who was all poet or nothing did to the stubble field in his ode *To Autumn:*

> Who hath not seen thee oft amid thy store?
> Sometimes whoever seeks abroad may find
> Thee sitting careless on a granary floor,
> Thy hair soft-lifted by the winnowing wind;
> Or on a half-reap'd furrow sound asleep,
> Drows'd with the fume of poppies, while thy hook
> Spares the next swath and all its twined flowers:
> And sometimes like a gleaner thou dost keep
> Steady thy laden head across a brook;
> Or by a cyder-press, with patient look,
> Thou watchest the last oozings hours by hours.

What has happened? That is not the particular stubble field of a particular town at a certain time of the year. Rather it is autumn distilled, it is all the hot gold warmth of all the autumns in the world, it is the stubblefieldishness of the stubble field. The actual has suffered a translation into the true.

Keats's nervous organization was so exquisite, so acute, that he could not watch a sparrow pecking at some gravel without becoming that sparrow. He thought with his nerves. He felt with his intellect. And he saw everything with a "certain trembling, delicate, and snail-horn perception of beauty," saw everything freshly and fiercely as after a rain. Where he stepped he made the earth his.

But with all this intense awareness there went the power, which every great poet must possess, of emotion recollected tranquilly, though no less vividly. His appetite for beauty was masculine, though not muscular, feminine, though not effeminate. One of his portraits reveals the curved nostril, the mobile mouth of a connoisseur of sensation—and the fists of the fighter. He could work at a poem and work hard, very hard, subjecting the lyrical tumult to a saner mercy than that of his diaphragm.

III

Time moves on with a feverish tread. Keats coughs and spits blood. In September, 1820, his friends said he must go to Italy for the winter. Keats knew that the parting with Fanny Brawne was final. This last chapter of his life shall be unrecorded here. It is enough to say that, toward the end, he lay for hours holding in his white transparent hands the oval carnelian Fanny Brawne had given him. He did not allow her last letters to be opened. He asked instead that they be put "inside his winding sheet on his heart." He had slipped from the pale husk which lay so quietly now. The "posthumous existence" of which he had been so bitterly, perhaps justly, complaining, was drawing to a close. Keats said very calmly on Friday, February 23, 1821:

"Severn—I—lift me up, for I am dying. I shall die easy. Don't be frightened! Thank God it has come."

At eleven o'clock in the evening of that day, the great mercy of Death shut those dark feverish eyes forever, touched that damp forehead like a fantastic and tenderly imperious nurse, erased the agony from those lips. It was a massively quiet gesture, it was a settling down of light or snow.

They laid his body near the Pyramid of Caius Cestius in the English cemetery in Rome; violets, the violets he so loved, ran over the grave, and tufts of daisies were dropped upon it.

IV

More than any other poet of his time, Keats restored that faith in the pure enchantment of poetry which had passed out of the English world with the passing of Chaucer and Spenser and Marlowe and Shakespeare. He brought back to us golden gossip from those two great realms of beauty—the realm of the classic Greek, and the realm of medieval romance. He gave us again the quality of delight, a sense of something as haunting as lost childhood, the dew and dawn of an age we had quite forgotten in the humdrum business of our daily lives. He gave us all these things tinged a little with regret as these things always are when we recall them. He saw not only *with* his eye, but *through* it; and what he saw he became. He had no motives when he wrote. He did not hook a moral to the rose. He warmed to Coleridge's magic; but he would never have almost ruined a poem as perfect as *The Ancient Mariner* with a pulpit summary. He was not a preacher, but a poet—purely and passionately a poet. Poetry was enough for him. His poetry preached by carrying its own beauty alive into the heart by passion.

What to Keats was Shelley's mania for reforming the world? Or Byron's revolutionary sympathies? Or Burns's democracy? He did not have to read Rousseau in order to be spontaneous, or Godwin in order to love liberty. The social impulses of his age left him cold. His idea in being a poet was not to save man's soul, but to make it worth saving. What was beautiful was true; what was ugly was false. Beauty was more rational than reason, more ethical than conduct. It persuaded by its own image. Being a joy forever, it was more wholesome than all the creeds.

Perhaps Keats was the purest poet that ever lived. That he might have done finer things than he did in his horribly brief twenty-five years, had he been spared, is not the point. What he did remains, for utter felicity and natural magic, unparalleled —with the exception only of Shakespeare. But he was no more Elizabethan than he was Greek. He was Keatsian. No other adjective can coin him. If you have any capacity for the enjoyment of beauty on beauty's own terms, if you be made of penetrable stuff, you will drink deep of Keats, you will find him the shadow of a great rock in a weary land.

Of all the singers there is none to whom
My heart goes out, as to your song it goes:
For none has ever known, and no one knows,
Your luxury of words. You hold your doom
Shut, as you are, in your cool Roman room,
Those feverish dark eyes quenched in long repose,
Ignorant of the violet as it blows
And of the daisies running over your tomb—
Your English daisies, that no canker eats,
Pushing their roots into your heart's hushed bell
That beat for beauty with such golden beats
And made such music even out of your hell. . . .
No more. No words. Sleep, sleep, O lovely Keats!
Enough of words. You have your own. Farewell!

CHAPTER XXII

LORD TENNYSON

One day late in April, 1824, a boy of fifteen was roaming the countryside near Somersby, England. He walked distractedly through valleys and woods, and came out now and then on cliffs to gaze over the restless prairie of the North Sea. Finally, he paused beside a large rock and began carving upon it with his knife. When he had finished, hours later, the stone told in three ragged words the secret of his trouble:

BYRON IS DEAD

The death that meant so much to young Alfred Tennyson was scarcely less important than he supposed. The passing of Byron brought something to an end in English poetry. Only two years before, a sudden storm had sucked Shelley to his ocean grave off the Italian coast. Keats, wasted with consumption, had faded away in 1821. Wordsworth and Coleridge still lived, but had written their best poetry. The great singers of nature and liberty and bright beauty had blown by suddenly, like the debates, revolutions, and wars that had fired them. The boy Tennyson was right in mourning the death of Byron.

Yet that he himself should mourn it seems a little strange

now. For after Byron's age of passion and freedom was to come a quieter period, and this could better be named for Tennyson than for any other single poet.

Already the boy was shaping his life to the days he was to live—days in which men hoped for rest after wars and shouting. Somersby was sweet with the calm of rural Lincolnshire. Here lived George Clayton Tennyson, rector of the parish, with his wife and twelve children. In their large house, the noise and activity of many people were softened with books and long walks and music at twilight.

Alfred, the fourth of the twelve brothers and sisters, had already written an "epic of 6,000 lines" before Byron died, and at eighteen he published with his brothers, Charles and Frederick, a little volume called *Poems by Two Brothers* (Frederick wrote only a few of them). When he went to Cambridge University in 1827, poetry was already his chief interest.

At Cambridge he met other young men interested in writing. Monckton Milnes was one of them; later, as Lord Houghton, he was to edit the poems of Keats. Arthur Hallam, the son of the historian, was another.

Tennyson was shy, but he was also a person to be noticed, and the brilliant young men of Cambridge quickly made him one of them. He looked like a poet. Tall, dark, handsome, silent, he spoke his few words in a deep voice that gave them a mysterious importance. The young men saw him, they heard of his book, they told themselves that he was a genius. When Alfred won the Chancellor's prize for poetry in 1829 with *Timbuctoo*, a fanciful poem of an African city, which few people read now and none admires greatly, young Milnes wrote that "the work is certainly equal to most parts of Milton."

Hallam was most active of all the brilliant young Cambridge students in praising Tennyson and urging him to write great poetry. With the others, he had thrown over Byron as the great poet of his time, setting up Keats and Shelley as his gods. Tennyson, in the two books he published in 1830 and 1832, showed that he, too, was living more with the beauty of the earth and the beauty of words than with the dark romanticism and two-edged humour of *Childe Harold*. The quiet of Cambridge and of Somersby was in him when he wrote of

> The sparrow's chirrup on the roof,
> The slow clock ticking and the sound
> Which to the wooing wind aloof
> The poplar made,

and in a little poem called *Claribel* he wove words artfully into music that echoed the sounds of fields:

> At eve the beetle boometh
> Athwart the thicket lone;
> At noon the wild bee hummeth
> Above the moss'd headstone;
> At midnight the moon cometh,
> And looketh down alone.

He wrote of the fairy Lady of Shalott looking at bold Sir Lancelot:

> The gemmy bridle glitter'd free,
> Like to some branch of stars we see
> Hung in the golden Galaxy.
> The bridle bells rang merrily
> As he rode down to Camelot:
> And from his blazoned baldric slung
> A mighty silver bugle hung
> And as he rode his armour rung
> Beside remote Shalott.

That was golden poetry, glittering music that already proved the young men at Cambridge right in hailing Tennyson as a genius, if the world had only known it. Hallam knew it, and praised this poetry, different from Keats's but, like Keats's, splendid. Yet he was a little worried about it, too. He was afraid Tennyson might sit at Somersby putting beautiful words one after another, not paying enough attention to men and women and noble ideas. He knew people were starving for want of food, fighting for freedom, trying to harness the earth and ocean and air through the magic of electric sparks and steam and gas. He wanted Tennyson to put something of this into his poetry. Tennyson wanted to capture it, too. He felt, as he said later, that "the great sage poets" like Æschylus, Shakespeare, Dante, and Goethe were greater than Keats and Shelley, and he wanted to become one of them.

That was an exciting time in Tennyson's life. He and Hallam set out to get experience that would teach them to live and write greatly. They went first to fight with a Spanish patriot who was going to collect an army in southern France and topple the King of Spain off his throne. But the revolution didn't come off, and after some pleasant travelling in the foothills of the Pyrenees, the two young men returned to England. Tennyson's father now became sick, and Tennyson left Cambridge. But he and Hallam wrote eager letters to each other, and Hallam, who became engaged to Tennyson's sister Emily, came up to Somersby and tramped the hills with his friend, talking and talking of great ideas and great poetry. It was a time, as Tennyson wrote later,

> When each by turns was guide to each
> And Fancy light from Fancy caught,
> And Thought leapt out to wed with Thought
> Ere Thought could wed itself with Speech.

And then the fine ecstasy of the two friends was shattered. Hallam—gay, vital, energetic, eager Hallam—suddenly died. Travelling in Europe, he lay down to sleep one afternoon in Vienna, complaining of an "ague." When his father came later to wake him, a little blood vessel in his wonderful brain had snapped, and he had slipped into a different kind of slumber and could not be roused.

The news of this swift sickness carrying away his friend came to Tennyson himself like a sickness. He was in a stupor. He had always been silent and reserved, more interested in his dreams than in people. Hallam had pulled him toward life and activity, but now Hallam was gone. Tennyson brooded upon his friend's death and turned back from his other friends to himself. He wrote fewer letters, saw less than formerly of men and women. He had several nervous breakdowns. So it went with him for ten years.

Yet, though Hallam's death had much to do with this unhappy period in Tennyson's life, there were other causes for it. For one thing, Tennyson had fallen in love! In 1830 he had met Hallam walking in the Fairy Wood near Somersby with young Emily Sellwood. She was seventeen and delicately beautiful in her gray dress. Tennyson asked her: "Are you a dryad or an oread wandering among these trees?"

In 1836 he stood beside her at her sister's marriage to his own brother, and he pressed her hand and whispered: "O happy bridesmaid, make a happy bride." This was a lovely beginning. Emily Sellwood smiled and promised. But before the two could be married they must have money to live on, and they had very little money. Alfred might have gone to work, but to work meant less time for poetry. Finally, after four years, they gave up the idea of marrying and decided not to see or even write to each other again. Time and accidents were to bring them together later, but in 1840 this did not seem possible.

Besides the loss of Hallam and the difficulties in the way of his marriage, Tennyson had another problem. He had still to write the great poetry he and Hallam had planned he should write. The critics had not been unkind to the 1832 poems, but they had said hard things. "He has a fine ear for melody," wrote Christopher North, one of the best known of them, "but at present he has small power over the common feelings and thoughts of men." Tennyson smarted under such words, and read and wrote at Somersby, polishing his old poems and building new ones. Through seclusion and nervous breakdowns and troubled love he carved at his verse, shaping emotion and chiming words into poetic patterns. He was determined to make a book that would be remembered, and when his two volumes appeared finally in 1842 they contained the work of ten full years, carefully moulded in thought and feeling, and woven into a music of words that has been known and loved since, through the world.

Some say that all the best work of Tennyson is in these books. Certainly much of what he had written in those ten years of doubt and difficulty is different from the poems he wrote in the last fifty years of his life.

Probably it is different because the feeling back of it was deeper and keener. Tennyson had not gone out, as Hallam would have hoped, to live with life, but life had come to live with him. He had lost his marvellous friend. He had felt the call of love. He had been challenged to prove that he was a great poet. These experiences were all in his own heart and mind, but they were the grief and love and ambitious struggle that men know in the world, and they came to Tennyson directly. He had already felt the charm of dreams. He had written his understanding of indolent withdrawal from the world in *The Lotos Eaters*. Now, in his *Morte d'Arthur*, he could reflect his mood of grief for the death of his own Arthur. Something of his mourning for Hallam went into his simple picture of the three queens who came to take King Arthur away—

> And loosed the shatter'd casque, and chafed his hands,
> And call'd him by his name, complaining loud,
> And dropping bitter tears against his brow
> Striped with dark blood.

On the other hand, there were poems like *Locksley Hall* and *Ulysses* that showed a triumphant struggle with despondency. In *Ulysses*, the old hero of the Trojan War and the Cyclops' Cave and the storms of twenty years turns restlessly from a safe, idle old age and gathers together his men for a last adventure. And through the eyes of his hero in *Locksley Hall* Tennyson seems to have seen the Twentieth Century with its wars and wings and hope of world peace:

For I dipt into the future, far as human eye could see,
Saw the Vision of the World, and all the wonder that would be;
Saw the heavens fill with commerce, argosies of magic sails,
Pilots of the purple twilight, dropping down with costly bales;
Heard the heavens fill with shouting, and there rain'd a ghastly dew
From the nations' airy navies grappling in the central blue;
Far along the world-wide whisper of the south wind rushing warm,
With the standards of the peoples plunging thro' the thunderstorm;
Till the war drum throbb'd no longer, and the battleflags were furl'd
In the Parliament of man, the Federation of the world.

This was life that men and women could understand; it was feeling, it rolled out in noble music. There had been nothing so stirring since Byron, and Byron had not known the craft of words so well.

For, during these ten years, Tennyson had learned the art of writing poetry as perhaps no other poet had learned it before him, or has learned it since. Eagerly and patiently he had studied how to blend thought and feeling and the music of speech. He knew the sounds of words as a pianist knows the keys of a piano. He could make the vowel sounds give high treble notes to match his idea:

> Let the wild
> Lean-headed eagle yelp alone, and leave
> The monstrous ledges;

or low soft sounds:

> The purple flower droops: the golden bee
> Is lily-cradled; I alone awake.

He could mould consonants in the same manner. For instance, the "l's" in the lines above make a finely woven alliteration. As the thought or feeling changed, Tennyson could alter the consonant sounds with it. With "h's" and "c's" and "r's" and "t's" he gave the sound of waterfalls in

> The long brook falling through the clov'n ravine
> In cataract after cataract to the sea.

How magnificently his art could express mood and atmosphere
is shown in the description of Sir Bedivere climbing down to
the lake in *Morte d'Arthur:*

> Dry clash'd his harness in the icy caves
> And barren chasms, and all to left and right
> The bare black cliff clang'd round him, as he based
> His feet on juts of slippery crag that rang
> Sharp-smitten with the dint of armèd heels.

Here Tennyson was inspired, and this is among the great descriptive passages in poetry, but even when less of the poet's fire was
in him, he seldom lost his unique skill in word melody—a skill
that had grown out of a study and practice in all types of rhyme
and metre and suiting of sound to sense. Tennyson lifted the
craft of writing poetry in English—in so far as it can be separated from poetic inspiration—to a new level. Though he was
never to write up to the best of Shakespeare, Milton, Keats, and
Wordsworth, in the perfection of poetic method he excelled
them all.

Tennyson's long poem *In Memoriam*, not published until
1850, but much of it written before 1842, like *Morte d'Arthur*
and *Ulysses*, grew from his personal experience. It was dedicated
to Hallam, and told the story of Tennyson's great grief. It was
and still remains the longest and most sensitive and compre-
hensive of all great poems about personal grief. Millions of
people who have lost their friends, children, wives, or parents
by death have got comfort from *In Memoriam*. In it Tennyson
ranges through all the thoughts and impulses of grief, yet offers
the healing belief that

> 'Tis better to have loved and lost
> Than never to have loved at all.

He trusts in God and His purpose. He feels that men are not
"idle ore," with whatever metal and dross happened to be in
them,

> But iron dug from central gloom,
> And heated hot with burning fears,
> And dipt in baths of hissing tears,
> And batter'd with the shocks of doom
>
> To shape and use.

He sings his faith in man and in God in lyrics that have become part of the language, such as the vigorous New Year song beginning

> Ring out, wild bells, to the wild sky,
> The flying cloud, the frosty light,
> The year is dying in the night;
> Ring out, wild bells, and let him die.

But not everything that Tennyson wrote was so real to him as this poem and the better poems of 1842. Though he had tried with Hallam to meet the life of men and know it, he did not fully like it. For one thing, it disturbed his writing. "I require quiet," he said, "and myself to myself more than any man when I write." Then, as we have seen, he had a natural shrinking away from the real world toward his dream world. He was doubtful of life. He was afraid that love might sink into passion, adventure turn into folly, liberty become licence. So, like his Lady of Shalott, he watched the reflection of a life he did not share or in many ways even watch attentively, and he wrote of the things that did not disturb him—the pure Sir Galahad, the pale, rapt St. Agnes, the miller's daughter, the May Queen. He wrote also of patriotism. In these poems, as in *The Princess* (1847), he spun charming descriptions and songs and stories. England, emerging from the Napoleonic wars as mistress of the ocean and of lands in many parts of the world, tired of wild uprisings in the name of liberty, listened to this music of quiet country life, of dewy trees and gentle sadness and faithful love, and was charmed by it. This sad sweet poetry, as well as the stirring *Ulysses* and the splendid *Morte d'Arthur*, was responsible for a growing popularity that now came to Tennyson.

For things went better with him as to both money and praise.

The critics had fine words for his poetry. In 1845 his friends got him a pension of £200 a year from the government as "one who has devoted to worthy purposes great intellectual powers." His books sold through edition after edition. When the aged Wordsworth died in 1850, Tennyson was made Poet Laureate. Emerson in America helped bring out an edition of his work. He met literary people—Thackeray, Elizabeth Barrett, Ruskin, Coventry Patmore, all telling him he had written great poetry, as indeed he had. Finally, he met Emily Sellwood again, and in 1850 he married her. "The peace of God entered my soul," he said, "when I wedded her at the altar."

All the rest of his life was peace and praise and success. Living after 1854 at Farringford, his home on the Isle of Wight, and later during the summer months at Aldworth in Surrey, he wrote his smoothly flowing poetry, helped bring up his two children, entertained his guests, answered letters.

For many people, from poets to kings, wrote to him and came to hear him talk. Walt Whitman hailed him from America; Prince Albert visited him; Longfellow sent him Christmas greetings; Victor Hugo, the old French novelist and poet, wrote thankfully of a sonnet Tennyson had addressed to him. Then there was the honour of being called to read his poetry to Queen Victoria, and later of knowing her as a friend. Finally, there was the offer of a peerage. At first Tennyson frowned on it, but later he asked himself: "Why should I be selfish and not suffer an honour to be done to literature in my name?" So in 1883 he became Alfred, Lord Tennyson.

Meanwhile, he had gone on writing successfully. There came the emotional story and love lyrics of *Maud* (1855), the slower but sentimentally moving story of *Enoch Arden*, the martial *Charge of the Light Brigade*, and the solemn power of the *Ode on the Death of the Duke of Wellington*. His six poetical dramas were less popular, although one, *The Cup*, ran for 130 days in London.

In almost all these poems and dramas Tennyson was continuing to sing to the English people of their country, their heroes, their thoughts, their problems. And, finally, he put into poetry the great hero stories clustering about King Arthur and his court. The twelve *Idylls of the King* brought into homes and schoolrooms the perfect Arthur, the beautiful Guinevere, the courteous and skilful Lancelot, the gay Gawain, the sad Elaine, the eager Gareth, the pure Galahad, the traitor Modred. Some of these had been known, for Malory's *Morte d'Arthur* was read by not a few lovers of chivalry and romance before Tennyson made over a great deal of it into poetry. But Tennyson made Arthur and his knights a part of modern life and literature. He drew together the English ideals of 1870 and put them into these old heroes. In the far-off world of Camelot, he got very near to the reality of his ten years of struggle. He wrote, too, with surpassing skill. He never let his poetry slow up or interfere with his story. In *Balin and Balan*, for instance, he tells of two knights sitting by a spring, and he might have paused to describe the water. Instead, he says that the spring

> Sang, and the sand danced at the bottom of it,

and we have poetry and go on with the story. There are splendid passages all through the *Idylls*. Gareth sees Castle Perilous

> A huge pavilion like a mountain peak
> Sunder the glooming crimson on the marge,
> Black, with black banner, and a long black horn
> Beside it hanging—

Fights and battles—cities—queens—enchantresses—wizards— love—holy hours of prayer shine throughout these poems. If Tennyson had done nothing but write the *Idylls* he would deserve a distinguished place in English poetry. Though they show his conventional ideas and limited knowledge of human nature, no one except Milton has done an English epic to be compared with them.

Such accomplishments should be remembered when we speak of Tennyson. He had such a great gift for writing that many who love poetry are disappointed that he did not do more with it. But such disappointment seems unjust when we remember the great range and high quality of Tennyson's work. His patriotic poems alone are memorable. Schoolboys say *Love Thou Thy Land*, and the dashing stanzas of

> Half a league, half a league,
> Half a league onward,
> All in the valley of Death
> Rode the Six Hundred.

On the other hand, children are still lulled to sleep with Tennyson's

> Sweet and low, sweet and low
> Wind of the western sea.

Phrases struck from his thought and feeling, like "tears, idle tears,"

> There lives more faith in honest doubt,
> Believe me, than in half the creeds,

> More things are wrought by prayer
> Than this world dreams of *etc.*

are embedded in the language. The spirited, delicate music of poems like *The Lady of Shalott* is everlasting. Finally, those who love quiet beauty whispering of the mystery of life will continue to read poems such as *Tithonus* with its first four lines that tell in themselves a whole story of life and death:

> The woods decay, the woods decay and fall,
> The vapours weep their burthen to the ground,
> Man comes and tills the field and lies beneath,
> And after many a summer dies the swan.

Such poetry was great enough to influence writers like Swinburne and Rossetti, and probably it has had an influence indirectly on all poets writing since Tennyson, except some of the followers of Walt Whitman. It represented a noble art that lifted the quality of the language and gave a new impulse to the music of poetry and—as in the case of the *Idylls*—new poetic stories for later poets to work over.

At Farringford and Aldworth, his two homes, Tennyson received constant testimonials to his work during the later years of his life. There were thousands of acknowledgments, gifts, and letters. Often he read his poems in the evening, and saw his listeners moved to tears by their beauty. When he clasped his copy of Shakespeare in his hand and carried his eighty-five years into quiet death, the world mourned the passing of the man it considered the greatest poet of the time. And since his death none, save possibly Walt Whitman with his wholly different conception of poetry, has loomed up bigger in the eyes of men and women turning to a modern age and to modern poets for comfort or inspiration.

CHAPTER XXIII

THE BROWNINGS

I

One afternoon in May, 1845, a young man with lemon-coloured gloves, quite "the glass of fashion and the mould of form," called at 50 Wimpole Street, London. He was taken upstairs and there he saw, for the first time, Elizabeth Barrett, lying on a sofa—and "there was nothing between the knowing and the loving."

In January, she had received the first letter from him—Robert Browning—the first letter of a wonderful correspondence. For in no other age do we know of such poets who were lovers, too. Elizabeth Barrett had promised to see him when spring came, for "winters shut me up like a dormouse's eyes." She had been an invalid for seven years, having injured her spine in a fall; and, because of her ill health and the unhappy death of her favourite brother, was just then tired of living—unaffectedly tired. But this July, soon after her first meeting with Browning, she was to begin walking again, and to come to health, and to write in her *Sonnets from the Portuguese:*

> . . . how a mystic Shape did move
> Behind me, and drew me backward by the hair;
> And a voice said in mastery, while I strove,—
> "Guess now who holds thee!"—"Death," I said.
>   But there,
> The silver answer rang—"Not Death, but Love."

Well and beautifully it has been said that "Browning stooped and picked up a fair-coined soul that lay rusting in a pool of tears."

From that first meeting, Robert Browning went home, up the staircase, past the bust of his god Shelley, into his large, low room crammed with books, and so on to the study with its little desk where he was to write his letters to Elizabeth Barrett. And while he is busy at some such occupation, let us leave Elizabeth Barrett for a time, and spend a few pages in discovering what kind of a person it was who had rescued her from despondency and tears.

Robert Browning had grown to manhood under happy circumstances. He had an artistic, book-loving father and a musical mother. He had been a precocious boy, reading widely, writing a little book of Byronic poems when twelve, studying at London University for a year, then (loving Keats's poetry and aware that Keats had studied medicine) attending lectures at Guy's Hospital.

But Shelley had been his inspiration. Robert Browning had worshipped the author of *Alastor* and *Adonais*, and had even dieted on bread and potatoes for a while because Shelley had been a vegetarian. And when *Pauline,* Browning's first printed book, was published at the expense of his family in the poet's twenty-second year, it bore a glowing burst of poetic praise for the older writer, beginning:

> Sun treader, life and light be thine forever!

Pauline was a longish poem, and its ecstatic lines were not easy reading for most poetry lovers. But the reviewers wrote about it, and Robert was happy. His "inexpressible delight" vanished when some months passed and not a copy was sold, but he pressed on with his next work in spite of publishers who "would have nothing to say to poets, regarding them as unprofitable people" (as they still do); and *Paracelsus*, appearing eighteen months after *Pauline*, was much more successful.

It is true that it sold little better than the first volume. However, the opinion of critics like John Forster of the *Examiner* made Browning respected by London writers. "We may safely predict for him a brilliant career," wrote Forster, "if he continues true to the present promise of his genius." Indeed, the young man's prospects seemed bright. He found himself a member of a London set called the "Colloquials." His poem, cast in a series of dramatic scenes, impressed Macready, the most distinguished actor of the day, and led to a proposal that Browning should write a poetic tragedy. He composed *Strafford*, and for five nights this representation of the struggle between Parliament and King Charles I was applauded by enthusiastic audiences.

But *Strafford* lasted only its five nights, and though critics kindly said that "the very faults of the drama are proofs of talent," Browning turned from writing for actors and resumed the making of his third long poem. While completing it, he went abroad and discovered Italy, rambling through "delicious Asolo," Verona, Venice. The latter part of *Sordello* is particularly rich in lines showing Browning's first contact with the land that was later to be his second home.

The three volumes of verse which Browning had issued were well enough for his poetic reputation. The only drawback was that they brought him few readers. *Sordello*, even longer than *Paracelsus*, had the enthusiasm and interest in character which had been attractive features in the former, but was much less readable. The long poems were acting as a wet blanket on popular interest in Browning.

Browning did not enjoy being read by nobody except his

friends, and he did not enjoy paying (as he had been doing) for books that did not sell. So, to lessen expense and attract more general attention, he adopted a new device, at the suggestion of his publishers, for producing the work of the next five years. It was one that had the happy effect of introducing him as the writer of shorter and more readable poems.

His plan was to issue his poetry in pamphlets. From 1841 to 1846 he brought out a succession of little books in this style, calling the series *Bells and Pomegranates*. They showed fully his faults and powers as a poet. *Pauline,* his first poem, had been romantic and ecstatic. *Paracelsus* had stirred to life some fine poetry like Shelley's and Keats's, such as these lines from one of the songs:

> And strew faint sweetness from some old
> Egyptian's fine worm-eaten shroud
> Which breaks to dust when once unrolled;
> Or shredded perfume, like a cloud
> From closet long to quiet vowed,
> With mothed and dropping arras hung,
> Mouldering her lute and books among,
> As when a queen, long dead, was young.

But the quality that justly caught the attention of those who noticed these poems and *Strafford* and *Sordello* had been an unusual interest in the workings of the minds and hearts of men, and a remarkable skill in setting these forth. The new poems developed this interest and ability.

All of *Bells and Pomegranates* is alive with a sense for people. The first pamphlet, *Pippa Passes,* was a story in vivid episodes of the silk worker Pippa's one holiday—New Year's. As she walks singing, we see the life of four separate groups of people, and get a subtle, if perhaps too sanguine, glimpse of how varied and exciting is the existence of men and women, and how one person, even without knowing it, can affect the destinies of many. In *Bells and Pomegranates* appeared a number of dramatic monologues. Such a poem as *My Last Duchess* showed the

vital swiftness and fullness with which Browning could reveal a
character by letting the man or woman speak his or her thoughts.
Narrative poems like *Saul* mingled a sensitive feeling for character with sonorous music. In *Cavalier Tunes* the rollicking
fighters of Charles I stepped into song. *Home Thoughts from
Abroad* gave Browning's own personal affection for England,
and his delight in the thrush that

> sings each song twice over,
> Lest you should think he never could recapture
> The first fine careless rapture!

Doubtless more readers would have enjoyed such poetry
if they had not stumbled over its sudden parentheses, grotesque
rhymes, and thoughts that crowded awkwardly against one
another because Browning had tried to get too many of them
in a stanza, or had left out here and there a connecting word.
"Grammatical Asthma," one scholar has called his more confused style. The asthmatic passages puzzled and routed those
who might have enjoyed the duchess in her pleasure with

> The dropping of the daylight in the west,
> The bough of cherries some officious fool
> Broke in the orchard for her, the white mule
> She rode around the terrace—

or delighted in the peace of the landscape—

> Where the quiet-coloured end of evening smiles
> Miles and miles,
> On the solitary pastures where our sheep
> Half-asleep
> Tinkle homeward thro' the twilight, . . .

or approved the ardour of this scorn for *The Lost Leader:*

> Just for a handful of silver he left us,
> Just for a riband to stick in his coat.

But Tennyson published his *Poems* in 1842, and those who
were dazzled and enchanted by the almost perfect music and the
real power of *Ulysses* and *Tithonus* and *Morte d'Arthur* turned

impatiently from the flaws of Browning. They did not read enough of him to learn that the contrast between these two poets, both destined to be great, was not all in Tennyson's favour. They did not realize that if Tennyson was melodious where Browning was harsh, he was feminine where Browning was masculine; that if Tennyson had the strength of dream and meditative doubt, Browning had the gusto of confidence and energy; that if Tennyson could evoke marvellous shadows of romance, Browning could enliven his poems with the colloquial pulse of modern thought and fancy. So they came close to ignoring the genius of a poet who was independent in a time of timidities, eccentric, electric, buoyant, who could write these exultant lines in *Saul* (1845) on the sheer leap of life:

> Oh, our manhood's prime vigour! No spirit feels waste,
> Not a muscle is stopped in its playing nor sinew unbraced.
> Oh, the wild joys of living! the leaping from rock up to rock,
> The strong rending of boughs from the fir-tree, the cool silver shock
> Of the plunge in a pool's living water, the hunt of the bear,
> And the sultriness showing the lion is couched in his lair.
> And the meal, the rich dates yellowed over with gold dust divine,
> And the locust-flesh steeped in the pitcher, the full draught of wine,
> And the sleep in the dried river-channel where bulrushes tell
> That the water was wont to go warbling so softly and well.
> How good is man's life, the mere living! how fit to employ
> All the heart and the soul and the senses forever in joy!

II

A few had been wise enough to see a fine poet in Browning, and Elizabeth Barrett was one of them. The young man with lemon-coloured gloves and long dark hair and high-strung, restless manner who visited her in 1846 had been moved to write to her because she had praised his poetry. She found the man even more to her liking than the verse, and it was not so very long—only the time between May, 1845, and September, 1846—before Robert Browning had stolen the poetess from the dour father who guarded her like a dragon (never wanting her to marry any man), and taken her with him to Italy and a new life.

One morning, soon after their marriage, Elizabeth Browning thrust a manuscript into her husband's pocket, and then ran upstairs in a swift confusion to her room. It was a sonnet sequence on their love written during the time of their courtship and love letters. Mrs. Browning never intended these poems to be published, but her poet-husband promptly declared that they must be. He suggested calling them *Sonnets from the Portuguese*—a title which might hide the fact that they were personal. They were in his mind "the finest sonnets written in our language since Shakespeare's."

Browning's opinion of *Sonnets from the Portuguese* was hardly more flattering to his wife than his opinion of most of her poetry. He thought her a better poet than he was, and the world at that time agreed with him. He called her his "moon of poets," as she considered him her sun, and later he wrote, in his dedication to *The Ring and the Book* (1868):

> O lyric Love, half angel and half bird,
> And all a wonder and a wild desire,—
> Boldest of hearts that ever braved the sun,
> Took sanctuary within the holier blue,
> And sang a kindred soul out to his face.

Though his wife was hardly the supreme poet her husband believed her to be, we can understand and respect his feeling. She was a pure singer with a lovely lyric tenderness, the best poet of her sex since Sappho. Her Sonnets, in their autobiographical candour, in their fine restraint and fullness, reveal a woman's secret soul as had no poetry in our literature up to that time. Her lyrical mastery in this stray stanza from *A Musical Instrument* shines in many passages of her writings:

> Sweet, sweet, sweet, O Pan!
> Piercing sweet by the river!
> Blinding sweet, O great god Pan!
> The sun on the hill forgot to die,
> And the lilies revived, and the dragon-fly
> Came back to dream on the river.

Italy was a kind of promised land for Elizabeth Browning. Living in Florence or in little villages in the summers, she drank in the sun of the south and warmth of her husband's love, and blossomed in a life of precarious happiness for fifteen years. In Italy she found friends, most of them cultured Americans. Hawthorne saw the Brownings there; the New England thinker and essayist Margaret Fuller visited them. The painter Story came, and the young sculptress Harriet Hosmer. One caller records that Robert Browning was "simple, natural, and playful," and that Mrs. Browning was all "genius and sensibility, . . . her tremulous voice often flutters over her words like the flame of a dying candle over the wick. I have never seen a human frame which seemed so nearly a transparent veil for a celestial and immortal spirit." Daytimes Browning walked forth with Elizabeth's little dog Flush, but he seldom could be lured from his home evenings. One privileged intruder, coming frequently at night to join the poets over hot chestnuts and mulled wine, found talk good and laughter plentiful. During the third year of their stay in Italy a son, Robert Wiedemann Browning, was born.

The Brownings had not been living all this time on money that flowed in from the sale of their poems. Browning's verse at this time did not even pay for itself. But Robert's father had a comfortable income, enough for his own family in England and his son's family in Italy. Robert and Elizabeth had no financial worries. Browning, who had an excellent digestion and a zest for life, had nothing to do but care for his wife and son and make his poetry. He loved music, and found joy in this; he read widely, went with Elizabeth on muleback up the Italian hill trails, soaking in the sound and colour of Italy, picnicking on strawberries and cream.

Sometimes there were trips to England, and the Brownings were much fêted by old and new friends, but these were brief experiences, for the climate was unsuited to Mrs. Browning. Only memories of a few rare evenings remain. On one of these, four poets gathered in one room. Tennyson gave Browning a first-edition copy of *Maud* in the presence of Dante Gabriel Rossetti and Elizabeth Browning. The latter said of Tennyson, "He opened his heart to us." They had rich conversations. "The best talk I ever heard, so full of repartee, quip, epigram, anecdote, depth, and wisdom; but it is quite impossible to attempt to reproduce them owing to their very brilliancy," says Tennyson's son.

Through this happy life a strain of dark foreboding began to creep. Elizabeth Browning's father died unrelenting in his disapproval of her marriage, refusing to see her or to allow any of his family to see her. A dearly loved sister died and left three children all younger than her own boy. She drooped and pined a little and Browning shielded her from ordinary visitors. She had a sudden and alarming attack of sickness but was not considered in any danger. One night, soon after, she awoke from a troubled sleep and, apparently with no idea that she was about to leave him, spoke in the tenderest fashion of her love for him, and, in his arms, her head drooped as though in a faint, but it was the end.

Profound and lasting was Browning's grief. "Looking back," he said, "I see that we have been all the time walking over a torrent on a straw." But even in this deep sorrow, his robust and resolute attitude was emphasized in his determination to go back to England, to live and work and write.

III

Happiness in Italy, the birth of his son, anxiety for his wife's health—all these had stemmed for a while Robert Browning's great poetic energy. He wrote and published little. There was a four-year gap between his wedding and *Christmas Eve and Easter-Day* (1850). Five more years passed until *Men and Women* was issued in 1855.

However, this book showed that he had been growing in poetic stature during this time when life had been more important to him than poetry. In *Men and Women*, dedicated to Elizabeth, Browning stands forth a complete poet. There is no doubt as to the freshness and value of what he has brought to poetry.

His gift was nothing less than a new study of the human soul. Of course, all poets had been interested in souls, if only in their own. Still, few had been more interested in souls than in anything else. Milton had thought too much about heaven and hell, Pope too much about wit and polish, Wordsworth too much about nature and himself, Shelley and Keats too much about star-white or violet-dim beauty to study very closely the thoughts and feelings of men. Only Shakespeare among the great poets had been great enough to fashion poetry not only of words and enthusiasms and truths, but of the play of mind and emotion in his many people.

Browning had already showed in *Bells and Pomegranates* that he, too, was great enough to do this. And in these earlier poems, and in the fuller and finer poetry of *Men and Women*, he showed that he was attempting a different and perhaps a harder thing than Shakespeare attempted. Shakespeare had shown his people as they appeared in their deeds. They were part of what an audience had to *see*. Browning, after writing some plays for the stage, seems to have discovered that there was a great deal happening to men and women that could not be seen. Then, too, he wrote at a time when ladies and gentlemen were living prosperously on the wealth of English factories and commerce. Their lives were peaceful, with much time for books and reflection and the refinements of feeling. They were ready for poetry about the mind and heart, and cared less for poetry

> Of moving accidents by flood and field,
> Of hair-breadth scapes i' the imminent deadly breach.

Browning was just such a person himself. In verse that was dramatic, but not tied to the theatre, he took a delight in breaking away from spoken words and physical acts when he chose, and showing the finest quivering emotion, the most delicate thought.

So he created people caught at some moment that exhibits their innermost nature. He picks up the thread that leads to their secret meaning, and takes us weaving in and out through the torture chambers of their minds. Bishops, fakers, tyrants— their thoughts and actions are cunningly sifted. We chat with the cheery monk-artist Fra Lippo Lippi, who paints the holiness of church windows but bubbles with life at times and goes out to kick his heels and have his fun. And we sit dreaming with the "perfect painter," Andrea del Sarto, who can draw correctly anything he sees, but cannot see like a great artist. He looks sadly at less skilful men with greater souls:

> Their works drop groundward, but themselves, I know,
> Reach many a time a heaven that's shut to me,
> Enter and take their place there sure enough,
> Though they come back and cannot tell the world.
> My works are nearer heaven, but I sit here.

During the next twenty years, Browning added many men and women to his gallery of soul-paintings. He sketched masterfully the grotesque savage Caliban,

> Flat on his belly in the pit's much mire,

talking to himself of his god Setebos. And he turned from the delicious whimsicality and weird uncouthness of this to the pungent thinker Rabbi Ben Ezra, and to the characters of his long epic, *The Ring and the Book* (1868), recently dramatized and put into a Twentieth Century play. In this poem the story is told by ten separate characters, each with his own point of view; and by Browning himself. It is an impressive study of the different appearance the same happenings take on for various humans.

Dramatic in their essence, many of these poems are narrative in form. The story of Hervé Riel, who led the scattered French fleet through the rocky passage into the harbour of St. Malo, saving it from the pursuing English, is quick and eloquent. And there is that thrilling narrative of the Arabian horse

Muléykeh the Pearl, beloved of Hóseyn her master; and how she was coveted for her beauty and her swiftness by all the tribesmen; and how Duhl the son of Sheyban desired her with a great desire and offered much gold for her, and Hóseyn laughed scornfully in his face; and how, inflamed to possess her, Duhl one night glided like a serpent through the tent flap, while Hóseyn slept, and saw Muléykeh splashed with moonlight at her tether and cut the thong and sprang upon her back and was gone; and how Hóseyn started up, feeling the theft, and pursued the thief, following hot on the back of Buhéyseh, the Pearl's sister; and how Pearl, missing her master's heel and touch of the bit, chafed at her strange rider and shortened her stride so that Buhéyseh, the hitherto second in speed, flashed nearer and nearer and was nose by tail, neck by croup, and in another instant would be even with her, when suddenly Hóseyn shouted:

> ". . . Dog Duhl, Damned son of the Dust,
> Touch the right ear and press with your foot my
> Pearl's left flank!"

Away shot the Pearl then, and Hóseyn turned back weeping to his tent and his neighbours came—

And they jeered him, one and all: "Poor Hóseyn is crazed past hope!
How else had he wrought himself his ruin, in fortune's spite?
To have simply held the tongue were a task for a boy or girl,
And here were Muléykeh again, the eyed like an antelope,
The child of his heart by day, the wife of his breast by night!"—
"And the beaten in speed!" wept Hóseyn: "you never have loved my Pearl."

This love of horses, like his inquisitive and tenderly careful love of creeping things too small for a name, was all part of Browning's healthy animal exultation, his English out-of-doorness, his intense sympathy with the whole living creation. He loved men and women in precisely the same way. Perhaps it was partly because of his excellent digestion. But it was more than that, certainly, it was because his soul was immensely alive and vigorous as well. He believed fiercely in life. He plunged himself up to the armpits in it. In one form or another, through all his poetry, and in himself, he was life's strenuous champion.

But Browning, for all his versatility and ingenuity and sympathy, never climbed to supremacy in dramatic or poetic power. He made many fine dramatic figures. In reality of style, Tennyson could not match Browning's genius for trapping the authentic tone of the speaker, all the natural shadings and changes of tempo, and even Chaucer and Shakespeare scarcely excel him here. The implied listener to his dramatic monologues, though silent, is so livingly talked at or to or with that the listener becomes almost as audible as the speaker. Every reader is that listener.

Yet, for all this, no figure in Browning's poetry stands out with a dignity that makes him comparable to Hamlet, Macbeth, Lear, Antony. Browning did not even create a character as powerful as Milton's Satan or Tennyson's Ulysses (if we can take characters from brief dramatic monologues like *Ulysses*.)

Again, he was not a great master of words. He wrote brilliant phrases and lines. There is his cry:

> Only I discern
> Infinite passion, and the pain
> Of finite hearts that yearn.

or wisdom like Rabbi Ben Ezra's:

> What I aspired to be,
> And was not, comforts me:
> A brute I might have been, but would not sink i' the scale;

or Andrea del Sarto's cry:

> Ah, but a man's reach should exceed his grasp,
> Or what's a heaven for!

Browning is rich with flashes of beauty and penetrating humanity like these, but they are—flashes. And while poems like *My Last Duchess* and *Saul* and *Andrea del Sarto* are finely written throughout, we cannot but admit that the best poems of Tennyson and Wordsworth and Keats and Shelley are finer poetry.

We can see where Browning failed by comparing *Andrea* or *Saul* with Tennyson's *Ulysses*. While all three are great poems, *Ulysses* is great in theme and great in words. It is the dramatic-lyric cry of a noble spirit who, in a double sense, will never die while he is alive! What Tennyson wants to say is said with a high clarity and a moving beauty. Neither of Browning's poems is so satisfactory in what it tries to say or in its way of saying it. Andrea del Sarto is a little too much of a fool and a little too limited in soul to make as great a subject as Ulysses. Saul is great enough, but we don't get a poem about Saul; we get one about life in general, ending in a burst of Christian eloquence. This is splendid, but not a little stretched and strained. And in this, as in poorer poems of Browning's, the poet is always turning from the big thing he has at heart to nose out some side-idea and play with it. Perhaps Browning failed of supreme greatness because he was always tempted to spend his strength on odd trifles that accidentally caught his attention. This in turn may have been somewhat due to his retired life among books, his lack of familiarity with struggle and (except for the death of his wife) with shock and sorrow. At any rate, he never mounts to the tragic beauty of the master poets. He never merged the art of words and his poet's knowledge and the deep feeling he possessed into as fine an expression as *Ulysses*. This is regrettable when we realize that in robustness of soul and subtlety of understanding and sharp truth of speech Browning was a better poet than Tennyson.

I V

Browning never left England for any considerable length of time after his return in 1861. He spent many summers in Brittany, he visited Italy, but his permanent home was in London. Here he wrote, read magazines and newspapers, digested nota-

ble books in French, German, and Italian, and went much to
dine with his friends. We have glimpses of him gadding about
like a pleasant old Beau Brummel, eating with a tremendous
heartiness, showing an eager if modest pleasure in the praise of
sentimental ladies.

He was known and popular now. His long poem, *The Ring
and the Book*, had been praised by the reviewers. In 1881 the
English Browning Society had been formed. American readers
were quite as enthusiastic, or more so, than the English. Honours were thrust upon the poet. One of these was an honorary
degrée conferred by the University of Oxford. An observer who
watched Browning on this occasion remarked how lightly he
carried his almost seventy years and how briskly he stepped
along in his new red gown, with his head thrown back and eyes
on the buildings, roofs, and sky. She also said of the previous
evening: ". . . He took me down to dinner and on the stairs I
discovered the kind, blue-eyed man to be friendly and not
formidable. He talked on every subject. . . . He gave me the
feeling of never being old; and was the gentlest, dearest of
men!"

Robert Browning, at his son's urgent invitation, went to
Italy for what proved to be his last visit. On December 18,
1889, he passed away. On the last day of the year, Westminster Abbey received one poet more, while those beautiful
words of his wife's were sung:

> What would we give to our beloved?

His last book, *Asolando*, was published on the day he died.

v

Browning's fame was at its flood tide then; it is at an ebb
now. This is not unnatural. In the 'nineties Browning was almost worshipped. His very faults were proclaimed virtues. The
sturdy, optimistic tone of his poetry was especially praised,
his assertion that he was

One who never turned his back but marched breast forward,
Never doubted clouds would break,
Never dreamed, tho' right were worsted, wrong would triumph,
Held we fall to rise, are baffled to fight better,
     Sleep to wake.

These are indeed brave lines, reminding us of the Anglo-Saxon soldier's cry to his comrades in the *Battle of Maldon*, when the fight was going against them:

Harder shall purpose be, heart be the bolder,
Courage grow the keener as our strength littleth.

But along with this sturdiness went Browning's ejaculations and crudities and conversational cavorting, and much booming about braveness and manliness and buoyancy. This seemed good in 1880. Roughness was what the Victorian Era lacked. Men and women were grateful to a poet who, while writing profoundly enough to puzzle them, could jest at them and cuff them and talk so bluff and bold as to be almost profane.

However, as time passed, other writers became really rough, and all the fizz went out of Browning's oddities and good-natured bluster. After Masefield's *Everlasting Mercy* and Masters's *A Spoon River Anthology* and plays like *What Price Glory*, the antics of Browning's most unusual characters seemed innocent and a little insipid. Then, too, as Browning's peculiarities of expression became well known, his poetry, once puzzling, became simple enough to understand, and its faults stood out the more clearly. The tremendous enthusiasm of Browning societies seemed foolish, and not a little of the sentimental folly got attached to the poetry that had inspired it.

However, Browning is likely to have a better day. He did not write his glowing dramatic monologues for nothing. After the present reaction against him, there is likely to come a new friendliness. It will be remembered that he revived the dramatic spirit in English verse, and put it to a novel and modern use, bringing in much modern psychology before modern psychology was born. It will be recalled that he showed how poetry could be enlivened with modern humour and the play of talk and ideas, how it could be sharpened with pungent rhyme and rhythm. And, although Browning never achieved the height of blended harmony and feeling that Shakespeare and Milton, Keats and Wordsworth and Tennyson won, there will also be a revival of enjoyment in the intense, if unsustained, passages of beauty which he created.

CHAPTER XXIV

THE POET OF RAVENS AND LOST LADIES

I

The continent of North America had been discovered half a hundred years before the first great modern English poetry was written. Even before Shakespeare came to London, an English poet had been busy trying to establish a settlement on what is now the shore of North Carolina. Sir Walter Raleigh failed with this dream. His colonists deserted, and almost nothing of his scheme has lasted save the word "Virginia," the name for the new land with which he honoured the virgin English queen, Elizabeth. Yet before Milton was born a successful colony had been planted at Jamestown, and a second one followed soon afterward in Massachusetts. If Milton had not been blind in 1660 he might have fled from the triumphant Royalists to hide in the little Puritan world across the sea and write *Paradise Lost* by Boston Bay.

But England sent no poet to America in the Seventeenth Century, and no poet was born in the New World. The colonies grew, and won their independence, and gathered a population of more than five million people, and were still without a stanza of verse we think worth reading to-day.

This was natural enough. Poetry does not live comfortably among log huts and Indian wars. There is, of course, a great deal of poetry in such things, and American poets were to find it. But the poets did not come until cities had appeared and newspapers and struggling magazines and even a few book publishers. The first poem written in America worth comparing with memorable English poetry was *Thanatopsis*, a grave lyric in blank verse written by William Cullen Bryant. It was written by Bryant when he was a boy of seventeen, and its concluding lines, speaking of death, have a fine and simple dignity:

> So live, that when thy summons comes to join
> The innumerable caravan, which moves
> To that mysterious realm, where each shall take
> His chamber in the silent halls of death,
> Thou go not, like the quarry-slave at night,
> Scourged to his dungeon, but, sustained and soothed
> By an unfaltering trust, approach thy grave
> Like one who wraps the drapery of his couch
> About him, and lies down to pleasant dreams.

A number of poets were soon writing poetry that, like Bryant's, startled and roused Americans. The lyrics and verse stories of Longfellow, Whittier, Emerson, and Lowell put into song American thought and feeling and American legend.

However, their verse was produced in a new, growing, bustling land, with too few readers able to appreciate good poetry when they saw it. Emerson, who had the greatest mind and soul of them all, wrote most of his poems in prose. Lowell was more a critic than a poet. Whittier and Longfellow wrote with an admirable simplicity. If a poet were to become great because he wrote poetry that millions of people love and read, Longfellow would be a great poet. In *Hiawatha* he created the first poetry of wigwams and moccasined Indian hunters. His *Evangeline* and *The Courtship of Miles Standish* have put old American legends into our life and talk. But like Bryant and Lowell and Whittier

Longfellow made no poems with the magic and eternal quality of Wordsworth's, Keats's, or Shelley's. He has a lasting place in poetry, but not among the few supreme singers. Yet, while he was writing, two poets appeared in America who have taken their place among the great makers of poetry.

II

Mrs. David Poe, a pretty young actress, died in Richmond, Virginia, in 1811. She left three little children behind her; and a flutter of sympathy for them went through the town. Mrs. John Allan, the wife of a prospering tobacco merchant, was particularly concerned. She had no children of her own. "General" Poe, grandfather of the orphans, took the oldest, William, but let Rosalie go to a sympathetic stranger, and Mrs. Allan brought the second child, Edgar, then two years old, to her own home.

As it happened, the Allans were not the best people to become the foster parents of the boy. It is true that they belonged to the aristocracy of the town, and that Mr. Allan was already successful at the business which was to make him one of the wealthiest men in Virginia. It is true also that he and his wife tried to be kind to Edgar. They took him with them to England when he was six years old and put him in a good school. When they returned to America five years later, they continued his education at the best academy to be found, and saw that he had dress and training to fit the social position he occupied as their son. Any ordinary boy would have thought himself lucky to get what they gave Edgar Allan Poe, then called Edgar Allan.

But Poe was not an ordinary boy. His English mother had come from a family of actors. His father, an American of North Ireland ancestry, was wild and irresponsible. He forsook the law to go on the stage, drank too much whisky, and finally abandoned his family. Edgar himself was born in the theatre. Everything in him was as different as possible from the honest, shrewd, hard-minded tobacco dealer who had taken him into his home.

Poe was sensitive, and he quickly felt this difference. He discovered, too, that though this Mr. Allan had taken charge of
him, he had not adopted him. Poe would have been a problem in
any case. He vibrated to his surroundings like a violin string to
the least brush of a finger. In England, for instance, he brooded
on the ghosts that were said to walk about his school, and
stored up gloomy pictures of walls that probably looked quite
natural to his schoolmates. But, though he would have been
difficult for any parents, he was undoubtedly a greater problem
for the Allans than he might have been for his mother. Mr.
Allan remarked bitterly in a letter he wrote when Poe was
fifteen on the boy's "moody and unruly manner toward all the
family" and his "complete absence of any sense of gratitude."
However, the self-righteous and rather stupid merchant continued to do what he regarded as his duty. Poe stayed at school
as Mr. Allan's son. He studied French, made Latin verses, and,
when fifteen, swam six miles upstream in the James River.
This seems to have been a Byronic feat, the sort of stunt a
proud, headstrong, morbidly sensitive boy would carry off to
win the admiration of unsympathetic comrades. About that
time he fell into a passion of grief at the death of Mrs. Stanard,
the mother of one of his schoolmates. She had been gently kind
to him, and the tale runs that he haunted her grave at night for
months after she died. All his life he was to carry her name as a
sacred and mysterious memory, dead ladies and haunted graves
were to appear in many of his stories, and any woman named
Helen stirred sweet and melancholy echoes in him.

A year later, Poe fell in love with a girl who lived in the
neighbourhood; but his letters were intercepted, and Sarah
Elmira Royster married someone else. Another year, and we
find him registered at the University of Virginia, where all the
young bucks of the Southern aristocracy drank and gambled
like gentlemen, fought, smashed windows, rang the college bell
at unholy hours, bellowed plantation melodies in their rooms,
and tore on their blooded horses through the college grounds.

Poe came to the University rankling with the taunts of the boys at school about his mother's profession (which, in years to follow, he always vehemently championed), and moody and bitter with Mr. Allan. He saw that Allan had taught him to live like an aristocrat, but, by refusing to adopt him, had left his future uncertain. Poe realized that he might be thrown on the world at Allan's whim. He resented this. The schoolfellows found the proud, dark young man with glowing eyes "self-willed, capricious, inclined to be imperious, and, though of generous impulse, not steadily kind or even amiable." He took to gambling. He discovered that a glass of liquor gulped down raised his spirits and made him talk of phantasies which sobered everyone but himself. Unhappy in his ordinary life, in these moments he could glitter splendidly. They were a reckless escape from the humiliation he felt in his parentage and situation, and the limited income Mr. Allan gave him.

But the gambling and drinking brought debts to Poe's guardian, and Mr. Allan called his ward back to Richmond and put him to work. Poe could not stomach this. Perhaps Richmond was laughing at him. Perhaps there was a quarrel following on many that had certainly gone before.

He fled, enlisted in the United States Army, repented, and at last begged Mr. Allan to forgive him and secure his release. The latter got Poe transferred to West Point, but he did it with bad grace. His first wife had died; remarried now, he had a son, and was fully determined to be quit of his foster child. "Frankly, sir," he informed the Secretary of War, "do I declare he is no relation to me whatsoever."

Poe did not last long as a cadet. He soon deliberately got discharged, came back and told Mr. Allan what he thought of him, and was probably informed that he had "the blackest heart and deepest ingratitude" of all mankind. Allan died soon after. Poe, thrown on the world without money and without any apparent way of making money, disappeared for several years into miserable poverty.

III

Poe's life thus far had been unsuccessful. He had failed with the Allans, he had failed or suffered in his few feeble gropings for human love, he had failed in school, he had failed in the army. He must have felt the more a failure in everyday life because the land in which he lived had less use for failure than any other. It was a new land, busy and thriving, with its people urging one another to lead respectable and successful lives. Men with tempers and temperaments had been miserable in Europe—poets like Byron and Shelley in England, for example. In America, full of work to be done and fame and money to be made, the temperamental Poe had every reason to be more "out of joint" than anywhere else.

But he had already turned from the practical life that had agreed so poorly with him. He was seeking consolation and confidence in a dream world. In 1827, when only nineteen, he had published a volume of poems. It contained forty pages of verse, and was called *Tamerlane and Other Poems, by a Bostonian*. Of course, Poe, though born in Boston, usually preferred to call himself a "Virginian." But the book appeared in Boston, and might sell better if advertised as being written by a native son. When it suited Poe, he could juggle localities and loyalties. Probably he got a thrill out of such posturing. He was to show all his life a love for nom de plumage and romantic parades and hoaxes. They gave him a sense of secret superiority, and blended into the growing mythology and masquerade he was to create for his own consolation and deception.

Tamerlane was not much of a poem—the kind a number of boys of nineteen have written. A second volume published in Baltimore in 1829 was also of little account. But Poe's *Poems*, brought out in New York in 1831, showed that, in turning from life into his own dreams, he had begun to make a strange and mysterious beauty. He put in this volume the brief lyric *To Helen*, with its romantic yearning:

On desperate seas long wont to roam,
Thy hyacinth hair, thy classic face,
Thy Naiad airs have brought me home
To the glory that was Greece
And the grandeur that was Rome.

He wrote of Israfel, the angel who sang so wildly well in Heaven that

Tottering above
In her highest noon,
The enamoured Moon
Blushes with love,
While, to listen, the red levin
(With the rapid Pleiads, even,
Which were seven),
Pauses in Heaven.

He wrote of *The City in the Sea:*

No rays from the holy heaven come down
On the long night-time of that town;
But light from out the lurid sea
Streams up the turrets silently,
Gleams up the pinnacles far and free:
Up domes, up spires, up kingly halls,
Up fanes, up Babylon-like walls,
Up shadowy long-forgotten bowers
Of sculptured ivy and stone flowers,
Up many and many a marvellous shrine
Whose wreathèd friezes intertwine
The viol, the violet, and the vine.

Resignedly beneath the sky
The melancholy waters lie.
So blend the turrets and shadows there
That all seem pendulous in air,
While from a proud tower in the town
Death looks gigantically down.

. . . .

And when, amid no earthly moans,
Down, down that town shall settle hence,
Hell, rising from a thousand thrones,
Shall do it reverence

There was nothing ordinary in such poetry. These lines showed a poet reaching with startling success into a world of imagination for the magnificence he could not find in the everyday world about him. To some extent, at least, all poets do this. Poe, who was to do it perhaps more than any of them, revealed in these early poems the zest and intensity with which he could abandon the real for unreality.

In the few years following 1831, he must have lived a great deal on dreams and delusions. He liked to tell in later years that he had gone to Europe to help the Greeks in their fight for independence, that he had travelled by way of Russia and met obstacles there that turned him back. This seems to have been entirely a myth. Probably Poe took refuge in Baltimore almost at once with his aunt, Mrs. Clemm, a seamstress, and was supported by her while he read and wrote and made a few futile attempts to find work. With Mrs. Clemm was her young daughter Virginia, a pale, delicate child. Poe became very fond of her. In 1834, when she was only twelve years old, he took out a license to marry her, and in 1836 he finally did so. The fragile, unearthly beauty of his child wife blended harmoniously into the world of dream he was making, and for the eleven succeeding years that Virginia lived, Poe was apparently happy with her.

But before he had made this strange marriage, the young poet had attracted some attention to his writing. In 1833, the Baltimore *Saturday Visitor* announced a literary contest, and offered a prize of fifty dollars for the best story and one of twenty-five dollars for the best poem submitted. Poe sent in both prose and poetry. The judges gave his story, *MS. Found in a Bottle*, the larger of the two prizes, and would have given his poem *The Coliseum* the other prize if they had not objected to the same writer winning both.

At first nothing came of this success. Poe visited the editor of the magazine, and the latter remembered that he was pale and gentlemanly. He was dressed in shabby black but "carried himself erect and well, as one who had been trained to it." He talked easily about *A Voyage to the Moon*, a prose account he claimed to be writing, and spoke learnedly "upon the laws of gravity, the height of the earth's atmosphere, and the capacity of balloons." However, though he aroused the interest of the editor and the judges, he struggled on in poverty for almost two years. Then, through the encouragement and help of the novelist, John P. Kennedy, who had been one of the judges, he sold a story to the *Southern Literary Messenger* of Richmond, and soon afterward became editor of that magazine at five hundred and twenty dollars a year, a salary that in those times was not a bad one.

I V

This was success of a kind, and for a time it grew, until the prospects of the strange young man in black seemed very bright. The *Messenger* had only seven hundred readers when Poe took charge of it. He began publishing tales that were weird with terror, horror, gloom. In them strange mansions tottered and collapsed, ladies of unearthly beauty walked through unearthly romance, the souls of men were transfixed by grotesque and fearful emotions. Poe wrote sensational book reviews also, fearless, often devastating, always exciting. The *Messenger* soon had five thousand instead of seven hundred readers, and its young editor began to be known throughout the country.

However, all the while, the same habits that had made him fail under other circumstances were again gnawing at his success. Apparently, the aristocracy of Richmond remembered him and would have little to do with him; he was depressed and embittered, and he drank. He was not a steady drinker, but a glass or two seemed to drive him out of himself into a kind of insanity. So, though he had at last found opportunity in the literary world, he wrote desperately to a friend at this time: "I am wretched and know not why. Console me—if you can. But let it be quickly, or it will be too late." Soon after this, his employer wrote him a friendly but warning letter. Poe, he said, must put liquor out of his life or leave the *Messenger*. Poe made promises, but soon broke them, and the *Messenger* and he parted company. He had failed again. He said years afterward of such occurrences: "It has not been in pursuit of pleasure that I have perilled life and reputation and reason. It has been in the desperate attempt to escape from torturing memories, from a sense of insupportable loneliness, and a dread of some strange impending doom."

The next seven years were a repetition of experiences like this. Sometimes, as in the case of *Graham's Magazine* in Philadelphia, the poet held a precarious place for years. Sometimes it was only for months. And always Mrs. Clemm followed where he went, making a home for Poe and Virginia (now his wife) in the face of Poe's poverty and Virginia's sickness, never complaining, giving him a crude haven where he could come in bitterness and desperation to find a kind of escape from the hostile world.

And Poe's escape was more and more into that strange unreality of his tales and poems. Not that he often suggested in a word or gesture that the magazine office was a place of failure. He walked about Baltimore and Philadelphia and New York with a sombre and superior pride. He wrote with enormous pretense to knowledge, gesticulating angrily in print over unhappy authors whose work displeased him. But all the time he was turning more and more to a realm of imagination in which phantoms made a gorgeous parade. Here he could win a kind of true mastery, marshalling his shadows and incredible lights and sounds into stories or verse that, like a madman's, had a marvellous exactness and made unreality seem real. And, having set his triumph down in words, he could carry it out of dream into print; he could force the practical world to come under the spell he created and admit his mastery. Then he could exult. He cried: "I love fame. I dote upon it. I idolize it. I would drink to the dregs the glorious intoxication; I would have incense arise in my honour from every hamlet."

And soon it began at last to arise. He was able in 1843 to publish a number of his stories in a volume entitled *Tales of the Grotesque and Arabesque,* and his prose work began to be talked of seriously in American cities among literary men and women, and in France and England. Then, in 1845, his poem *The Raven* appeared in the New York *Evening Mirror,* and as if an explosion had sent the sound of it everywhere, his name was on all lips. *The Raven and Other Poems* was published soon afterward, and the book brought praise from Hawthorne in America and Elizabeth Barrett Browning in England.

The Raven was not the best of Poe's poems, but it was the easiest to read. It attracted attention first to itself, and then to his other verse. The eerie episode of the black bird tapping on the chamber door of the poet, stirring nameless fears in him, entering, perching on the bust of Pallas and croaking, "Nevermore!" was just understandable enough and just mysterious enough to please millions of readers. They, like the poet, thrilled to

> ... the silken 'sad uncertain rustling of each purple curtain.

They delighted in the weaving rhymes with their sepulchral insistence:

> Open here I flung the shutter, when, with many a flirt and flutter,
> In there stepped a stately Raven of the saintly days of yore;
> Not the least obeisance made he; not an instant stopped or stayed he;
> But, with mien of lord or lady, perched above my chamber door,—
> Perched upon a bust of Pallas just above my chamber door,—
> Perched, and sat, and nothing more—

and, at the end, they pondered over the symbolic horror of the last stanza, where the Raven is pictured sitting, sitting, throwing his shadow on the floor.

> And my soul from out that shadow that lies floating on the floor
> Shall be lifted—nevermore!

Poe had come to New York to live, and though Boston and not New York was then the literary centre of the country, in the second-rate literary salons of the latter city he tasted a few years of fame and praise. Then Virginia died, and Poe, never at ease with the new American life about him, staggered through several years of nervous excitement and poverty (for he got little money from his poems or tales or the strange philosophical work, *Eureka*, which he published in 1848), and died finally in Baltimore under mysterious circumstances. Undoubtedly he had been drinking, but his death was not due to alcohol.

v

Poe wrote few poems, and, although his tales are more numerous, not a great amount of prose either. He is a proof of the fact that quality in writing is far more important than quantity, for he has come to have a place both in poetry and prose among the unforgettable creators.

There is something in this that seems puzzling. Poe's poems are many of them imitative and melodramatic. He absorbed the glamour of Coleridge, in reading whose poetry he says he trembled "like one who stands upon a volcano, conscious from the very darkness bursting from the crater, of the fire and light that are weltering below." Though he bitterly assailed Longfellow and others because he thought they had stolen phrases and ideas from him and other writers, he borrowed many himself; and *The Raven*, published in 1845, certainly owes a great deal to Mrs. Browning's poem, *Lady Geraldine's Courtship*, brought out in the previous year. Mrs. Browning had written:

With a murmurous stir uncertain, in the air, the purple curtain
Swelleth in and swelleth out around her motionless pale brows;
While the gliding of the river sends a rippling noise for ever
Through the open casement whitened by the moonlight's scant repose.

Said he—"Vision of a lady! stand there silent, stand there steady!
Now I see it plainly, plainly; now I cannot hope or doubt—
There, the brows of mild repression—there, the lips of silent passion,
Curv'd like an archer's bow to send the bitter arrows out."

The similarity in metre and rhyme and even in certain words is easily seen.

Yet, as we read Poe, his debts and his stealings seem a small matter. There is something about his poetry that is wholly original.

If we wish to understand this, we have only to remind ourselves of his strange life. As we look on it, we see that he was strangely frustrated in the everyday world. Probably, under the best of circumstances, he would have found it a difficult place, but he lived in a growing, successful country where leisure for art was small; he was brought up by foster parents who taught him pride, could not give him sympathy, and denied him money; he was tragically susceptible to drink; he entered manhood with a series of failures behind him. All this threw him into his haunted dream world as no poet was ever thrown, and because he had been so fully rejected in his experience with reality, he made unreality more real than any other poet!

This is not the explanation Poe gave of his art, but it is harmonious with that explanation. Poe said he wrote as he did because he sought "Art for Beauty's sake." He found his duty in Taste—"Taste waging war upon Vice solely on the ground of her deformity—her disproportion—her animosity to the fitting, to the appropriate, to the harmonious . . . in a word, to Beauty." This was a sufficiently good description of Poe's own poetry, but the poetry came first and the description afterward. And it was because Poe had actually lived and suffered more in the realm of imagination than in his everyday world that he could give such intense and exact images, that his Beauty, freed from reality, could be so severely true to its own eerie and terrible self.

And what shall be said of this beauty? We enter it to walk amid bizarre and terrific towers. We are shadowed by mysterious skies, we stand by dark waters. The poet shuts out the sun. It sifts only through thick leafage or stained glass or heavy arras. Perfume comes to us, but it emanates not from flowers, but censers invisibly agitated; it is stealthy and overpowering. We see light, but of tapers and torches wind-shaken, whose writhing shadows are more important than their flame. Graves yawn, caskets disgorge. Feelings of nameless horror float in the air like mist.

This is very different poetry from the human verse of Shakespeare, the simple but exalted truth of Wordsworth, the rich but quiet beauty of Keats. Poe's lines are unnatural, brilliant, fearful in comparison with the work of these more normal poets.

Yet his poetry has its value. There is a kind of terrible mathematical power in his lurid words. He seems to dissolve the substance of speech and give old syllables a new intensity:

> The skies they were ashen and sober;
> The leaves they were crisped and sere,—
> The leaves they were withering and sere,—
> It was night in the lonesome October
> Of my most immemorial year;
> It was hard by the dim lake of Auber,
> In the misty mid-region of Weir,—
> It was down by the dank tarn of Auber,
> In the ghoul-haunted woodland of Weir.

"Auber," "Weir," what and where are they? The poet says them, and they are. So are his "dank tarn," the "misty mid-region," the unnatural leaves. He has brought up from his brooding a severe distillation of sound and atmosphere, has created out of his tortured dream-experience something that is weirdly superb.

Such poetry seems unnatural to many; certainly it is abnormal, yet Poe, with an iced lucidity, gives it a firm artistic form that we must admire for its almost inhuman magnificence. Writing from among the shadows of his own soul, he made a beauty so stringent, so close to perfection that it gives, as the French poet Baudelaire says, a "taste of eternity."

Yet it is human, too. We are all to some degree frustrated. We have all known despair. We get in the music of Poe's suppressed experience magnified echoes of our own troubled souls. We know in some degree the hell that was in his heart, the black fire banked up and threatening to break through. Even his wild hallucinations, grotesque lamps and waving arras, dim cities and leaden seas, rouse a familiarity in us. Poe, the high priest of despair, has suffered darker contradictions in his soul than most of us have known, but they are, after all, human contradictions.

So we accept him, terror and horror and agony. We may like the quietly mournful *Annabel Lee*, and lines of simple grief like

Ah! broken is the golden bowl! the spirit flown forever.

Yet we find his most inspired poetry and his most haunting rhythms in his more "unnatural" moods. In these, striding through a dream of mingled pain and splendour, he uttered lines like

The viol, the violet and the vine,

and made those refrains that beat the mood of his verse into the depth of our souls. This poetry, with its sound and emotion, intensifies our sense of human experience. It has little obvious meaning, but through its dark and glittering perfection it somehow lifts higher for us the significance of life.

CHAPTER XXV

"I SING DEMOCRACY"

Long Island, lying like a great fish with its nose at the mouth of the Hudson River, its body curving for 125 miles along the shore of Connecticut, its tail flirting into the wind and spray of the great Atlantic, is geographically a world in itself. To-day its 2,500,000 people are chained by subways and bridges to Manhattan, but in 1820 it lay apart. Water encircled it, and crossing the water was an event for any of the 60,000 Long Islanders. They stayed much to themselves. They went to the little town of Brooklyn to buy provisions, to sell fruit and grain, fish, wool, meat, butter, and eggs.

At West Hills, near the north shore, lived Walter Whitman, a carpenter. His ancestors, people of sturdy English stock, had owned a large farm, and he had begun life as a farmer. He was a big, silent man. He had married Louisa Van Velsor, part Dutch and part Welsh by descent.

His second son Walt (they called him that to distinguish him from his father) had been born at West Hills in 1819. A sturdy, fresh-coloured little boy, he tumbled about the yard of his father and grandfather. Later on, Walter Whitman moved to Brooklyn and began to build houses there. Young Walt now got glimpses of the world beyond the harbour water. Pilots brought their ships to the wharves. Every day the mail boat went to the bigger town of New York on Manhattan Island, across the bay. There were sometimes celebrations, parades, speeches. General Lafayette, who had fought for America in the Revolutionary War, was visiting the United States then, and came one day to Brooklyn. He saw rosy-cheeked Walt Whitman in the crowd and picked him up and kissed him.

About the town were shops and warehouses. Walt wandered among them, curiously watching and listening. He also went out of town to the beaches, delighting in the white-tongued waves and the music of the breakers. From his grandfather Whitman's farm, or from the old Van Velsor homestead, he tramped or rode as he grew older, seeing the island. He talked with clam diggers and Indians and the wild sheep herders on the great eastern plains toward Montauk Point.

At some time in these years Walt Whitman seems to have got an idea that he would discover what life was and tell men about it. In one of his poems, written years later, he describes how, as a boy, he heard a bird singing near the seashore for its lost mate. The bird's song and the wild sea music woke something in him.

I, that was a child, my tongue's use sleeping,
Now I have heard you,
Now in a moment I know what I am for—I awake,
And already a thousand singers—a thousand songs, clearer, louder, and more
    sorrowful than yours,
A thousand warbling echoes have started to life within me,
Never to die.

It was not that he knew he wanted to be a poet. He did not know exactly what had happened to him. But he had felt the curiosity, the mystery and wonder, the yearning to know and express knowledge, out of which all poets are to some extent fashioned. This was to stay with him a long time before he saw clearly how he should go about making poetry.

Indeed, for many years he seemed to be very far from poetry.

When he was twelve, he had to leave school. He went to work for a kindly lawyer, who one day brought him a library card and said:

"Walt, go and get some books and read them when you aren't busy."

Soon Walt was in the *Arabian Nights* and Walter Scott's novels. Then he left the lawyer to work for a doctor, left the doctor to go back with the family to Huntington and learn the printer's trade, taught school for a year or two, and finally started a little weekly newspaper with his brother George. He had begun to write for New York newspapers, too. "He's a smart boy," the neighbours must have said, "even if he is kind of lazy." For Walt, though he wrote and set up and delivered the *Long Islander* mostly by himself, always found time to gossip, or to lie under a tree dreaming, or to stroll down to the sea with a book.

How he left Huntington and went to Brooklyn and New York, how he wrote for various papers and edited some of them, how some of his stories appeared in magazines—Edgar Allan Poe printed several that he had written in the *Messenger*—how he finally published a novel against drunkenness—all that is a long and not too interesting story. Nor is the verse Whitman wrote then for the papers of much interest. It was much like other verse of the time, rhymed and well metred and unimportant.

In reality the most important thing he was doing in all these years was what people called his loafing. Young Walt Whitman never seemed to be in a hurry. Something of a Broadway dandy, carrying a cane, wearing a bud in his buttonhole, he stopped on his way to the office to see workmen tinning a roof, or to talk with a policeman. He saw the crowd pour from the ferryboat. He rode on the Broadway omnibuses for hours. He sat there beside Broadway Jack the driver, or Pop Rice or Old Elephant. Jack or Pop would spin a yarn, or Walt would recite *Julius Cæsar*.

At night, in the city, he went constantly to theatres and opera houses. One night at the theatre he met a genial Southern gentleman. The two had a friendly drink together (in spite of Whitman's novel on temperance), and the Southern gentleman persuaded the young journalist to go to New Orleans and help start a newspaper there. So away went Whitman across the Alleghanies and down the Mississippi, drinking in and storing up new glimpses of that great untamed and exciting country, America.

Perhaps his life in New Orleans helped him to understand what he wanted to do. He seems finally to have grown up there. Partly it may have been getting away from his home and seeing his past life from a distance. Partly it may have been falling in love. For, while Whitman never would tell much of what happened on his Southern trip, we know that he met in New Orleans some woman, apparently of great fineness and intelligence, who had a deep influence on his life. However this may be, he seems to have been more mature from this time on, and it was not long after his return from New Orleans that he began to plan a daring and tremendous work.

This was nothing less than the making over of American poetry. Whitman, now thirty years of age, felt at last that the poems Americans had made had little to do with the new, throbbing America he had seen. Where, he must have asked himself, is the real America in poems like Poe's *The Raven* or Longfellow's *Evangeline?* He surely read and thought upon Emerson's words: "Why should we grope among the dusty bones of the past? Why should not we also have an original relation to the universe?" At any rate, the idea came to him of writing a poetry, free and big-voiced, that should have in it the pulse of the prairies, the pine woods, the seashores, the plantations.

He left the world of newspapers and magazines and went to work as a carpenter with his brothers. At night he wrote and wrote. His poems grew into a book. He tramped down to Orient Point and read the book and flung it into the ocean. It was no good. But finally he wrote again and again, and when he had made his fifth version, he put down his carpenter's tools and went to a little printing shop in Brooklyn and set with his own hands the type of a small volume called *Leaves of Grass*.

It was an attractive book, with a picture of Whitman himself as a frontispiece. It was no longer Whitman of the frock coat and stovepipe hat, but a man in rough workman's clothes, his shirt open at the throat, a soft hat shading the hair and beard and dreamy eyes, the Whitman the world was to know from that time forward.

In July of 1855, the volume appeared for sale in a few bookstores, and Whitman sent copies of it to magazines and newspapers and to a few well-known authors. Most of those who read it were surprised, puzzled, outraged.

For *Leaves of Grass* was to them an entirely strange book of poetry. Whitman, seeking for a new form to express the new land, America, had turned his back on blank verse and heroic couplets and ballad stanzas. His poems had no regular metre, no rhyme. They had only a strong rhythm. Probably the book that helped him most to fashion this poetry was the English Bible. The essays of Emerson gave him something, too. Otherwise it seems to have been his own. He chanted in his new verse:

A child said, *What is the grass?* fetching it to me with full hands;
How could I answer the child? I do not know what it is, any more than he.

I guess it must be the flag of my disposition, out of hopeful green stuff woven.

Or I guess it is the handkerchief of the Lord,
A scented gift and remembrancer, designedly dropped,
Bearing the owner's name someway in the corners, that we may see and re-
    mark, and say, *Whose?*
        .   .   .   .

And now it seems to me the beautiful, uncut hair of graves.

Tenderly will I use you, curling grass;
It may be you transpire from the breasts of young men;
It may be if I had known them I would have loved them;
It may be you are from old people, and from women, and from offspring
    taken soon out of their mothers' laps.

What do you think has become of the young and old men?
And what do you think has become of the women and children?

They are alive and well somewhere;
The smallest sprout shows there is really no death;
. . . All goes onward and outward—nothing collapses;
And to die is different from what any one supposed, and luckier.

This was not what editors and authors had thought of as poetry. This great, confident belief in life, running riot through this poem and through the whole book, surprised and shocked them. Whitman announced that life was boundless.

I have heard what the talkers were talking, the talk of the beginning and the end;
But I do not talk of the beginning and the end.

No, he said, life has no beginning or end, and one part of it is ss good as another. He himself was good. He says half-humorously yet seriously, "I find no sweeter fat than sticks to my own bones." The Body and the Soul were good, heaven and hell had their places. And, he cried:

I am the poet of the woman the same as the man;
And I say it is as great to be a woman as to be a man;
And I say there is nothing greater than the mother of men.

Good and evil? Each in its place and part.

I am not the poet of goodness only—I do not decline to be the poet of wickedness also.

Earth "of the slumbering and liquid trees; earth of departed sunset" was splendid. So was the sea with its "crooked inviting fingers," so were all the activities of men on earth and sea. The trapper with luxuriant beard and curls, marrying the Indian girl; the blacksmith, the pilot, the printer, the slave girl on the auction block, the canal boy on the towpath, the lunatic, the bride, the President at his Cabinet meeting—all these were rich with life for Whitman. "Such as it is to be one of these, more or less, I am."

He would not refuse the least of them:

> O despairer, here is my neck;
> By God! You shall not go down! Hang your whole weight upon me.

He found life open to everyone—man or woman—"Let your soul stand cool and composed before a million universes." He was unabashed:

> The spotted hawk swoops by and accuses me—he complains of my gab and my loitering.
>
> I too am not a bit tamed—I too am untranslatable;
> I sound my barbaric yawp over the roofs of the world.

All this was extraordinary. The editors and authors didn't know what to make of it. "Muck!" cried some, reading one of Whitman's descriptions of criminals or sweating workmen. "Obscenity!" others said, shocked at his frank remarks about the love of men and women. "Full of bombast, egotism, vulgarity, and nonsense," pronounced a third critic. One went so far as to assert that Whitman "deserved the whip of the public executioner." There were some reviews expressing a good opinion, but they were cautious and apologetic.

It took all of Whitman's vitality and courage to keep him from feeling that he had attempted something useless and impossible. But, he said later, he went out to the east end of Long Island, and after talking things over with the sea and the shore,

> I came back to New York with the confirmed resolution, from which I never afterward wavered, to go on with my poetic enterprise in my own way and finish it as well as I could.

Undoubtedly, he was helped in this resolve by a letter from Emerson. Emerson was one of the authors to whom Whitman had sent copies of *Leaves of Grass*. Probably his belief in individuality and self-reliance, expressed in his well-known essays, had helped Whitman to shape his own larger philosophy of generous courage. Emerson now wrote from his home at Concord:

I give you joy of your free and brave thought. I have great joy in it. I find things said incomparably well . . .

I greet you at the beginning of a great career, which yet must have a long foreground somewhere, for such a start. I rubbed my eyes a little, to see if this sunbeam were no illusion; but the solid sense of the book is a sober certainty. It has the best merits, namely, of fortifying and encouraging.

It was a noble, generous letter. Emerson cooled a little when Whitman issued a new edition of the book, printing the letter. Yet when he saw Whitman later he was won immediately by the large, vital, genial personality of the poet.

So were others who read *Leaves of Grass* and saw its author. A thousand copies of the 1856 edition were sold. The book went to England and was praised by Rossetti, Swinburne, and Tennyson, who saw that it was unique and throbbing with life. Meanwhile, Whitman had added many new poems—the *Song of the Open Road*, *Crossing Brooklyn Ferry*, part of the *Song of the Answerer*, and poems about men and women.

These were augmented in 1860 by *Children of Adam*, and they hurt the sale and popularity of Whitman's work. Whitman believed in being very frank about sex. He thought the bodies of men and women were beautiful, and that the love springing up between men and women was beautiful. He thought that motherhood and fatherhood were experiences deserving a great place in poetry. About all these matters he wrote freely what he felt. But at that time, many Americans thought such matters should be written about very little or not at all, and Whitman's poems shocked them. There are passages in them that still shock people. For this reason *Children of Adam* and other poems like them made much trouble for Whitman.

But now there was trouble of another kind. The great Civil War began. Men from the prairies and seas and plantations and forests that Whitman loved rushed together in terrible conflict. His brother George marched off with the 51st New York volunteers. Although Walt was now forty-two years old, he himself considered going. But while he was undecided came the news that his brother was seriously wounded. Walt went down to Washington and from Washington to the front. Here, luckily, he found his brother already recovered and ready to go out again as a captain.

But by coming down to the camp Whitman had discovered what he could do about the war. He could help the wounded.

For three years, supplied with a little money by friends and relatives, working himself at journalistic work and in the paymaster's office, he spent all the time he could visiting the sick and wounded in the Washington hospitals. These were overcrowded and not too well organized, equipped, and manned. There was much a big-hearted man or woman could do. Whitman brought tobacco, books, letter paper. He talked to homesick boys and held the hands of the suffering, whispering courage. It is estimated that he did something for nearly 100,000 men, and the sight of him was like medicine to those who knew him.

Years later, a New York reporter was talking with a labourer named Rafferty, working in a field by the road. Rafferty told the reporter how he had been in the hospital during the war. He had been wounded badly in the leg, and the doctors told him they must take off the leg to save his life. He protested, but no one would listen to him. Then he told his troubles to a tall rough-looking man "with the face of an angel" whom he had seen going about helping the other soldiers. This man, after inquiring carefully about the leg, said: "May your mind rest easy, my boy; they sha'n't take it off." Rafferty went on to tell the reporter how he was cheered by this promise, but his eyes filled with tears and his voice choked as he thought of it. Finally, he slapped his leg with his hand and cried: "This is the leg that man saved for me." He couldn't remember the name of his benefactor. He thought it might be Whitcomb. When the reporter suggested Walt Whitman, Rafferty seized his hand and cried: "That's the man, that's the man; do you know him?"

So while the great war between the North and South was being waged, Whitman fought his fight against the loneliness and pain that stalked the wounded in the hospitals. But he saw and suffered more than he saw there. In *Drum-Taps*, 1865, he sang the story of the whole war. He sang of the call to arms:

Beat! beat! drums!—Blow, bugles! blow!
Through the windows—through doors—burst like a ruthless force.

He pictured the army corps

With its cloud of skirmishers in advance,
With now the sound of a single shot, snapping like a whip, and now an irregular volley;

he told of cavalry crossing the ford, of camps at night. He wrote of how he kept watch with a dying soldier, of dressing wounds, of what the soldiers dreamed, how they died, what they fought for. Later he sang also of life to be lived now that the war was over. He had faith in America and Americans.

Have the elder races halted?
Do they droop and end their lesson, wearied, over there beyond the seas?
We take up the task eternal and the burden, and the lesson,
Pioneers, O pioneers!

In America he saw the materials of a better world:

Ages, precedents, have long been accumulating
undirected materials,
America brings builders, and brings its own styles.

Yet he felt that America was not great as a land, but great because of the men and women it promised to make.

I swear nothing is good to me now that ignores individuals:

and to his mind the mission of the country was the creation of nobler people for the world. For this task its strength and youth gave it great opportunity.

Whitman saw, with the ending of the war, the death of

President Lincoln. Lincoln, it has recently been discovered, read and admired *Leaves of Grass*. Whitman knew nothing of this, but he saw in the kindness, humour, patience, vision, and courage of Lincoln the greatness that might come from America. He wrote a number of fine poems mourning Lincoln's death. *O Captain, My Captain!*—one of the few poems Whitman wrote in rhyme and regular metre after 1855—is in every schoolboy's reader. *When Lilacs Last in the Door-Yard Bloomed* is a longer and more beautiful elegy for "the sweetest, wisest soul of all my days and lands."

The tragedy of the war made Whitman's poetry graver and deeper and richer with poems like those described above. The poetry of the years following the war: *Passage to India, Proud Music of the Storm, Out of the Cradle Endlessly Rocking*—these combine music and depth of feeling and are perhaps the grandest of Whitman's poems.

Yet the war struck Whitman a great blow. The sound of agonies, the sight of the dying and dead, the thoughts of his country torn with strife pierced to his heart and put a poison in his blood. There was also his unjust dismissal in 1865 from a clerkship in the Department of the Interior because of his "immoral" poems. All this seems finally to have showed itself in 1873, when Whitman became paralyzed in one arm and leg. He recovered partially, was almost his old self again, but never quite. From the increasing sales of his books, which were stimulated by friends who knew his unhappy condition, he bought a little house at Camden, N. J. Here he lived, sallying forth to ride on the street cars or ferries and watch the crowds he loved, visited by humble people and distinguished people; pondering, talking, writing. His ruddy, noble face, framed by his white hair and beard, gave him the appearance of a prophet. He bore his sickness without complaint, and his singular gentleness of disposition was remarked on by many who saw him.

One friend gives an example of this. Once, he says, Whitman was searching for a letter he had received from Stanton, the

Secretary of War in Lincoln's Cabinet. He found it at last, dilap-idated and apparently deliberately torn by someone. The poet did not show any anger. He looked at the letter a long time, and then said quietly, like a child someone has hurt without cause: "Why, I would give ten dollars if this was not done."

Throughout Whitman's life his poems had gradually been winning respect and admiration. There was always talk about whether they were poetry or prose, and many seemed to have the idea that if they were not poetry they had no value. Nowa-days we do not worry about this. We know that Whitman's poetry is not the same poetry as Tennyson's. There is no reason why the poetry he tried to write—without regularly recurring rhyme or metre—cannot be as beautiful as what we call regular or traditional poetry. Some of Whitman's poetry was very beau-tiful. But to get the fullest music from such a "freer" form each line must be melodious in itself, and melodious in relation to the lines before and after it. To make it so is the most difficult of all tasks in poetry. Whitman never spent the effort necessary to get such an effect. His poetry is loose and free and probably more powerful because it is. Yet he showed as had no one before him the possibilities of loose rhythmic verse. This had been written as an experiment by other poets in England and Germany, but it had never won any important place in poetry. Whitman made it important. In his most musical passages he showed that there was a new poetic form for great poets. The little poem *As I Pondered in Silence* suggests the melodious power of free verse:

> As I ponder'd in silence,
> Returning upon my poems, considering, lingering long,
> A Phantom arose before me, with distrustful aspect,
> Terrible in beauty, age, and power,
> The genius of the poets of old lands,
> As to me directing like flame its eyes,
> With finger pointing to many immortal songs,
> And menacing voice, *What singest thou?* it said—

So also there is haunting beauty in the bird's songs in *Out of the Cradle Endlessly Rocking*, with stanzas like this final stanza of the final song:

> O past! O life! O songs of joy!
> In the air—in the woods—over fields;
> Loved! loved! loved! loved!
> But my love no more, no more with me!
> We two together no more.

One could go to the descriptions in this poem for deep organ music, or to *When Lilacs Last in the Door-Yard Bloomed*, or to many other of Whitman's poems for varied rhythmic loveliness.

In such passages Whitman became the maker of a new type of poetic music. It was a music the modern world needed. Whitman expressed with its cadences the America of his time. He brought in the thousand activities and words that had come with new conditions of life—manufacturing, pioneering, popular education, newspapers, trains, telegraphs. Whitman passed on his music to modern writers of free verse, some of whom have made it more lovely, though never so inspiring or powerful.

He also blew new breath into traditional poetry. From Whitman's verse the older type of poems took new words, more varied cadences, a more vital energy. The old poetry was a house with a set number of rooms out of which the poets dared not wander. Whitman inspired the building of new rooms. He encouraged the poets to make porches and terraces and gardens and to look at the woods and seas and mountains beyond.

These were great contributions to poetry. They are just beginning to be recognized, because the effects of what Whitman did are just beginning to be felt fully. But these artistic contributions would never have been made at all without Whitman's poetic spirit. Poets are musicians and they are also prophets and teachers. Whitman, if not a great musician himself, showed others how they might be great musicians. But they learned from him not because of his musical skill, but because they had to listen to his rousing prophecies, his carelessly or sharply uttered truths. He gave the world a message of vitality and generosity. This had been given in various forms before, but Whitman suited it to modern life, made it wholly generous and inclusive. It was the song of Democracy—Democracy that means not that all men shall have a little and no one very much, but Democracy that means the rich expression of life for every man and woman. Whitman knew the faults of Democracy. He said once that the United States had been "endowed with a vast and more thoroughly appointed body, and left with little or no soul." But he sang proudly of the souls men could have in a land like America if they were willing to develop themselves. He made the world realize as no other writer had that all life and all men had something fine, that evil and pain could be translated into positive, productive things, that life was always beginning for anyone brave enough to live it.

In doing this, Whitman made a new and rich poetic world, and he is still making it. His words are becoming more and more known. He himself knew he would find a slow response to what he had to say.

> Who are you, that only wanted to be told what you knew before?
> Who are you, that wanted only a book to join you in your nonsense?

But gradually America has responded, and England, France, and Germany have responded. Already Whitman is considered by many to be the greatest poetic force of the last century. True, when someone mentions him with Shakespeare, Milton, Æschylus, or Dante, there is a cry that Whitman is hardly a poet at all, and should not be placed with the great world poets. Yet we continue to talk of him when great poetry is discussed, and perhaps his greatness is proved by our not having an exact place to put him. He was, after all, not a person to be placed, as he knew himself.

I know I have the best of time and space, and was never measured, and never
    will be measured. . . .

I depart as air—I shake my white locks at the runaway sun . . .

I bequeath myself to the dirt, to grow from the grass I love;
If you want me again, look for me under your boot-soles.

You will hardly know who I am, or what I mean,
But I shall be good health to you nevertheless . . .

Failing to find me at first, keep encouraged;
Missing me one place, search another;
I stop somewhere, waiting for you.

CHAPTER XXVI

UNDER STEAM AND STONE

I

While Whitman had been making his new music in a land where the smoke of mills hung over old forests, and six-horse ploughs turned under the prairie grasses through which the red men had crept, new poets were being born in England.

The land they knew was different from Chaucer's or Shakespeare's or even Wordsworth's country. Steam had come, and gas and coal. Noisy factories shot up like dark, square fungi along the Northern rivers, spitting their soot on the wind. Men and women and children crowded in from the cornland and the hill land to tend new steam-driven machines that wove cloth, or the great furnaces that made the stuff of rails and tools and ribs of iron ships. All over England the dark breath of the factories hung in the sky. Sometimes the tenders of the machines, underpaid or out of work, cursed their hard life and the rich owners of the factories. But the mill wheels kept turning, and over all the seas ships were carrying the mill-made cloth and machines to far countries. In the mill towns and the sea towns life was hurried, smoke-grimed, humming at wharves and depots and in the crowded streets.

The new poets looked at this life. It had been creeping on England for some time. Shelley and Byron had seen it, but it was a new thing then, and Shelley at least believed that when men got Liberty, the dark houses, the too much toil, and the want of bread would disappear. Tennyson had seen the workers and the smoke, but mostly he lived apart from them and knew a quiet England of field and forest. He lashed at the towns where men sold "poisoned poison," and was afraid of what might come; still, at times, he got hope and beauty out of the new life, with the promising zest of its swift wheels and the great empire it helped England to build.

But the new poets saw no promise of beautiful life in the ugliness of the mills. Young Matthew Arnold, studying at Oxford and winning a poetry prize there in 1843, already suspected that their noise and hurry were not good. He had been reading Homer and Sophocles. These Greek poets told him of a nobler life than that he saw whirling about him. And when Arnold had graduated from Oxford and taught a little at Rugby and served for a while as secretary to the great Lord Lansdowne, he was more and more certain that there was much in modern life that was wrong. What would come of the stark machines, the crowded streets, the quarrels between labourers and mill owners? Would they lead to something fine and beautiful, he asked? Was there even any good to be hoped for in the uprisings of oppressed peoples against their kings, flaring up every few years in Europe? He did not think so. He felt that the frenzied sweating and quarrelling were probably the tossings of a world sick with ignorance, fretful from a lack of thought, from a failure to understand beauty.

And when he turned to poetry, the thing to be done seemed to him to capture a Greek sense of order and serenity. He wanted to wipe out what he thought the wordiness and silly romanticism of much English poetry and chisel poems in which each word counted and built toward a noble and impressive whole. In *The Strayed Reveller* (1849) he wrote with a simplicity

and in a metre which remind us of the unrhymed choruses of
Sophocles:

> I am Ulysses.
> And thou, too, sleeper?
> Thy voice is sweet.
> It may be thou hast followed
> Through the islands some divine bard . . .
> And heard him delighting
> The chiefs and people
> In the banquet, and learned his songs,
> Of gods and heroes,
> Of war and arts,
> And peopled cities,
> Inland, or built
> By the gray sea. If so, then hail!
> I honour and welcome thee.

This was a poem of the Greek world, but even in his poems of
the North, like *The Forsaken Merman*, Arnold wrote with the
same directness. The merman, sorrowing for his lost human
wife in

> Sand-strewn caverns, cool and deep,
> Where the winds are all asleep;
> Where the spent lights quiver and gleam,
> Were the salt weed sways in the stream . . .
> Where the sea-snakes coil and twine,
> Dry their mail and bask in the brine;

is painted with a few clear word strokes, like the young strayed
reveller who wanders into the garden of Circe and drinks her wine
and sees Ulysses and talks his dreamy talk.

There was no denying the power of this verse. If few people
noticed it when it was first published, and if it fell short of the
more gorgeous poetry of Keats and Tennyson, it was different
and suggested new possibilities. Arnold tried to develop these.
His *Empedocles on Etna* was a dramatic poem modelled on the
Greek drama. His *Poems* (1853) illustrated what he believed,
and even had a preface explaining what he was trying to
do.

In this preface he said that Greek poetry was the best model for poets to study. There were two great differences, he explained, between the Greek poets and the modern poets. One was that the Greeks refused to write at all unless they had something worth writing about, while often the latter-day poets didn't much care what they wrote about if it gave them a chance to make some beautiful lines. And that led to the second difference—which was that the Greeks never let beautiful words interfere with what they had to say. It wasn't that they couldn't write beautiful words. They could and did. But they felt that the highest beauty was always necessary and proportioned. The beauty of words must be only a part of a perfect whole.

For these reasons Arnold thought the Greeks were better guides in poetry than even Shakespeare. Shakespeare, he said, didn't have "their purity of method," though he could perhaps outwrite them. Like other modern poets, Shakespeare often stopped to make beautiful phrases that had little to do with what he was writing about. And writers who tried to learn from Shakespeare, Arnold believed, almost always imitated his habit of wasting words and paid little attention to his fine sense for great stories and his genius for telling them. The Greeks were safer. Arnold said of his own poems: "I find the only sure guidance, the only sound footing, among the ancients."

The *Poems* of 1853 showed that Arnold had practised what he preached, and it was pretty good practice. In *Sohrab and Rustum*, he took an episode of the great Persian poem, the *Shah Nameh*, and wrote it in the Greek epic style. There are few finer stories in English verse than this tale of Rustum, the great Persian warrior who slew a young champion of the Tartars and discovered too late that it was his own son. Entirely different but also fine was *The Scholar-Gypsy*, a quietly beautiful poem about a student who, the old legend said, had left university to live with the gypsies and learn the secret of their happiness.

His hope and peaceful life seemed good to Arnold in contrast with

> this strange disease of modern life,
> With its sick hurry, its divided aims.

Among the shorter poems in this volume, several, like his sonnet, *Shakespeare*, are now among the few hundred English poems that cannot be forgotten.

The next book Arnold published was not so successful. *Merope* (1853) was a poetic tragedy. Arnold took here a Greek story and tried to get in English the effect of the old Greek dialogue and choruses. It was a difficult and probably an unwise thing to do, and Arnold failed with it. The truth is that he had just been appointed Professor of Poetry at Oxford, and thought he had to attempt something scholarly and impressive.

"I wrote it," he said of *Merope* to a friend, "to inaugurate my professorship with dignity rather than to move deeply the present race of humans."

Probably Arnold himself saw fairly soon that *Merope*, fine as it was in parts, came close to being frozen with dignity. If he had gone on writing poetry constantly, he would have turned to things less cold and stately.

But he did not go on writing poetry. His lectures at Oxford took time, he had got married and found a family growing up about him, and in 1851 he had been appointed an Inspector of Schools. This inspectorship was a good position, but it often tired Arnold greatly. It took him on smoky trains about England. It put him to examining teachers, reading the papers of schoolboys, and writing long, conscientious reports about education. Exhausted from such work, he found writing prose easier than writing poetry. Then, too, his essays and lectures were very successful. In them he was able to speak directly on his ideas of how life should be lived, to attack the spirit of the mills and hurried streets, and to talk about great literature. People paid more attention to these essays and lectures than they did to Arnold's poetry.

So he wrote less and less poetry. *Poems* (second series) came out in 1855, then, twelve years later, *New Poems*, then *Collected Poems.* After that he wrote scarcely a dozen pieces of verse before his death thirty-one years later.

Beyond doubt Arnold would have preferred writing poems to inspecting schools. He might have preferred poetry to lectures and essays. With more leisure than he had, he would probably have left behind him more verse and a greater name. Most of what he did is remarkably fine. It is never oversentimental, it speaks clearly and directly, it is loved by all who like truth and restraint. Nor does it lack spirit and strength—Sohrab and Rustum rush

> Together, as two eagles on one prey
> Come rushing down together from the clouds,

and it is a prophet's voice crying of modern life in *Dover Beach*—

> And we are here as on a darkling plain
> Swept with confused alarms of struggle and flight
> Where ignorant armies clash by night.

Still, Arnold's poetry came to be the poetry of a man who had borne much hard work and sorrow (he lost by death all of his three sons) and had lived in an ugly world he wished in vain to make more beautiful. The grave harmony of his lines lacks the colour and leap and dramatic thrill which we find in the greatest English poetry.

Arnold held Pegasus by his golden bridle and rode the divine horse about the hills. He even got off the earth for low skimming flights. But never did he shoot up on shining wings straight toward the sun. Modern life with its wheels and smoke oppressed him and kept him down. Even when he was young, he hated its confused hurry, and all his life he found its noise and ugliness about him. The imperfect but lovely song he wrote in the early 1850's for a lady who had died can be read with his own life in mind. He, too, was often tired and longed for peace, and was perhaps not sorry when it came to him:

REQUIESCAT

Strew on her roses, roses,
 And never a spray of yew:
In quiet she reposes;
 Ah, would that I did too!

Her mirth the world required;
 She bathed it in smiles of glee.
But her heart was tired, tired,
 And now they let her be.

Her life was turning, turning,
 In mazes of heat and sound;
But for peace her soul was yearning,
 And now peace laps her round.

Her cabin'd, ample spirit,
 It flutter'd and fail'd for breath;
To-night it doth inherit
 The vasty hall of death.

II

Meanwhile there were other poets.

Two of these were friends, and both were painters as well as makers of poetry. Dante Gabriel Rossetti, the older of the two, had brought something strange and exotic into English poetry. His father was an Italian—a scholar and librarian who had been driven from Italy for plotting against Ferdinand I, King of Naples. He had settled in England, where he married and taught Italian. His wife also was half Italian, and their son Gabriel was a vivid, enthusiastic young man, with an Italian love for colour, whether in words or in pictures.

William Morris was in his way quite as strange in Nineteenth Century England. He was English, but with his great physical strength, his passionate love of beautiful old churches, and his restless imagination, he seemed like a medieval knight or an adventurous Viking born out of his time to toss against the dullness and conventionality of the mills and towns.

Like Arnold, Rossetti and Morris saw little poetry in modern life. Rossetti had been brought up on Dante's poems and on old Italian paintings. Morris had roamed the woods of southern England, climbing among Druid and Roman ruins, or visiting old castles or abbeys with curiously carved doors. Separately— for they did not meet until Rossetti was twenty-eight and Morris twenty-two—both came to find in the life of the Middle Ages, whether in France or England or Italy or Scandinavia, a hope for modern life. While Arnold turned to the calm and art of the Greeks, Rossetti and Morris saw a rich beauty in Gothic cathedrals, bright wall paintings, high chiselled doorways, gorgeous tapestries and armour, and chivalric bravery and faith.

Rossetti was chiefly a painter, and while only twenty years of age was the leader of a little band of other painters who thought the Italian artists living before Raphael had something in colour and art and spirit peculiarly worth studying. Rossetti and his friends became known as "Pre-Raphaelites," and when the painter began to publish poetry, the clear colours and medieval influences visible in his pictures showed also in his verse. So the poetry Rossetti wrote and that of some of his friends is often called "Pre-Raphaelite poetry."

It was a poetry new and strange in its medieval quality. The Romantic poets had written legends and ballads about the Middle Ages, and Rossetti and Morris did the same thing. But their poems treated the age of chivalry with a peculiar seriousness. A few poems like Keats's *Eve of St. Agnes* and Tennyson's *The Lady of Shalott* had a great deal of what Rossetti and Morris strove for, and were better than any they ever wrote. Still, while Keats and Tennyson were greatly admired by Morris and Rossetti and taught them much, the things these earlier poets saw in the Middle Ages were different from what Morris and Rossetti saw.

Rossetti's first great poem, *The Blessèd Damozel*, was written when the poet-painter was only nineteen. It showed the influence of Keats and Tennyson and Poe, but it had a love of colour and a deliberate simplicity that were new:

> The blessèd damozel lean'd out
> From the gold bar of Heaven;
> Her eyes were deeper than the depth
> Of water still'd at even;
> She had three lilies in her hand,
> And the stars in her hair were seven.

There is the quaint shining picture of Heaven where

> . . . the souls mounting up to God
> Went by her like thin flames;

There is the hope of the blessed damozel to see again the lover she had left behind on earth. She dreams that

> We two will stand beside that shrine,
> Occult, withheld, untrod,
> Whose lamps are stirred continually
> With prayer sent up to God;
> And see our old prayers, granted, melt
> Each like a little cloud.

With all this is a hint of fear that her loved one can never come to her, and her sorrow at the end to be in Heaven without him.

What was the new thing in this poem and in most of the poetry of Rossetti and Morris? Perhaps it was that the two painters, with their artists' eyes, had seen something in the Middle Ages that all the Romantic poets had missed. Shelley and Keats and Tennyson had looked to chivalry for beauty, just as Morris and Rossetti had. But the older poets were satisfied with the rather mysterious meanings they got from this beauty as they saw it far away and long ago. Rossetti and Morris weren't satisfied with that. They fingered old tapestries and longed to buy them or make new ones like them. They saw the work of old painters and sculptors and said: "These fellows had something that the world has lost, and we must get it back." They studied altars and doorways and high vaulted ceilings and asked: "Why don't we build like that to-day?" The Middle Ages were romantic for them, but practical also. The colour and courtesy and craftsmanship and faith of these older times seemed to be things on which the drab, distracted, bargaining modern world might well reshape itself in a new pattern.

There is nothing in *The Blessèd Damozel* that *says* such things. Still, when we know what Rossetti believed, we can see that it had an effect on what he wrote. The love for the definite, usable things of medieval times—garments, windows, names, music—shows in *The Blessèd Damozel*. It shows even more clearly in a poem of Rossetti's like *The Bride's Prelude*. Something of it is in simpler poems like his *Sister Helen*. In Rossetti's great sonnet sequence, *The House of Life*, it still gives its peculiar flavour of beauty, though these poems written to his wife are more poems of the modern world.

Unfortunately, they marked the end of Rossetti's poetry. For, after Elizabeth Siddal Rossetti died suddenly, young and beautiful, two years after her marriage to the poet-painter, Rossetti was never fully himself again. Impulsively, in his grief, he thrust the manuscript of his sonnets into his wife's coffin. He was persuaded seven years later that this had been wrong to her and to the world. So the grave was reopened and *The House of Life* was taken from its house in the ground. Still, so far as Rossetti was concerned, it was almost as if all his poetry had been buried once and for all with the beautiful lady he had loved. He wrote little and struggled with sickness and the habit of taking drugs which the sickness brought, and was never his old vigorous self again before his death in 1882. Perhaps he had looked clearly into the future when he had written in Sonnet IV of *The House of Life*:

O love, my love! if I no more should see
Thyself, nor on the earth the shadow of thee,
    Nor image of thine eyes in any spring,—
How then should sound upon Life's darkening slope
The ground-whirl of the perished leaves of Hope,
    The wind of Death's imperishable wing?

III

With Morris the course of poetry was happier and longer. Before he met Rossetti he had studied at Oxford, and there he discovered suddenly that he could write verse.

"He's a big poet," cried his friend Burne-Jones to some others who came into the room just after Morris had been reading his first poem.

"Well, if this is poetry, it is very easy to write," said Morris, and all his life he seemed to find it so. It came or did not come; if it came there was little effort.

Morris wrote at once of the age of castles and churches and armour. Every year he lived he seemed to love this colourful past more and the drab present-day world less.

"Verily railways are ABOMINATIONS," he wrote from France to a friend, outraged that smoke and whistles should jar him from his dreams among cathedrals and old turrets.

Much a lover of the earlier poems of Tennyson, a lover of Keats, of Shakespeare, and of Chaucer, he dreamed out in rhyme the adventure and pageantry and mystic excitement of chivalry. He knew well Malory's collection of prose tales, the *Morte d'Arthur*, and Tennyson's poem with the same title. Some of his early verse shaped itself around King Arthur's knights, so that his first book, coming out finally in 1858, was called *The Defence of Guenevere*, and contained four poems about the world of Camelot and the Round Table. There were others that showed how the chronicler Sir John Froissart, how old ballads, old churches, and the medieval verse tales of Chaucer had given something for his imagination to work with. He had met Rossetti in 1856, and Rossetti's ideas about painting and his enthusiasm for it had also had an effect upon Morris's first work.

Almost nobody in England noticed *The Defence of Guenevere*. Yet it was a volume of new and fine poems. They were stories— stories told in narrative, or in the form of short dramas, or in rousing lyrics. Guenevere is on trial for loving Sir Launcelot. Princess Rapunzel lets down her golden hair for the Prince to climb. The young knight shouting the name of his !ady's flower as a war cry wins the tournament:

> A golden gilliflower to-day
> I wore upon my helm alway,
> And won the prize of this tourney.
> *Hah! hah! la belle jaune giroflée.*
>
> However well Sir Giles might sit,
> His sun was weak to wither it,
> Lord Miles's blood was dew on it,
> *Hah! hah! la belle jaune giroflee.*

These poems were beautiful and they were rousing and human. As Arnold had pointed out, it is seldom that even the best poets can keep from smothering the stories they tell and the truth they cry with too many words. Morris in his first book kept to what he had to say, and his poems are simple and strong.

Meanwhile, other things than poetry had taken his attention. He had served an architect for a while, working long hours. After this, Rossetti persuaded him for a time that painting was the important thing to do. Suddenly then he got married, and at once planned to build on some pleasant orchard land near London the now famous Red House.

In doing this he put into practice his belief in the inspiration of medieval life. He decided that the furniture and curtains and tableware that English people were then using were ugly things, and began making his own chairs, tables, glasses, and draperies. These were often shaped after medieval furnishings Morris had seen. The embroidered hangings or wall paintings put into picture some of the old legends he loved. As Morris worked at this, what he was doing became so interesting and seemed so important (for just then nobody seemed to be making beautiful things for houses), that finally he and his friends organized a company and began taking orders to furnish houses, make church windows, embroider curtains and design wall paper. This was only the beginning of a life work at such art crafts; later Morris studied the making of books and established a printing press. How splendid a thing his work proved to be for the homes of England and America, how it set styles in furniture and wallpaper and printing that are still inspiring to makers of lovely things is a story related indirectly to the story of his poetry, but not a part of it.

Fortunately, Morris was a man of prodigious and restless imagination. While he worked painting glass and designing wallpaper he shaped poems in his mind.

"If a chap can't compose an epic poem while he's weaving a tapestry," he said once, "he'd better shut up, he'll never do any good at all."

So when he took time to write, he had his poems partly done, and wrote rapidly. He turned now wholly to stories in verse and wrote *The Life and Death of Jason*, the Greek tale of the Golden Fleece. Then came *The Earthly Paradise*.

This book (1868) was his great contribution to poetry. Like *The Canterbury Tales*, it is a collection of story-poems. Some of the stories are Greek, some Norse, some Italian, some French, but all are told in the medieval manner. In fact, except for the modern English, one could often fancy one were reading Morris's master, Geoffrey Chaucer. Morris asks us to

> Forget six counties overhung with smoke,
> Forget the snorting steam and piston stroke,
> Forget the spreading of the hideous town,

and turn our thoughts to lovely palaces, amazing courage, gay apparel, and fine faith. Many of the poems are close to fairy tales. There is the dragon in *The Lady of the Land* that

with its teeth
The body of a slain goat did it tear
The blood whereof in its hot jaws did seethe,
And on its tongue he saw the smoking hair. . . .

There are princesses in the shape of swans, there are wars, foot races, sea voyages.

Throughout the poems shines the beauty of the things Morris pictured as a part of the older world. King Proetus leads the hero Bellerophon into his palace, and past an elaborate fountain. Morris describes lovingly its metal sculpture and carving:

Midmost the pavement, wrought by toil of years,
A tree was set, gold-leaved like that which bears
Unto the maids of Hesperus strange fruit;
A many-coloured serpent from the root
Curled upward round the stem, and, reaching o'er
A four-square silver laver, did outpour
Bright glittering water from his throat of brass;
And at each corner of the basin was
A brazen hart who seemed at point to drink.

He wrote also of heroes—of Kiartan in *The Lovers of Gudrun,* who was

with the sword so skilled,
That when he played therewith the air seemed filled
With light of gleaming blades,

and of Bellerophon, who stood on the wall of the enemy's town, fighting alone, and

Then it was as though
A clear, bright light about his head did glow
Amidst the darts and clamour, and he turned
A face to us that with such glory burned
That those behind us drave us back again,
And cried aloud to die there in the plain
Rather than leave him.

There are also tales that are very modern as well as medieval in their close searching of the souls of the people they describe.

In such poems, Morris is more than "the idle singer of an empty day," as he called himself once, trying to bring back the beauty of the medieval world.

In all his poems, in those that have been mentioned here, in the later epic of *Sigurd the Volsung* and in the translation of Virgil's Æneid, it is the spirit of Morris that is the fine thing, and not his art. He was never a great artist as Keats was or Tennyson or even Arnold. He had the gift of telling a story well and the gift of writing with naturalness and energy. He never got—except a little in his first book—the ecstasy or magic that is in the greater poets. Some of his tales are very like Chaucer's, but putting them side by side with Chaucer's, we can see how Morris lacked the sparkling humour and bursts of perfect poetry that the older poet had. In the same way, he lacked the sweet and sonorous music of Tennyson.

Morris might have gone farther in poetry than he did. He gave only a little of his time to poet's work. He was busy all his life with art crafts, and he wrote great quantities of prose tales. In his later years, he spent time and wore down his body preaching the gospel of socialism in which he came to believe. All this took something from his poetry. Morris wrote his poems because he loved to write them, and they have the delightful freshness of things done happily. But they lack the severe work that would have made them clearer and nobler. This is natural; the wonder is that Morris found time to write so much verse, and that the verse he composed is so full of colour and energy and the rich interest of good stories.

IV

Morris had left Oxford University in 1856 to work at architecture. However, his profession kept him in Oxford town, and he and Rossetti, who was also there to do some work, soon came to know a young man who had arrived at Balliol College in January, 1856. He was a strange, almost imp-like person— a small, girlish body topped with an enormous head which looked even larger than it was because of a great mop of reddish golden hair.

Yet the Pre-Raphaelite painter-poets were quickly drawn to Algernon Charles Swinburne. There was a kind of steely firmness in this elfin young man which commanded their respect, and there was a winning courtesy in his manner. Then, too, it was apparent that he had read amazingly. He knew French and French literature like a native. He was almost as much at home with Italian, loved and wrote Greek, and seemed to have all English poetry at his tongue's end. Morris was soon reading him *The Haystack in the Floods*, due to be printed the following year in his first book, and Rossetti called him "my little Northumbrian friend" and praised the verse that Swinburne showed him.

Swinburne came of a distinguished family. His father was an admiral and his mother was the daughter of an earl. Still, they were also haters of tyrants and believers in Liberty, especially Sir John Swinburne, Algernon's grandfather. The young poet had inherited this love of democracy and made a passion of it. Swinburne told a friend how he was driving once with his father and mother in the Champs Élysées in Paris, and passed the carriage of the French emperor, Napoleon III. He was infuriated because his father had bowed to the Emperor and raised his hat.

"And did you raise yours?" asked the friend.

"Not wishing to cut my hand off immediately on returning to the hotel," came the answer, partly in fun, but also serious, "I did—*not*."

On the other hand, Swinburne was intensely proud of his noble blood. He considered his family one of the oldest and best in England and liked to think of his ancestors as brave and violent men. During his boyhood he seems to have urged his little body with resolute eagerness to attempt feats of skill and endurance. Near his father's home on the Isle of Wight he exulted in battles with the sea, and there and on his grandfather's estate in Northumberland he dashed wildly about on horseback. On the Isle of Wight there is a promontory, Culver Cliff, that drops sheer from its summit to the sea a thousand feet below. When he was eighteen, Swinburne went out one day without saying anything to his family and worked his way by crevice and rocky shelf up the perpendicular wall to the very crest of the height. It was a war between his slight body and his fiery pride, and the pride was the victor.

Later, Swinburne tried to enlist in the cavalry, but was rejected. He regretted this for years. He was the only literary member of a family of fighters, and he seems to have felt that the least he could do by his clan was to seek some kind of active service. Later, he got comfort by feeling that he expressed the vehemence of the Swinburnes in his verse. He wrote once to a correspondent:

"I think you will allow that when this race [his family] chose at last to produce a poet, it would have been at least remarkable if he had been content to write nothing but hymns and idylls for clergymen and young ladies to read in chapels and drawing-rooms."

And much of Swinburne's poetry was not for clergymen and young ladies. There was little in his first book to shock them, for though there was violent action in *The Queen Mother* and *Rosamond* (1860) these poetic plays were in the now traditional blank verse and, like the early poems of Morris and Rossetti, pictured the Midd.e Ages. They contained fine poetry but attracted no attention. It was different with the second volume. In *Atalanta in Calydon* (1865), Swinburne poured out a poem that horrified a few people with what they thought was its impiety and dazzled the rest of literary London with its music.

The critics were ready to praise Swinburne now, for they had heard of him from men like Ruskin and Rossetti. Still more important, Monckton Milnes, Tennyson's old college friend, now close to being a king among reviewers, had said fine things of *Atalanta* and had sworn to make it the literary success of the year.

So Swinburne's book was soon the marvel of London. Justly so, too. In its stately blank verse and glittering rhymed choruses, this poetic drama of the old Greek hero Meleager and the warrior maiden he loved brought to English poetry a new voice and a new skill. With its form and bright movement, it gave a fresh version of Greek poetry, and it showed that a kind of English verse, different from anything that had been done before, could be written.

When we remember how much Tennyson had accomplished, this seems unbelievable. But Swinburne had seen new possibilities. For instance, he knew the alliterative verse of the Anglo-Saxons. He realized that modern poets had not made the most of alliteration. He set out boldly to make it once more an ornament almost as important as rhyme, and wove it into his lines with great skill and often with great beauty. The first lines of *Atalanta* show his method:

> *M*aiden, and *m*istress of the *m*onths and stars
> Now *f*olded in the *f*lowerless *f*ields of heaven,
> *G*oddess whom all *g*ods love with threefold heart,
> Being treble in thy *d*ivided *d*eity,
> A light for *d*ead men and *d*ark hours, a foot
> Swift on the *h*ills of morning, and a *h*and
> To all things *f*ierce and *f*leet that *r*oar and *r*ange
> Mortal, with gentler *s*hafts than *s*now or *s*leep;
> *H*ear now and *h*elp and lift no violent *h*and.

Swinburne had also a fine ear for metre and rhyme, and a skill with them that apparently had been sharpened by his great knowledge of English poetry. From his French and Italian reading he seemed to have caught the magic of clear vowel sounds and dancing rhymes. He tried rhymes such as poets had seldom attempted before except in humorous verse, flinging them about like fireworks—many two-syllabled rhymes like

pity	and	found me
city		bound me

and daring three-syllabled rhymes such as

| bedrape us | and | over us | and | rent from us |
| Priapus | | cover us | | sent from us. |

Finally, from Greek poetry he took the three-footed anapestic and dactyllic measures. Poems had been written in these by English poets, but the best English verse had run to iambic and trochaic metres. Swinburne showed that quite as lovely things could be done in a rippling music like that which Pindar and Euripides had loved. Nothing in English excels the hymn to Artemis at the opening of *Atalanta* for the sheer dancing ecstasy of music:

> Come with bows bent and with emptying of quivers,
>   Maiden most perfect, lady of light,
> With a noise of winds and many rivers,
>   With a clamour of waters, and with might;
> Bind on they sandals, O thou most fleet,
> Over the splendour and speed of thy feet,
>   For the faint east quickens, the wan west shivers,
> Round the feet of the day and the feet of the night.
>
> Where shall we find her, how shall we sing to her,
>   Fold our hands round her knees, and cling?
> O that man's heart were as fire and could spring to her,
>   Fire, or the strength of the streams that spring!
> For the stars and the winds are unto her
> As raiment, as songs of the harp-player;
>   For the risen stars and the fallen cling to her
> And the southwest-wind and the west-wind sing.

What was going to happen to poetry when a young man of twenty-seven was just beginning to write it, and was writing like this? Ruskin exclaimed that *Atalanta* was "the grandest thing ever done by a youth." At times Swinburne's friends came close to worshipping him. He had been writing some dazzling ballads and lyrics and it is said that on evenings when he would chant these to his friends, certain ones of his listeners would unconsciously slip to their knees in adoration! These new poems came out in 1866, but they got a different reception from *Atalanta*. For *Poems and Ballads* (1866) shocked England. Swinburne wrote of Dolores with

> Cold eyelids that hide like a jewel
>   Hard eyes that grow soft for an hour;
> The heavy white limbs, and the cruel
>   Red mouth like a venomous flower,

of Felise and Aholibah and Faustine and other ladies whom Victorian readers found most amazing and improper. We should find them so to-day. In fact, they are so unfit for the clergymen and young ladies whom Swinburne scorned that should *Poems and Ballads* appear in New York or London to-day someone would probably propose, as a Mr. Ludlow did in 1866, to prosecute the author and suppress the book. The *Saturday Review* wrote: "We are in the midst of fire and serpents, wine and ashes, blood and foam, and a hundred buried horrors."

Naturally such words made Swinburne known, but not pleasantly known. In fact, because of *Poems and Ballads* many people regarded him for years as a kind of fantastic and wicked writer. A little of this reputation clings to his name twenty-five years after his death. Still, there was no denying the skill and power and beauty of many of these poems of 1866. Lurid and daring, they were full of colour and art. The *Hymn to Proserpine*, mourning for the lost Greek gods Swinburne loved, makes majestic music.

> O Gods dethroned and deceased, cast forth, wiped out in a day!
> From your wrath is the world released, redeemed from your chains, men say.
> New gods are crowned in the city, their flowers have broken your rods;
> They are merciful, clothed with pity, the young compassionate gods.

There were lighter poems, delicately charming, and there was *The Garden of Proserpine*, expressing persuasively the satisfaction in the idea that there was no life beyond death:

> From too much love of living,
>   From hope and fear set free,
> We thank with brief thanksgiving
>   Whatever gods may be

> That no life lives forever;
>> That dead men rise up never;
> That even the weariest river
>> Winds somewhere safe to sea.

Probably Swinburne felt keenly the injustice of the critics who always thought of him as the poet of "wine and ashes, blood and foam." He had written much else than such poetry, and was to continue writing different things. *Poems and Ballads* had contained verse like *A Song in the Time of Revolution* (1860), in which Swinburne cried:

> The poor and the halt and the blind are keen and mighty and fleet:
> Like the noise of the blowing of wind is the sound of the noise of their feet;
> The wind has the sound of a laugh in the clamour of days and deeds:
> The priests are scattered like chaff, and rulers broken like reeds.

This cry for liberty swelled into a volume in 1867 with *Songs of Two Nations*, dedicated to the Italian patriot Mazzini. Later came *Songs Before Sunrise* (1871). It contained poems to patriots of various nations, among them one *To Walt Whitman in America*, beginning

> Send but a song oversea for us,
>> Heart of their hearts who are free,
> Heart of their singer, to be for us
>> More than our singing can be.

In another poem, *The Litany of Nations*, Swinburne told how life was warped and wrong

> By the pastures that give grass to feed the lamb in,
>> Where men lack meat;
> By the cities clad with gold and shame and famine;
>> By field and street,

and sang burningly his hope that it would be righted. Later he wrote patriotic poems. *The Armada*, a poem made for the three hundredth anniversary (1888) of the destruction of the great Spanish fleet that came to conquer England, rings with sonorous pride of his country:

England, queen of the waves whose green inviolate girdle enrings thee round,
Mother fair as the morning, where is now the place of thy foemen found?
Still the sea that salutes us free proclaims them stricken, acclaims thee
    crowned.

Some consider Swinburne's poetic tragedies his most important achievement, and the three plays which tell the story of Mary Queen of Scots are indeed magnificent verse and make a rich poetic biography for this beautiful and unhappy queen.

So Swinburne wrote on, always skilful, always flaming up when he wrote of great literature or liberty or of heroes he loved. But he never reached the heights that *Atalanta in Calydon* seemed to promise, though after the death of Tennyson the world spoke of him as the greatest of living English poets. In fact, he never did anything better than his second and third books, and little as good.

What was the trouble? Perhaps it was partly that he ceased to grow as an artist. He had found out how to write a new kind of poetry, but instead of mounting on what he had written to something still more glorious, he seemed satisfied to repeat what he had already done. After a number of years, the deft alliteration and glittering metres and rhymes of *Atalanta* and *Poems and Ballads* grew a little common, at their worst something like tricks.

Then, too, Swinburne probably never knew exactly what he wanted to say. He himself said he was like one of the old harpers who composed poems while he sang them. Perhaps this was so. At any rate, he lashes out wildly, the musical, dancing words pour easily from his lips, but almost always it is as if he had not thought or felt deeply what he is saying. He was like Shelley in his simplicity and passionate love of liberty and in his musical skill, but Shelley, though not on the whole a wise person, often seems wholly wise when inspired. Swinburne almost never does. Ecstatic and gorgeous, he is not quite true. We miss in him the positive, definite thing that the truth always is. He was a passionate rebel, hating the tyranny of kings and priests. He sang much of destroying and of the glory that would be after the destruction was over, but he never saw what he wanted to build in place of what he was going to tear down.

So he will be remembered not for any great truth he told, but chiefly for the new magic of words he brought. This was much in itself. The shining patterns Swinburne made are glorious even if they do not mean as much as the less perfect work of other poets. Men and women will go on singing them and new writers will discover treasures in their colour and energy.

V

Swinburne did not find modern life as ugly and empty as Arnold and Morris and Rossetti found it, but like them he got his greatest delight and satisfaction from the past. We remember him not for his poems about liberty but for his plays about Mary Queen of Scots and Atalanta, for his singing verses that drew their sweetness partly from ancient Greece, partly from old England, partly from the Elizabethans. So we may think of Swinburne, too, as turning from the mill life to other and older worlds.

What did he and the others get from Greece and Iceland and Arthur's England and Froissart's France? Probably more than they would have got from Nineteenth Century England. Probably the time to write of men in the world of machines had not yet come: the world of machines was only in process of growing up. Whitman had put some of it into his chants, but few could have done what Whitman did. Arnold and Morris and Rossetti and Swinburne brought back cargoes more useful than cinnamon and peacock plumes, tea and jewel stones.

The hurried new world, buying and building, had forgotten much. It had forgotten beauty of form—form in churches and statues, and sometimes form in the arrangment of words. Arnold recovered from old Greece this harmony and proportion in ideas. His poetry was his refuge from the formless life he saw about him. Men and women go to it now. They find that its quiet, searching thought and grave music make a kind of solid ground after the rush and perplexity of the modern world's work, give them peace and knowledge after the day's noise and doubt.

They find a different kind of comfort in Rossetti, Morris, and Swinburne. But the clear-coloured pictures and rich words of *The House of Life*, the quaint rhymes, the sharp pictures, the swiftly moving stories of *The Earthly Paradise* also take them away from the machine age. People go to this poetry and to the gleaming melody of Swinburne to find a world that, for a time, at least, is better than the real world they live in.

This poetry seems very far from our paved avenues and hurrying motor cars. It is farther from our everyday lives than the poetry of Keats or Wordsworth or Tennyson. But sometimes we wish to forget the wheels and the dark ribbons of smoke and the cities armoured in stone. We are glad then that these poets dug their glory out of the past. We read of Sohrab dying by the Oxus stream or the Blessèd Damozel leaning on the parapet of heaven, or white Atalanta slaying the boar, and are very happy in this world of beauty and brave men and women.

And then we find, too, that these heroes and heroines of the unreal world are not so unreal. From their stories we bring back something of colour and beauty into our everyday life. We see the offices and factories with new eyes. We say, "Life should be more than toil and speed and humming machinery." We think of making the real world more like the marble world of Arnold or the carved and tapestried world of Morris. Then the poets who turned their backs on life and made a dream life to suit themselves—an apparently useless thing—become suddenly useful! It seems very strange. Still, it is the way with all great poets.

CHAPTER XXVII

UNDER STEAM AND STONE (*Continued*)

I

But come back from Avalon and ancient Iceland, leave the Hesperides and their apples of gold, forget the gods of Calydon and the land east of the sun and west of the moon! The poets dreamed in these places, but now they have new dreams. They have seen a ship swing out to sea under full steam, with red and black funnels and a city of two thousand people on its decks. They have seen a locomotive hurry on its feet of spinning wheels into a palace of iron and marble which men call a depot. They have seen armies marching with rifles agleam in the sunlight and moonlight. They have seen men building cities as high as mountains. They have heard men roaring through the air on wings faster than wind.

The poets will not believe any longer that there is no poetry in such life. They have begun to make rhymes about its stone palaces and steel chariots, about its heroes who plough the sea with steam-driven ships and swing their spidery metal bridges from mountain to mountain so that the new road, the railroad, may make a magic path between far places. They have longed to sing the song of wagons rolling out through the vast sea of prairie grass toward the gold of California. They have heard with glistening eyes the tales and songs of lumberjacks who felled tall pines and rode them down boiling rivers. They have found heroes among the farmers, heroes who burned and cleared the stumps of the pine trees and made fields of wheat and corn. They have hailed the workers who riveted together the skeletons of skyscrapers and drove tunnels under broad rivers. They have wanted to make songs of new sea voyages, new battles, and the thousand dramas of love and ambition and sacrifice that men and women play in the new world as they did in the old.

II

By the middle of the Nineteenth Century the little island of England, the island of Keats and Shakespeare, had set her flag on all the continents of the world. Her ships and her soldiers went to Canada, to Guiana, to Cape Town, to New Zealand and Australia, to the great peninsula of India with its rice lands and serpents and elephants and 300,000,000 people.

At Bombay, India, Rudyard Kipling was born in 1865. His father was one of the thousands of English officials who helped govern the Indian provinces. John Kipling sent his son Rudyard to England to be schooled there, with the idea that he, too, would come back to India and help run things.

So Rudyard Kipling crossed the Indian Ocean and the Mediterranean Sea and passed through busy London. He saw the smokestacks of factories, he saw old churches and palaces. He saw the ships slipping out to sea with sails blowing full or funnels streaming smoke, and the red-coated British soldiers marching through drizzling streets to embark for Egypt or Hong Kong or his own Calcutta. He thrilled with the idea that his own blood was the blood of these islanders, these people on a fragment of land who had conquered islands and provinces in all the seas. He saw how they were busy making clothes for the world, making engines to drive their ships, guns to make their soldiers feared. He saw ugly things in the life about him, but power and glory, too.

When he had finished school at the United Service College, Kipling went back to India, but he did not become a government official. Instead, he began to write for newspapers. He wrote stories of Englishmen and Indians in India, and he wrote verses—mostly humorous and many about British soldiers. When these came out as *Barrack-Room Ballads* in 1892, people in England and America saw that a new poet had appeared.

What Kipling wrote was not new with any new beauty. It was swinging, thumping ballad verse. There were ballads of the Indian hills—of the robber chief Kamal who stole the colonel's mare and of the colonel's son who pursued him on a horse

With the mouth of a bell and the heart of a Hell and the head of a gallows-tree,

and had a wild ride with a strange ending. There were poems of the soldiers who guarded England's empire. In the speech of these men we learn of Gunga Din the coolie water carrier who served them:

> The uniform 'e wore
> Was nothing much before,
> An' rather less than arf o' that be'ind,

but he did his job so well that the soldier who tells his story ends:

> Though I've belted you and flayed you,
> By the living God that made you,
> You're a better man than I am, Gunga Din.

We hear in soldier language of the great queen, "the Widow at Windsor," whom they served. They were proud of her, but they knew they risked their lives for her and the country she represented.

> Walk wide o' the Widow at Windsor,
>   For 'alf o' Creation she owns:
> We 'ave bought 'er the same with the sword an' the flame,
>   An' we've salted it down with our bones,
>   (Poor beggars!—It's blue with our bones!)

There is *The English Flag*, a poem of the great British Empire, in which all the winds of the world tell of the flag. To the North—

> The lean white bear hath seen it in the long, long Arctic nights,
> The musk-ox knows the standard that flouts the Northern Lights.

while in the South—

> Never was isle so little, never was sea so lone,
> But over the scud and the palm-trees an English flag was flown.

Eastward it flutters above desert and city, and Westward the wheat plains know it and

> The dead dumb fog hath wrapped it—the frozen dews have kissed—
> The naked stars have seen it, a fellow-star in the mist.
> What is the Flag of England? Ye have but my breath to dare,
> Ye have but my waves to conquer, go forth, for it is there!

As we have said, this poetry was not new with a beauty like Keats's or Tennyson's or Swinburne's. Its direct ballad style, though unusual in the effect it made, could be traced back not only to the old English ballads but to Tennyson, Browning, Macaulay, and Swinburne. The new and invigorating thing was that Kipling had taken the ballad metres and written stories about modern men and things. Whitman had made a new poetry for the new life; Kipling got at some of the things Whitman wanted by taking older poetic forms and making them do unheard-of things. For no one had made a modern army and a modern soldier talk as Kipling now made them. No one—save Whitman in his different way—had had Kipling's vision of the heroism of the life men were living. No one had put such a vision into ballad poetry almost as simple as the old ballads and therefore interesting and understandable to millions of people. Finally, no one had taken the language of the streets, of the army, of the ships, and made it part of poetry that was not humorous only, but often told unforgettable truths about life—its exhilaration, its nobility, its cruelty.

And as the years passed, Kipling found more poetry in modern life than the poetry of Indian kings and chiefs, the poetry of British soldiers and the British flag. He wrote also of men on the sea. It was not only the old sea, under whose surface are romantic

> darker deeps that hide
> The blind white sea-snake and his bride,
> Who, drowsing, nose the long-lost ships
> Let down through darkness to their lips—

but the sea of ships with funnels and fenders and engines. He told of the crew of the modern steamship driving homeward—

> Then home, get her home, where the drunken rollers comb,
>   And the shouting seas drive by,
> And the engines stamp and ring, and the wet bows reel and swing,
>   And the Southern Cross rides high!

We even go down into the engine room to meet that hard-boiled, religious Scotch engineer, M'Andrew, who thanks God for good steam engines:

> "From coupler-flange to spindle-guide I see Thy Hand, O God—
> Predestination in the stride o' yon connectin'-rod.
> John Calvin might ha' forged the same—enorrmous, certain, slow—
> Ay, wrought it in the furnace-flame—*my* 'Institutio.'

Nor is Kipling unaware of the heroes of the land, though he writes less of them. There is *The Explorer*, the story of the pioneer who went to the edge of the settlements, but couldn't stay there because

> —a voice, as bad as Conscience, rang interminable changes
>   On one everlasting Whisper day and night repeated—so:
> "Something hidden. Go and find it. Go and look behind the Ranges—
>   Something lost behind the Ranges. Lost and waiting for you. Go!"

Kipling tells how he pushed out over the plains and deserts, almost dying there for want of water and food, and climbed

Up along the hostile mountains, where the hair-poised snow-slide shivers—
Down and through the big fat marshes that the virgin ore-bed stains,
Till I heard the mile-wide mutterings of unimagined rivers,
And beyond the nameless timber saw illimitable plains!

In *The Sons of Martha* and other poems, Kipling wrote of the toiling millions and made poetry of their wrongs and sadness.

He came to see and proclaim the price men and nations paid for wars and conquests, and in doing so made some of his greatest poetry. His song of *The White Man's Burden*—telling the troubles of the countries who try to rule

Your new-caught, sullen peoples,
Half-devil and half-child—

is known over the world. His poem *Boots* sings the terrible monotony and hardship of marching, and *The Song of the Dead* tells the cost of fighting and empire-making in a way that will long be remembered:

We have fed our sea for a thousand years
And she calls us, still unfed,
Though there's never a wave of all her waves
But marks our English dead:
We have strawed our best to the weed's unrest,
To the shark and the sheering gull,
If blood be the price of admiralty,
Lord God, we ha' paid in full!

It is not time yet to try to say how great such poetry is. Kipling still lives and writes. But we do know already that his verse gave the shock of fresh life to poetry everywhere. His winning of the Nobel Prize in 1907 was only a just expression of his electric influence. Other poets have rushed in to write, like him, of other modern heroes, to use the talk of modern people, to sing the thoughts that are in the hearts of men to-day. Kipling was less a prophet than Whitman. But, like Whitman, he has been a great liberator, shaking off dead ideas in poetry and encouraging poets to write of living things.

III

We are still in the midst of the poetry made possible by the free and generous spirit of Whitman, by the energy of Kipling, by the beauty Keats and Tennyson wrought, by the work of Arnold and Morris and Swinburne. In England we find the quieter, lovelier poetry continuing in the poets that have no interest in the great humming world of steel and steam. Francis Thompson, who was inspired chiefly by poets of the Seventeenth Century as well as by Shelley and Keats and Tennyson, wrote poems like *The Hound of Heaven* that are marvellous in mystic tenderness and soaring music. So did Oscar Wilde, who said a beautiful poem was enough in itself regardless of what it meant. James Elroy Flecker, dying at thirty-one, left gorgeous verse of the East, full of daring and colour, like his description of an old ship that ends:

> It was so old a ship—who knows, who knows?
> And yet so beautiful, I watched in vain
> To see the mast burst open with a rose
> And the whole deck put on its leaves again.

William Butler Yeats, who won the Nobel Prize for Literature in 1923, wrote rhyme and blank verse smoothly wrought like Tennyson's. But he has put into English the strange charm of old Irish legends, and he has written of modern Ireland in language with the swing and charm of English as Irish men and women speak it. Finally, we cannot forget among the many poets of our own time A. E. Housman, who wrote *The Shropshire Lad* and *Last Poems*. Two slender books they are, and the poems in them are short, yet probably they will be long remembered. Mr. Housman teaches Greek and Latin at Cambridge University. Perhaps he learned early from Simonides and Horace and Sappho that the poet does well who says much in a few words. At any rate, *The Shropshire Lad* is full of poems that do this, and in doing so it captures the very spirit of youth, its beauty and quickness and sadness. The poem *To an Athlete Dying Young* mingles playfulness and grief, and already some of its lines are part of the talk of millions of people. It is a blessing, says Housman, to leave life while you are still happy and triumphant:

> Smart lad, to slip betimes away
> From fields where glory does not stay,
> And early though the laurel grows
> It withers quicker than the rose.
>
> Eyes that shady night has shut
> Cannot see the record cut,
> And silence sounds no worse than cheers
> After earth has stopped the ears!

Along with English poets who write under the spell of some older tradition are others closer to Kipling and Whitman. Like Kipling, William Ernest Henley wrote of England, and he also took the free verse of Whitman and gave it a sharper form. He wrote of

> The stalwart Ships,
> The beautiful and bold adventurers!

He pictured the lighthouse on the island,

> The tall Policeman,
> Flashing his bull's-eye, as he peers
> About him in the ancient vacancy,
> Tells them this way is safety—this way home.

In *Hospital Verses* he brought the modern doctors and operating rooms into poetry. His *Invictus* is a poem of courage for modern men and women, and his *Margaritæ Sorori* (to my Sister Margaret) one of peace.

> The smoke ascends
> In a rosy-and-golden haze. The spires
> Shine and are changed. In the valley
> Shadows rise. The lark sings on. The sun
> Closing his benediction,

Sinks, and the darkening air
Thrills with a sense of the triumphing night—
Night with her train of stars
And her great gift of sleep.

To this period, though perhaps as much to later years, belong also the poems of two writers famed as novelists—George Meredith and Thomas Hardy. Both have written lyrics and poems of philosophic stature which some admirers rank high among modern verse.

Through the work of both runs a restless mental inquiry, a closeness of thought and emotion that makes, as with Browning, for difficult reading. Yet in both there are great rewards also. Meredith, for instance, often bursts into an almost liquid loveliness, as when

Large and smoky red the sun's cold disk drops,
Clipp'd by naked hills on violet shaded snow,

or when he exclaims in a lover's ecstasy:

Could I find a place to be alone with heaven,
I would speak my heart out: heaven is my need,
Every woodland tree is flushing like the dogwood,
Flashing like the whitebeam, swaying like the reed.

His poem *The Woods of Westermain* is runic with significant shadow and satyr-like melody. Now it is the voice of a druid intoning twisted parable, now it is oracular with veiled solemnity, now it crackles into terrific grotesqueries:

Hate, the shadow of a grain;
You are lost in Westermain;
Earthward swoops a vulture sun,
Nighted upon carrion. . . .
Flowers along the reeling floor
Drip henbane and hellebore. . . .
Imp that dances, imp that flits,
Imp o' the demon-growing girl,
Maddest! whirl with imp o' the pits
Round you, and with them you whirl. . . .

And you ask where you may be,
In what reek of a lair
Given to bones and ogre-broods;
And they yell you Where.
Enter these enchanted woods,
You who dare.

Again, Meredith can mingle bitter tenderness, savage irony, and tragic wisdom, as he does in his great "sonnet" sequence *Modern Love*. There is much in this work that eats into the memory; the best of the poem, perhaps, finds its distillation in the concluding picture of the unfortunate man and wife:

Thus piteously Love closed what he begat
The union of this ever-diverse pair!
These two were rapid falcons in a snare,
Condemned to do the flitting of the bat.
Lovers beneath the singing sky of May,
They wandered once; clear as the dew on flowers.
But they fed not on the advancing hours:
Their hearts held cravings for the buried day,
Then each applied to each that fatal knife,
Deep questioning, which probes to endless dole.
Ah! what a dusty answer gets the soul
When hot for certainties in this our life!

Hardy, though his poetry often gives an effect of roughness, of oddity and too tightly packed thought not unlike Browning's, usually writes in a simpler style than Meredith. His verse is very modern in flavour. Despite the fact that he was born in 1840, much of it consists of lyrics, or of brief little narratives that cannot well be quoted in part. On the other hand, his poem *The Dynasts* is a gigantic work in three parts, nineteen acts, and one hundred and thirty scenes, covering the struggles of the Napoleonic period. It bulks in realistic power among the finer poems in English of the last fifty years.

Hardy himself feels that he will be remembered more as a poet than as a novelist, and if this is true, he will be remembered as a great poet. Still writing at eighty-seven, he has drawn many admirers to him, who love the wryness of his

songs and short verse-stories, the fearless truth with which
he looks at life, the courage he keeps to companion his often
discouraging observations. Something of his rugged imagination and abrupt music can be found in the ten lines of

WAITING BOTH

A star looks down on me,
And says: "Here I and you
Stand, each in our degree:
What do you mean to do—
    Mean to do?"

I say: "For all I know,
Wait, and let Time go by,
Till my change come."—"Just so,"
The star says; "So mean I—
    So mean I."

Many other poets are writing in England, but there is no room
here to tell of them. This is a book about great poets. Probably Francis Thompson and Henley will not be thought of as
great; perhaps none mentioned in this chapter will be. They do
not seem now to reach high when put beside Keats or Wordsworth; we tell of them here partly because they may be greater
than they seem, partly because they seem to be the greatest
poets we have; partly because they show what poetry has been
in the last seventy-five years. For such reasons the poetry of
other writers like Ernest Dowson, Alfred Noyes, Walter de la
Mare, G. K. Chesterton, Rupert Brooke, John Drinkwater,
James Stephens, W. H. Davies, and Francis Ledwidge might
be spoken of if this were a bigger book.

But one more English poet should be here, because of all
poets born in the last fifty years he seems now most likely to be
great. John Masefield, lover of the sea and of men, himself a
sailor for a time in his youth, has blended the beauty of older
English poetry with the leap of modern life. Anyone who read
his *Cargoes*, in one of the early volumes of his poetry, could see
that he knew the past and present.

In his dedication to *Salt-Water Ballads*, Masefield announced at the beginning of his career a purpose to sing

> Not of the princes and prelates with periwigged charioteers
> Riding triumphantly laurelled to lap the fat of the years,—
> Rather the scorned—the rejected—the men hemmed in with the spears;
>
> The men of the tattered battalion which fights till it dies,
> Dazed with the dust of the battle, the din and the cries.
> The men with the broken heads and the blood running into their eyes.
>   .   .   .   .
> Of the maimed, of the halt and the blind in the rain and the cold—
> Of these shall my songs be fashioned, my tales be told.

In his first long poem he looked into the world of factories and saloons and told the story of burly, rowdy, drunken Saul Kane—how, starting with a prize fight and a terrible spree, he was suddenly converted to God and Christ, and went preaching the gospel. This story comes in the words of Saul himself. It has the rough humour and simple pathos of Chaucer, and the quicker language and harder, faster life of the Twentieth Century. Its strong, rollicking rhymes and passages of tender beauty showed that stories about to-day longer than the short ballads (such as Kipling had done) could be written in poetry and written better than in prose. In the *Everlasting Mercy* we see Saul fight his friend Bill. We hear how Saul felt that he was wrong, and how he was getting whipped when Bill suddenly sprained his thumb. Then when Saul has won and goes over to shake hands, we hear Bill:

> "I'll never shake your hand," he said,
> "I'd rather see my children dead.
>   I've been about and had some fun with you,
>   But you're a liar and I've done with you.
>   You've knocked me out, you didn't beat me;
>   Look out the next time that you meet me;
>   There'll be no friend to watch the clock for you
>   And no convenient thumb to cock for you.
>   That puts my meaning clear I guess,
>   Now get to hell; I want to dress."

We read how Saul got drunk and decided to scare the town out of itself, and rushed out clashing two blazing lamps and pulled the fire bell until

> I felt the air mingle and clang
> And beat the walls a muffled bang
> ... And then surge up and gather shape,
> And spread great pinions and escape;
> And each great bird of clanging shrieks
> O Fire! Fire, from iron beaks.

We hear how other adventures came to him, and a sudden light at last, so that

> I felt I walked at Heaven's gate

as he passed along the road in the early morning and heard the birds and saw the sun and a ploughman ploughing on a hill.

This is a poem that is tender, rousing, beautiful. Its fun and roughness and beauty are better for being in verse. Masefield has gone on writing poems where hard reality and broad humour often blend with solemn beauty. In *Dauber* there are both, and descriptions of the sea like the following are among the finest anyone has done:

> Darkness came down—half darkness—in a whirl;
> The sky went out, the waters disappeared.
> He felt a shocking pressure of blowing hurl
> The ship upon her side. The darkness speared
> At her with wind; she staggered, she careered;
> Then down she lay. The Dauber felt her go,
> He saw her yard tilt downwards. Then the snow
>
> Whirled all about—dense, multitudinous, cold—
> Mixed with the wind's one devilish thrust and shriek,
> Which whiffled out men's tears, defeated, took hold,
> Flattening the flying drift against the cheek.
> The yards buckled and bent, man could not speak.
> The ship lay on her broadside; the wind's sound
> Had devilish malice at having got her downed.

In later poems, Masefield writes at times with a calm, golden beauty. In the strange land to which Saint Withiel goes in *The*

Hounds of Hell there are stanzas all luminous with light and colour and quiet:

> Trampled by many-footed rain,
>   The sun-burnt corn lay dead;
> The myriad finches in the grain
>   Rose bothering at his tread. . . . .
>
> The gate swung creaking on its hasp,
>   The pear splashed from the tree,
> In the rotting apple's heart the wasp
>   Was drunken drowsily.

But what Masefield has done for poetry and men must be left with future readers and writers to discuss. They will be better able than any present-day writers to weigh the strength and wonder against the flaws of his writing, to decide what the whole is worth. We are grateful that he has taken real life, often ugly life, and made it into song and beauty, for this is much.

IV

America in the last fifty years has had its living poetry, too. During the latter part of the Nineteenth Century there was little that was good. In the 1870's Sidney Lanier was fashioning scrupulous music that appeared fugitively and was finally collected after his death. Millions now know his dashing *Song of the Chattahoochee*, and the intricate baritone swell of *The Marshes of Glynn*. Lanier, who was a professional musician, wedded two arts in his relatively few but distinguished poems. However, except for him and one other writer, it was as if all the genuine poetry in the country had been put into the making of Whitman. The poets who published verse from 1875 to 1895, with these exceptions, wrote timidly, echoing Longfellow and Tennyson.

But one unforgettable poet had been writing, a single hidden singer before a chorus of songs that were to come later. Emily Dickinson had filled letters and scraps of paper with hundreds of poems. Few were published while she lived, and none in a book. Only in 1890, four years after her death, was the first volume of her verse published, and it was years later before she was discovered and read by thousands and called by some critics the greatest woman poet since Sappho.

All this shouting would have seemed strange to Emily Dickinson. Brought up in a strict New England family, she read widely and fell in love with a man she could not marry, and retired to live very quietly in her father's house at Amherst, Massachusetts. Often she hardly left the house for months, though she could be witty and gay and sparkling among her few friends. She loved God in her own very original way, and she loved her flowers and her sister and her sister's children. She remembered the brief love that she could not have. Knowing only these few people and emotions, she wrote poems of her narrow world that are eternal.

Her poetry is very much like itself and little like any other. It is always brief and for the most part strange. Now it is a jewel of wild shape and colour; now a sword curled like a sea wave, now a white moon sliver. It may be a straight needle thrust of light, or a little cabinet of darkness that, if you put a head inside of it, will open into black infinity.

All these short lyrics are in simple forms—usually couplets or quatrains—and often at first they seem unfinished. The sentences may be twisted awkwardly. There may be odd grammar in them. Then the poet often prefers assonance, or the matching of sounds that are similar but not the same, to rhyme. "Star" will be paired with "door," "glass" with "house," "self" with "life." But the more the poems are read, the less important these oddities seem. The poems dart at beauty and truth with such an intensity and dancing magic that nothing seems to matter but the life of them.

They tell of simple, sometimes of trivial things. It may be that Emily listened at her window and heard how the bees

> Like trains of cars on tracks of plush

went humming. It may be she breathed the garden air and exclaimed:

> I taste a liquor never brewed
> From tankards scooped of pearl.

Or she may have lain awake at night to make a playful picture of the morning that seemed long in coming:

> Will there really be a morning
> Is there such a thing as day?
> Could I see it from the mountains
> If I were as tall as they?
>
> Has it feet like water-lilies?
> Has it feathers like a bird,
> Is it brought from famous countries
> Of which I have never heard?

Perhaps the very narrowness of her life made her see these simple things marvellously. And she saw as marvellously into her own mind and heart and the minds and hearts of the few about her. She knew how speech could hurt:

> There is a word
> Which bears a sword
> Can pierce an armed man.

She made romance of moods of hope or uncertainty:

> The house of supposition,
> The glimmering frontier
> That skirts the acre of perhaps—

while with shame and laughter she saw how she had been fooled by something cheap or false:

> It dropped so low in my regard
> I heard it hit the ground,
> And go to pieces on the stones
> At bottom of my mind.

In sadness she tells how

> I felt a funeral in my brain,
> And mourners, to and fro,

and she can write gently:

> I had no time to hate, because
> The grave would hinder me,
> And life was not so ample I
> Could finish enmity.
>
> Nor had I time to love; but since
> Some industry must be,
> The little toil of love, I thought,
> Was large enough for me.

It is strange, living, true poetry. No poetry ever told directly so much of one heart and mind. The things that kept Emily Dickinson to her house and made her know herself and her garden and sky so well gave the world a rich gift. The love she could not have; the little she liked, perhaps, in the America about her; and her instinct for quiet—all did something for her much like what America had done earlier for Poe. But while Poe was thrown back from the shock of life in a new country to an intenser life in art, Emily Dickinson was thrown back on her own thoughts and feelings to write of them more searchingly and surprisingly than any man or woman ever wrote.

While this unheard but exquisite solo was being sung, other poets were preparing to make a poetry different from hers, and even more different from that of Longfellow, Bryant, Lowell, and Whittier. The pioneer of the new singers had remained for years almost as unknown as Emily Dickinson, though he had published a number of volumes of verse. In fact, Edwin Arlington Robinson, born only four years later than Kipling, had begun to publish in 1897, five years after *Barrack-Room Ballads* appeared. And, like Kipling, he had written of modern men and women. Unfortunately, *The Children of the Night*, ballads and sonnets and lyrics about the New Englanders of Tilbury Town, got little attention. And though later books like *Captain Craig* and *The Town Down the River* made some name for Robinson, it was not until 1916 that he became famous. When *The Man Against the Sky* appeared in that year, everyone suddenly realized that Robinson had been the first of American poets since Whitman to write in a modern way of modern America.

At once lovers of poetry proclaimed him one of the finest of our living poets. Since then, with later books, Robinson has become even more important. Some lovers of his work set him beside Whitman and Poe. He has written successfully a great variety of poems—lyrics, sonnets, ballads, quaint character sketches, novels in verse—and all with fine art. He has explored the tortured minds and souls of men, turning into poetry our growing knowledge of the subconscious; and whether he deals with pathetic Miniver Cheevy, or curious Captain Craig, or Will Shakespeare with

> The mystery that's his—a mischievous
> Half-mad serenity that laughs at fame
> For being won so easy—

or Merlin or Richard Cary who "glittered when he walked," he strikes off golden lines and glinting truth.

Robinson has made a poetic language of his own, taking the casual American speech about him and giving it a firm literary form, with many of its weaknesses refined, and much of its strength intensified. Tens of thousands of readers enjoy his taciturn humour, his owlish and salty wit, his clipped and acrid deliberation. Perhaps he hesitates and worries in his thought and feeling, giving often a hard, crabbed, frustrated effect. Yet he can be one of the music makers.

The vigour and intensity and austere harmony of his best passages are memorable—the bleak and dramatic ending of *Merlin*, for instance:

Fiercer now,
The wind was like a flying animal
That beat the two of them incessantly
With icy wings, and bit them as they went.
The rock above them was an empty place
Where neither seer nor fool should view again
The stricken city. Colder blew the wind
Across the world, and on it heavier lay
The shadow and the burden of the night;
And there was darkness over Camelot.

There are other lovers of poetry who might choose other poets. Some might be tempted to linger over William Vaughn Moody, born in the same year as Robinson, whose work, cut short by death, might have grown to imposing proportions. Robert Frost, another New Englander, has sung his way into a first place with many. A New Englander like Robinson, he has written of New England farm people and the New England woods and houses. Robinson brought the homely speech of every day into poetry; Frost has made even a more careful marriage of the lilt of common talk and the beauty of poetic truth. He can tell how

Part of a moon was falling down the west,
Dragging the whole sky with it to the hills,

and get language that is as simple and friendly as conversation, and yet has a grandeur in it. Some of his lines have a haunting quality that grows out of their very talklike nature:

Something there is that doesn't love a wall,

for instance.

Frost has also been like Robinson in suggesting, through stories humorous or tragic, what goes on in the hearts of men and women. But where Robinson tells mostly of people who lived in little towns or long ago, Frost writes of himself or of the farmers about him. He has been a farmer most of his life, and no poet except Burns has known farm work and farm thoughts so well. But Frost also knows the beauty of books and the beauty of thought, and what he writes is both close to the earth and close to eternity. He gives a meaning to mending wall and mowing hay, to forests mantled with snow, to brooks and birches. Perhaps this is one important quality in his poetry: before we read it we have seen the things it tells of, but after having read it we are friends with them. There is more than this, for Frost has sung of youth and love and death, and some of the things he has written seem already to be lasting poems, almost as clear and tender as Wordsworth's. One of the shortest and best tells how

NOTHING GOLD CAN STAY

Nature's first green is gold,
Her hardest hue to hold.
Her leaf's an early flower;
But only for an hour.
Then leaf subsides to leaf.
So Eden sank to grief,
So dawn goes down in day.
Nothing gold can stay.

While Robinson and Frost were finding poetry in New England, poets were dreaming great dreams in the Middle West. Edgar Lee Masters took an Illinois town and made a book of the stories which the gravestones might tell if they would talk. *The Spoon River Anthology* (1914) was the result. The English poet Crabbe had told the story of an English village in his *Parish Register* more than a hundred years before. But Masters told of an American town, and his poetry was free verse. He made Americans feel the sweep and surge, the joy and pity of modern life, and they bought his book by the tens of thousands. Since then he has done other poetry that has both originality and power.

Quite as dramatic as Masters, but in a different way, is Nicholas Vachel Lindsay. Born in Illinois, walking the plains of broad Middle Western America, drinking in old stories, he was stirred by the clattering bigness of his country. In his early twenties, he went tramping through many parts of the country, singing and reciting to the farmer folk in return for meals and lodging. Then he began to write poems about America that were widely read. He wrote of Springfield, his own town; he wrote *General Booth Enters into Heaven*. Later came *The Congo*, his poem of American Negroes, with its refrain:

Boomlay, boomlay, boomlay, BOOM!

There was the song of the Santa Fe trail; there were poems of Abraham Lincoln and Johnny Appleseed and Mary Pickford and many others. He made romance of the pioneer America, and the zest and electric speed of the new America shine in verse, though he could write also of a sweet bird's song or of

THE FLOWER-FED BUFFALOES

The flower-fed buffaloes of the spring
In the days of long ago,
Ranged where the locomotives sing
And the prairie flowers lie low;
The tossing, blooming, perfumed grass
Is swept away by wheat,
Wheels and wheels and wheels spin by
In the spring that still is sweet.
But the flower-fed buffaloes of the spring
Left us long ago.
They gore no more, they bellow no more,
They trundle on the hills no more:—
With the Blackfeet lying low,
With the Pawnees lying low.

Carl Sandburg wrote of the new America, too. In verse much like Whitman's he made his *Chicago Poems*, songs of smoke and trains and meat factories. In free verse that was quieter and smoother he made later poems of the prairie where

The pearl-gray haystacks
In the gloaming
Are cool prayers
To the harvest hands.

He made poems of band concerts and motor cars, of cool tombs—

Pocahontas' body, lovely as a poplar, sweet as a red haw in November or a pawpaw in May, did she wonder? does she remember? . . . in the dust, in the cool tombs?

He wrote of foundries, jails, war, airplanes, parades. Often he took for his poems the talk and slang of the streets. Always he wrote with understanding for the hard-worked and oppressed, with sympathy for the misunderstood.

Masters has written much in free verse, and Sandburg has written all his poems in it. Both followed in the path Whitman had made, though both have tried to get into their irregular lines more form and beauty than Whitman usually got. While they were writing, other poets began to see other possibilities in free verse. Ezra Pound studied Greek and Japanese and French poetry, and wrote verses in which he tried to make the images and thoughts he had give each its own form to poetry. He and others who experimented with such ideas believed that every feeling or picture the mind knew could be closely suggested by words. Poetry written under this belief is called "imagist" poetry. Amy Lowell was interested in such verse, though she wrote much other verse, too. "H. D." (Hilda Doolittle) has done the most exquisite verse of this type. Like Amy Lowell's, hers has not been strictly "imagist," but has been greatly influenced by the Greek rhythms and phrases. She has shown more than any other one poet how "free verse" can be as finely polished as verse in rhyme and regular metre. Nothing could be more carefully carved than her poem—

HEAT

O wind, rend open the heat,
cut apart the heat,
rend it to tatters.

Fruit cannot drop
through this thick air—
fruit cannot fall into heat
that presses up and blunts
the points of pears
and rounds the grapes.

Cut through the heat—
plough through it,
turning it on either side
of your path.

But Hilda Doolittle and the others who tried to give form to "free verse" showed that in one sense it was no "freer" than any other verse. Each line must have a music of its own, yet must blend into the music of the other lines. A false rhythm jarred on the ear. Regular metre and rhyme made a form into which words could be poured, and gave a regular music covering up the rough and unharmonious words. Still, the writers of free verse were very successful in that they made a new kind of music with a pleasing variety all its own. In addition, and more important, they finished a great work begun by Whitman. They taught writers and readers of poetry that beauty in poetry could exist without regular rhyme or metre. They showed that whatever kind of beauty suited the feeling or picture to be expressed was a right kind of beauty. The poets writing in rhyme as well as the poets writing in free verse profited by this. They could do new things with rhyme and metre. They could bring in new words. It was not a little because of what the writers of free verse had done that a spirit of fresh life swept all of American poetry.

Nothing fully great seems to have come of this yet. There are young poets experimenting with new rhythms, and there are others writing in the old forms, putting modern language and modern feeling into these. One can range through diverse in talent and temperament: Sara Teasdale, Genevieve Taggard, William Ellery Leonard, John Gould Fletcher, E. E. Cummings, and Robinson Jeffers.

Elinor Wylie injects into loveliness jewel drops of acid.

Edna St. Vincent Millay, in her sonnets and poetic plays and short lyrics, has wrought some of the finest poems since Emily Dickinson. The lilt and spirit of Miss Millay's verse are indeed much like those remarkable Amherst songs. There is less of terrific intensity in the younger poet's work, but more of human life. There is also a greater art, though at the cost of that peculiar telegraphic defiance of grammar which gives a wry and elfin magic to Emily Dickinson's brevities. There is a frankness which is sometimes charming and often clever rather than moving. There is a tendency, once too frequent, toward saying smart ironic things in a kind of consciously infantile talk which, while it may rejoice the superficial, cannot but make the judicious grieve, as, for instance, that much-quoted triviality beginning "my candle burns at both ends":

> My candle burns at both ends,
>   It will not last the night;
> But ah, my foes, and oh, my friends—
>   It gives a lovely light!

There is, however, the enthusiastic radiance of *Renascence;* the stripped athletic loveliness of

THE POET AND HIS BOOK

> Stranger, pause and look;
>   From the dust of ages
> Lift this little book,
>   Turn the tattered pages,
> Read me, do not let me die!
>   Search the fading letters, finding
>   Steadfast in the broken binding
> All that once was I!

And there is that simple and serious beauty which is Miss Millay at her worthiest, now biting in its hard, clean, single-syllabled strength:

> I drank at every vine.
>   The last was like the first.
> I came upon no wine
>   So wonderful as thirst;

now like a cathedral in its dignity:

> Your face is like a chamber where a king
> Dies of his wounds, untended and alone.

Other poets have taken the freedom won by the battle Whitman began, and have taken also much from the forms of older poetry. Such a poet is Conrad Aiken, who has woven melodies that might have charmed the Lady of Shalott back into her dream world. Though what he has to say is often suggested by long orchestral waves of verse that only let his meaning gleam vaguely through sound, he can make pictures lovely in their strangeness.

Beautiful and very tender are passages like this beginning of his *Portrait of One Dead:*

> This is her house. On one side there is darkness,
> On one side there is light.
> Into the darkness you may lift your lanterns,
> O any number—it will still be night.
> And there are echoing stairs to lead you downward
> To long sonorous halls.
> And here is spring forever at these windows
> With roses on the walls.

Aiken, with other poets such as T. S. Eliot, reflects the philosophical disturbance made in the souls of thoughtful men by the brutal aggressiveness and vulgarity of modern life, with its exaltation of immense manufacturing, building, and bartering, its destruction of old loveliness, its chaos of ideas, its poverty of noble purpose. Often such poets find a great emptiness in life, speaking out their spiritual despair in fragments like this from Eliot's "The Waste Land":

> What are the roots that clutch, what branches grow
> Out of this stony rubbish? Son of man,
> You cannot say, or guess, for you know only
> A heap of broken images, where the sun beats,
> And the dead tree gives no shelter, the cricket no relief,
> And the dry stone no sound of water.

CHAPTER XXVIII

PEGASUS IN TO-MORROW

We are at the ending of a story. We can look back on all that has happened to poetry and poets since Homer breathed the life of song into Helen and Achilles.

We are also at the beginning of a story. We cannot fail to turn from the pageant that has been and peer into the long to-morrow that lies at the horizon. Will the wings of a horse gleam there among tall chimney snouts and cubical towers? Will he lift poets skyward to let them pull once more from heaven words that will be lamps for a dark earth below?

It is not certain what we may expect of Pegasus in that uncharted country. There are many who doubt if he will fly high. Some say he will not fly at all. And startling though such a prophecy may sound, we can see, if we look back through the almost three thousand years of our poetry, and then look at the poetry about us to-day—we can see some reason for uncertainty and discouragement.

For though poetry has had its many glorious days under Sappho and Sophocles and Virgil, under Shakespeare and Keats and Whitman, it has also little by little been losing portions of its original kingdom.

Very early it began to shed its ancient function of helping men to work. Gradually this has lessened through the centuries, fading and reviving and fading; there is almost nothing left of it now.

Poetry has lost also much of its office of wisdom-giver. The philosophers came with their speculations about the meaning of life and took a great deal from poetry. With the making of books, first by hand and then by printing press, others arrived to take more: historians, essayists, scientists. There are many to-day who claim to know more than the poets!

Then, too, poetry has fallen into disuse as a means of keeping knowledge. It was once the strong-box where the facts of history and the rules of conduct were preserved. It was an encyclopedia of information. But it has long been easier and safer to store dates and recipes and advice in volumes of stamped paper. When we need them, we turn to a library index instead of quoting a rhyme.

Poetry has lost its hold on the telling of stories. First history began to be done in prose. Then, among the later Greeks, the prose romance was born, and gradually more and more fiction slipped outside of metre. In the Eighteenth Century, while poetry was sleeping in common sense, the modern novel was fashioned. Prose walled in a great preserve in those days, and ever since it has been making its domain greater and greater. Nowadays, we even hear it said that a story that can be told in prose ought not to be told in poetry at all..

Men turn to poetry for music less than they did. In earlier days musical instruments were simple. They were often used to set off and embellish the glory of human feeling and the rhythm of human words. But in the Middle Ages there were developed remarkable toys like the violin and organ and piano. Men became fascinated with the sounds of these instruments. Their ears became less responsive to the more delicate and complicated music of poetry, woven as it is of thought and feeling, form and harmony. So now in our theatres actors have for-

gotten how to recite poetry and audiences how to listen to it.
Prose has taken over our plays, and poetry appears for the most
part only in opera or musical comedy. There it is usually a
jingle ministering to the twanging strings, the shrilling brass,
the resonant wood that once served it in Athens and Alexandria.

These are the chief losses; others could be listed. Some of
them are discouraging to those who love poetry. They seem
to have left poetry relatively weak, much less a necessity than
it was. Compared with prose, poetry is not widely read. New
volumes seldom command the attention of busy men and
women. Why should they? People want their reading to be useful. They want to learn of the ideas and people and feelings of
the hour, and through these to get enjoyment, or suggestions
for the living of their own lives. They want knowledge and solid
wisdom and the reality of history. When they turn to poetry,
they often find timid experiments in new rhythms, descriptions,
thoughts, and feelings that seem to be the left-overs from prose.
It is sad to think of these poets, wrapped up in the trivialities of
life, in contrast with the older poets. But let poetry speak
what should be its own feeling:

> We who were prophets and priest-men
> For the Kings of the East and the East-men,
> The bugles of God to the beast-men,
> His terrible seal on our brow—
> Physicians of music and makers
> Of language and law and the breakers
> Of battle, strength-lifters, heart-shakers—
> We are nice poets now.
>
> And we sip cups of tea, nibble crumpets,
> And we celebrate ninnies and strumpets,
> While the rust bites the throat of the trumpets
> And the ram's horn hangs on the wall;
> And the fifes of the Lord are polluted
> With melodies tickled and tooted
> Out of the stops that once fluted
> Tall silver songs for King Saul.

It is from such a picture that the darker prophets make their prophecies on poetry. With the lessening of poets and the growing power of drama and music and novels, with the machine art of newspapers, of movies, of radio sets will come, they say, a time when there will be no place at all for the one-time glory of verse. Pegasus will vanish forever, they think, beyond the haze of factory towns, shunning the earth that is full of hissing and hammering, and the hands of singers that are too weak to urge a dream upward, vaulting and planing among the clouds.

However, poetry does not seem to be ready to disappear.

It persists even at some of the jobs it is supposed to have given up. Children play their games to it. Important people catch themselves reciting jingles to remind themselves of some elusive fact or process:

> Thirty days hath September,
> April, June, and November—

or

> Turn to the right
> To make it tight—

or

> "I" before "e"
> Except after "c"—

When a slogan is wanted to put a purpose into a million people, it comes often in rhyme. Advertisements try the persuasiveness of couplets and quatrains. We demand war songs, poems of grief, poems for gala days. Newspapers hire desperate rhymesters to make a "poem" a day because people like to read "poetry." Boys and girls scribble their love or grief in stammering metre, or hunt for verses on postcards, or even read books of poetry! If books of new poetry do not sell well, collections of poetry already known are as popular as novels.

And if poetry has lost many of its old functions, it has kept and strengthened certain very important ones. It began by assisting men in their need and fear and perplexity, and in the world of cities and books it still does this. Its work is more subtle than it once was, but it is still far-reaching. Men and women who work in offices and factories lead a life that is limited. They find little opportunity to express positive emotions, and less opportunity to act them. They turn to poetry and discover emotion that fulfills their own impulses. In the beauty of verse their own hunger for beauty is satisfied. The bravery and confidence of poetry feeds their craving for personal recognition. Poetry keeps alive in them the desire to go on, preserves the sense of brightness through days too seldom bright. And, less directly, the noble tone of all great verse sets for millions a kind of ideal of behaviour. Boys and girls chant to themselves lines that mould a purpose or make a way of thinking or feeling. Men and women come back from difficult days of work to remind themselves through poetry that there is something nobler in life than they tasted at the stint in the workshop or behind the counter. In a similar fashion, most genuinely great men and women turn to poetry for a spiritual force nothing else seems to give them. Philosophers and essayists quote poets. It is often said that this novelist or that playwright can never be great because he is not a poet. Finally, there are times when a new poem strikes fire in men and women, and there is a rush for books which suggests that the need for poetry still lives like a hunger in men.

The fact is that nothing has as yet been devised to do for men what poetry has always done and still does to-day. Nothing else blends thought and feeling and harmony into such intense and satisfying form. Poetry speaks most fully and briefly as much of the high mystery and meaning of life as man can utter. To speak in its fashion is the most difficult way of talking. It is also the most glorious. In prose and music men have tried other and easier ways of doing the work of poetry. They have not yet been able to say what the best poetry has always said.

It is difficult to see how men, who have never done without poetry in the past, can do without it in the future. They have changed their lives, but they have not lost the necessity for expressing their intense emotions, their high wonder. And although they neglect poetry because it asks more effort of them than any other art, they come back to it because it gives more.

During the last hundred years, life has been changing. Poets and listeners have both been distracted. At times there seemed to be little to sing of. Songs were drowned in the shriek of a locomotive, blotted out by the headlines of a newspaper, forgotten for the startling voice of a radio. But now the poets and the world are both getting used to the new existence. The coming of the machines that have remade the face of the earth has itself been a great adventure, physical and spiritual—a challenge to poets. Perhaps they are more needed now than they have been for thousands of years, for in many senses more has happened in the last hundred years than in twenty centuries of earlier life.

Of course, the use of poetry by men and women depends not a little on fashion. People listen to orchestral music that bores them because it is the thing to do. At present they do not listen to poetry in a similar way. Many of them would get more enjoyment from hearing *The Everlasting Mercy* or *Out of the Cradle Endlessly Rocking* than they get from Bach or Debussy or Mr. Ornstein. They would get more out of reading Mr. Robinson's *Tristram* than from many novels that might be compared with it. However, they are out of the habit of listening to verse or reading it; they find it an effort. They go to poetry only when they have to.

Perhaps this will continue to be the way of the world with regard to poetry. If a new attitude is to be established, it will come with the shock of a great poet's personality. Great poets may appear. They have a way of rising to opportunities. Shakespeare stands scarcely a century away from a time when England had no poets but ballad-makers. Whitman and Poe shot up from the American wilderness. To-day, thanks to Whitman and many who have followed him, the language of poetry is fresh and human. There are new stories that might be put into song. There are new thoughts, new crafts, new parades, new cities. There is a world that ought to have as much usefulness as ever, and perhaps more, for the music of words it has kept all the days of its life.

THE END

READING LISTS

The Winged Horse has flown so far, over lands both far and near, and during so many years, both long ago and yesterday, that it would be easy indeed to make a very long list of books about the beautiful things that are related to those flights. Instead, a comparatively few books have been chosen such as may prolong the pleasure of the book and help to show how to satisfy the longing that it rouses and send each reader questing to discover beauty for himself.

That is the way to read for delight of course —to let a book like this open the gates and then through the open gates to go wandering to find beauty each by himself.

"By myself?" said David. "To be sure," said the Man in the Moon. "How else would you go?"

THERESA WEST ELMENDORF

READING LISTS

Page 421   *Anthologies.*

Page 423   *Studies biographical and critical of the poets and poetry*

Page 431   *References to texts of poets and to studies*

"Then whoso will with vertuous deeds assay
To mount to heaven, on Pegasus must ride,
And with sweete poets verse be glorifide."

EDMUND SPENSER

ANTHOLOGIES

*"To make the Muses' access easier
when, in the right hour, they come
to uplift or to console."*

SIR ARTHUR QUILLER-COUCH.

Alden, Raymond Macdonald, Ed. Poems of the English Race. Scribner. 1921.

Andrews, Clarence Edward, and M. O. Percival. Poetry of the Nineties. Harcourt. 1926.

Auslander, Joseph, and Frank Ernest Hill. The Winged Horse Anthology. Doubleday. 1929.

Bridges, Robert, Ed. Chilswell Book of English Poetry. Longmans. 1924.

De La Mare, Walter, Ed. Come Hither: A Collection of Rhymes for the Young of All Ages. Knopf. 1923.

Drinkwater, John, Ed. The Way of Poetry; an Anthology for Younger Readers. Houghton. 1922.

Everett, William, Ed. The Italian Poets Since Dante; Accompanied by Verse Translations. Scribner. 1904.

Meynell, Alice, Ed. The School of Poetry; an Anthology Chosen for Young Readers. Scribners. 1924.

Monroe, Harriet, and Alice Corbin Henderson, Eds. The New Poetry; An Anthology of Twentieth Century Verse in English. New ed. Macmillan. 1926.

Newbolt, Sir Henry, Ed. Book of Verse Chosen for Students at Home and Abroad. Bell. 1922.

Page, Curtis Hidden, Ed. The Chief American Poets: Selected Poems. Houghton. 1905.

Palgrave, Francis Turner, Ed. The Golden Treasury; Selected from the Best Songs and Lyrical Poems in the English Language. Rev. and Enl. Ed. Macmillan. 1909. 2 v. in 1.

Quiller-Couch, Sir Arthur, Ed. The Oxford Book of English Verse, 1250–1900. Oxf. Univ. Pr. 1901.

The Oxford Book of Victorian Verse. Oxf. Univ. Pr. 1911.

Roxburgh, John Fergusson, Ed. The Poetic Procession: a Beginner's Introduction to English Poetry. Blackwell. 1922.

Stevenson, Burton Egbert, Ed. The Home Book of Verse, American and English, 1580–1912. 5th Ed. Holt. 1925.

Untermeyer, Louis, Ed. Modern American Poetry. 3d Ed. Harcourt. 1925.

    Modern British Poetry. Rev. Ed. Harcourt. 1925.

    Yesterday and To-day; a Collection of Verse Mostly Modern Designed for the Average Person of Nine to Nineteen and Possibly Higher. Harcourt. 1926.

Wooldridge, Dorothy, Ed. The Poetry of Toil: An Anthology. Faber. 1926.

STUDIES
Biographical and Critical of the Poets and Poetry

Adams, Joseph Quincy.
1. Life of William Shakespeare. Houghton Mifflin, 1923.

Alden, Raymond Macdonald.
1a. Alfred Tennyson: How to Know Him. Bobbs. 1917.
2. An Introduction to Poetry. Holt. 1909.
3. Shakespeare. (Master Spirits of Literature.) Duffield. 1922.

Andrews, Clarence Edward.
4. The Writing and Reading of Verse. Appleton. 1918.

Bailey, John.
5. Milton. (Home Univ. Libr.) Williams and Norgate. 1913.
6. Walt Whitman. (Eng. Men of Letters. new ser.) (Macmillan. 1926)

Bazalgetta, Leon.
6a. Walt Whitman, The Man and His Work. Doubleday, Page, 1920.

Benson, Arthur Christopher.
7. Essays. Heinemann. 1896.

Bianchi, Martha Dickinson.
8. Life and Letters of Emily Dickinson. Houghton. 1924.

Boissier, Gaston.
9. The Country of Horace and Virgil: Trans. by D. H. Fisher. Putnam. 1896.

Boynton, Percy Holmes.
10. Some Contemporary Americans; the Personal Equation in Literature. Univ. of Chicago Pr. 1924.

Bradley, Andrew Cecil.
11. Oxford Lectures on Poetry. Macmillan. 1909.
12. Shakespearean Tragedy; Lectures on Hamlet, Othello, King Lear, Macbeth. 2d Ed. Macmillan. 1905.

Bridges, Horace James.
13. Our Fellow Shakespeare. 2nd Ed. rev. Covici. 1925.

Brooke, Stopford Augustus.
14. Studies in Poetry. Duckworth. 1907.

Burroughs, John.
   15. Birds and Poets. Houghton. 1895.
Butler, Arthur John.
   16. Dante, His Times and His Work. Innes. 1895.
Campbell, Lewis.
   17. Tragic Drama in Aeschylus, Sophocles and Shakespeare;
      an Essay. Longmans. 1904.
Cary, Elisabeth Luther.
   18. Browning Poet and Man. Putnam. 1899.
   19. The Rossettis: Dante Gabriel and Christina. Putnams. 1900.
Chapman, John Jay.
   20. Greek Genius, and Other Essays. Moffat. 1915.
Chaytor, Henry John.
   21. The Troubadours. Camb. Univ. Pr. 1912.
Chesterton, Gilbert Keith.
   22. Robert Browning. (Eng. Men of Letters.) Macmillan. 1903.
   23. William Blake. Dutton. 1910.
Church, Alfred John.
   24. The Iliad for Boys and Girls Told from Homer in Simple
      Language. Macmillan. 1907.
Church, Richard William.
   25. Dante, and Other Essays. Macmillan. 1888.
Clutton-Brock, Arthur.
   26. Shelley, The Man and The Poet. Methuen. 1909.
   27. William Morris, His Work and Influence. (Home Univ.
      Libr.) Holt. 1912.
Cody, Sherwin.
   28. Poe—Man, Poet, and Creative Thinker. Boni. 1924.
Collins, William Lucas.
   29. Aristophanes.(Ancient Clas. for Eng. Readers.) Lippincott. 1879.
Colum, Padraic.
   30. The Adventures of Odysseus and the Tale of Troy. Macmillan.
      1918.
Colvin, Sir Sidney.
   31. John Keats; His Life and Poetry, His Friends, Critics and
      After-fame. Scribners. 1917.
Copleston, Reginald Stephen.
   32. Aeschylus. (Ancient Clas. for Eng. Readers.) Lippincott. 1879.
Cowling, George H.
   33. A Preface to Shakespeare. Methuen. 1925.
Davies, James.

34. Hesiod and Theognis. (Ancient Clas. for Eng. Readers.) Lippincott. 1873.

Dawson, William James.

35. The Makers of English Poetry. 3d Ed. Revell. 1906.

De Selincourt, Basil.

36. William Blake. Scribners. 1909.

Dinsmore, Charles Allen.

37. Life of Dante Alighieri. Houghton. 1919.

Dixon, William Macneile.

38. English Epic and Heroic Poetry. Dent. 1912.

Dowden, Edward.

39. New Studies in Literature. Kegan Paul. 1902.

Drinkwater, John.

40. The Muse in Council; Essays on Poets and Poetry. Houghton. 1925.

Eastman, Max.

41. Enjoyment of Poetry. 9th Ed. rev. Scribners. 1921.

Edmunds, Edward William.

42. Shelley and His Poetry. Harrap. 1911.

Erskine, John.

43. The Elizabethan Lyric. Columb. Univ. Pr. 1903.

44. The Kinds of Poetry, and Other Essays. Duffield. 1920.

Fausset, Hugh I'Anson.

45. Samuel Taylor Coleridge. Cape. 1926.

45a. Tennyson: A Modern Portrait. Appleton, 1923

Federn, Karl.

46. Dante and His Time; Introd. by A. J. Butler. Heinemann 1902.

Flamini, Francesco.

47. Introduction to the Study of the Divine Comedy. Ginn. 1910,

Fletcher, Jefferson Butler.

48. Dante. (Home Univ. Libr.) Holt. 1916.

Gardner, Edmund Garratt.

49. Dante. (Revision of his "Dante primer.") Dent. 1923.

Garnett, Richard.

50. Essays of an Ex-librarian. Heinemann. 1901.

Garrod, Heathcote William.

51. Keats. Clar. Pr. 1926.

52. Wordsworth; Lectures and Essays. Oxf. Univ. Pr. 1923.

Gayley, Charles Mills, and Others.

53. English Poetry. Macmillan. 1920.

Glover, Terroc Reaveley.
    54. From Pericles to Philip. Macmillan. 1917.
Goodell, Thomas Dwight.
    55. Athenian Tragedy; a Study in Popular Art. Yale Univ. Press.
        1920.
Gosse, Edmund.
    56. Questions at Issue. Appleton. 1893.
Grandgent, Charles Hall.
    57. Dante. (Master Spirits of Literature.) Duffield. 1916.
Gummere, Francis Barton.
    58. The Beginnings of Poetry. Macmillan. 1901.
    59. The Popular Ballad. Houghton. 1907.
Hadow, Grace Eleanor.
    60. Chaucer and His Times. (Home Univ. Libr.) Holt.
Haight, Elizabeth Hazelton.
    61. Horace and His Art of Enjoyment. Dutton. 1925
Horridge, Frank.
    62. Lives of Great Italians. Unwin. 1897.
Hubbell, Jay Broadus, and John O. Beaty.
    63. An Introduction to Poetry. Macmillan. 1922.
Hudson, William Henry.
    64. Keats and His Poetry. Harrap. 1912.
Hueffer, Frances.
    65. The Troubadours; a History of Provençal Life and Literature
        in the Middle Ages. Chatto. 1878.
Ingram, John H.
    66. Elizabeth Barrett Browning. Little. 1898.
Jack, Adolphus Alfred.
    67. Poetry and Prose; Essays on Modern English Poetry. Con-
        stable. 1911.
Jebb, Sir Richard Claverhouse.
    68. Homer: an Introduction to the Iliad and the Odyssey.
        Maclehose. 1887.
Jerrold, Maud F.
    69. Francesco Petrarca, Poet and Humanist. Dent. 1909.
Jones, Henry.
    70. Idealism as a Practical Creed. Maclehose. 1910.
Jones, Llewellyn.
    71. First Impressions; Essays on Poetry, Criticism and Prosody.
        Knopf. 1925.

Kellow, Henry Arthur.
72. Burns and His Poetry. (Poetry and Life.) Harrap. 1911.
Ker, William Paton.
73. The Art of Poetry; Seven Lectures, 1920–1922. Oxf. Univ. Pr. 1923.
74. Collected Essays: Ed. with Introd. by Charles Whibley. Macmillan. 1925. 2 v.
75. Epic and Romance; Essays on Medieval Literature. Macmillan. 1897.
Kernahan, Coulson.
76. Six Famous Living Poets. Butterworth. 1922.
Kittredge, George Lyman.
77. Chaucer and His Poetry. Harvard Univ. Pr. 1915.
Krutch, Joseph Wood.
78. Edgar Allan Poe; a Study in Genius. Knopf. 1926.
Lang, Andrew.
79. Essays in Little. Scribner. 1901.
Lawton, William Cranston.
80. The Soul of the Anthology. Yale Univ. Pr.
Leaf, Walter.
81. A Companion to the Iliad for English Readers. Macmillan. 1892.
Livingstone, Richard Winn, Comp.
82. The Pageant of Greece. Clar. Pr. 1923.
Lord, Louis E.
83. Aristophanes; His Plays and His Influence. (Our Debt to Greece and Rome.) Marshall Jones. 1925.
Lowell, Amy.
83a. John Keats. Houghton, 1925. 2v.
84. Tendencies in Modern American Poetry. Macmillan. 1917.
Lowell, James Russell.
85. Literary Essays. Houghton. 1890. 4 v
Lynd, Robert.
86. Books and Authors. Putnam. 1923.
Mackail, John William.
87. Lectures on Greek Poetry. New Ed. Longmans. 1926.
88. Lectures on Poetry. Longmans. 1911.
89. The Springs of Helicon; a Study in the Progress of English Poetry from Chaucer to Milton. Longmans. 1909.
90. Studies of English Poets. Longmans. 1926.
91. Virgil and His Meaning to the World of To-day. (Our Debt to Greece and Rome.) Jones. 1922.

92. William Morris; Life and Letters. Longmans. 1899. 2 v.

Malory, Sir Thomas.

93. The Boy's King Arthur; Ed. by Sidney Lanier, illus. by N.C. Wyeth. Scribner. 1917.

94. Morte d'Arthur; Book of King Arthur and of His Noble Knights of the Round Table; Ed. by Sir Edward Strachey. Macmillan. 1897.

Marvin, Francis Sydney.

95. The Adventures of Odysseus Retold in English. Dent. (Everyman.) 1921.

Masefield, John.

96. William Shakespeare. (Home Univ. Libr.) Holt. 1911.

Maurois, Andre.

96a. Ariel: The Life of Shelley. Appleton, 1924.

Morris, Lloyd.

97. The Poetry of Edwin Arlington Robinson. Doran. 1923.

Moulton, Richard Green.

98. The Ancient Classical Drama; a Study in Literary Evolution. 2d Ed. Clar. Pr. 1898.

Murray, Gilbert.

99. Euripides and His Age. (Home Univ. Libr.) Holt. 1913.

Myers, Frederick William Henry.

100. Essays: Classical. Macmillan. 1883.

Neilson, William Allen.

101. Essentials of Poetry. (Lowell lectures.) Houghton. 1912.

102. Robert Burns; How to Know Him. Bobbs. 1917.

Newbolt, Sir Henry.

103. A New Study of English Poetry. Constable. 1917.

Nicolson, Harold.

104. Swinburne. (Eng. Men of Letters: New Rev.) Macmillan. 1926.

Noyes, Alfred.

105. Some Aspects of Modern Poetry. Stokes. 1924.

106. William Morris. Macmillan. 1908.

Palmer, George Herbert.

107. Formative Types in English Poetry. Houghton. 1918.

Phelps, William Lyon.

108. The Advance of English Poetry in the Twentieth Century. Dodd. 1919.

109. Robert Browning, and How to Know Him. Bobbs. 1915.

Pound, Louise.
110. Poetic Origins and the Ballad. Macmillan. 1921.
Pyle, Howard.
111. Histories Relating to the Life and to the Kingship of Arthur, King of England. 4v. Scribners. 1903–1910.
Quiller-Couch, Sir Arthur.
112. Notes on Shakespeare's Workmanship; from Lectures (at Cambridge). Holt. 1917.
113. Poetry. (Fellowship Books.) Dutton. 1914.
114. Studies in Literature. Camb. Univ. Pr. 1918. 2 v.
Raleigh, Sir Walter.
115. Milton. Arnold. 1900.
116. Shakespeare. (Eng. Men of Letters.) Macmillan. 1907.
117. Some Authors: a Collection of Literary Essays. Oxf. Univ. Pr. 1923.
Redman, Ben Ray.
118. Edwin Arlington Robinson. McBride. 1926.
Rhys, Ernest.
119. Lyric Poetry. Dent. 1913.
Royds, Kathleen E.
120. Coleridge and His Poetry. (Poetry and Life.) Harrap. 1912.
Schofield, William Henry.
121. Chivalry in English Literature. Harv. Univ. Pr. 1912.
Scott, John A.
122. Homer and His Influence. (Our Debt to Greece and Rome.) Jones. 1925.
Sedgwick, Henry Dwight.
123. Dante. Yale Univ. Pr. 1918.
Sellar, William Young.
124. The Roman Poets of the Augustan Age: Horace and the Elegiac Poets. Clar. Pr. 1892.
125. The Roman Poets of the Augustan Age: Virgil. 3d. Ed. Oxf. Univ. Pr. 1908.
Sherman, Stuart Pratt.
126. Matthew Arnold; How to Know Him. Bobbs. 1917.
Showerman, Grant.
127. Horace and His Influence. (Our Debt to Greece and Rome.) Marshall Jones. 1922.
Smyth, Herbert Weir.
128. Aeschylean Tragedy. Univ. of Cal. Pr. 1924.

Stalker, James
   129. How to Read Shakespeare: a Guide for the General Reader.
      Hodder. 1913.
Sturgeon, Mary C.
   130. Studies of Contemporary Poets. Rev. Ed. Dodd. 1919.
Swinburne, Algernon Charles.
   131. Essays and Studies. Chatto. 1911.
Thompson, Francis.
   132. Shelley. Scribner. 1910.
Tyrrell, Robert Yelverton.
   133. Essays on Greek Literature. Macmillan. 1909.
Untermeyer, Louis.
   134. American Poetry Since 1900. Holt. 1923.
   135. Forms of Poetry; a Pocket Dictionary of Verse. Harcourt.
      1926.
   136. The New Era in American Poetry. Holt. 1919.
Van Doren, Mark.
   137. The Poetry of John Dryden. Harcourt. 1920.
Van Dyke, Henry.
   138. Studies in Tennyson. Scribner. 1920.
Warren, Sir Thomas Herbert.
   139. Essays of Poets and Poetry Ancient and Modern. Murray.
      1909.
Watts-Dunton, Theodore.
   140. Old Familiar Faces. Dutton. 1916.
Whiting, Lilian.
   141. The Brownings; Their Life and Art. Little. 1911.
Wilkinson, Marguerite.
   142. New Voices; an Introd. to Contemporary Poetry. New Ed.
      Macmillan. 1921.
Williams, Stanley Thomas.
   143. Studies in Victorian Literature. Dutton. 1923.
Winchester, Caleb Thomas.
   144. William Wordsworth; How to Know Him. Bobbs. 1916.
Yeats, William Butler.
   145. Essays. Macmillan. 1924.

REFERENCES
To Texts of Poets and to Studies
Numbers refer to Reading List

Chapter I

Comments: Studies no. 58, 59, 98, 101.

Chapter IV

HOMER

Texts: The Iliad of Homer; Trans. by Alexander Pope. Bell.

The Iliad of Homer; Done into English Prose by Andrew Lang, Walter Leaf and Ernest Myers. Rev. ed. Macmillan, 1891.

Homer's Odyssey; trans. by Alexander Pope. Bell.

The Odyssey: Trans. by George Herbert Palmer. Houghton. 1891.

The Odyssey: Done into English Prose by S. H. Butcher and A. Lang. Rev. ed. Macmillan, 1879.

Texts: simple versions: Studies no. 24; 30; 95.

Comments: Studies no. 68; 81; 82 p. 15–78; 87 p. 3–79; 122.

Chapter V

GREEK POETRY: general books.

Texts: Appleton, William Hyde, Ed. Greek Poets in English Verse by Various Hands. Houghton. 1893.

Dole, Nathan Haskell, Ed. The Greek Poets; an Anthology. Crowell. 1904.

Comments: Studies No. 82; 87; 98.

THE ANTHOLOGY

Texts: Little Poems from the Greek by Walter Leaf. Grant Richards. 1922–24. 2 v.

Comments: Studies No. 80; 82; 87; 98.

HESIOD

Davies, James. Hesiod and Theognis. (Ancient Clas. for English Readers.) Lippincott. 1875.

PINDAR

Texts: The Extant Odes of Pindar; Trans. with Introd. and Notes
by Ernest Myers. Macmillan. 1874.
The Golden Porch; a Book of Greek Fairy Tales by W. M. L.
Hutchinson. New ed. Longmans. 1925.
Comments: Studies No. 123 p. 1–40.

SAPPHO

Text: The Fragments of the Lyrical Poems of Sappho; Ed. by
Edgar Lobel. Oxf. Univ. Pr. 1927.

THEOCRITUS

Texts: Theocritus, Bion and Moschus; Rendered into English
Prose by A. Lang. Macmillan. 1889.
Theocritus, Bion and Moschus; Trans. into English Verse
by Arthur S. Way. Camb. Univ. Pr. 1913.
Comments: Studies No. 87 p. 208–238.

Chapter VI

ÆSCHYLUS

Texts: Lyrical Dramas; Trans. into English Verse by John Stuart
Blackie. (Everyman.) Dutton. 1906.
Comments: Studies No. 17; 32; 55 p. 183–201; 128.

SOPHOCLES

Texts: Tragedies; Trans. into English Prose by Sir R. C. Jebb,
Camb. Univ. Pr. 1904.
Comments: Studies No. 17; 55 p. 202–232; 133 p. 41–84.

EURIPIDES

Texts: Euripides; Trans. into English Rhyming Verse by Gilbert
Murray. Oxf. Univ. Pr. 1902—and 7 v.
Comments: Studies no. 20 p. 1–131; 55 p. 233–283; 54 p. 136–152; 99.

ARISTOPHANES

Texts: The Acharnians, and Two Other Plays; Trans. by J. H.
Frere. (Everyman.) Dutton. 1909.
Comments: Studies No. 29, 83.

Chapter VII

LATIN POETRY; GENERAL BOOKS, Dole, Nathan Haskell,
Ed. The Latin Poets; an Anthology. Crowell. 1905.
Sellar, William Young. Roman Poets of the Augustan Age.
Oxf. Univ. Pr. 1892, 1908. 2v.

HORACE

Texts: Complete Works: Trans. by Various Hands. (Everyman.) Dent. 1911.

Comments: Studies No. 9; 61; 114 v. 1 p. 51–75; 124; 127.

VIRGIL

Texts: The Aeneid: Trans. into English Verse by T. C. Williams. Houghton. 1910.

Works; Trans. into English Prose by John Conington; Ed. by John Addington Symonds. McKay.

Comments: Studies No. 9; 91; 100 p. 106–176; 125.

Chapter VIII

BEOWULF

Texts: The Story of Beowulf: Trans. by Ernest J. B. Kirtlan into Modern English Prose. Crowell. 1914.

Beowulf: a New Verse Trans. for Fireside and Class Room by William Ellery Leonard. Century. 1923.

Comments: Studies No. 75 p. 182–202.

TROUBADOURS

Texts: Troubadour Poets: Selections from eight Troubadours: Trans. from the Provençal, with Introd. and Notes by Barbara Smythe. Oxf. Univ. Pr. 1925.

Comments: Studies No. 21; 65.

CHANSON DE ROLAND

Texts: The Song of Roland: Newly Trans. with an Introd. by Jessie Crosland. Chatto. 1924.

The Song of Roland: Trans. into English Verse by Leonard Bacon. Yale Univ. Pr. 1914.

NIBELUNGENLIED

Texts: The Nibelungenlied: Trans. into English Verse by George Henry Needler. Holt. 1904.

The Nibelungenlied: Trans. with Introductory Sketch and Notes by Daniel Bussier Shumway. Houghton. 1909.

The Lay of the Nibelung Men: Trans. by Arthur S. Way. Camb. Univ. Pr. 1911.

THE SAGAS

Texts: The Sagas of Olaf Tryggvason, and of Harald the Tyrant. (Harald Haardraade.) Williams and Norgate. 1911.

Stories and Ballads of the Far Past: Trans. from the Norse with Introd. and Notes by N. Kershaw. Camb. Univ. Pr. 1921.

The Saga of Grettir the Strong: a Story of the Eleventh
Century: Trans. by George Ainslie Wright. (Everyman.)
Dutton. 1913.

Comments: Studies No. 75 p. 205–325.

KING ARTHUR

Texts: Malory, Sir Thomas, Morte d'Arthur: Ed. by Sir Edward
Strachey. Macmillan. 1897.

The Boy's King Arthur: Ed. by Sidney Lanier. Illus. by N. C.
Wyeth. Scribner. 1917.

Histories Relating to the Life and Kingship of Arthur King
of England by Howard Pyle. Scribner. 1903–1910. 4 v.

Chapter IX

DANTE ALIGHIERI

Texts: The Divine Comedy: Trans. by Henry Johnson. Yale Univ.
Pr. 1915.

The Divine Comedy: Trans. by Charles Eliot Norton. Rev.
Ed. complete in 1 v. Houghton. 1919.

Comments: Studies No. 16; 25 p. 1–191; 37; 46; 47; 48; 49; 57; 74
v. 1. p. 305–320; 85 v. 4 p. 118–264; 123.

Chapter X

PETRARCH

Texts: Sonnets, Triumphs and Other Poems; Trans. into English
by Various Hands. Bell. 1901.

Comments: Studies No. 62 p. 51–141; 39.

Chapter XI

CHAUCER, GEOFFREY

Texts: Chaucer: Ed. by H. N. McCracken. Yale Univ. Pr. 1913.

Modern Reader's Chaucer; the Complete Poetical Works
Put into Modern English by J. S. Tatlock and Percy
Mackaye. Macmillan. 1912.

Selections from Chaucer: Ed. by W. A. Neilson and H. R.
Patch. Harcourt. 1921.

The Student's Chaucer: Ed. by Rev. Walter W. Skeat, with
a Glossary. Oxford University Press, American Branch.

Comments: Studies No. 60; 77; 85 v. 3 p. 291–366; 89 p. 1–69;
103 p. 119–159; 107 p. 33–59; 114 v. 2 p. 207–248; 121 p.
11–72.

Chapter XII

THE BALLAD MAKERS

Texts: Child, Francis James, Ed. English and Scottish Popular
Ballads, Ed. by Helen Child Sargent and George Lyman
Kittredge. (Cambridge Ed.) Houghton, 1904.

Gayley, Charles Mills, and Martin C. Flaherty, Eds. Poetry
of the People. Enl. Ed. Ginn. 1920.

Johnson, Reginald Brimley. Ed. A Book of British Ballads.
(Everyman.) Dutton. 1912.

Lang, Andrew, Ed. A Collection of Ballads. Chapman and
Hall. 1897.

Quiller-Couch, Sir Arthur. Ed. The Oxford Book of Ballads.
Oxf. Univ. Pr. 1910.

Comments: Studies No. 38 p. 27–48; 103 p. 215–239; 110; 114 v. 1.
p. 23–50.

Chapter XIII

SPENSER, EDMUND

Texts: Complete Works: Ed. by R. Morris. Macmillan. 1897.

Complete Works: with an Introd. by W. P. Trent. Crowell.
1903.

Comments: Studies No. 85 v. 4 p. 265–353; 89 p. 71–133; 107 p.
63–95; 121 p. 127–179.

LYRICAL POETRY

Ault, Norman, Ed. Elizabethan. Lyrics. Longmans. 1925.

Erskine, John. The Elizabethan Lyric. Col. Univ. Pr. 1903.

Squire, John Collins. Ed. Songs from the Elizabethans.
Dial Pr. 1925.

Chapter XIV

SHAKESPEARE, WILLIAM

Texts: The Oxford Shakespeare: Ed. by W. J. Craig. Oxf. Univ.
Pr. 1905.

Shakespeare's Principal Plays: Ed. with Introd. and Notes
by Tucker Brooke, John William Cunliffe and Henry
Noble MacCracken, Century Co. 1914.

Works: Ed. by W. J. Rolfe. Amer. Book Co. 40 v.

Comments: Studies No. 3; 11 p. 245–395; 12; 13; 33; 85 v. 3 p.
1–94; 96; 112; 116; 121; 129.

Chapter XV

MILTON, JOHN

Texts:　Complete Poems, (Oxf. Stand. Ed.) Oxf. Univ. Pr.
　　　　Minor Poems; Ed. by W. J. Rolfe. Amer. Book Co. 1887.
Comments:　Studies No. 5; 85 v. 4 p. 58–117; 89 p. 135–204; 103 p.
　　　　224–250; 114 v. 2 p. 88–167, 115.

Chapter XVI

DRYDEN, JOHN

Text:　Poetical Works. (Globe Ed.) Macmillan. 1897.
Comments:　Studies No. 74 v. 1 p. 10–71; 85 v. 3 p. 95–191; 137.

POPE, ALEXANDER

Text:　Poetical Works: Ed. by Sir A. W. Ward. (Glove Ed.) Mac-
　　　　millan. 1869.
Comments:　Studies No. 73 p. 93–116; 85 v. 4 p. 1–57; 90 p. 55–80;
　　　　107 p. 135–180.

Chapter XVII

BURNS, ROBERT

Texts:　Complete Poems. (Oxford Stand. Ed.) Oxf. Univ. Pr.
　　　　Selected Poems; with an Introd. by Andrew Lang. Kegan
　　　　Paul. 1896.
Comments:　Studies No. 67 p. 52–85; 72; 102; 117 p. 220–250.

BLAKE, WILLIAM

Text:　Poems. (Oxf. Stand. Ed). Oxf. Univ. Pr.
Comments:　Studies No. 14 p. 1–54; 23; 36; 117 p. 251–288.

Chapter XVIII

WORDSWORTH, WILLIAM

Texts:　Complete Poetical Works. (Camb. Ed.) Houghton. 1904.
　　　　Poems: Chosen and Ed. by Matthew Arnold. (Golden
　　　　Treasury.) Macmillan. 1879.
Comments:　Studies No. 11 p. 99–148; 25 p. 193–260; 35 p. 100–163;
　　　　67 p. 86–121; 70 p. 141–192; 85 v. 4 p. 354–415; 107
　　　　p. 181–219; 144.

COLERIDGE, SAMUEL TAYLOR

Texts:　Complete Poems. (Oxf. Stand. Ed.) Oxf. Univ. Pr. 1912.
　　　　Coleridge. Poetry and Prose with Essays by Hazlitt, Jeffrey,
　　　　De Quincey, Carlyle and Others. Clar. Pr. 1925.
Comments:　Studies No. 39 p. 313–354; 45; 50 p. 57–97; 114 v. 1 p.
　　　　212–230; 120.

Chapter XIX

BYRON, GEORGE GORDON NOEL, LORD

Texts: Complete Poetical Works: with Introductory Memoir by
         Sir Leslie Stephen. (Globe Ed.) Macmillan. 1907.
         Poetry of Byron: Chosen and Arranged by Matthew Arnold.
         Macmillan. 1881.

Comments: Studies No. 67 p. 122–145; 74 v. 1 p. 207–223; 114 v. 2
            p. 3–31.

Chapter XX

SHELLEY, PERCY BYSSHE

Text: Poetical Works; Ed. by Edward Dowden. (Globe Ed.)
        Macmillan. 1890.

Comments: Studies No. 14 p. 115–201; 26; 42; 73 p. 29–52; 105
            p. 15–48; 114 v. 2 p. 32–87; 132; 145 p. 79–116.

Chapter XXI

KEATS, JOHN

Text: Poems: Ed. with Introd. and Notes by E. De Selincourt.
        Dodd. 1905.

Comments: Studies No. 14 p. 202–253; 31; 51; 64; 74 v. 1 p. 224–
            241; 85 v. 1 p. 218–246; 86 p. 41–60.

Chapter XXII

TENNYSON, ALFRED, LORD

Texts: Works, with Notes by the Author. Ed. by Hallam, Lord
         Tennyson. (Globe Ed.) Macmillan. 1913.
         Idylls of the King; Ed. by W. J. Rolfe. Houghton. 1896.
         Selected Poems. Ed. by Marjorie H. Nicolson. Houghton.
         1924.

Comments: Studies No. 1a; 35 p. 178–274; 74 v. 1 p. 258–276; 90 p.
            229–251; 107 p. 223–269; 138.

Chapter XXIII

BROWNING, ELIZABETH BARRETT

Text: Complete Poetical Works. (Camb. Ed.) Houghton. 1900.

Comments: Studies No. 7 p. 205–227; 18 p. 64–104.

BROWNING, ROBERT

Texts: Complete Poetical Works. New Ed. Macmillan. 1914.
         Poems: His Own Selection with Additions from His Latest

Works. Ed. by Charlotte Porter and Helen A. Clark. Crowell. 1896.

Robert Browning Humanist; a Selection from Browning's Poetry, with Introd. and Bibliographical Note by Arthur Compton Rickett. Dial Pr. 1925.

Comments: Studies No. 22; 35 p. 275-332; 74 v. 1 p. 277-293; 107 p. 271-310; 109.

Chapter XXIV

POE, EDGAR ALLAN

Text: Poems, Ed. by E. C. Stedman and G. E. Woodberry. Scribner. 1895.

Comments: Studies No. 28; 78.

Chapter XXV

WHITMAN, WALT

Texts: Leaves of Grass; Abridged Edition with an Introd. by Emory Holloway. Doubleday. 1926.

The Rolling Earth; Outdoor Scenes and Thoughts. Comp. by Waldo R. Brown with an Introd. by John Burroughs. Houghton. 1912.

Comments: Studies No. 6; 15 p. 185-235.

Chapter XXVI

ARNOLD, MATTHEW

Texts: Poetical Works. Macmillan. 1898.

Selections: Ed. by R. E. C. Houghton. Methuen. 1924.

Comments: Studies No. 67 p. 177-200; 73 p. 139-160; 114 v. 1 p. 231-245; 126; 131 p. 123-183; 143 p. 71-160.

ROSSETTI, DANTE GABRIEL

Text: Poems and Translations, 1850-1870. (Oxf. Stand. Ed.) Oxf. Univ. Pr. 1913.

Comments: Studies No. 19; 131 p. 60-109; 140 p. 69-119.

ROSSETTI, CHRISTINA GEORGINA

Text: Poetical Works. Macmillan. 1904.

Comments: Studies No. 7 p. 268-291; 19 p. 228-275; 56 p. 135-162; 140 p. 177-191.

MORRIS, WILLIAM

Texts: The Earthly Paradise. New Ed. Longmans.

The Story of Sigurd the Volsung and the Fall of the Niblungs. Longmans. 1904.

Comments: Studies No. 27; 90 p. 173–197; 92; 140 p. 240–276; 145 p. 64–78.

SWINBURNE, ALGERNON CHARLES
Text: Selections from Swinburne: Ed. by W. O. Raymond. Harcourt. 1925.
Comments: Studies No. 56 p. 1–58; 90 p. 201–225; 104; 114 v. 1 p. 246–273.

Chapter XXVII

KIPLING, RUDYARD
Text: Rudyard Kipling's Verse, 1885–1918. Doubleday, 1919.
Comments: Studies No. 76 p. 53–93.

MASEFIELD, JOHN
Text: Poems. Macmillan. 1925.
Comments: Studies No. 76 p. 13–50; 108 p. 71–97; 130 p. 197–216.

DICKINSON, EMILY
Text: Complete Poems: with an Introd. by M. D. Bianchi. Little. 1924.
Comment: Studies No. 8.

ROBINSON, EDWIN ARLINGTON
Texts: Collected Poems. Macmillan. 1924.
Tristram. Macmillan. 1927.
Comments: Studies No. 10 p. 16–32; 40 p. 248–262; 71 p. 13–37; 84 p. 3–75; 97; 118; 136; p. 111–136.

FROST, ROBERT
Texts: New Hampshire. Holt. 1923.
Selected Poems. Holt. 1923.
Comments: Studies No. 10 p. 33–49; 71 p. 37–52; 84 p. 79–136; 136 p. 15–40.

MASTERS, EDGAR LEE
Texts: Selected Poems, Macmillan. 1925.
Spoon River Anthology. Macmillan. 1915.
Comments: Studies No. 71 p. 69–84; 84 p. 139–232; 136 p. 161–182.

LINDSAY, VACHEL
Text: Collected Poems. Rev. Ed. Macmillan. 1925.
Comments: Studies No. 71 p. 85–96; 108 p. 213–244; 136 p. 65–94.

SANDBURG, CARL
Text: Selected Poems. Ed. by Rebecca West. Harcourt. 1926.
Comments: Studies No. 71 p. 53–68; 84 p. 139–232; 134 p. 67–87; Introd. to his "Selected Poems," above.

INDEX

A

ACCENT, in poetry, 38.
ACHILLES, 23–25, 100, 414.
ADDISON, JOHN, 211, 212.
Adonais, 276, 281, 317.
AENEAS, 69, 70, 71, 72, 74.
AENEID, 69–72; 74, 87, 148, 285; Morris's Translation, 379.
AESCHYLUS, 42–46; 53, 54, 186, 189, 306, 361; early life of, 42, 43; contributions to tragedy, 44, 45; translation from, 45.
AGAMEMNON, 23, 24.
AIKEN, CONRAD, 412, 413.
Alastor, 271, 272, 273, 317.
ALEXANDER THE GREAT, 36, 55.
ALEXANDRIA, 36.
ALEXANDRIAN SCHOOL, 36.
ALLAN, JOHN, 335, 336, 337.
ALLAN, MRS. JOHN, 335.
ALLITERATION, 81, 82, 382.
AMEN, HYMN TO, 20.
Amoretti, Spenser's, 156.
ANACREON, 35.
Ancient Mariner, see Rime of the Ancient Mariner.
Andrea del Sarto, 328, 329.
Annabel Lee, 347.
Antigone, 47, 48, 49, 52, 54.
Antony and Cleopatra, 183, 190.
ANTONY, MARK, 56, 66.
ARCHILOCHUS, 32.
ARDEN, MARY, 167.
ARIOSTO, 154, 187.
ARISTOPHANES, 51.
ARISTOTLE, 99.
ARMADA, SPANISH, *see* SPANISH ARMADA.
Armada, The, 385.
ARMOUR, JEAN, 219, 223.
ARNOLD, MATTHEW, 366–371; 372, 379, 387; dissatisfaction with modern life, 366; takes Greek poetry as model, 368;

Professor of Poetry, 369; character of A.'s poetry, 370.
ARTHUR, KING, 86, 87, 199, 308, 313.
As I Pondered in Silence, 359.
Asolando, 330.
As You Like It, 183.
ATALANTA IN CALYDON, 381, 382, 383, 384, 386.
ATHENIAN POETS, *see* AESCHYLUS, EURIPIDES, POETRY, SIMONIDES, SOPHOCLES.
AUGUSTUS, EMPEROR, *see* CAESAR, OCTAVIUS.

B

BACH, J. S., 419.
Balin and Balan, 313.
BALLADS, 139–146; 228; description of form, 140; possible origins, 140, 141; form, 141; types of, 142, 143; literary quality, 143, 145; influence of, 146.
Barrack-Room Ballads, 391, 405.
BAUDELAIRE, CHARLES P., 346.
BEATRICE (Portinari), 89, 90, 91, 92, 93, 94, 96, 103, 104.
BEAUMONT, FRANCIS, 183, 188.
Bells and Pomegranates, 319, 325.
BIBLE, the, 27, 46, 169, 199; (Latin) 148.
BLAKE, WILLIAM, 227–232, 243, 250, 258; first poems, 227–229; early life, 228–229; marriage, 229; visions, 228, 229, 231, 232; later poems, 229, 230, 231; influence, 231–232.
Blessed Damozel, The, 373, 374.
BLONDEL, 84.
BOCCACCIO, 130, 131, 148.
Beowulf, 80, 81, 82, 140; translated from, 81; alliterative verse of, 81, 82; influence, 82.
Book of the Duchess, The, 128, 129.
Book of Thel, The, 231.
Boots, 394.
Borderers, The, 240, 241.

Bothie of Tober-na-Vuloich, The, 28.
BRAWNE, FANNY, 292, 298, 300.
Bride's Prelude, The, 374.
BROOKE, RUPERT, 399.
BROWN, CHARLES, 292, 297.
BROWNING, ELIZABETH BARRETT, 312, 316, 317, 321, 322, 323, 324, 343, 344.
BROWNING, ROBERT, 189, 316–332, 392; early life, 317–318; first published poems, 317–318; drama, 318; *Bells and Pomegranates*, 319; originality and power, 320, 321; marriage to Elizabeth Barrett, 321; life in Italy, 323–324; *Men and Women* shows B's genius, 324–326; later poems, 326–329; quality and influence of verse, 328–329, 331; death, 330.
BROWNING, ROBERT WIEDEMANN, 323.
BRUTUS, 56.
BRYANT, WILLIAM CULLEN, 334, 405.
BURBAGE, RICHARD, 178.
BURNS, ROBERT, 217–227, 243, 250, 258, 301; early life, 217–219; first poems, 218, 219; reception in Edinburgh, 219–222; description of Burns, 221; sickness and death, 222, 223; quality and influence of poems, 224–227.
BYRON, LADY (Anna Isabella Milbanke), 260.
BYRON, GEORGE GORDON, LORD, 64, 226, 255–264, 273, 274, 276, 282, 289, 301, 303, 304, 309, 338, 366; early life, 256–257; description of, 257, 258; literary success, 257–260; marriage, 259–260; life abroad, 261; later poetry, 261–263; quality, 263; Greek expedition and death, 263–264.

C

CAESAR, JULIUS, 56, 65, 66, 69, 70, 99.
CAESAR, OCTAVIUS (AUGUSTUS), 56, 57, 69, 70.
CALLISTRATUS, 35.
CAMPBELL, THOMAS, 258.
Canterbury Tales, The, 132, 133, 134, 135; quoted from, 134, 135, 149, 182, 206, 377.
CANZONE, 90.
Captain Craig, 405.

Cargoes, 399.
CASHMERE SHAWL CHANT, 11.
Cato, 212.
CATULLUS, 75.
CAVALCANTI, GUIDO, 91, 94.
Cavalier Tunes, 320.
CAXTON, WILLIAM, 148.
Cenci, The, 276.
CHAPMAN, GEORGE, 160, 287.
Charge of the Light Brigade, The, 312.
CHARLEMAGNE, 85, 86.
CHATTERTON, THOMAS, 227, 243, 250.
CHAUCER, GEOFFREY, 74, 127–136, 140, 147, 148, 149, 150, 152, 157, 179, 182, 188, 205, 250, 286, 301, 328, 365, 375, 377, 379; early life and poetry, 127–130; influence of Italy on, 130, offices and work, 131; *Canterbury Tales*—content and influence, 132–135; death, 136.
CHESTERTON, G. K., 399.
Chicago Poems, 409.
CHILD, FRANCIS, J., 146.
Childe Harold's Pilgrimage, 257, 258, 261, 305.
Children of Adam, 355.
Children of the Night, The, 405.
Christabel, 249.
Christmas Eve and Easter-Day, 324.
CICERO, 110, 112, 130, 169.
City in the Sea, The, 339.
Claribel, 305.
CLARKE, CHARLES COWDEN, 285, 286, 287, 288.
CLEMM, MRS., 340, 342.
CLEOPATRA, 100.
CLOUGH, ARTHUR HUGH, 28.
COLERIDGE, SAMUEL TAYLOR, 241, 242, 243, 244, 245, 249, 256, 258, 271, 291, 303, 344.
Colin Cloute's Come Home Again, 155.
Coliseum, The, 340.
COLONNA, CARDINAL, 109, 117.
Comedy of Errors, 167, 177.
Complaint of Chaucer to His Empty Purse, 136.
Comus, 195, 203.
Confessions, Rousseau's, 216.
Congo, The, 409.
CONNINGTON, JOHN, 35.
CONSTABLE, HENRY, 163.

Cotter's Saturday Night, The, 224.
Courtship of Miles Standish, The, 334.
COWPER, WILLIAM, 227, 243.
CRABBE, GEORGE, 408.
Crossing Brooklyn Ferry, 355.
CUMMINGS, E. E., 411.
Cup, The, 312.

D

DANTE (Dante Aligheri), 74, 89–105,
117, 122, 130, 193, 202, 306, 361;
early life, 89–92; *Vita Nuova*, 91–94;
military and political life, 94–96;
Divine Comedy, 96–98; exile and death,
96–98; outline of *Divine Comedy*,
98–104; significance of, 104–105.
DARK LADY OF SONNETS, THE, 175, 176.
Dauber, 401.
DAVISON, WALTER, 161.
*Death and Dying Words of Poor Mailie,
The*, 224.
DEBUSSY, C. A., 419.
Defence of Guenevere, 375, 376.
DEKKER, THOMAS, 160, 161.
DE LA MARE, WALTER, 399.
DENNIS, JOHN, 212.
Descriptive Sketches, 236, 241.
DEVEREAUX, PENELOPE, LADY, 174.
DICKINSON, EMILY, 402–405, 411, 412;
secluded life, 402, 403; character
of poetry, 403–405.
Dictionary of Merchandise, 285.
DIDO, 70, 71, 72.
DIONYSUS, 41.
DITHYRAMB, 42.
Divine Comedy, 96, 97, 98; outline of,
98–104; significance, 104–105.
Doctor Faustus, 166.
Don Juan, 261, 262.
DONNE, JOHN, 160, 162.
Dover Beach, 370.
DOWSON, E., 399.
DRAMATIC POETRY, 38, *see also* POETRY,
and Chaps. VI, XIV.
DRAYTON, MICHAEL, 163, 187.
DRINKWATER, JOHN, 399.
Drum-Taps, 357.
DRYDEN, JOHN, 206, 207, 214.
Dunciad, The, 212, 213.
Dynasts, The, 398.

E

Earthly Paradise, The, 377, 378, 379.
Eclogues, Virgil's, 67, 68.
Edinburgh Review, The, 243, 255, 256.
Edward II, 167, 178.
ELAINE, 313.
ELEGY, 39. *See also Adonais, Lycidas,
When Lilacs Last in the Door-Yard
Bloomed.*
Elegy Written in a Country Churchyard,
214, 215, 216, 221, 224.
ELIOT, T. S., 413.
ELIZABETH, QUEEN, 151, 152, 155, 156,
159, 173, 186, 333.
ELIZABETHAN THEATRE, descriptions of,
164, 165, 171.
EMERSON, RALPH WALDO, 334, 351.
Empedocles on Etna, 367.
ELEUSINIAN MYSTERIES, 42.
ELIZABETHAN POETRY, 147–189; char-
acteristics of period, 147, 148, 151, 170,
171; Spenser, 148–159; the lyric poets,
159–163; Shakespeare and other drama-
tists, 164–189.
Endymion, 289, 290, 291.
English Bards and Scotch Reviewers, 256,
257.
English Flag, The, 392.
Enoch Arden, 312.
EPIC, description of, 28; *see also* chapters
IV, VII (Virgil), VIII (*Beowulf*), IX,
XV, XXII (Idylls of the King), and
Aeneid, Divine Comedy, Idylls of the
King, Iliad, Odyssey, Paradise Lost,
and Paradise Regained.
Epipsychidion, 277.
EPITAPH, 34, 39, 162, 193; definition, 34;
Epitaph for a Hound, 34; for the Spar-
tans at Thermopylae, 34.
Epitaph on Elizabeth, L. H., 162.
*Epitaph on the Marchioness of Win-
chester*, 193.
Epithalamion, 156.
Erce, Hymn to, 6.
Erectheus, 53.
Essay on Criticism, An, 208, 209, 210,
212.
Essay on Man, 213, 214.
Eureka, 344.

EURIPIDES, 49–53, 54, 165, 189, 193, 383; early life, 49; character of his work, 50–53; influence, 53, 54.

Evangeline, 28, 334, 351.

Eve of St. Agnes, 292, 372.

Eve of St. Mark, The, 295, 296.

Evening Mirror, the N. Y., 343.

Evening Walk, An, 236.

Everlasting Mercy, The, 331, 400, 401, 419.

Excursion, The, 248.

Explorer, The, 393.

F

Faery Queen, The, 153–156, 158, 159, 182, 285.

FARINATA DEGLI UBERTI, 101, 102.

FATE (in Greek tragedy), 49.

Faust, Goethe's, 274.

Filostrato, Boccaccio's, 131.

FLECKER, JAMES ELROY, 39, 395.

FLETCHER, J. G., 411.

Flower-Fed Buffaloes, The, 409.

FOLIO EDITION OF SHAKESPEARE'S PLAYS, 188.

Forsaken Merman, The, 367.

FORSTER, JOHN, 318.

F. P. A. (Franklin P. Adams), 59, 209.

FRANCESCA DA RIMINI, 100, 102.

FRANCIS, SAINT, OF ASSISI, 90.

FREE VERSE, 352, 359, 396, 409, 410, 411.

FRENCH REVOLUTION, 225, 233, 237, 248, 261.

Frogs, The, 51, 52.

FROISSART, SIR JOHN, 169, 375.

FROST, ROBERT, 406, 407, 408.

FULLER, MARGARET, 323.

FUTURE OF POETRY, 414–421.

G

GALAHAD, 313.

GARETH, 313.

Garden of Proserpine, The, 384.

GAWAIN, 86, 313.

General Booth Enters Heaven, 409.

Georgics, Virgil's, 69.

Ghost of Abel, The, 231.

GLOBE THEATRE, 183, 187.

GODWIN, WILLIAM, 231, 239, 242, 267, 268, 270, 301.

GOETHE, J. W., VON, 261, 274, 306

GOLDSMITH, OLIVER, 227.

Graham's Magazine, 342.

Grave, The, 229.

GRAY, THOMAS, 214, 215.

GREECE, POETRY OF, 19–54, 55, 79.

GREEK POETRY, 19–54, 56, 67, 68.

GREEKS, HOMERIC, 22–31; life of, 22, 29, 30.

GREEN, ROBERT, 160.

GUICCIOLI, COUNTESS, 263.

Guilt and Sorrow, 240, 241.

GUINEVERE, QUEEN, 87, 313.

GUINICELLI, GUIDO, 90.

H

HALLAM, ARTHUR, 304, 305, 306, 307.

Hamlet, 183, 184, 185, 198.

HARDY, THOMAS, 397, 398, 399.

Hark! Hark! The Lark, 161.

Harmodious and Aristogeiton, 35.

HAWTHORNE, N., 323, 343.

Haystack in the Floods, The, 380.

Heat, 410.

HECTOR, 23, 24, 25, 99.

"H. D." (Hilda Doolittle), 410, 411.

HELEN OF TROY, 22, 25, 28, 100, 166, 414.

HELOÏSE AND ABELARD, GEORGE MOORE'S, 71, 72.

HENLEY, WILLIAM ERNEST, 396, 397, 399.

Henry IV, I and II, 178.

Henry V, 178.

Henry VI, I, II, and III, 171, 172, 177, 179.

Henry VIII, 187.

HEROIC COUPLET, THE, 206, 208, 209, 210, 215, 258.

HERVÉ RIEL, 326.

HESIOD, 31, 32.

HEXAMETER, 27, 28, 32, 38.

HEYWOOD, THOMAS, 160.

Hiawatha, 334.

Hilderbrand, Lay of, 82.

Hippolytus, 52.

Home Thoughts, from Abroad, 320.

HOMER, BLIND, 19–29, 32, 55, 99, 130, 147, 193, 211, 212, 287, 366, 414; outline of poems, 22–27; nature of poetry, 27, 28; influence, 29; selections from, 22, 23, 24, 25, 26.

HORACE (Quintus Horatius Flaccus).

56–64, 65, 67, 75, 99, 147, 148, 193, 395; early life, 56, 57; first poetry, 57, 58; character and art, 60–64; influence of, 64.

HOSMER, HARRIET, 323.

Hospital Verses, 396.

HOUGHTON, LORD, *see* MILNES, MONCKTON.

Hound of Heaven, The, 395.

Hounds of Hell, The, 401, 402.

Hours of Idleness, 255.

House of Fame, The, 131.

House of Life, 374, 388.

HOUSMAN, A. E., 395, 396.

HOW POETRY BECAME BEAUTIFUL, 9–12.

HUGO, VICTOR, 312.

HUNT, LEIGH, 281, 288, 289.

HUTCHINSON, MARY, 246.

HYMN OF JEWS IN BABYLON, 11.

Hymn to Aphrodite, 33.

Hymn to Apollo, 287.

Hymn to Proserpine, 384.

Hyperion, 295.

I

IAMBIC VERSE, 32, 38.

IBSEN, 54.

Idylls of the King, 313, 315.

IDYLS, 36, 37, 38, 149, 150.

Iliad, The, 21–25, 27, 28, 29, 87, 160, 211.

Il Penseroso, 195.

Imitation of Spenser, 285.

In Memoriam, 310.

Inquiry Concerning Political Justice, An, 239.

Invictus, 396.

Israfel, 339.

J

JAMES I, KING, 186.

JEFFERS, ROBINSON, 411.

Jerusalem, 231.

Jew of Malta, The, 167, 182.

JONSON, BEN, 64, 156, 160, 162, 163, 177, 186, 187, 188, 189, 193.

JOHNSON, SAMUEL, 227.

Julius Cæsar, 178, 182, 184.

K

KEATS, FANNY, 284, 291, 292, 293.

KEATS, GEORGE, 284, 291, 295.

KEATS, JOHN, 157, 202, 226, 261, 263, 276, 283–302; 303, 304, 305, 306, 317, 319, 325, 329, 332, 346, 367, 372, 373, 375, 379, 388, 392, 395, 399, 414; early life, 283–287; early poetry, 287–291; love for Fanny Brawne, 292; best poetry, 292–299; contribution to poetry, 295–297, 300, 301, 302; sickness and death, 300.

KEATS, TOM, 284, 291, 298.

KENNEDY, JOHN P., 341.

Kinmount Willie, 145.

KIPLING, JOHN, 390.

KIPLING, RUDYARD, 390–395, 396, 400, 405; boyhood and early published poems, 390, 391; quality of verse, 392–393; wins Nobel Prize, 394; significance, 394.

Kubla Khan, 249.

KYD, THOMAS, 171, 172.

L

LADY GERALDINE'S COURTSHIP, 344.

Lady of Shalott, The, 305, 314, 372.

Lady of the Land, The, 377.

L'Allegro, 195.

LANDOR, WALTER SAVAGE, 130.

LANIER, SIDNEY, 402.

Last Poems, 395.

LAUNCELOT, 86, 87, 88, 305.

LAURA, 106–108, 113–116, 117–123.

Lear, King, 183.

Leaves of Grass, 352, 353, 354, 355, 358.

LEDWIDGE, FRANCIS, 399.

Legend of Good Women, The, 131, 132.

LEONARD, WILLIAM ELLERY, 411.

LESBOS, 32.

Life and Death of Jason, 377.

LINCOLN, ABRAHAM, 358, 409.

LINDSAY, NICHOLAS VACHEL, 408, 409.

Lines Composed Above Tintern Abbey, 245, 271.

Litany of Nations, The, 385.

Locksley Hall, 308.

LODGE, THOMAS, 160.

LONDON, 57.

LONGFELLOW, HENRY WADSWORTH, 28, 334, 351, 402, 405.

LORD CHAMBERLAIN'S COMPANY, THE, 176.

LORD HOUGHTON, *see* MILNES MONCKTON.
Lord Randal, 144.
Lost Leader, The, 320.
Lotus Eaters, The, 308.
Love in a Valley, 397.
Love Thou Thy Land, 314.
Lovers of Gudrun, The, 378.
Love's Labour's Lost, 167, 172, 173, 177, 179.
LOWELL, AMY, 410.
LOWELL, JAMES RUSSELL, 334, 405.
LUCAN, 99.
LUCRETIUS, 75.
LUDGATE, JOHN, 139, 147, 149.
Lycidas, 195, 287.
LYDIA, IN HORACE'S POETRY, 59.
LYLY, JOHN, 172.
LYRIC, 33, 38, *see also* POETRY.
Lyrical Ballads, 242, 243, 244, 245, 246, 247.

M

MACAULAY, THOMAS BABBINGTON, 392.
Macbeth, 183, 184, 185, 198.
MACREADY, WM. C., 318.
MAECENAS, 57, 58, 59, 60, 61, 63, 67, 68.
MALORY, SIR THOMAS, 313, 375.
Man Against the Sky, The, 406.
MANTUA, 65
Margaritae Sorori, 396.
MARIE DE FRANCE, 83.
MARLOWE, CHRISTOPHER, 160, 163, 165, 166, 167, 171, 172, 178, 179, 182, 294, 301.
Marriage of Heaven and Hell, The, 231.
Marshes of Glynn, The, 402.
MARY, QUEEN OF SCOTS, 386, 387.
MASEFIELD, JOHN, 331, 399–402.
Mask of Anarchy, The, 278.
MASTERS, EDGAR LEE, 331, 408, 410.
Maud, 312, 324.
MAZZINI, G., 385.
Medea, 50 (with translated passage), 51.
MEDIAEVAL POETRY, INFLUENCE OF, 187.
Men and Women, 324, 325.
Merchant of Venice, The, 182.
MEREDITH, GEORGE, 397, 398.
MERLIN, 86, 406.
Merlin, 406.
Merope, 369.
Merry Wives of Windsor, The, 169.

METER, 14, 15, 27, 28, 32, 33, 38, 59, 68, 81, 82, 133, 166 (blank verse), 199, 382; anapest, 38; dactyl, 38; hexameter, 27, 28; iambic, 32, 38; tetrameter, 32, 38; trimeter, 32, 38; trochaic, 38.
Michael, 244.
Midsummer Night's Dream, A, 179, 180, 181, 183.
MILLAY, EDNA ST. VINCENT, 411, 412.
MILNES, MONCKTON (Lord Houghton), 304, 381.
MILTON, JOHN, 64, 75, 123, 140, 157, 190–204, 205, 226, 247, 250, 261, 287, 313, 325, 332, 333, 361; early life, 190–191; early poems, 192–195; travel abroad, 195, 196; services to Commonwealth, 197, 198, retirement and later poetry, 198–203; quality, 202; Milton's influence, 202–204; death, 204.
MILTON, MARY POWELL, 197.
Minstrelsy of the Scottish Border, 146.
Modern Love, 398.
MODRED, 313.
MOLIÈRE, 186.
MOODY, WILLIAM VAUGHAN, 407.
MOORE, GEORGE, 71, 72.
MOORE, THOMAS, 258.
Moral Epistles, Pope's, 213.
MORRIS, WILLIAM, 371, 372, 373, 374, 375–379, 387, 395; love of mediæval art, 372–373; first published poems, 375; work in crafts, 376, 377; long narrative poems, 377–379; quality of his work, 379.
Morte d'Arthur (Mallory's), 313, 375.
Morte d'Arthur (Tennyson's), 308, 310, 311, 320.
Mother Hubbard's Tale, 155.
MS. Found in a Bottle, 340.
MULÉYKEH, 327.
MURRAY, GILBERT, 51.
Musical Instrument, A, 322.
My Last Duchess, 319, 328.

N

NARRATIVE POETRY, 13, 22–29, *see also* poetry, Epic.
NASH, THOMAS, 160.
Nibelungenlied, The, 86; translation from, 86.

NOBEL PRIZE (for Literature), 394, 395.
NORTH, CHRISTOPHER, 307.
Nothing Gold Can Stay, 408.
NOYES, ALFRED, 399.
Nuova rima, Dante's, 93.

O

OCCLEVE, THOMAS, 139, 147.
O Captain, My Captain, 358.
ODE, 39.
Ode on a Grecian Urn, 296.
Ode on Intimations of Immortality, 247.
Ode on the Death of the Duke of Wellington, 312.
Ode to a Nightingale, 297.
Ode to the West Wind, 279.
ODYSSEUS, 26, 27, 28.
Odyssey, The, 21, 26, 27, 28, 29, 87, 211.
Oedipus the King, 54.
Oedipus Tyrannus, 277.
OLIVER, 85, 87.
ONOMATOPOEIA, 38.
On Receiving a Curious Shell, 287.
On the Morning of Christ's Nativity, 92.
On the Necessity of Atheism, 267.
ORLANDI, GUIDO, 91; sonnet by, 92.
Orlando Furioso, Ariosto's, 154.
ORNSTEIN, L., 419.
Othello, 183.
Out of the Cradle Endlessly Rocking, 358, 360, 419.
OVID, 75, 99, 193.

P

PAMELA, 216.
Paradise Lost, 199–203, 206, 333.
Paradise Regained, 201.
PARIS (Son of Priam), 22, 87.
Parish Register, The, 408.
PASTORAL POETRY, 36, 67, 68, 149, 150, 151; *see also* IDYLS.
PATMORE, COVENTRY, 312.
Paracelsus, 318.
Parliament of Birds, The, 131.
Passage to India, 358.
Pauline, 317, 318.
Pearl, The, 133.
PEELE, GEORGE, 171.
PEGASUS, IN ENGLAND, 127–136.
PEGASUS, IN GREECE, 30–40.

PENTAMETER, 38 (text and note).
PERCIVAL, 86.
PERCY, BISHOP, 146, 217, 229.
PERICLES, 47.
Persians, The, 45 (with translated passage), 46.
PETRARCH, FRANCESCO, 64, 106–123, 130, 148, 149, 157, 193, 287; sees Laura, 106; early life of, 108–110; travels and studies, 110–113; love for Laura, 114, 117, 118–123; sonnets of (translated), 107, 116, 118, 120, 121, 122; death of, 122; influence of, 122, 123.
PETRARCHAN SONNET, *see* SONNET.
PHYLLIS, in Horace's poetry, 59.
Piers Plowman, Langland's, 133.
PINDAR, 35, 36, 383.
PLATO, 56, 99.
Plutarch, 53, 111.
PLUTARCH'S *Lives*, 177.
POE, EDGAR ALLAN, 335–347, 351, 373, 419; adoption by Allans, 335; childhood, 335–337; university and army life, 337; early published verse, 338; marriage, 340, 342; journalistic work, 340–342; success, 343; death, 344; character and value of work, 344–347.
Poems and Ballads, 384, 385, 386.
Poetical Sketches, 227, 228, 229.
POETRY, accent in, 38; American, Chaps. XXIV, XXV, XXVII, XXVIII; Arab, 83; Athenian, see Chaps V and VI; Ballads, *see* pages on beginnings of poetry, 2–8, also Chap. XII; Chinese, 20, 21; Choric, 38; common sense, 205–214; dramatic, 38; decline of functions, 415; and fighting, 3, 4; first known, 19; free verse, *see* free verse; future of, 414–421; Egyptian, 21; Elizabethan, see Elizabethan; German, 82, 86; Greek, 19–54; Greek and English, 38 (note); of Heroes and Dragons, 79–88; heroic couplet, *see* heroic couplet, How Poetry Became Beautiful, 9–12; idyllic, 36, 37, 38; Italian (Dante and Petrarch), Chaps. IX, X; lyric, 33, 38; mediæval, 79–88; meter, 14, 38, *see also*, meter; narrative, 13, 22–29; pastoral, 36, 37, 67, 68; Provençal, 82; Roman, 55–75, 83; Romantic, see

Chaps. XVII, XVIII, XIX, XX, XXI;
Satire, 32, 57–64; Scandinavian, 82;
sonnet, see sonnet; stress and vowel
quantity, 38; terminology, 38; *terza
rime*, 97; to-day, 414–420; troubadours,
82, 83; used for entertainment, 13, 14;
usefulness of, 1–16, 417–420; When
Poetry Was Necessary, 1–8; and work,
5.

POETRY OF HEROES AND DRAGONS, 79–88.

POETS, *see* POETRY.

POETS OF NATURE, 214–251; *see also*
Blake, Burns, Chatterton, Coleridge,
Wordsworth.

POETS, the First, 13–16.

POPE, ALEXANDER, 64, 207–214, 215,
242, 289, 325; early life, 207–208;
success, 208; nature of poetry, 208–210;
makes poetry pay, 211; later satires
and other verse, 212–214; influence,
214; death, 214.

Portrait of One Dead, 412.

POUND, EZRA, 410.

"PRE-RAPHAELITES," 372, 380; *see also*
371, 388.

PRIAM, KING, 23, 24, 25.

Princess, The, 311.

PROMETHEUS, of Aeschylus, 44.

Prometheus Unbound, 275.

PROTHALAMION, 156.

Proud Music of the Storm, 358.

Prelude, The, 234, 248.

Prisoner of Chillon, The, 261, 262.

PUCCINI, G., 54.

Q

Quarterly Review, 289.

Queen Mab, 269, 271, 273.

Queen Mother and Rosamund, 381.

RABBI BEN EZRA, 326, 328.

RACINE, J., 53, 54.

RAIN CHANT, 10.

RALEIGH, SIR WALTER, 155, 160, 333.

RAMESES II, poetry about, 20.

Rape of Lucrece, The, 174.

Rape of the Lock, The, 210, 211.

Raven, The, 343, 344, 351.

RED HOUSE, THE, of William Morris,
376.

Reliques of English Poetry, Percy's, 146,
217.

RENAISSANCE, THE, 92, 93, 130, 147, 148.

Renascence, 411.

Requiescat, 371.

Revolt of Islam, The, 273, 275.

RHYME, 15, 28, 59, 68, 82, 83, 117 (Petrarchan sonnet), 128, 140 (ballad),
154 (Spenserian stanza), 163 (Elizabethan sonnet), 206 (heroic couplet),
310, 382.

RHYME ROYAL, THE, 133.

RHYTHM, 3–5, and meter, 14.

RICHARD I, the Lion-hearted, 83, 84.

Richard II, 178.

Richard III, 178, 184.

RICHARDSON, SAMUEL, 216.

Rime of the Ancient Mariner, The, 244,
245, 301.

Ring and the Book, The, 322, 326, 330.

ROBINSON, E. A., 405, 406, 407.

ROLAND, 85, 86, 87, 88.

ROMANCE OF THE ROSE, 128.

ROMANS, THE: HORACE AND VIRGIL, 55–
75.

ROME, 55, 56, 57, 60, 61, 62, 63, 66, 67,
68, 69, 70, 72, 73, 79.

Romeo and Juliet, 179, 180, 184.

ROSSETTI, DANTE GABRIEL, 314, 324,
355, 371–375, 379, 380, 381, 387; his
painting, 372; love of mediæval art,
372–373; quality of verse, 373–374.

ROUND TABLE, THE, 86, 375.

ROUSSEAU, JEAN JACQUES, 216, 225, 243,
246, 250, 267, 301.

RUSKIN, JOHN, 312, 381.

S

Sacrifice, The, 21.

SADE, HUGH DE, 108, 113, 114, 115.

SADE, LAURA de (see *Laura*).

SALAMIS, battle of, 45, 46; Euripides'
study on, 52.

Salt-water Ballads, 400.

Samson Agonistes, 204.

SANDBURG, CARL, 409.

SAPPHIC STANZA, THE, 33.

SAPPHO, 32, 33, 34, 55, 322, 395, 402, 414.

SATIRE, 32, 57–64, 213, *and in general*
Chapter XVI; Byron's, 256.

Satires, Pope's, 213.
Saturday Review, The, 384.
Saturday Visitor, The, 340.
Saul, 321, 329.
Scholar-Gypsy, 368.
SCOTT, WALTER, 146, 248, 256, 258.
SENECA, 75, 165.
Shah Nameh, 368.
SHAKESPEARE, JOHN, 167, 169.
Shakespeare (sonnet), 369.
SHAKESPEARE, WILLIAM, 53, 54, 64, 75, 157, 160, 161, 162, 163, 164–189, 190, 193, 198, 205, 212, 214, 250, 251, 261, 263, 277, 287, 294, 301, 306, 315, 325, 328, 332, 346, 361, 365, 368, 375, 414, 419; early life, 167–170; appearance, 169, 188; first years in London, 170–172; poems, 173–176; comedies and early tragedies, 170–172, 177–182; success, 182, 183, 186, 187; great tragedies, 183–185; literary supremacy, 186, 188, 189; death, 187.
SHAW, BERNARD, 186.
SHELLEY, HARRIET (Westbrook), 268, 269, 270.
SHELLEY, MARY (Godwin), 270, 271, 281.
SHELLEY, PERCY BYSSHE, 202, 226, 260, 265–282, 289, 301, 303, 304, 306, 317, 319, 325, 329, 338, 366, 386; boyhood, 265–267; expulsion from Oxford, 267; first marriage, 268; poetry of revolt, 269; Mary Godwin, 270; poems, 271–276; character of poetry, 277–281; death, 281–282.
SHELLEY, SIR TIMOTHY, 266, 267.
Shepherd's Calender, The, 148, 149, 150, 151, 155, 160.
Shropshire Lad, The, 395.
SIDNEY, SIR PHILIP, 152, 160, 163, 174.
SIEGFRIED, 86, 87.
Sigurd the Volsung, 379.
SIMONIDES OF CEOS, 34, 56.
Sir Gawain and the Green Knight, 133.
Sir Patrick Spens, 143.
Sister Helen, 374.
SKELTON, JOHN, 149.
Sleep and Poetry, 288.
SOCRATES, 56, 99.
Sohrab and Rustum, 368.
Solitary Reaper, The, 247.

Song in the Time of Revolution, A, 385.
Song of Roland, The, 84, 86; translation, 85; influence of, 86.
Song of the Answerer, The, 355.
Song of the Chattahoochee, 402.
Song of the Dead, The, 394.
Song of the Open Road, The, 355.
Songs Before Sunrise, 385.
Songs of Experience, 230.
Songs of Innocence, 229, 230.
Songs of Two Nations, 385.
SONNET, DANTE'S, 90, 92; early Italian, 90, 91, 92; Petrarch's quoted, 107, 116, 118, 120, 121, 122; form of P.'s, 117; literary influence of P.'s, 122, 123; Arnold's, 369; Elizabethan, 162, 163, 174, 175, 176; Keats's, 287, 288, 302 (sonnet to Keats); Milton's, 198; Wordsworth's, 238, 247; Mrs. Browning's, 316, 322; Rossetti's, 374, 375.
Sonnets from the Portuguese, 316, 322.
Sons of Martha, The, 394.
SOPHOCLES, 46, 49, 55, 147, 184, 189, 366, 414; early life, 46; character of work, 46–49; influence, 53, 54.
Sordello, 318, 319.
SOUTHAMPTON, HENRY WRIOTHESLEY, Earl of, 173, 174, 176.
Southern Literary Messenger, The, 341.
SOUTHEY, ROBERT, 241, 249, 268.
SPANISH ARMADA, 160, 177.
Spanish Tragedy, The, 171.
Specimen of an Induction to a Poem, 286.
Spectator, The, 211.
SPENSER, EDMUND, 148–159, 188, 198, 285, 286, 293, 294, 301; *Shepherd's Calendar*, 149–151; goes to Ireland, 153; *Faery Queen*, 153–156; quality of poetry, 157, 158; influence, 157, 159.
SPENSERIAN STANZA, 154, 157, 258.
Spoon River Anthology, A, 331.
Stanzas Written in Dejection, 274, 275.
State of Innocence and the Fall of Man, 206.
St. Irvyne, 267.
STORY, J., 323.
Strafford, 318, 319.
Strayed Reveller, The, 366, 367.
SURREY, HENRY HOWARD, Earl of, 149.
SWIFT, JONATHAN, 211.
SWINBURNE, ALGERNON CHARLES, 314,

355, 379–388, 386, 392, 395; family
and childhood, 380–381; love of liberty,
380; success of *Atalanta*, 381; poetic
contributions, 382–385; limitations,
386.

T

TAGGARD, GENEVIEVE, 411.
Tales of the Grotesque and Arabesque, 343.
Tamburlaine, 165, 166, 172.
Tamerlane, 338.
Tam o'Shanter, 224.
TEASDALE, SARA, 411.
TENNYSON, ALFRED, LORD, 75, 87, 202,
226, 303–315, 320, 321, 324, 328, 329,
332, 355, 367, 372, 373, 375, 379, 381,
386, 388, 392, 395, 402; early life, 303,
304; description of, 304; Cambridge
friends, 305; first poems, 305–306;
Hallam, 305–307; grief at Hallam's
death, 307; Emily Sellwood, 307;
poems of 1842—T's art, 307–310;
In Memoriam, 310; success, 311, 312;
Poet Laureate, 312; later poems and
dramas, 312–313; *Idylls of the King*,
313; T's poetic contribution, 313–315.
TENNYSON, CHARLES, 304.
TENNYSON, EMILY (Sellwood), 307, 312.
TENNYSON, FREDERICK, 304.
TERRENCE, 75.
TERZA RIMA, 97.
TETRAMETER, 32, 38 (text and note).
THACKERAY, W. M., 312.
Thanatopsis, 334.
THE FIRST POETS, 13–16.
THEOCRITUS, 36, 37, 67.
Theogony, Hesiod's, 32.
THERMOPYLAE, Epitaph for Spartans at,
34.
THESPIS, 42.
THOMPSON, FRANCIS, 277, 395, 399.
THOMSON, JAMES, 215.
Tithonus, 314, 320.
Titus Andronicus, 171.
To an Athlete Dying Young, 396.
To Autumn, 299.
To Helen, 338.
To Hope, 287.
To Some Ladies, 287.
To Walt Whitman in America, 385.

Town Down the River, The, 406.
TRAGEDY, 41–54; origin of, 41, 42;
Athenian, 42–54; of Aeschylus, 42–46;
47, 48, 51, 52, 53, 54; of Sophocles,
46–49, 51, 52, 53, 54; of Euripides,
49–53, 54; influence on later drama,
54; on modern music, 54; Shakespearean
tragedy, *see* Chapter XIV.
TRELAWNEY, E. J., 273, 282.
TRIMETER, 32, 38.
TRISTRAM, 86, 419.
TROCHAIC VERSE, 38.
Troilus and Cressida, 130, 131, 133.
TROJAN WAR, 22–26.
Trojan Women, The, 50, 51.
TROUBADOURS, poetry of, 83–88.
TROY, 22–26.
Twelfth Night, 183.
Two Gentlemen of Verona, The, 177.

U

ULYSSES, 308, 310, 311, 320, 321, 329.

V

VALLON, ANNETTE (and William Words-
worth), 237, 238.
Vaudracour and Julia, 238.
Venus and Adonis, 173.
VERDI, G., 54.
Vers libre, *see* free verse.
VICTORIA, QUEEN, 312.
VIRGIL (Publius Vergilius Maro), 65–75,
98, 99, 100, 102, 103, 110, 130, 147,
148, 149, 157, 189, 250, 285, 379, 414;
birth and early life, 65–66; first poems,
67, 68; *Georgics*, 69; *Aeneid*, 69–72;
translations from, 71, 74; characteris-
tics, 72–74; influence of, 74–75.
Vita Nuova, 92, 93, 94, 96.
VOLTAIRE, F. M. A. DE, 64.
VONDEL, J. VAN DEN, 199.
Voyage to The Moon, A, 341.

W

WAGNER, R., 54.
Waiting Both, 399.
Waste Land, The, 413.
What Price Glory, 331.

When Lilacs Last in the Door-Yard Bloomed, 358, 360.

White Man's Burden, The, 394.

WHITMAN, GEORGE, 355, 356.

WHITMAN, LOUISA VAN VELSOR, 348.

WHITMAN, WALT, 312, 314, 315, 348–362; 365, 385, 387, 392, 394, 395, 402, 405, 409, 410, 411, 414, 419, 420; boyhood, 348–350; journalism, 350–351; southern trip, 351; dedication to poetry, 349, 351; *Leaves of Grass*, 352–354; Emerson's letter, 355; work in war, 355–357; later poems, 357–358; later life, 358; contributions as artist and teacher, 359–362.

WHITMAN, WALTER, 348.

WHITTIER, J. G., 334, 405.

WILDE, OSCAR, 395.

Witch of Atlas, The, 277.

Woods of Westermain, The, 397.

WORDSWORTH, DOROTHY, 236, 239, 240, 243.

WORDSWORTH, WILLIAM, 140, 226, 233–251, 256, 261, 263, 271, 290, 303, 325, 329, 332, 335, 346, 365, 388, 399, 407; life in France, 233–234, 237–238; early life, 234–237; period of doubt, 238–241; Coleridge's influence, 241–242; *Lyrical Ballads*, 242–246; marriage, 246; Poems of 1807; decline of poetic ability, 248–249; honours and death, 249; influence, 250, 251.

Works and Days, Hesiod's, 32.

World Is too Much with Us, The, 247.

WYATT, SIR THOMAS, 149.

WYLIE, ELINOR, 411.

Y

YEATS, WILLIAM BUTLER, 395

YOUNG, EDWARD, 215.